Book of Mormon Discourses

Doctrines and Commentary: A Study Guide

Written and Edited
by
Robert I. Webber

© Robert I. Webber 2019

Introduction

The Book of Mormon is comprised of (i) events, and (ii) discourses. **Events** are historical incidents and episodes, such as Nephi building a ship; Ammon serving King Lamoni; and various accounts of political turmoil, war and deliverance. These events often illustrate gospel principles. For example, Lehi's experience with the Liahona demonstrates that small means can lead to marvelous works; however, if we do not exercise faith, those marvelous works may cease. (See 1 Nephi 16; Alma 37).

The Book of Mormon also includes 28 major prophetic **discourses**, or sermons, delivered to a particular audience. These discourses generally communicate doctrines, such as the importance of faith, the conditions of repentance, and the universality of the resurrection.

Book of Mormon Discourses: A Study Guide is intended to be a resource for scripture study and gospel instruction, at church and in the home. Each chapter focuses on a discrete prophetic discourse, and includes a brief introduction, a summary of key doctrines, and a commentary on those doctrines.[1] The commentary section includes teachings from General Authorities of The Church of Jesus Christ of Latter-day Saints, and supplemental materials.

My intent in organizing Book of Mormon content into doctrinal discourses is to provide (1) a simple framework to approach Book of Mormon study; (2) a novel structure to assist in analysis, and comprehension, of Book of Mormon teachings; and (3) a supplemental collection of authoritative commentaries that address key Book of Mormon doctrines.[2]

Book of Mormon discourses can be compared to conference talks given by general authorities of The Church of Jesus Christ of Latter-day Saints. Indeed, the total number of major discourses contained in the entire Book of Mormon is approximately the same number of talks in one semi-annual general conference, although the Book of Mormon discourses span a thousand-year history rather than just two days.

Approaching the Book of Mormon as a compilation of prophetic discourses has revealed thematically consistent doctrines and distinct prophetic voices. Importantly, each discourse includes prophesies, teachings and testimonies of Jesus Christ. I hope this study guide can assist those who read the Book of Mormon increase their testimony of the truthfulness of the record as another testament of Jesus Christ.

---

[1] This treatment does not include the doctrines taught by Jesus Christ in 3 Nephi 11-28. For a comprehensive review of the Lord's teachings in 3 Nephi, see Holland, Christ and the New Covenant, 249-311.

[2] Joseph Smith may have been referring to the discourses in the Book of Mormon rather than geography and culture when he stated: "the Book of Mormon was the most correct of any book on earth, and the keystone of our religion, and a man would get nearer to God by abiding its precepts, than by any other book." History of the Church, 4:461. Elder George Q. Cannon taught: "'the Book of Mormon is not a geographical primer. It was not written to teach geographical truths. What is told us of the situation of the various lands or cities . . . is usually simply an incidental remark connected with the doctrinal or historical portions of the work.'" (*Quoted in* Faust, Conf. Report, Oct. 1983).

How to Use This Book

For each discourse, the reader should first review the "Introduction" and "Key Doctrines" sections. Next, carefully read the text of the discourse from the Book of Mormon and identify scriptural passages that contain the key doctrines. Return to the related discourse materials in the study guide, and review the Commentary section, which is organized by doctrinal topics and supplements scriptural text with insights from General Authorities and additional materials.

The discourses in this study guide are organized by prophet and then by the order they appear in the Book of Mormon. The discourses can be reviewed chronologically; or, they can be studied topically, by doctrine(s). For example, the reader can review Jacob's discourse on the Atonement in 2 Nephi 9, concurrently with Amulek's teachings about the Atonement in Alma 34; or, can compare Alma's discourse on repentance in Alma 36, with Samuel's teachings about the conditions of repentance in Helaman 13.

For ease of reference, the Topical Index designates one primary discourse for each key doctrine. (See "Key Doctrines: Topical Index"). For example, several prophets teach about the resurrection, but most of the commentaries on the resurrection are included with Amulek's discourse in Alma 11. To facilitate additional study, a list of commentary source material is provided in Appendix D, organized by discourse and doctrinal topic.

The twenty-eight discourses were delivered to four categories of audiences: (1) family members; (2) church members in or around a temple or synagogue; (3) inhabitants of a city or other geographic area as part of missionary efforts; and (4) future readers of the record, including the descendants of Lehi. The content and tone of these sermons vary by audience. For example, a prophet's address to a faithful congregation of believers is very different from his call to repentance to an apostate community.

Whether studied chronologically, by prophet, by doctrinal topic, or by audience, the discourse framework can assist the reader internalize key doctrines from the Book of Mormon. With a little effort, the reader can also use the framework to memorize which prophets taught what doctrines to whom, and the scriptural source of key doctrines (e.g., teachings on the resurrection can be found in Alma 11; 2 Nephi 9; Mosiah 15; and Alma 40).

Whatever the approach, it is critical to read and ponder the original discourse as recorded in the Book of Mormon, and to seek the Lord's guidance in applying those sacred teachings to the reader's individual situation, and thus "liken all scriptures unto us, that it might be for our profit and learning" (1 Nephi 19:23).

A PDF version of this study guide is available upon request to BookofMormonDiscourses2019@gmail.com.[3]

---

[3] I would like to thank my friend and colleague, Jay W. Deverich, for his comprehensive cite-checking, and review of source materials and scriptural quotations, and for providing stylistic edits throughout this edition of Book of Mormon Discourses.

Table of Contents

Introduction 2
    How to Use This Book 3
    Table of Contents 4
    Key Doctrines: Topical Index 6
    Book of Mormon Discourses: Audiences 10

Discourse 1: Lehi, "The Tree of Life" (1 Nephi 8-10) 15
Discourse 2: Lehi, "Awake and Repent" (2 Nephi 1) 26
Discourse 3: Lehi, "Agency and the Plan of Salvation" (2 Nephi 2) 30
Discourse 4: Lehi, "Joseph - A Choice Seer" (2 Nephi 3) 40
Discourse 5: Nephi, "Panoramic Vision of the Future" (1 Nephi 11-14) 46
Discourse 6: Nephi, "Hope in the Lord (Isaiah)" (1 Nephi 19-22) 61
Discourse 7: Nephi, "Press Forward in Christ" (2 Nephi 25-33) 70
Discourse 8: Jacob, "The Infinite Atonement" (2 Nephi 6-10) 86
Discourse 9: Jacob, "A Warning about Sin" (Jacob 2-3) 99
Discourse 10: King Benjamin, "Service and Salvation" (Mosiah 2-4) 105
Discourse 11: Abinadi, "Redemption through Christ" (Mosiah 13-16) 119
Discourse 12: Alma, "A Mighty Change of Heart" (Alma 5) 129
Discourse 13: Alma, "Divine Attributes" (Alma 7) 136
Discourse 14: Amulek, "Resurrection" (Alma 10-11) 145
Discourse 15: Alma, "Probationary State; High Priesthood" (Alma 12-13) 151
Discourse 16: Alma, "Nourish Faith with the Word of God" (Alma 32-33) 158
Discourse 17: Amulek, "Atonement, Prayer & Procrastination" (Alma 34) 165
Discourse 18: Alma, "Repentance; Small and Simple Things" (Alma 36) 172
Discourse 19: Alma, "Effective Teaching" (Alma 38) 182
Discourse 20: Alma, "Chastity, Justice & Mercy" (Alma 39-42) 188
Discourse 21: Helaman, "The Rock of Christ" (Helaman 5) 206
Discourse 22: Samuel the Lamanite, "Signs of Christ" (Helaman 13-15) 212
Discourse 23: Mormon, "Faith, Hope & Charity" (Moroni 7) 216
Discourse 24: Mormon, "Baptism of Little Children" (Moroni 8) 230
Discourse 25: Mormon, "Persevere Despite Wickedness" (Moroni 9) 234
Discourse 26: Mormon, "Invitation to Believe" (Mormon 7) 239
Discourse 27: Moroni, "Voice of Warning; The Last Days" (Mormon 8-9) 242
Discourse 28: Moroni, "Promise of the Book of Mormon" (Moroni 10) 251

Appendix A: Another Testament of Jesus Christ 267
Appendix B: Testimonies of the Book of Mormon by Latter-Day Prophets 272
Appendix C: Book of Mormon Discourses – Major Doctrinal Topics 279
Appendix D: Commentary Sources by Discourse 282
Word Index 313
    The 28 Discourses 317

Other Content[4]

Opposition: Don't Let Your Want Power Overcome Your Will Power (2 Nephi 2).........	36
Mary, the Mother of Christ: Handmaid of the Lord (1 Nephi 11)...............................	51
Delight in the Words of Isaiah: A Primer for Latter-day Saints (1 Nephi 19-22)............	63
Doctrine of Inclusion: From Sneetches to Penguins (2 Nephi 26)...............................	74
Obedience Leads to Happiness: The Abundant Life, Flying First Class (Mosiah 3).........	111
A Biotechnology Analogy: Expressing Christ-like Attributes (Alma 7)......................	142
Small and Simple Things: Miracle on the Hudson (Alma 38)...................................	180
Bridle Your Passions: Brakes Help You Go Faster (Alma 39)..................................	184
Developing Real Intent: The "As If" Principle (Moroni 7).......................................	218
The Light of Christ: Scattering Cockroaches (Moroni 7)...	220
Reading the Book of Mormon: B-17 Flight Checklists (Moroni 10)...........................	252

---

[4] Includes excerpts from articles, lessons or talks prepared by the author.

Key Doctrines: Topical Index

Topic	Discourse #	Prophet, Subtitle (Chapter in Book of Mormon)	Page
Affliction	# 6.	Nephi, "Hope in the Lord" (1 Nephi 20)	65
Agency	# 3.	Lehi, "The Gift of Agency" (2 Nephi 2) (See also: 2 Nephi 9; Alma 32-33; Helaman 15, Moroni 7)	36
Angels	# 5.	Nephi, "Panoramic Vision of the Future" (1 Nephi 11) (See also: Mosiah 3; Mosiah 27)	49
Atonement	# 8.	Jacob, "The Infinite Atonement" (2 Nephi 9) (See also: 1 Ne. 8; 2 Ne. 2; Mos. 13-16; Alma 7, 34, 39-42; Hel. 13)	89
Awake	# 2.	Lehi, "Awake and Repent" (2 Nephi 1)	27
Baptism	# 7.	Nephi, "Press Forward in Christ" (2 Nephi 31) (See also: Moroni 8)	82
Categories of People	# 1.	Lehi, "The Tree of Life" (1 Nephi 8)	20
Charity	# 23.	Mormon, "Faith, Hope & Charity" (Moroni 7) (See also: Alma 7; Mosiah 4)	225
Chastity	# 20.	Alma, "Chastity" (Alma 39) (See also: Jacob 2 "Polygamy")	190
Conversion	# 12.	Alma, "A Mighty Change of Heart" (Alma 5) (See also: Mosiah 2-4; Alma 32-33; Alma 36)	131
Divine Attributes	# 13.	Alma, "Divine Attributes" (Alma 7) (See also: Mosiah 4; Alma 38; Moroni 7; Moroni 10)	138
Education	# 8.	Jacob, "Jacob's Warnings – The Learned" (2 Nephi 9) (See also: Alma 7)	95
Endure	# 7.	Nephi, "Press Forward in Christ" (2 Nephi 31) (See also: 1 Nephi 8)	83
Faith	# 16.	Alma, "Nourish Faith with the Word of God" (Alma 32-33) (See also: 2 Nephi 31; Alma 36-37; Moroni 7; Mormon 8-9)	160
Family	# 1.	Lehi, "Tree of Life" (Wayward Children) (1 Nephi 8) (See also: Mosiah 4).	24

Gathering of Israel	# 6.	Nephi, "Hope in the Lord" (1 Nephi 19-22)...............................	66
		(See also: 2 Nephi 25-29; Mormon 8-9)	
Gifts	# 28.	Moroni, "Gifts of the Spirit" (Moroni 10)…………….....…………..	262
Gratitude	# 10.	King Benjamin, "Gratitude and Obedience" (Mosiah 2-4)………....…….	110
		(See also: 1 Nephi 11 "Mary")	
Happiness	# 10.	King Benjamin "Obedience Leads to Happiness" (Mosiah 3)………….	111
		(See also: Alma 41)	
Holy Ghost	# 28.	Moroni, "The Holy Ghost; Revelation" (Moroni 10)………………..	260
		(See also: 2 Nephi 31; Moroni 7)	
Hope	# 23.	Mormon, "Faith, Hope & Charity" (Moroni 7)…………………………	224
		(See also: 2 Nephi 31)	
Humility	# 16.	Alma, "Humility; Nourish Faith with the Word" (Alma 32)……………	159
		(See also: Jacob 2 "Pride"; Alma 5, 7, 32; 1 Nephi 11 "Mary")	
Inclusion	# 7.	Nephi, "Doctrine of Inclusion" (2 Nephi 26)………………………..	74
		(See also: Alma 5)	
Jesus Christ	# 7.	Nephi, "Talk of Christ" (2 Nephi 31)……………….......…………..	72
Condescends	# 5.	Nephi, "Condescension of God" (1 Nephi 11)……………....………	50
Father & Son	# 11.	Abinadi, "Christ as the Father and the Son" (Mosiah 15)………....……	127
Foundation	# 21.	Helaman, "The Rock of Our Redeemer" (Helaman 5)…………………	209
Light of Christ	# 23.	Mormon, "The Light of Christ" (Moroni 7)……………………………	220
Mortal Life & Ministry	# 8.	Jacob, "The Savior Will Redeem Israel" (2 Nephi 6-8)……………….	88
	# 11.	Abinadi, "Redemption through Christ" (Mosiah 14-15)………………	122
	# 13.	Alma, "Christ Takes On Our Infirmities" (Alma 7)……………………	137
	# 22.	Samuel, "Prophesy of Christ" (Helaman 13-15)………………………	214
Name of Christ	# 10.	King Benjamin, "The Name of Jesus Christ" (Mosiah 4)………………	113
Perfection	# 28.	Moroni, "Come Unto Christ and Be Perfected" (Moroni 10)…………...	265
		Appendix A: Another Testament of Christ…………………………...	282

Judgment	# 20.	Alma, "Judgment" (Alma 41)...	199
		(See also: 2 Nephi 9, Alma 12; Alma 34)	
Justice & Mercy	# 20.	Alma, "Justice & Mercy" (Alma 42)...	200
		(See also: 2 Nephi 2, 9; Jacob 2)	
Miracles	# 27.	Moroni, "God Performs Miracles" (Mormon 8-9).............................	247
Obedience	# 10.	King Benjamin, "Gratitude and Obedience" (Mosiah 2-4).................	110
		(See also: 1 Nephi 8; 2 Nephi 2, 9; Mosiah 13-14; Alma 39)	
		(Helaman 5; Mormon 7-8, 9)	
Opposition	# 3.	Lehi, "The Gift of Agency: Opposition" (2 Nephi 2)........................	36
Patience	# 13.	Alma, "Divine Attributes - Patience" (Alma 7).................................	139
		(See also: Alma 32-33; Moroni 7)	
Plan of Salvation	# 3.	Lehi, "Plan of Salvation" (2 Nephi 2)..	31
		(See also: 2 Nephi 9; Alma 12-13; Alma 40-42)	
Ponder	# 5.	Nephi, "Pondering Leads to Revelation" (1 Nephi 11).....................	48
		(See also: 2 Nephi 31; Moroni 10)	
Prayer	# 17.	Amulek, "Pray at All Times, in All Places" (Alma 34)....................	168
		(See also: Moroni 10)	
Preparation	# 18.	Alma, "Small and Simple Things" (Alma 37)...................................	178
		(See also: Alma 34)	
Priesthood	# 15.	Alma, "Melchizedek Priesthood" (Alma 13).....................................	155
Procrastinate	# 17.	Amulek, "Do Not Procrastinate Repentance" (Alma 34)...................	170
Prophets	# 2.	Lehi, "Follow the Prophet" (2 Nephi 1)..	29
		(See also: Helaman 13)	
Joseph Smith	# 4.	Lehi, "Joseph Smith: A Choice Seer" (2 Nephi 3)...........................	41
Real Intent	# 23.	Mormon, "Real Intent" (Moroni 7)...	217
Remember	# 21.	Helaman, "Remember" (Helaman 5)	207
Repentance	# 18.	Alma, "Principles of Repentance" (Alma 36)..................................	173
		(See also: 2 Nephi 1, 31; Mosiah 4; Alma 32, 39-41, Hel. 13-15)	
Restoration	# 20.	Alma, "Restoration: Wickedness Never Was Happiness" (Alma 41)....	197

Resurrection	# 14.	Amulek, "Resurrection Is Universal" (Alma 10-11)..........................146	
		(See also: 2 Nephi 9; Mosiah 13-15; Alma 40)	
Revelation	# 28.	Moroni, "The Holy Ghost; Revelation (Moroni 10)........................260	
		(See also: 1 Nephi 11; 2 Nephi 31)	
Riches	# 9.	Jacob, "Riches and Pride" (Jacob 2-3)..100	
		(See also: 2 Nephi 9)	
Satan	# 6.	Nephi, "Satan Will Have No More Power" (1 Nephi 22).................. 68	
		(See also: 1 Nephi 8; Moroni 7) (See "<u>Wickedness</u>")	
Natural Man	# 10.	King Benjamin, "The Natural Man" (Mosiah 3-4)........................... 114	
Scriptures	# 6.	Nephi, "Hope in the Lord: Scriptures" (1 Nephi 19-22)................... 61	
		(See also: 1 Nephi 8; 2 Nephi 9; 2 Nephi 31: Alma 32-33; Alma 37)	
Bible	# 5.	Nephi, "The Bible and the Book of Mormon" (1 Nephi 13-14)............ 58	
		(See also: 2 Nephi 3; 2 Nephi 25-27; Mormon 7)	
Book of Mormon	# 28.	Moroni, "Promise of the Book of Mormon" (Moroni 10)................... 252	
		(See also: 1 Nephi 13; 2 Nephi 27-29; Mormon 8-9)	
Isaiah	# 7.	Nephi, "Delight in the Words of Isaiah" (1 Nephi 19-22)................... 62	
		(See also: 2 Nephi 12-24; Jacob 6-8; Mosiah 13-15)	
Service	# 10.	King Benjamin, "Service and Salvation" (Mosiah 2-4)..................... 106	
		(See also: Alma 5; Alma 32-33)	
Small Things	# 18.	Alma, "Small and Simple Things" (Alma 39)................................ 178	
Teaching	# 19.	Alma, "Attributes of an Effective Teacher" (Alma 38)..................... 183	
		(See also: 1 Nephi 11; Alma 5; Alma 32-33)	
Testimony	# 28.	Moroni, "Obtaining a Testimony" (Moroni 10)............................ 255	
		(See also: Alma 5; Alma 32-33; Appendix B - Testimonies)	
Wickedness (Warnings)	# 7.	Nephi, "Nephi's Warnings: False Doctrines" (2 Nephi 28)................. 77	
		(See also: 2 Nephi 9 "Jacob's Warnings"; Jacob 2-3 "Pride/Immorality")	
		(Alma 41 "Not Happiness"; Moroni 8 "Anger"; Mormon 9 "Last Days")	

Book of Mormon Discourses: Audiences

The twenty-eight major discourses included in this treatment were delivered by eleven prophets. Alma the Younger is the most prolific with seven sermons, followed by Lehi and Mormon, with four recorded discourses each.

Prophet	No. of Discourses	Scriptural References	Period (Dates)
			600 B.C. – 421 B.C.
Lehi	4	1 Nephi 8; 2 Nephi 1; 2; 3	600 B.C. – 570 B.C.
Nephi	3	1 Nephi 11-14; 19-22; 2 Nephi 25-33	600 B.C. – 545 B.C.
Jacob	2	2 Nephi 6-10; Jacob 2-3	559 B.C. – 421 B.C.
			148 B.C. – 6 B.C.
Benjamin	1	Mosiah 2-4	124 B.C.
Abinadi	1	Mosiah 13-16	148 B.C.
Alma	7	Alma 5; 7; 12-13; 32-33; 36-37; 38; 39-42	83 B.C. – 73 B.C.
Amulek	2	Alma 10-11; Alma 34	82 B.C. – 74 B.C.
Helaman	1	Helaman 5	52 B.C. – 39 B.C.
Samuel	1	Helaman 13-15	6 B.C.
			A.D. 385 – A.D. 421
Mormon	4	Mormon 7; Moroni 7; 8; 9	A.D. 385 – A.D. 400
Moroni	2	Mormon 8-9; Moroni 10	A.D. 401 – A.D. 421

Audience Categories

The audience for each discourse falls into one of the following four categories: (i) family discourses; (ii) church discourses; (iii) missionary discourses; or (iv) prophetic discourses addressed to future readers of the record. The audience discourses tend to be clustered together chronologically in the Book of Mormon (e.g., Discourses 8 through 13 are primarily church discourses).

Family Discourses

Ten of the twenty-eight discourses were delivered to family members. These discourses are often a father's instruction to his children, addressing personal issues, ranging from recognition of faithful missionary service to an admonition to obey the law of chastity. Thematically, these parental instructions encourage family members to remember their heritage, to be grateful to the Lord for His blessings, and to keep the commandments.

Several family discourses include information about the family's ancestors or experiences from the prophet's life. For example, Lehi instructs his son Joseph about their ancestor, Joseph of Egypt (2 Nephi 3). Helaman teaches his sons that they have been named after their forbearers, Nephi and Lehi, as a constant reminder to model their lives after their ancestors' righteous example (Helaman 5). Alma shares the account of his miraculous conversion with his son, Helaman (Alma 36); and, Lehi instructs his children about his vision of the tree of life (1 Nephi 8).

Some of the discourses contain parental warnings and admonitions to wayward children. Lehi warns Laman and Lemuel to repent and be obedient (2 Nephi 1); and Alma preaches to his disobedient missionary son, Corianton, about the consequences of sin (Alma 39-42). Other discourses contain encouragement and instructions to righteous children. Alma praises his son, Shiblon, for his faithfulness and steadiness (Alma 38); and Mormon encourages his son, Moroni, to continue in righteousness, and persevere, despite the wickedness surrounding him (Moroni 9).

Several family discourses contain doctrinal insights concerning the Plan of Salvation. For example, one of the most comprehensive sermons on the creation, fall and atonement is contained in Lehi's instructions to his son, Jacob (2 Nephi 2). Alma's admonitions to his son, Corianton, include a wide-ranging review of the resurrection, and the principles of redemption, justice, and mercy (Alma 39-42). In each of the family discourses, the prophet teaches his children about Jesus Christ.

Family Discourses

Discourse 1:   Lehi, "The Tree of Life," to his children (1 Nephi 8)

Discourse 2:   Lehi, "Awake and Repent," to his sons, Laman and Lemuel (2 Nephi 1)

Discourse 3:   Lehi, "Agency and the Plan of Salvation," to his son, Jacob (2 Nephi 2)

Discourse 4:   Lehi, "Joseph – A Choice Seer," to his son, Joseph (2 Nephi 3)

Discourse 18: Alma, "Repentance and Simple Things," to his son, Helaman (Alma 36-37)

Discourse 19: Alma, "Effective Teaching," to his son, Shiblon (Alma 38)

Discourse 20: Alma, "Judgment and Mercy," to his son, Corianton (Alma 39-42)

Discourse 21: Helaman, "The Rock of Christ," to his sons, Nephi and Lehi (Helaman 5)

Discourse 24: Mormon, "The Baptism of Little Children," to his son, Moroni (Moroni 8)

Discourse 25: Mormon, "Persevere Despite Wickedness," to his son, Moroni (Moroni 9)

Church Discourses

There are six instructional discourses directed to church members, several of which are delivered in or from a temple or a synagogue. These discourses include admonitions and warnings to a congregation that may be deviating from the path of righteousness. Or, they include encouragement and instructions to those who are striving to live the commandments. For example, several church discourses encourage those who aspire to be disciples of Christ to develop specific divine attributes. (See Mosiah 4:11-16; Alma 5:27-30; Alma 7:22-23; and Moroni 7:20-48). The church discourses often focus on the "how": how to develop faith, hope and charity (Moroni 7); how to serve our fellow man (Mosiah 2-4); and how to be truly converted and retain a remission of our sins (Alma 5).

Church Discourses

Discourse 8. Jacob's admonitions and teachings about the Atonement to the followers of Nephi in the land of Nephi (2 Nephi 6-10)

Discourse 9. Jacob's warnings about pride and immorality to members of the church in the land of Nephi (from the temple) (Jacob 2-3)

Discourse 10. King Benjamin's teachings about service to the people in Zarahemla who take upon themselves the name of Christ (from the temple) (Mosiah 2-5)

Discourse 12. Alma's message about conversion, obtaining and retaining a testimony, to members of the church in the city of Zarahemla (Alma 5)

Discourse 13. Alma's message on fulfilling our duty to God and the attributes of Christ to the members of the church in the city of Gideon (Alma 7)

Discourse 23. Mormon's teachings on faith, hope, and charity to the members of the church from a synagogue in an unidentified location (Moroni 7)

Missionary Discourses to People in a Certain City or Land

There are six missionary discourses focused on reclaiming, admonishing and instructing people in a specific geographic location. These discourses contain calls to repentance, and often also include teachings about basic gospel principles, such as faith, prayer, and obedience to the commandments.

In each of these discourses, the prophet is in great personal risk of physical harm. Abinadi is killed after he delivers his message to the court of King Noah (Mosiah 12-17). Samuel preaches from the wall in Zarahemla while being attacked with stones and arrows (Helaman 13-16). Alma is initially rejected, reviled, and cast out of the city of Ammonihah, and only returns when instructed by a heavenly messenger (Alma 8). He meets Amulek, and they preach to the people, but are beaten and imprisoned, and then escape through miraculous means (Alma 14). Later, after Alma and Amulek attempt to reclaim the apostate Zoramites in Antionum, they are rejected by the rulers and leaders of the land (Alma 31). They have some success with the poor and persecuted members of the Zoramite society, but those converts are soon "cast out of the land," and the remaining Zoramites "stir up" the Lamanites and persuade them to commence a war with Alma's people (Alma 35).

Missionary Discourses

Discourse 11. Abinadi's teachings about Christ and the fulfillment of the law of Moses to the court of King Noah and the people in the land of Shilom (Mosiah 13-16)

Discourse 14. Amulek's teachings on the resurrection to the people in Ammonihah (Alma 10-11)

Discourse 15. Alma's instructions on church authority to the people in Ammonihah (Alma 12-13)

Discourse 16. Alma's instructions on faith to the Zoramites in Antionum (Alma 32-33)

Discourse 17. Amulek's teachings about prayer to the people in Antionum (Alma 34)

Discourse 22. Samuel's prophesy about the coming of Christ to the people in the city of Zarahemla (Helaman 13-15)

Prophetic Discourses to Future Readers of the Record

There are six discourses that are directed not only to the Nephites and Lamanites, but the House of Israel, generally, and to future generations. Both Nephi, who begins the record, and Moroni, who finishes his father's abridgement, direct their own writings to future readers of the record, including "all the house of Israel" (1 Nephi 19:19), and "all those that shall receive hereafter the things which I write" (2 Nephi 25:3).

Nephi summarizes a panoramic vision of the future, and prophesies about the restoration of the gospel in the latter days. (1 Nephi 11-14). He teaches about the gathering of Israel, a "marvelous work and wonder" that is the restoration, and the coming forth of the Book of Mormon. He quotes extensively from the messianic prophecies of Isaiah, and adds his own prophesies and admonitions (1 Nephi 19-22; 2 Nephi 12-25). Nephi warns the future inhabitants of the earth about the influence of Satan, and false doctrines that will be propagated by the evil one (2 Nephi 28). In his final recorded discourse, Nephi invites all people to search the scriptures and come unto the Savior. He preaches the "doctrine of Christ," including the first principles of faith, repentance, baptism, and the gift of the Holy Ghost. (2 Nephi 31-32).

Similarly, Moroni prophesies about the restoration of the gospel, and coming forth of the Book of Mormon, and describes conditions that will exist in the latter days. (Mormon 8-9). He challenges non-believers to "come unto the Lord" and preaches the gospel of redemption. Moroni includes specific prophetic warnings and admonitions to future generations (Mormon 8-9; Moroni 10). "Behold, I speak unto you as if ye were present, and yet ye are not. But behold, Jesus Christ hath shown you unto me and I know your doing" (Mormon 8:35). In Moroni's concluding discourse, the prophet invites all to read the record, and learn of its truthfulness through the power of the Holy Ghost. He exhorts all to "come unto Christ" and "be perfected in him," and preaches about the gifts of God, including faith, hope and charity (Moroni 10).

<u>Prophetic Discourses</u>

Discourse 5.   Nephi's panoramic vision of the future (1 Nephi 11-14)

Discourse 6.   Nephi's instructions to his people, and the House of Israel (1 Nephi 19-22)

Discourse 7.   Nephi's summary of Isaiah's Messianic prophesies (2 Nephi 25-33)

Discourse 26. Mormon's invitation to believe to the descendants of the Lamanites (Mormon 7)

Discourse 27. Moroni's warnings and prophesies about the last days (Mormon 8-9)

Discourse 28. Moroni's promise (Moroni 10).

The twenty-eight discourses take place in tents and homes, temples and synagogues, the court of a king, and from the top of a city wall. Regardless of audience or location, each discourse includes prophesies, teachings and testimonies of Jesus Christ. Indeed, every single sermon "talks of Christ, rejoices in Christ, preaches of Christ, or prophesies of Christ" (2 Nephi 25:26). This emphasis is consistent with the Book of Mormon's stated purpose as "Another Testament" of the ministry, mission and divinity of Jesus Christ. (See Appendix A).

Discourse 1: Lehi, "The Tree of Life" (1 Nephi 8-10)

Prophet	Key Doctrines	Scriptures	Audience	Date
Lehi	<ul><li>The Tree of Life</li><li>Four Categories of People</li><li>Wayward Children</li></ul>	1 Nephi 8	To his family in the wilderness "as he dwelt in a tent in the valley of Lemuel" (1 Nephi 9:1)	600 – 592 B.C.

INTRODUCTION

The prophet Lehi was likely born between 650 B.C. and 640 B.C.[5] He was a descendant of Jacob's eleventh son, Joseph (1 Nephi 6:2; 2 Nephi 3), through Joseph's son, Manasseh (Alma 10:3). Lehi was an educated man, who was familiar with both the Egyptian and Hebrew languages (1 Nephi 1:2). He was evidently quite wealthy, possessing "gold and silver, and all manner of riches" (1 Nephi 3:16). Lehi's wealth also included property, both in Jerusalem, which was his primary residence (1 Nephi 1:4, 7), as well as outside Jerusalem in the "land of his inheritance" (1 Nephi 3:16, 25).

Some scholars suggest that Lehi was a trader, and that his riches may have resulted from the exchange of commodities, such as oils, wine, figs, and honey – he also seemed to be well-versed in beekeeping.[6] Lehi's ability to travel with his family into the wilderness, and desert regions, also suggests familiarity with a nomadic lifestyle.[7] When he was instructed to leave Jerusalem, he knew exactly what to take, and what to do. Lehi is described as a "visionary man" (1 Nephi 5:4); the record refers to at least nine of Lehi's visions or dreams.[8] One of these visions is described in detail by Lehi to his family, and is the first prophetic discourse recorded in the Book of Mormon.

In this vision, Lehi wanders through a dark and dreary wilderness until he reaches a tree, later called the "tree of life," and partakes of its fruit, which fills his soul with "exceedingly great joy" (1 Nephi 8:12). He immediately wants to share this fruit with his family. Lehi's wife, Sariah, and two of his sons, Nephi and Sam, listen to Lehi, follow him to the tree, and partake of the fruit. Lehi's other sons, Laman and Lemuel, however, will not listen to their father and refuse to take the path to the tree.

---

[5] Peterson, H. Donl, "Father Lehi," in Nyman, <u>First Nephi, The Doctrinal Foundation</u> BYU, 55-56.
[6] Nibley, Hugh. <u>Lehi in the Desert and the World of the Jaredites</u>, (1952).
[7] <u>Ibid</u>.
[8] See 1 Nephi 1:6 (pillar of fire appears while Lehi prays on behalf of the people of Jerusalem); 1 Nephi 1:8 (Lehi is overcome by the spirit and carried away in a vision while on his bed); 1 Nephi 2:1 (the Lord commands Lehi in a dream to depart into the wilderness); 1 Nephi 3:2 (the Lord commands Lehi in a dream to send sons back to Jerusalem to recover Lehi's genealogy on plates of brass); 1 Nephi 7:1 (the Lord commands Lehi in dream to send his sons to the land of Jerusalem to obtain daughters from the family of Ishmael); 1 Nephi 8 (Lehi's vision of the tree of life); 1 Nephi 16:9 (voice of the Lord speaks to Lehi by night); 1 Nephi 18:5 (voice of the Lord instructs Lehi that his family should board the ship to the promised land); 2 Nephi 1:4 (Lehi tells his family that he has seen the destruction of Jerusalem in vision).

Lehi's vision is rich in metaphor and meaning, and includes the first symbolic references to Jesus Christ in the Book of Mormon. Elder Jeffrey R. Holland wrote that the tree of life is "a symbol through which Christ is seen as restoring and redeeming the human family by the fruitfulness of his love. . . . Thus, at the very outset of the Book of Mormon, in its first fully developed allegory, Christ is portrayed as the source of eternal life and joy, the living evidence of divine love, and means whereby God will fulfill his covenant with the house of Israel and indeed the entire family of man, returning them to all their eternal promises." (Holland, Christ and the New Covenant, 159, 162).

President Boyd K. Packer counseled that we should read and re-read the account of Lehi's vision: "You may think that Lehi's dream or vision has no meaning for you, but it does. You are in it; all of us are in it. . . Lehi's dream or vision of the iron rod has in it everything a Latter-day Saint needs to understand the test of life. . . Read the dream or vision carefully; then read it again." ("Finding Ourselves in Lehi's Dream," *Ensign*, Aug. 2010).

DISCOURSE: 1 Nephi 8:2-35

KEY DOCTRINES

- **The Tree of Life**. In the allegory, the ultimate goal of life is to arrive at the tree, representing the love of God (1 Nephi 11:21-22, 25); partake of the fruit, representing the Atonement (Bednar, "Lehi's Dream," *Ensign*, October 2011); and endure to the end.

- **Four Categories of People**. Lehi observes four groups of people: (i) some never start on the path to the tree of life, but head directly for a great and spacious building; (ii) some enter the path, but succumb to temptation, and are lost in mists of darkness; (iii) some follow the path to the tree and taste of fruit, but then become ashamed and fall away; and, (iv) some press forward on the path, continually holding fast to the iron rod (the word of God), arrive at the tree, partake of the fruit, and remain steadfastly by the tree (endure to the end).

- **Wayward Children**. Never give up on wayward children; continue to "exhort them . . . with all the feeling of a tender parent" (1 Nephi 8:37).

COMMENTARY

Journey to the Tree of Life: Hold Fast to the Iron Rod

Lehi begins his journey in "a dark and dreary wilderness" (1 Nephi 8:5). He soon receives assistance from a man in a white robe, an angel, whom he follows.[9] Although the angel helps Lehi commence on the right path, he soon departs, and Lehi again finds himself alone in a "dark and dreary waste" (1 Nephi 8:7). The first metaphorical lesson from Lehi's vision is that although we may be guided to the right path – even through divine assistance, we may still need to pass through darkness, and endure trials and temptations, before we reach our ultimate destination.

Elder Orson Pratt taught, "Lehi was . . . a man who had been raised up as a great prophet in the midst of Jerusalem. . . But notwithstanding this gift of prophesy, and the gifts of the spirit which he enjoyed, the Lord showed him by this dream that there would be seasons of darkness through which he would have to pass. . . . God may in some measure, withhold even from those who walk before him in purity and integrity, a portion of his Spirit, that they may prove to themselves . . . whether they are full of integrity even in times when they have not so much of the Spirit to guide and influence them." (Journal of Discourses, 15:31, 1872).

After traveling alone in the darkness, Lehi prays earnestly to the Lord for mercy, "according to the multitude of his tender mercies" (1 Nephi 8:8), and is ultimately able to arrive at his destination: a tree, later called the "tree of life,"[10] where he finds fruit "most sweet," and "white to exceed all the whiteness that I had ever seen" (1 Nephi 8:11). Partaking of this fruit fills Lehi's soul "with exceeding great joy" (1 Nephi 8:12). These verses at the beginning of Lehi's vision suggest that the path to "exceeding great joy" may be difficult, but if we continue in prayer and faithfulness, we can rely on the tender mercies of the Lord to escape the darkness and arrive safely at our destination.

When Lehi partakes of the fruit in his dream, he immediately "began to be desirous that [his] family should partake of it also" (1 Nephi 8:12). Lehi looks around and, "a little way off," sees his wife, Sariah, and his sons, Sam and Nephi, standing "as if they knew not whither they should go" (1 Nephi 8:14). Lehi beckons to them and calls with a "loud voice" for them to come to him and partake of the fruit. These three listen to Lehi and immediately come to the tree, and partake of the fruit (1 Nephi 8:16). Here, Lehi serves in the role of the angelic guide, leading others on the path to the tree of life. We may have similar opportunities.

On a basic level, it seems to be human nature to want to share good things we experience with friends and family. This need not be something as consequential as fruit from the tree of life, but may be an enjoyable movie, a good book, a favorite song, or a delicious food.

---

[9] Elder Jeffrey R. Holland taught: "When in Lehi's dream he found himself in a frightening place, 'a dark and dreary waste,' as he described it, he was met by an angel, 'a man . . . dressed in a white robe'" whom he follows to safety. (Conf. Report, Oct. 2008).

[10] 1 Nephi 11:25. There are several references to a "tree of life" in the scriptures. In Revelation 2:7, "the tree of life . . . is in the midst of the paradise of God." A "tree of life" was in the Garden of Eden. (See Genesis 3:22, 24; Moses 3:9; 4:28, 31; Abr. 5:9). In Alma 5:34, Alma quotes Christ: "Come unto me and ye shall partake of the fruit of the tree of life." In Revelation 22:14, John speaks of a tree of life that is to come down from heaven. And, Proverbs 11:30 states that "the fruit of the righteous is a tree of life."

For example, on the island of Maui, there is a wonderful restaurant called "Mama's Fish House." This restaurant serves an exquisite local dessert, lilikoi crème brulee. When my young daughter first tasted this dish, she immediately wanted to share a (small) portion of the treat with members of her family so they could enjoy it as well: a simple example of what seems to be an innate desire to share good things we experience with family members, friends, and those around us. Similarly, in his dream, after tasting the fruit that was sweet above all other fruit, Lehi desired that his family should share that experience, and also partake.

The Iron Rod

Thereafter, Lehi observes a rod of iron along a "straight and narrow path" leading to the tree by which he stood. When Nephi's brothers later ask, "What meaneth the rod of iron which our father saw, that led to the tree? [Nephi] said unto them that it was the word of God; and whoso would hearken unto the word of God, and hold fast unto it, they would never perish; neither could the temptations and the fiery darts of the adversary . . . lead them away to destruction" (1 Nephi 15:23-24).

The rod of iron is "the word of God, which word, if accepted and lived, will lead mankind to the tree of life. . . . Man's duty, therefore, is to seek earnestly for the word of the Lord; and when he finds it, if he is sincere in his desires, he will enter into that straight and narrow path that will take him to the tree of life where he can partake of the fruit thereof." (Stapley, Conf. Report, Apr. 1966). "As the mists of darkness gather around us, we are only lost if we choose to let go of the iron rod, which is the word of God." (Baxter, Conf. Report, Oct. 2006).

Elder Neil L. Andersen explained: "The word of God contains three very strong elements that intertwine and sustain one another to form an immovable rod. These three elements include, first, the scriptures, or the words of the ancient prophets. . . . The second element of the word of God is the personal revelation and inspiration that comes to us through the Holy Ghost. . . . The third element, a critical addition intertwining with the other two . . . represents the words of the living prophets." ("Hold Fast to the Words of the Prophets," CES Fireside, March 4, 2007).

The iron rod secures us on the path to the tree of life. Although mists of darkness, representing trials and temptations, may arise, if we press forward and "continually hold fast" to the word of God, we can avoid losing our way. "However diligent we may be in other areas, certain blessings are to be found only in the scriptures, only in coming to the word of the Lord and holding fast to it as we make our way through the mists of darkness to the tree of life." (Benson, Conf. Report, Apr. 1986).

When the Savior was confronted with three types of temptation after His 40-day fast, as recorded in Matthew 4:1-11, He used the scriptures to rebut the tempter. In each instance of temptation, the Savior first responds, and refutes the devil by quoting scripture: "It is written . . ." (Matt. 4:4, 7, 10). Similarly, we can use the word of God as we press forward to overcome life's temptations.

The Tree of Life

The central feature in Lehi's dream is the tree of life, or what Nephi later revealed to be the "love of God" (1 Nephi 11:21-22, 25). Elder Neal A. Maxwell declared: "The tree of life . . . is the love of God. The love of God for his children is most profoundly expressed in His gift of Jesus as our Redeemer: 'God so loved the world, that he gave his only begotten Son' (John 3:16)." (Conf. Report, Oct. 1999). The tree of life represents the love of God manifested through the mission, ministry and mercies of His Son.

Elder Jeffrey R. Holland wrote that "the Spirit made explicit that the Tree of Life and its precious fruit are symbols of Christ's redemption . . . . The life, mission, and atonement of Christ are the ultimate manifestations of the Tree of Life, the fruit of the gospel, [and] the love of God." (Holland, Christ and the New Covenant, 160-161). Elder David A. Bednar explained that the *fruit* of the tree represents the Atonement of Jesus Christ: "The fruit on the tree is a symbol for the blessings of the Atonement. Partaking of the fruit of the tree represents the receiving of ordinances and covenants whereby the Atonement can become fully efficacious in our lives." ("Lehi's Dream," *Ensign*, October 2011).

"To partake of the love of God is to partake of Jesus' Atonement and the emancipations and joys which it can bring." (Maxwell, Conf. Report, Oct. 1999). Similar to the act of "partaking" of the fruit, we must "partake" of the Atonement through repenting, receiving ordinances, entering covenants, and faithfully obeying the Lord's commandments. In the vision of the tree of life, "partaking of the fruit of the tree . . . represent[s] the partaking of the powers of Christ and his atonement: forgiveness of sins, as well as feelings of peace, joy, and gratitude. Ultimately, through partaking of the powers of the gospel one is qualified to partake of the greatest fruit of the atonement – the blessings associated with eternal life." (McConkie & Millet, Doctrinal Commentary on the Book of Mormon. 1:56, 1987). The Savior instructs Alma, "Come unto me, and ye shall partake of the fruit of the tree of life" (Alma 5:34).

The fruit, or the blessing of the Atonement, "is desirable above all other fruit," "most sweet" and "white to exceed all whiteness," and can fill the soul "with exceedingly great joy" (1 Nephi 8:12). This metaphor aptly describes the cleanliness, the purity and the blessings we can receive through the impact of the Atonement of Christ in our lives, and the opportunity it provides to obtain eternal life, the "greatest of all the gifts of God" (1 Nephi 15:36; see D&C 14:7).

Four Categories of People

As the vision continues, Lehi observes multitudes of people, who can be categorized into four groups:

- The first group never starts on the path, but immediately seeks the large and spacious building, and when they arrive, "point the finger of scorn" at Lehi and those partaking of the fruit (1 Nephi 8:31-33). This group has no interest in the things of God.
- The second group starts on the path which leads to the tree, but loses their way in the mist of darkness (1 Nephi 8:21-23). This group succumbs to temptation.
- The third group starts on the path, catches hold of the iron rod, and by "clinging" to it are able to partake of the fruit, but then become ashamed because of those scoffing at them, and fall away (1 Nephi 8:24-28). This group succumbs to persecution.
- The fourth group starts on the path and presses forward, "continually holding fast to the rod of iron," until they partake of the fruit. They ignore scorn and persecution, and remain at the tree (1 Nephi 8:30). This group endures to the end.

The **first group** never starts on the path to the tree, but immediately begins to feel their way toward the great and spacious building. This group wants nothing to do with the word of God, or any strait and narrow path. From the very outset of their journey, these people, and there were "multitudes," find the attractions of the spacious building to be much more compelling than the fruit of the tree of life.

The "great and spacious building" may appear attractive and appealing, even compelling, and tempt us to head in that direction. In some instances, even those who have started on the path to the tree may disregard the word of God and head toward the building. "To those of you who are inching your way closer and closer to that great and spacious building, let me make it completely clear that the people in that building have absolutely nothing to offer except instant, short-term gratification inescapably connected to long-term sorrow and suffering. The commandments you observe were not given by a dispassionate God to prevent you from having fun, but by a loving Father in Heaven who wants you to be happy while you are living on this earth as well as in the hereafter." (Pace, Conf. Report, Oct. 1987).

In other instances, we may become distracted by things of the world, and follow a detour that leads to the building. We may seek pleasures or preoccupations that appear innocent, but ultimately take us away from the things of the Lord. Nephi later teaches that the building represents worldly pride and riches, a focus on the things of this world (1 Nephi 11:35-36). Elder L. Tom Perry warned that a preoccupation with material possessions may lead us toward the building: "The current cries we hear coming from the great and spacious building tempt us to compete for ownership in the things of this world. We think we need a larger home, with a three-car garage and a recreational vehicle parked next to it. We long for designer clothes, extra TV sets, the latest model computers, and the newest car." (Conf. Report, Oct. 1995). When the things of this world become our priority, we are furnishing our rooms in the spacious building rather than following the path to the tree of life. (See "Riches" in Topical Index, Jacob 2).

At times, Laman and Lemuel exhibit characteristics similar to the inhabitants of the great and spacious building. They were materialistic, preoccupied with their riches in Jerusalem. They were slow to keep the commandments of God. They murmured against their fathers' teachings and did not want to make the journey to the promised land, but wanted to remain in Jerusalem. And, they often "mocked" and "scorned" Nephi.[11]

The **second group** starts on the path and begins to press forward, but encounters the "mist of darkness," or the "temptations of the devil" (1 Nephi 12:17), and lose their way and wander off. No mention is made of them seeking or holding the rod of iron. About this group, Elder Bednar stated: "Those who ignore or treat lightly the word of God do not have access to that divine compass which points to the way to the Savior. Consider that this group obtained the path and pressed forward, exhibiting a measure of faith in Christ and spiritual conviction, but they were diverted by the temptations of the devil and were lost." (*Ensign*, Oct. 2011). This message highlights the importance of scripture study – holding fast to the word of God – to overcome the temptations of the devil.

In Lehi's vision, the second group did not hold the iron rod, and without the word of God (through rejection or ignorance) succumbed to the temptations of the devil, and "wandered off and were lost" (1 Nephi 8:23).

Although the **third group** of people reaches the tree and tastes of the fruit, they are soon mocked by the occupants of the great and spacious building, and they become ashamed and fall away. Members of this group move forward along the path with initial enthusiasm and actually partake of the fruit, but when confronted with persecution, adversity and peer pressure, they succumb, and fall away. "We see a few around us who simply can't stand to be separated from the 'politically correct' multitudes in the great and spacious building. These multitudes are 'in the attitude of mocking and pointing their fingers towards those who had come at and were partaking of the fruit' (1 Nephi 8:26-27). The 'finger of scorn' has its own way of separating the faithful from those who have little or no faith." (Maxwell, Lord, Increase Our Faith, 99).

Elder Bednar suggests that the depth of this group's commitment was insufficient to withstand scorn from those in the building, perhaps (especially) from some of those who had accompanied them along the path, but had fallen away, and were now persecuting their former colleagues. (*Ensign*, Oct. 2011). He also observed: "notice that this group is described as *clinging* to the rod of iron (1 Nephi 8:24)." (*Ensign*, Oct. 2011). There is a subtle, but significant, difference between "clinging" to the rod and "continually holding" to the rod. "This [third] group eventually was lost - perhaps because they only periodically read or studied or searched the scriptures. Clinging to the rod of iron suggests to me only occasional 'bursts' of study or irregular dipping rather than consistent, ongoing immersion in the word of God." (*Ensign*, Oct. 2011).

---

[11] See, e.g., 1 Nephi 17:19-20. Note, however, that there were periods of obedience by Laman and Lemuel (1 Nephi 16:5 – "they did humble themselves before the Lord"; 1 Nephi 7:2-4 – they followed the commandment to return to Jerusalem). The Lord will judge Lehi's sons with perfect judgment.

The **fourth group** of people press forward and reach the tree of life. Unlike the third group, who were "clinging" to the iron rod, the fourth group were "continually holding fast" (1 Nephi 8:30). Elder Bednar taught: "Let me suggest that *holding fast* to the iron rod entails the prayerful and consistent use of [the scriptures]. . . . Are you and I daily reading, studying, and searching the scriptures in a way that enables us to hold fast to the rod of iron?" ("A Reservoir of Living Water," CES Fireside, Feb. 4, 2007). (See: 2 Nephi 32:3).

Despite taunts and scorn from those in the great and spacious building, this fourth group "heeded them not," and never did fall away (1 Nephi 8:33). "There at the end of the verse is Nephi's powerful principle, and answer to unwanted peer pressure: 'But we heeded them not.' . . . However out of step we may seem, however much the standards are belittled, however much others yield, we will not yield, we cannot yield." (Zwick, Conf. Report, Apr. 2008). "Let us expect that many . . . will see us as quaint or misled. Let us bear the pointing fingers . . . Let us not revile the revilers and heed them not. Instead, let us use our energy to hold up the shield of faith to quench the incoming fiery darts." (Maxwell, Conf. Report, Oct. 2003).

Bishop W. Christopher Waddell taught: "A key difference between those who were ashamed, fell away, and were lost and those who did not heed the mocking from the building and stood with the prophet is found in two phrases: first, 'after they had *tasted*,' and second, 'those that were *partaking*.' The first group had arrived at the tree, stood for a time with the prophet, but only *tasted* the fruit. By not continuing to eat, they allowed the taunting from the building to affect them, drawing them away from the prophet and into forbidden paths, where they were lost. In contrast to those who tasted and wandered off were those who were found *continuously partaking* of the fruit. These individuals ignored the commotion from the building, stood by the prophet, and enjoyed the accompanying safety and peace." (Conf. Report, Apr. 2016, *emphasis in original*). The strength gained from *continually partaking* of the fruit allowed these committed saints to be unmoved by the scorn from people in the building. (See, "Endure" in Topical Index, 2 Ne. 31).

Perhaps another distinguishing factor in this fourth group is that they "fell down" when they reached the tree and partook of the fruit, suggesting humility. The combination of consistent immersion in the scriptures with humble recognition of the love of God distinguished them from other groups, and likely served as protection from outside influences. The fourth group were those who held fast to the iron rod continually, reached the tree, partook of the fruit humbly and continuously, and then endured to the end.

Lehi teaches that we must be proactive in our journey to the tree. Action verbs fill his discourse. First, we must *"catch hold"* of the rod. This represents our desire to read and study the scriptures. Next, we must *"press forward"* through the mist. This represents our faith and obedience to continue moving forward in the face of temptation, even when we cannot always see the path clearly – to "hope for things which are not seen" (Alma 32:21). As we press forward, we must *"continually hold fast"* to the iron rod, relying on the "tender mercies" of the Lord. This represents our commitment to continually follow the words of the Lord and His prophets. When we reach the tree, we *"come forth and fall down,"* in the attitude of humility and gratitude for the love of God, and actively *"partake* of the fruit of the tree" so that through the blessings of the Atonement, we may obtain eternal life.

Comparison to Parable of the Sower (Four Soils)

Several characteristics of the four groups are similar to the characteristics of the four soils in the Savior's Parable of the Sower. (Matthew 13:18-23).[12] Just as Lehi's vision includes four categories of people who make different choices in their journey through life, the Lord's parable includes four categories of people who react differently to the "seed" or the word of God.[13]

Lehi's Vision of the Tree of Life	Parable of the Sower (Matt. 13:18-23)
Group 1 (no interest): They never get on the path or take hold of the iron rod. Instead, they head directly to the great and spacious building.	**Hardened soil**. Those that receive seed by the way side don't understand the word, and it is immediately taken away by the wicked one. Teachings "fall upon a heart hardened and unprepared." They are more focused on other things. (Matt. 13:19)
Group 2 (succumb to temptations): They start on the path, but lose their way in the mist of darkness (temptations).	**Thorny soil**. Those that receive seed among thorns. They hear the word, but the cares of the world and deceitfulness of riches [temptations] choke the word, and they lose their way. (Matt. 13:22)
Group 3 (succumb to persecution): They follow the path and reach the tree of life, where they abide for a while, until they are persecuted, become ashamed, and are lost.	**Thin soil**. Those that receive the seed into stony places. They hear the word and receive it with joy. They endure for a while, but are "offended" by tribulation and persecution and do not continue. (Matt. 13: 21-22)
Group 4 (endure to the end): They follow the path, and reach the tree of life, where they endure, despite persecution, are fruitful and invite others to the tree.	**Good soil**. Those that receive seed into good ground. They hear the word, and understand it[14] (hold fast to it), and they bring forth fruit. (Matt. 13:23). Jesus explained that "the good ground are they, which in an honest and good heart, having heard the word, keep it, and bring forth fruit with patience" (Luke 8:15).

"The different soils on which the seeds fell represent different ways in which mortals receive and follow [the word of God]. . . . What do we do with the Savior's teachings as we live our lives? The parable of the sower warns us of circumstances and attitudes that can keep anyone who has received the seed of the gospel message from bringing forth a goodly harvest." (Oaks, Conf. Report, Apr. 2015).

---

[12] See "The Parable of the Sower," (Oaks, Conf. Report, Apr. 2015).
[13] The seed that was sown was the "word of the kingdom" (Matthew 13:19); "the word" (Mark 4:14); or, "the word of God" (Luke 8:13) – the teachings of the Master and His servants.
[14] Luke says "keep it [the word]" (Luke 8:15).

Feelings of a Tender Parent: Dealing with Wayward Children

In Lehi's vision, Nephi and Sam listen to their father and follow him to the tree of life. But Laman and Lemuel refuse to take the path toward the tree, and do not partake of the fruit. This response greatly troubles Lehi, and he "exceedingly feared" that his two eldest sons will "be cast off from the presence of the Lord" (1 Nephi 8:4, 36). Nephi states that after father Lehi had shared his dream, he exhorted his older sons "with all the feeling of a tender parent, that they would hearken to his words" (1 Nephi 8:37).

This verse shows the great love and concern that Lehi had for Laman and Lemuel, and provides guidance on how to deal with wayward children. We do not know the final judgment of Laman and Lemuel, but we know they were often disobedient and caused their parents great anguish. Lehi's difficulty with his children is similar to the difficulty many parents face with wayward children today. "Did Lehi fail as a parent? The record is clear that he had taught them and showed them how to live, but they exercised their agency to deny themselves the blessings of righteous living. Nevertheless, as a dedicated father, Lehi refused to give up on them. He continued to 'exhort them . . . with all the feeling of a tender parent' (1 Nephi 8:36)." (Ogden and Skinner, Verse By Verse: The Book of Mormon, 1:38-39).

When faced with wayward children, parents may second guess their efforts, blame themselves, or lose hope. In spite of righteous parents, Laman and Lemuel consistently choose to murmur, rebel, and disobey the commandments of the Lord. Nevertheless, Lehi never gives up on his sons, even after a heavenly vision indicates that they will not partake of the fruit and obtain eternal life. Lehi does not waste time blaming himself or Sariah, but rather continues to work with them.

Elder Robert D. Hales taught how parents can follow Lehi's example when dealing with wayward children: "We too must have faith to teach our children and bid them to keep the commandments. We should not let their choices weaken our faith. Our worthiness will not be measured according to their righteousness. Lehi did not lose the blessing of feasting at the tree of life because Laman and Lemuel refused to partake of its fruit. Sometimes as parents we feel we have failed when our children make mistakes or stray. Parents are never failures when they do their best to love, teach, pray, and care for their children. Their faith, prayers, and efforts will be consecrated for the good of their children." (Conf. Report, Apr. 2004).

"The scriptures tell us that when some of Heavenly Father's spirit children chose not to follow His plan, the heavens wept. (D&C 76:26; Moses 7:37). Some parents who have loved and taught their children also weep when their grown children choose not to follow the Lord's plan. What can parents do? We cannot pray away another's agency. Remember the father of the prodigal son, who patiently waited for his son to '[come] to himself,' all the while watching for him. (Luke 15:17). . . . We can pray for guidance about when to speak, what to say, and yes, on some occasions, when to be still. Remember, our children and family members already chose to follow the Savior in their premortal realm. Sometimes it is only by their own life experiences that those sacred feelings are awakened again. Ultimately, the choice to love and follow the Lord has to be their own." (Hales, Conf. Report, Oct. 2016).

"It is hard to understand all the reasons why some people take another path. The best we can do in these circumstances is just to love and embrace them, pray for their well-being, and seek for the Lord's help to know what to do and say. Sincerely rejoice with them in their successes; be their friends and look for the good in them. We should never give up on them but preserve our relationships. Never reject or misjudge them." (Soares, Conf. Report, Apr. 2019).

We simply don't know when righteous efforts will ultimately impact a wayward son or daughter. When a rebellious Alma the Younger turned to the Lord in true repentance (with an angelic assist), he "remembered also to have heard my father prophesy unto the people concerning the coming of one Jesus Christ, a Son of God, to atone for the sins of the world" (Alma 36:17). Gospel discussions, home evening lessons, scripture readings, and family prayers can all positively influence, despite the reluctance of the family member to "hear" at the time. Parents can persuade, and plant the seeds for future change, even if the results are not immediately forthcoming.

"For those of you who are right now experiencing . . . feelings of sadness, agony, and maybe regret, please know that they are not totally lost because the Lord knows where they are and is watching over them. Remember, they are His children too! . . . Ultimately, keep living a worthy life, be a good example to them of what you believe, and draw closer to our Savior, Jesus Christ. He knows and understands our deep sorrows and pains, and He will bless your efforts and dedication to your dear ones, if not in this life, in the next life. Remember, brothers and sisters, always that hope is an important part of the gospel plan." (Soares, Conf. Report, Apr. 2019).

Though hearts will ache, there is reason for faithful parents, who have received the sealing blessings of the temple and kept their covenants, to have hope for their disobedient children. "When a seal is put upon the father and mother, it secures their posterity, so that they cannot be lost, but will be saved by virtue of the covenant of their father and mother." (Teachings of the Prophet Joseph Smith, 321). Elder Orson F. Whitney expounded on this doctrine of hope: "The Prophet Joseph Smith declared - and he never taught more comforting doctrine - that the eternal sealings of faithful parents and the divine promises made to them for valiant service in the Cause of Truth, would save not only themselves, but likewise their posterity. Though some of the sheep may wander, the eye of the Shepherd is upon them, and sooner or later they will feel the tentacles of Divine Providence reaching out after them and drawing them back to the fold. Either in this life or the life to come, they will return. They will have to pay their debt to justice; they will suffer for their sins; and may tread a thorny path; but if it leads them at last, like the penitent Prodigal, to a loving and forgiving father's heart and home, the painful experience will not have been in vain. Pray for your careless and disobedient children; hold on to them with your faith. Hope on, trust on, till you see the salvation of God." (Conf. Report, Apr. 1929).

In discussing this topic, Elder David A. Bednar cautioned that "the influence of parents who honor covenants and obey commandments indeed can have a decisive spiritual impact upon children who stray by activating the tentacles of Divine Providence – in ways that have not been revealed fully and are not understood completely. However, righteous parental influence (1) does not replace . . . the need for the redeeming and strengthening power of the Atonement of Jesus Christ, (2) does not overrule the consequences of the unrighteous exercise of moral agency, and (3) does not negate the responsibility of an individual as an agent 'to act . . . and not to be acted upon.'" (*Ensign*, March 2014). Parental efforts cannot prevail over agency, but the scriptures and prophetic teachings confirm that hope, prayer, patience, forgiveness and righteous example can influence wayward or unbelieving children both in this life, and the life to come.

Discourse 2: Lehi, "Awake and Repent" (2 Nephi 1)

Prophet	Topics	Scriptures	Audience	Date
Lehi	<ul><li>Keep the Commandments and Prosper</li><li>Awake and Repent</li><li>Follow the Prophet</li></ul>	2 Nephi 1	To his children, Laman, Lemuel, sons of Ishmael, Zoram	About 588 B.C. – 570 B.C.

INTRODUCTION

Lehi was a visionary man, who was a prophet of God. His three sermons included in the first three chapters of Second Nephi include his final recorded words to his children. In Second Nephi chapter one, he addresses all of his children (Nephi's "brethren") with specific words of encouragement and warning for his eldest sons, Laman and Lemuel. In Second Nephi chapter two, he addresses his son, Jacob. And, in Second Nephi chapter three, Lehi teaches his youngest son, Joseph. Both Jacob and Joseph were born in the wilderness on the family's journey to the land of promise.

In Second Nephi chapter one, Lehi speaks to Laman and Lemuel with the words of a tender parent, and demonstrates that he has never given up on them, despite their actions, and his vision of their disobedience. He encourages them to "awake" and repent, to follow the counsel of the Lord's prophet, and prophesies that if they and their children obey the commandments of God, they will prosper.

DISCOURSE: 2 Nephi 1

KEY DOCTRINES

- **Awake and Repent.** Lehi's charge to his sons to awake and arise from the dust, shake off the chains by which they are bound, and put on the armor of righteousness.

- **Keep the Commandments.** If we keep the commandments, we will prosper.

- **Follow the Prophet.** We must follow the leaders the Lord has chosen. The Lord will not allow the prophet to lead the Church astray.

COMMENTARY

Awake and Repent

In his vision of the tree of life, Lehi was particularly concerned about Laman and Lemuel. This concern continued throughout his life. Shortly before his death, Lehi exhorts his wayward sons, Laman and Lemuel, to: "Arise from the dust . . . and be men" (2 Nephi 1:21). He warns them to "awake from a deep sleep . . . even from the sleep of hell, and shake off the awful chains by which ye are bound," to repent, and "put on the armor of righteousness" and "rebel no more"; otherwise, they will "incur the displeasure of a just God" (1 Nephi 1:13, 16, 22-24).[15]

Elder Carlos E. Asay explained the meaning of each element in Lehi's charge:

- "The challenge to 'arise from the dust' means to overcome evil behaviors that destroy character and ruin lives. Physical appetites must be controlled.
- 'Awake from a deep sleep . . . even from the sleep of hell' suggests a process of learning and becoming aware of God's holy purposes. No sleep is deeper or more deadly than the sleep of ignorance.
- 'Shake off the awful chains by which ye are bound' indicates the need to overcome bad habits, even the seemingly little habits that grow into strong 'chains of hell' (2 Nephi 26:22).
- 'Put on the armor of righteousness' reminds us of the need to wear the helmet of salvation, pick up the sword of truth, use the shield of faith, and accept the full protective coverings of the Lord. (Ephesians 6:11-18).
- 'Come forth out of obscurity' instructs one to model goodness and serve as a light to others. True men are living light fountains which are pleasant to be near.
- 'Rebel no more' makes it perfectly clear that ignoring or willfully breaking commandments is a wasteful effort." (Conf. Report, Apr. 1992).

Awaking from a deep sleep, arising from the dust, and putting on the armor of righteousness are all hallmarks of true repentance. To repent, we must "awake" and recognize our sins and the need to change. Then, we must correct our course – to "arise from the dust" of sinful behavior, through confession and restitution. Finally, we must "put on the armor of righteousness" and "sin no more," forsaking sin. These steps -- to recognize, to confess, and to forsake -- are all part of the repentance process. "By this ye may know if a man repenteth of his sins – behold, he will confess them and forsake them" (D&C 58:43). (See, "Repentance" in Topical Index).

Elder Marvin J. Ashton observed: "Lehi warned his sons to 'shake off the chains' because he knew that chains restrict our mobility, growth, and happiness. They cause us to be confused and less able to be guided by God's Spirit. . . . Samuel Johnson wisely shared, 'The chains of habit are too small to be felt until they are too strong to be broken.' . . . Righteous living is a shield, a protector, an insulation, a strength, a power, a joy, a Christlike trait. Yes, living a life of righteousness is a chain breaker. Many of us today are shackled by the restrictive chains of poor habits. . . . We are chained by an unwillingness to change for the better. Is it any wonder, in our day as it was in Nephi's, that God's pleas are 'awake,' 'listen' . . . and 'seek the straight course'?" (Conf. Report, Oct. 1986).

---

[15] The call to "awake" echoes Isaiah's admonition to "Awake, awake, put on thy strength" (Isaiah 52:1).

President Gordon B. Hinckley warned: "The words of Lehi are a clarion call. . . . Said he with great conviction: 'Awake, my sons; put on the armor of righteousness. Shake off the chains with which ye are bound, and come forth out of obscurity, and arise from the dust' (2 Nephi 1:23). There is not a [person] in this vast congregation tonight who cannot improve his life. And that needs to happen." (Conf. Report, Oct. 2006).

We are warned to not only awake from sinful behavior, but also from spiritual indifference, which can numb our spiritual senses, erode testimony, and distract us from our duties as disciples. "The Apostle Paul wrote, 'Awake thou that sleepest' . . . . Don't allow selfishness! Don't allow habits that can lead to addiction! Don't allow competing priorities to lull you into indifference or detachment from blessed discipleship." (Uchtdorf, Conf. Report, Apr. 2014).

President Henry B. Eyring taught: "One of the effects of disobeying God seems to be the creation of just enough spiritual anesthetic to block any sensation as the ties to God are being cut. Not only [does] the testimony of the truth slowly erode, but even the memories of what it was like to be in the light [begin] to seem . . . like a delusion." (BYU Speeches, 2000-2001, 81). The image of a person wandering through life in a stupor caused by the spiritual anesthetic of indifference or sin contrasts sharply with the image of one who is spiritually awake and alert, actively seeking to improve his or her life, and to bless the lives of others.

President Russell M. Nelson declared to the men of the church: "The Lord needs selfless men who put the welfare of others ahead of their own. He needs men who intentionally work to hear the voice of the Spirit with clarity. He needs men of the covenant who keep their covenants with integrity. He needs men who are determined to keep themselves sexually pure – worthy men who can be called upon at a moment's notice to give blessings with pure hearts, clean minds, and willing hands. The Lord needs men eager to repent – men with a zeal to serve and be part of the Lord's battalion of worthy priesthood bearers." (Conf. Report, Apr. 2019). He needs men "awake and alert."

Keep the Commandments and Prosper

Lehi teaches his children that the Lord blesses those who keep his commandments. The Lord says: "Inasmuch as ye shall keep my commandments, ye shall prosper in the land" (2 Nephi 1:20), a concept Lehi repeats four times in his discourse (See 2 Nephi 1:7, 9, 20, 32), and a recurring theme that appears at least 22 other times in the Book of Mormon.[16] (See also, Psalms 67:6; Proverbs 22:4-5). President Russell M. Nelson observed, "as Saints learn and obey the commandments of God, they will prosper. This promise has been recorded by prophets throughout time and in diverse places." (Conf. Report, Apr. 1986).

Elder Quentin L. Cook taught: "The scriptures are clear: those who are righteous, follow the Savior, and keep His commandments will prosper in the land. . . . However, righteousness, prayer, and faithfulness will not always result in happy endings in mortality. Many will experience severe trials." (Conf. Report, Oct. 2011). Certainly righteous Lehi, Sarah, and Nephi experienced severe trials. Nonetheless, and notwithstanding trials, Lehi's message is that if we keep the commandments, we will ultimately prosper.

---

[16]See 1 Nephi 4:14; 1 Nephi 17:13; 1 Nephi 22:31; 2 Nephi 1:9; 2 Nephi 1:31; 2 Nephi 4:4; 2 Nephi 5:10-11; Jacob 2:29; Jarom 1:9; Omni 1:6; Mosiah 1:7; Mosiah 2:22; Mosiah 2:31; Alma 9:13-14; Alma 36:1; Alma 36:30; Alma 37:13; Alma 38:1; Alma 45:6-8; Alma 50:20; Hel. 3:20; 3 Nephi 5:22

Lehi provided his children with several examples of how he personally prospered through a lifetime of keeping the commandments: (i) his soul was redeemed from hell; (ii) he beheld the glory of the Lord (perhaps referring to his visions); and (iii) he was encircled about eternally in the arms of God's love. (2 Nephi 1:15). (See "Obedience" in Topical Index, Mosiah 2-3).

Follow the Prophet

At the end of his sermon, Lehi admonishes Laman, Lemuel, Sam, and the sons of Ishmael to follow Nephi's leadership, to "hearken unto the voice of Nephi" (2 Nephi 1:28). Lehi reminds his children of Nephi's righteous actions: he has kept the commandments; he has been an instrument of God; he has not sought for power, but for the glory of God and the welfare of his brethren; and, he has preached the truth and word of God with plainness. Lehi testifies that the "power of God" is with Nephi, and "it was the Spirit of the Lord which was in him, which opened his mouth to utterance that he could not shut it" (2 Nephi 1:27). These are hallmarks of a leader-prophet chosen of God.

Lehi instructs his children that "if [they] will hearken unto the voice of Nephi, [they] will not perish" (2 Nephi 1:28). The blessings of spiritual prosperity and security are promised to all who follow the prophets of God. President Wilford Woodruff taught: "I hope we may all pursue the course laid down for us by the servants of the Lord, for if we do this I know that we shall be safe in this world, and secure happiness and exaltation in the world to come. . . . I have never in my life known it to fail, that when men went contrary to the counsel of their leaders . . . they always became entangled and suffered a loss by so doing." (Journal of Discourses, 5:82).

Elder Claudio R. M. Costa observed: "The Lord will reveal to His prophets absolutely anything that He feels is necessary to communicate to us. He will reveal His will to us, and He will instruct us through His prophets. . . . They will transmit the word of God and his counsel to us. Pay attention and follow their instruction and suggestions and I testify to you that your life will be completely blessed." (Conf. Report, Oct. 2010; *quoting* from an address by President Ezra Taft Benson, "Fourteen Fundamentals in Following the Prophet," BYU Devotional, 1980).

The Lord said: "And if my people will hearken unto my voice, and unto the voice of my servants whom I have appointed to lead my people, behold, verily I say unto you, they shall not be moved out of their place" (D&C 124:45). "Listening to and hearkening to living prophets will have profound, even life-changing effects in our lives. We are strengthened. We are more assured and confident in the Lord. We hear the word of the Lord. We feel God's love. We will know how to conduct our lives with purpose." (Davies, Conf. Report, Oct. 2018)

We are assured that the prophet will never lead the Church astray. President Wilford Woodruff declared: "The Lord will never permit me or any other man who stands as President of this church to lead you astray. It is not in the programme. It is not the mind of God. If I were to attempt that, the Lord would remove me out of my place, and so He will any other man who attempts to lead the children of men astray from the oracles of God and from their duty." (Conf. Report, Oct. 1890; see D&C, Official Declaration-1).

Discourse 3: Lehi, "Agency and the Plan of Salvation" (2 Nephi 2)

Prophet	Key Doctrines	Scriptures	Audience	Date
Lehi	• Plan of Salvation: • The Gift of Agency • Opposition in All Things	2 Nephi 2	To Jacob (and Lehi's other children)	About 588 B.C. – 570 B.C.

INTRODUCTION

In Second Nephi chapter two, a discourse rich with doctrine, Lehi teaches his son, Jacob, about the Plan of Salvation: the necessity of the fall of man through the transgression of Adam and Eve; the need for opposition; the importance of agency; and the essential role the Savior plays in the redemption and salvation of mankind. He summarizes the purposes of the Plan in the statements: "Adam fell that men might be; and men are, that they might have joy. And the Messiah cometh in the fullness of time, that he may redeem the children of men from the fall" (2 Nephi 2:25-26).

As he teaches Jacob about agency and the consequences of choice, Lehi admonishes his son to "look to the great Mediator, and hearken unto his great commandments . . . and choose eternal life" (2 Nephi 2:28). Christ is the means by which the Plan of Salvation is implemented in our lives. Through the intercession of the Savior, and His Atonement, we are able return to our Father in Heaven to live in perfect happiness. The "ends of the Atonement," Lehi teaches, are the joy and happiness we obtain through redemption from the fall. And, this redemption, Lehi testifies, only "cometh in and through the Holy Messiah" (2 Nephi 2:6).

Referring to Lehi's discourse in 2 Nephi, chapter two, Elder Robert D. Hales said: "And to his righteous son Jacob [Lehi] taught one final, very important lesson. If we could leave one lesson of greatest importance for our children and grandchildren, what would it be? Of all the glorious principles of the gospel, Lehi chose to teach his son about the plan of salvation – and the gift of agency." (Conf. Report, Apr. 2006).

DISCOURSE: 2 Nephi 2

KEY DOCTRINES

- **The Plan of Salvation**: the Creation, the Fall and the Atonement. We are redeemed through Christ, who satisfies the demands of justice, and intercedes for those who repent.

- **Agency and Opposition**. There is opposition in all things; opposition allows progress, builds strength, and enables choice and growth. Our duty is to use our agency to follow Christ, and "choose the good part" (2 Nephi 2:30).

COMMENTARY

Plan of Salvation: Creation, Fall and Atonement

"Before we were born, we lived with God, the Father of our spirits. All of us on earth are literally brothers and sisters in His family, and each of us is precious to Him. We lived with Him for eons of time before our mortal birth – learning, choosing, and preparing. Because Heavenly Father loves us, He wants us to have the greatest gift He can give, the gift of eternal life. He could not simply give us this gift; we had to receive it by choosing Him and His ways. This required that we leave His presence and begin a wonderful and challenging journey of faith, growth, and becoming. The journey our Father prepared for us is called the plan of salvation or the plan of happiness." (Clayton, Conf. Report, April 2017). The Plan of Salvation includes a creation, a fall (with life on earth becoming a probationary period), a physical resurrection and a spiritual redemption, accomplished through the Atonement of Christ, whereby we can obtain eternal life.

Lehi teaches Jacob that God "created all things" in the heavens and the earth, "and all things that in them are," culminating in the zenith of earthly creation, our "first parents," Adam and Eve. (2 Nephi 2:14-15). To "bring about his eternal purposes," God allowed Adam and Eve to choose between good and evil, symbolized in the Garden of Eden by the "forbidden fruit in opposition to the tree of life" (2 Nephi 2:15).

In the scriptural account, the devil tempted Adam and Eve to partake of the forbidden fruit, and to disobey God. The "father of lies" told them "[p]artake of the forbidden fruit, and ye shall not die, but ye shall be as God, knowing good and evil" (2 Nephi 2:18). Here, the devil demonstrates one of his tactics of deceit by mixing a lie, "you shall not die" with a truth, "you shall know good from evil," wrapped in a partial truth, "ye shall be as God" (2 Nephi 2:18). This deceitful tactic, demonstrated in the Garden of Eden, has been deployed by the devil throughout the ages.

Lehi, "according to the things which [he has] read," teaches his son that the devil was an "angel of God . . . fallen from heaven" who had "sought that which was evil before God" (2 Nephi 2:17). Banished from heaven, the devil had "become miserable forever," and therefore "sought the misery of all mankind" (2 Nephi 2:18). "Because of his rebellion, Lucifer was cast out and became Satan, the devil, 'the father of all lies, to deceive and to blind men, and to lead them captive at his will, even as many as would not hearken unto [God's] voice' (Moses 4:4). And so this personage who was an angel of God . . . was removed from the presence of God and his Son. This caused great sadness in the heavens, 'for the heavens wept over him – he was Lucifer, a son of the morning' (D&C 76:26)." (Faust, Conf. Report Oct. 1987). (See "Satan" in Topical Index).

A Forward Fall

Adam and Eve chose to partake of the forbidden fruit, and, contrary to Satan's promise, "you shall not die," the transgression in the Garden introduced death, both physical and spiritual. After partaking the fruit, the bodies of Adam and Eve would ultimately decay and they would suffer physical death. After leaving the Garden, Adam and Eve would be separated from the presence of God, and they would suffer spiritual death.

Concurrently, the transgression in the Garden introduced life, in the sense that Adam and Eve were able to bring new life into the world. They could now exercise the power of procreation, and were able to "multiply and replenish the earth," and have joy in their posterity. (Genesis 1:28). Elder Orson F. Whitney described the Fall as having "a twofold direction – downward, yet forward. It brought man into the world and set his feet upon progression's highway" (*quoted in* Packer, Conf. Report, Oct. 1993). In a sense, the fall was a second creation, bringing both life and death into the world.

President Russell M. Nelson explained: "Adam and Eve were created in the image of God, with bodies of flesh and bone. Created in the image of God and not yet mortal, they could not grow old and die. 'And they would have had no children' (2 Nephi 2:23) nor experience the trials of life. . . . The creation of Adam and Eve was a *paradisiacal creation*, one that required a significant change before they could fulfill the commandment to have children and thus provide earthly bodies for premortal spirit sons and daughters of God. . . . The Fall of Adam (and Eve) constituted the mortal creation and brought about the required changes in their bodies, including the circulation of blood and other modifications as well. They were now able to have children. They and their posterity also became subject to injury, disease, and death." (Conf. Report, Oct. 1996).

The Lord knew that Adam and Eve would transgress and leave the Garden – mortal life was part of the plan. Indeed, Lehi taught that the Fall was purposeful, "done in the wisdom of him who knoweth all things" (2 Nephi 2:24). As Adam and Eve progressed from the Garden, they, and their posterity, could obtain additional blessings and could "become free forever" (2 Nephi 2:26), with the potential to obtain eternal life, the kind of life that God, Himself, enjoys. This progression was part of God's plan, formulated before the foundation of the world.

Scripture (Moses 5:10-11)	Implications
Adam said, "because of my transgression, my eyes are opened, and in this life I shall have joy" (Moses 5:10).	They understood the consequences of their actions, and that choosing good could lead to joy.
Adam said, "and again in the flesh I shall see God" (Moses 5:10).	They understood that a resurrection would take place.
Eve "heard all these things and was glad, saying: Were it not for our transgression we never should have seed. We never [would] have known good and evil" (Moses 5:11)	They were blessed with the power of procreation. They understood the existence of good and evil, and able to choose the good of their own free will.
She observed, "We never [would] have known . . . the joy of our redemption, and the eternal life which God giveth unto all the obedient" (Moses 5:11).	They understood that through the plan of salvation they could be redeemed and obtain eternal life.

With respect to the Plan, Joseph Smith taught: "God himself, finding he was in the midst of spirits and glory, because he was more intelligent, saw proper to institute laws whereby the rest could have a privilege to advance like himself . . . that they may be exalted with himself." (Teachings of the Prophet Joseph Smith, 354). With respect to the intelligence of God, the Book of Abraham reads: "I am the Lord thy God, I am more intelligent than they all" (Abraham 3:19). Joseph Smith said: "I believe that this means more than God is more intelligent than any other one of the intelligences. It means that he is more intelligent than all of the other intelligences combined. His intelligence is greater than that of the mass . . . . What he tells other intelligences to do must be precisely the wisest, fittest thing that they could anywhere or anyhow learn." (Teachings of the Prophet Joseph Smith, 353).

Nevertheless, the path to the exaltation God sought for His children would be challenging. Mortal life became a "state of probation" (2 Nephi 2:21), with tests, afflictions, and temptations. Mortals suffer injury, disease and death. Life is no restful sojourn and the mortal, telestial world is no paradisiacal garden. It is a land of "thorns and thistles" (Moses 4:4), and noxious weeds that torment man. Mortality is full of physical and spiritual challenges. Each and every one of Adam and Eve's posterity would make mistakes; "for all have sinned and come short of the glory of God" (Romans 3:23). And, as Lehi observed, "all men must repent" (2 Nephi 2:21). "In the course of mortal life, we would all be soiled by sin as we yielded to the evil temptations of the adversary." (Oaks, Conf. Report, Oct. 2018).

Elder David A. Bednar taught: "As sons and daughters of God, we have inherited divine capacities from Him. But we presently live in a fallen world. The very elements out of which our bodies were created are by nature fallen and ever subject to the pull of sin, corruption, and death. Consequently, the Fall of Adam and its spiritual and temporal consequences affect us most directly through our physical bodes. . . . The precise nature of the test of mortality, then, can be summarized in the following question: Will I respond to the inclinations of the natural man, or will I yield to the enticings of the Holy Spirit and put off the natural man and become a saint through the Atonement of Christ the Lord? That is the test. . . . We are here on the earth to develop godlike qualities and to bridle all of the passions of the flesh. The Father's plan is designed to provide direction of His children, to help them become happy, and to bring them safely home to Him with resurrected, exalted bodies." (Conf. Report, Apr. 2013).

Elder L. Tom Perry explained: "The main purpose of earth life is to allow our spirits, which existed before the world was, to be united with our bodies for a time of great opportunity in morality. The association of the two together has given us the privilege of growing, developing, and maturing as only we can with spirit and body united. With our bodies, we pass through a certain amount of trial in what is termed a probationary state of our existence. This is a time of learning and testing to prove ourselves worthy of eternal opportunities. It is all part of a divine plan our Father has for His children." (Conf. Report, Apr. 1989).

"Mortality . . . is a proving ground, a probationary state, a time to walk by faith, a time to prepare to meet God." (Wickman, Conf. Report, Oct. 2002). "Heavenly Father knew the grave dangers we would face on our journey through life, but He remains resolute in His desire to have each and every one of His children return home. Therefore, He gave us time – time to work out our mistakes, time to overcome our sins, time to prepare for reunion." (McMullin, Conf. Report, Apr. 1999).

President Harold B. Lee exclaimed: "Today I could desire with all my heart that all within the sound of this broadcast would . . . thank God for one more day! For what? For the opportunity to take care of some unfinished business. To repent; to right some wrongs; to influence for good some wayward child; . . . in short, to thank God for one more day to prepare to meet God (Alma 12:24)." (Conf. Report, Oct. 1970).

Our loving and omniscient Father in Heaven knows we will err, that we, just like our first parents, may be deceived, and sometimes choose the forbidden fruit, the bitter rather than the sweet, and transgress. As part of the Plan, He therefore provided a means of redemption through His Son, Jesus Christ, the Messiah and the Savior of the world. Elder Robert D. Hales said, "All of us make mistakes. That is why Lehi, who understood the Savior's role in preserving and reclaiming our agency, taught Jacob -- and us -- that 'the Messiah cometh in the fullness of time, that he might redeem the children of men from the fall.'" (Conf. Report, Apr. 2006).

The fall of man had been foreseen by God. Through the wise use of agency, and the power of the Savior's atonement, the fall – and mortality - became the way to allow the children of Adam and Eve to return to God's presence and enjoy redemption, and a life that would not have been possible if Adam and Eve had "remained in the garden of Eden . . . in the same state in which they were after they were created" (2 Nephi 2:22).

This redemption comes through the Atonement. I do not believe that it is mere coincidence that Lehi's statement "men are that they might have joy" is immediately followed by "<u>and</u> the Messiah cometh in the fullness of time, that he might redeem the children of men" (2 Nephi 2:25, 26, *emphasis added*). Our joy is possible <u>because</u> the Savior redeems us. His Atonement is essential to the "great plan of happiness" (Alma 42:8).

<u>The Atonement: Redemption through Christ</u>

It is through the Atonement of Christ that we have the opportunity to return to God's presence. Lehi taught: "there is no flesh that can dwell in the presence of God, save it be through the ***merits***, and ***mercy***, and ***grace*** of the Holy Messiah" (2 Nephi 2:8, *emphasis added*). Elder Richard G. Scott declared: "I testify that except for the Atonement of the Holy Redeemer, the demands of justice would prevent every soul born on earth from returning to the presence of God, to partake of His glory and exaltation, for all make mistakes for which we cannot personally appease justice . . . . Jesus Christ possessed ***merits*** that no other child of Heavenly Father could possibly have. He was a God, Jehovah, before his birth in Bethlehem. His Father not only gave Him His spirit body, but Jesus was His Only Begotten Son in the flesh. Our Master lived a perfect, sinless life and therefore was free from the demands of justice. He was and is perfect in every attribute, including love, compassion, patience, obedience, forgiveness, and humility. His ***mercy*** pays our debt to justice when we repent and obey Him. Even with our best efforts to obey His teachings we will still fall short, yet because of his ***grace*** we will be saved 'after all we can do.'" (Conf. Report, Apr. 1997, *emphasis in original*).

The miracle of the Atonement provides a path for us to obtain salvation. There are two blessings we receive through the Atonement: (i) immortality, and (ii) eternal life. The Savior's gift of immortality is universal, and is given to all mankind through the resurrection. But the gift of eternal life – living the kind of life that God lives – is conditional. It requires repentance and obedience. "Immortality denotes length of life – deathless. Eternal life denotes quality of life – the quality of life God enjoys." (Romney, Conf. Report, Apr. 1975).

President Joseph Fielding Smith explains: "This distinction between *eternal life*, as received by the faithful, and *immortality*, obtained by both the faithful and unfaithful is shown in the words of the Lord to Moses: 'For behold, this is my work and my glory – to bring to pass the immortality *and* eternal life of man.' The conjugation clearly separates the two thoughts. It explains that the Lord is giving to the vast majority of men . . . the blessing of immortality; and to those who will serve him, the blessing of eternal life." (Smith, The Way to Perfection, 329).

The Savior not only provides the universal blessing of immortality through the resurrection, He also provides the conditional gift of eternal life through the Atonement, whereby He paid "the price for all to be cleansed from sin on the conditions He prescribed. Those conditions included faith in Christ, repentance, baptism, the gift of the Holy Ghost, and other ordinances performed by priesthood authority. God's great plan of happiness provides a perfect balance between eternal justice and the mercy we can obtain through the Atonement of Christ." (Oaks, Conf. Report, Oct. 2018). In Lehi's words, the Savior "offereth himself a sacrifice for sin, to answer the ends of the law, unto all those who have a broken heart and contrite spirit; and unto none else can the ends of the law be answered" (2 Nephi 2:7).

The Atonement thus provides redemption from the Fall. The Atonement is the key that can unlock the door to life with God. It is the source of the "exceedingly great joy" Lehi experienced when he partook of the fruit (representing the Atonement) from the tree of life (representing the love of God). (1 Nephi 8:11-12). We "partake" of the Atonement through our belief in Christ, repentance with a broken heart and contrite spirit, obedience to His commandments, and acceptance of His ordinances and covenants; then, "by [His] grace . . . we are saved, after all we can do" (2 Nephi 25:23).

Because of the Atonement, through the *merits*, *mercy*, and *grace* of Jesus Christ, we can be redeemed, and return to the presence of God. "Immortality and the possibility of eternal life were provided by the Atonement of Jesus Christ." (Nelson, Conf. Report, Apr. 2000). This is the Plan of Salvation (Alma 42:5; Moses 6:62; Jarom 1:2) "also called the plan of happiness (Alma 42:8); . . . the plan of redemption (Jacob 6:8; Alma 17:16; Alma 18:39; Alma 34:16; Alma 39 18); the plan of restoration (Alma 41:2); the plan of mercy (Alma 42:15,31; 2 Nephi 9:6); and the plan of deliverance (2 Nephi 11:5). The purpose of the plan is to provide opportunity for the spirit children of God to progress toward an eternal exaltation." (Nelson, Conf. Report, Apr. 2000).

"That plan is built upon three grand pillars: the pillars of eternity. The first pillar is the Creation of the earth, the setting for our mortal journey. The second pillar is the Fall of our first earthly parents, Adam and Eve. Because of the Fall, some marvelous things were given to us. We were able to be born and receive a physical body. . . . Knowing that we would not always choose well – or in other words, sin – Father gave us the third pillar: the Savior Jesus Christ and His Atonement." (Clayton, Conf. Report, April 2017).

Elder Bruce R. McConkie taught "The most important events that ever have or will occur in all eternity are the Creation, the Fall and the Atonement. . . these three verities – the Creation, the Fall, and the Atonement – are inseparably woven together to form one plan of salvation. . . No one of them stands alone; each of them ties into the other two. . . But be it remembered, the Atonement came because of the Fall. Christ paid the ransom for Adam's transgression. If there had been no Fall, there would be no Atonement with its consequent immortality and eternal life. Thus, just as surely as salvation comes because of the Atonement, so salvation comes because of the Fall." ("Christ and the Creation," *Ensign*, June 1982). (See "Atonement" in Topical Index).

The Gift of Agency: Opposition in All Things

Whether we choose to repent and follow Christ, and partake of <u>all</u> the benefits of the Atonement, is up to us. One of the great gifts in the Plan of Salvation is the gift of agency. Lehi taught Jacob that God created "both things to act and things to be acted upon" (2 Nephi 2:14). Man was created to act. (2 Nephi 2:16). This ability to act, to choose, is the foundation of agency.

"When we came into this world, we brought with us from our heavenly home this God-given gift and privilege which we call our agency. It gives us the right and power to make decisions and to choose." (Paul, Conf. Report, Apr. 2006). Elder Dallin H. Oaks declared "we progress by making choices, by which we are tested to show that we will keep God's commandments. To be tested, we must have the agency to choose between alternatives. To provide alternatives on which to exercise our agency, we must have opposition." (Conf. Report, Apr. 2016).

Lehi taught Jacob "there is an opposition in all things" (2 Nephi 2:11). "All things" include both spiritual and physical applications. For example, in nature, opposition exists in forces such gravity, electro-magnetism, and nuclear forces that push and pull on everything from celestial spheres to subatomic particles. Opposite forces exist in the atoms that make up all physical matter. Electrons are kept in orbit around the nucleus because the nucleus is positively charged and attracts the negatively charged electrons. The nuclear force between protons and neutrons both binds them into atomic nuclei, and keeps them from collapsing into each other. Opposition in all things means:

1. Opposition allows progress (or forward motion).
2. Opposition builds strength.
3. Opposition enables choice, or agency.

Opposition allows progress (forward motion).

Progression from "opposition" can be compared by analogy to Isaac Newton's third law of motion, which states that for every action there is an equal and opposite reaction. In the physical world, opposite forces affect every object in motion – without the opposing force, the motion does not occur. Consider the flying motion of birds. Bird wings act as a force to push air down. The opposite reaction is the force of the air pushing up. If there was no opposing force, the bird could not fly. Walking works in a similar fashion. Our legs pushing down on the earth are met by an equal force pushing up, allowing us to move forward. Without opposition, there is no movement, or forward motion, and no progress.

Similarly, Lehi teaches, without opposition, Adam and Eve would have been stuck "in the same state in which they were created," in a condition of stasis – with no change, movement, or progress, forever (2 Nephi 2:22). "Opposition was necessary in the Garden of Eden. If Adam and Eve had not made the choice that introduced mortality, Lehi taught, 'they would have remained in a state of innocence . . . doing no good for they knew no sin.' (2 Nephi 2:23)." (Oaks, Conf. Report, Apr. 2016). They could have no joy, because they knew no misery. (2 Nephi 2:23). All things would "remain as dead," a "thing of naught," with "no purpose" to its creation. (2 Nephi 2:11). With no opposition, there is no progress.

Opposition builds strength.

In the physical world, strength training uses the force of gravity (in the form of weighted bars, dumbbells, etc.) to oppose the force generated by muscle through contraction. Using weighted resistance, the muscle grows. The progressive resistance of the opposite force on the muscle builds strength, and can result in increased muscle size, tendon and ligament strength, bone density, flexibility, tone, metabolic rate, and postural support.

Similarly, opposition can build spiritual strength. President Boyd K. Packer taught, "Life will not be free from challenges, some of them bitter and hard to bear. We may wish to be spared all the trials of life, but that would be contrary to the great plan of happiness, 'for it must needs be, that there is an opposition in all things.' **This testing is the source of all strength**." (Conf. Report, Apr. 2004, *emphasis added*). The trials, and testing we experience in life, are essential for our spiritual strength, and lead to increased capacity, patience, flexibility, and growth.

Elder Neal A. Maxwell taught: "Joseph [Smith], who translated the instructive words 'there is opposition in all things,' came to understand, by experience, that the calisthenics of spiritual growth involve isometrics, the pitting of the emerging self against the stern resistance of the old self." (Conf. Report, Oct. 1983).

"Opposition in the form of difficult circumstances we face in mortality is also part of the plan that furthers our growth in mortality. All of us experience various kinds of opposition that test us. Some of these tests are temptations to sin. Some are mortal challenges apart from personal sin. Some are very great. Some are minor. Some are continuous, and some are mere episodes. None of us is exempt. Opposition permits us to grow toward what our Heavenly Father would have us become [and fulfill the purpose of life]." (Oaks, Conf. Report, Apr. 2016). The purpose of mortal life for the children of God is to provide the experiences needed "to progress toward perfection and ultimately realize their divine destiny as heirs of eternal life." (The Family: A Proclamation to the World). Without opposition, this growth and progression, this spiritual strength, would not occur.

Opposition enables agency.

Finally, opposition is necessary for choice, and ultimately, for agency. "Opposition provides choices, and choices bring consequences – good or bad. . . . Daily, constantly, we choose by our desires, our thoughts and our actions whether we want to be blessed or cursed, happy or miserable." (Benson, Conf. Report, Apr. 1988). "It is opposition that enables choice and it is the opportunity of making the right choices that leads to the growth that is the purpose of the Father's plan." (Oaks, Conf. Report, Apr. 2016). "Indeed, without the existence of choices, without our freedom to choose and without opposition, there would be no real existence. . . . It is a fact that we can neither grow spiritually nor thereby be truly happy unless and until we make wise use of our moral agency." (Maxwell, One More Strain of Praise, 80).

Enticements to Choose Good or Evil: Making Wise Use of Our Agency

To truly choose, we must be "enticed" by real alternatives. Referring to the choice Adam and Eve had between opposites represented by the tree of life and forbidden fruit, Lehi teaches that "man could not act for himself save . . . he was enticed by the one or the other" (2 Nephi 2:16). Enticements are essential to agency. If the forbidden fruit was not enticing, the choice to partake or abstain would not exist.

We are enticed when we are invited or persuaded by forces of good or evil. Mormon explained: "For behold, the Spirit of Christ is given every man, that he may know good from evil . . . for every thing which *inviteth* to do good, and *persuade* to believe in Christ, is sent forth by the power and gift of Christ . . . [and] is of God. But whatsoever thing *persuadeth* men to do evil, and believe not in Christ, and deny him, and serve not God . . . is of the devil . . . for he *persuadeth* no man to do good" (Moroni 7:16, 17, *emphasis added*). "To be meaningful, mortal choices had to be made between contesting forces of good and evil. There had to be opposition and, therefore, an adversary, who . . . was allowed to tempt God's children to act contrary to God's plan." (Oaks, Conf. Report, Oct. 2018).

Satan's enticements and persuasions – or temptations - often target what Lehi called "the will of the flesh" or physical appetites (2 Nephi 2:29). Satan "chafes at the fact that his premortal apostasy permanently disqualifies him from this privilege [having a body], leaving him in a constant state of jealousy and resentment. Thus many, if not most, of the temptations he puts in our path cause us to abuse our bodies or the bodies of others. Because Satan is miserable without a body, he wants us to be miserable because of ours (2 Nephi 2:27)." (Nelson, Conf. Report, Apr. 2019).

Both our spirit and body have desires and appetites. One of life's challenges in exercising our agency in the face of opposition is to not allow our physical appetites to overwhelm our spiritual resolve. My wife taught this principle to her youth Sunday School class with the phrase, **"*don't let your want power overcome your will power.*"**

Submitting to physical appetites may lead to addictions, which can, often slowly, and almost imperceptibly, begin to destroy the very agency through which we made the choice in the first place. "From an initial experiment thought to be trivial, a vicious cycle may follow. From trial comes a habit. From habit dependence. From dependence comes addiction. Its grasp is so gradual. Enslaving shackles of habit are too small to be sensed until they are too strong to be broken. . . . Addiction surrenders later freedom to choose." (Nelson, Conf. Report, Oct. 1988). This is likely one of the reasons the Lord specifically forbids various addictive substances such as alcohol, tobacco, habit-forming drugs, etc. (see D&C 89:5-8), and his prophets instruct us to avoid forms of addictive behavior such as gambling and pornography. Addiction eviscerates agency.

Elder Robert D. Hales provided counsel for any who have fallen into the thick darkness of addiction, and thereby damaged their agency. "How do you reclaim that agency? How do you begin again to exercise it in the right way? You *choose* to act in faith and obedience. May I suggest a few basic choices that you can begin to make now – this very day.

- *Choose* to accept – truly accept – that you are a child of God, that He loves you, and that He has the power to help you.
- *Choose* to put everything – literally everything – on the altar before Him . . . decide that you will use your agency to do His will.
- *Choose* to put yourself in a position to have experiences with the Spirit of God through prayer, in scripture study, at Church meetings, in your home, and through wholesome interactions with others. . . .
- *Choose* to obey and keep your covenants . . . . Renew these covenants weekly by worthily partaking of the sacrament.
- *Choose* to prepare to worthily attend the temple . . . .

"Finally, and most importantly, *choose* to believe in the Atonement of Jesus Christ. Accept the Savior's forgiveness, and then forgive yourself. After you are on the path and are 'free to choose' again, *choose* to reject feelings of shame for sins you have already repented of, refuse to be discouraged about the past, and rejoice in hope for the future."(Conf. Report, Apr. 2006).

<u>Consequences of Our Choices: "Choosing the Good Part"</u>
While the gift of agency provides the freedom to choose, we are not free to choose the consequences of our choices. "The Lord has given you the gift of agency and instructed you sufficiently to know good from evil. You are free to choose and are permitted to act, but you are not free to choose the consequences. With absolute certainty, choices of good and right lead to happiness and peace, while choices of sin and evil eventually lead to unhappiness, sorrow and misery." (Wirthlin, Conf. Report, Oct. 1989). Once we have made choices, we are subject to the consequences of those choices. Some of these consequences are immediate; and, some occur over time. "As Father Lehi testified to his family of the blessings of agency. . . Our use of agency determines who we are and what we will be." (Hales, Conf. Report, Apr. 2006).

We are ultimately responsible for our own choices. And, through choosing to "do good continually" (Mor. 7:13), we can ultimately obtain "liberty and eternal life." Lehi calls the righteous exercise of agency "choosing the good part" (2 Nephi 2:30), and addressing his sons, provides them with three succinct ways to do so:

1. "look" to Christ;
2. "hearken" to his commandments; and
3. "be faithful" to his words. (2 Nephi 2:28).

Through these fundamental actions, we can "choose the good part." Indeed, one of the highest expressions of agency is when we choose to submit our will to God and are willing voluntarily to follow Christ in all that we do. If we desire eternal life, or the kind of life that God lives, it is logical to that we learn to make choices that God would make.

The greatest expression of mortal agency, therefore, may be to voluntarily submit our will, and choose to follow the will of our perfect, all-knowing, all-loving Father in Heaven. This was the great example provided by our Savior, implicit in His life's work and creed, "Not my will, but thine be done." (See Matt. 26:42; John 5:30; 3 Nephi 11:11; Mosiah 15:2, 7; Matt. 6:10; D&C 19:24). From the pre-existence, the Savior affirmed, "Father, thy will be done, and the glory be thine forever" (Moses 4:2). "All through His mortal life, Jesus lived that promise . . . 'I came . . . not to do mine own will, but the will of [the Father, who] sent me' (John 6:38). In His agony in Gethsemane, He prayed, 'Nevertheless not my will, but thine, be done' (Luke 22:42). When the Lord calls the elders in Israel to 'look unto me in every thought' . . . it is a call to trust Him completely, surrender our will and yield our hearts to Him." (Clark, Conf. Report, Apr. 2019).

As we submit our will to God's will, our power to choose, and our power to act in righteousness, may increase. The Lord told the prophet Nephi, "[thou] hast not sought thine own life, but hast sought my will, and to keep my commandments. And now, because thou hast done this with such unweariyngness, behold, I will bless thee forever; and I will make thee mighty in word and in deed, in faith and in works; yea even that all things shall be done unto thee according to thy word, for thou shalt not ask that which is contrary to my will" (Helaman 10:4-5).

Discourse 4: Lehi, "Joseph - A Choice Seer" (2 Nephi 3)

Prophet	Key Doctrines	Scriptures	Audience	Date
Lehi	• A Choice Seer • The Power of the Bible and the Book of Mormon together	2 Nephi 3	To his son, Joseph, shortly before his death	About 588 B.C. – 570 B.C.

INTRODUCTION

In Second Nephi chapter three, Lehi addresses his final recorded discourse to his son, Joseph, his "last-born." He blesses Joseph that the Lord will consecrate the land for the inheritance of his seed. He promises Joseph that his seed will not be destroyed if they are obedient. (2 Nephi 3:3). He tells Joseph, that he, Lehi, is a descendant of "Joseph who was carried captive into Egypt" (2 Nephi 3:4). Lehi informs his son that their forefather Joseph received a promise from the Lord that his descendants would include a "righteous branch" of the house of Israel, "which was to be broken off" (2 Nephi 3:5). This righteous branch includes Lehi's family and descendants. Lehi quotes several of Joseph's prophesies about his descendants in the promised land, including the coming forth of another Joseph, who would be a "choice seer" (2 Nephi 3:7, 15).

Elder Sterling W. Sill describes the scene in the following manner: "Six hundred years B.C. a little group of Israelites who were descendants of Joseph were led away from Jerusalem by the Lord, headed for a far-off land which we now know as America. They brought with them their records and the writings of their prophets, including the writings of . . . Joseph who was sent to Egypt 'to preserve life' (Gen. 45:5). After their arrival in the promised land, Lehi read to them a prophesy made by their famous ancestor, Joseph, about events that should take place in the latter days in this new land." (Conf. Report, Apr. 1956).

As he prepared to leave his earthly family, Lehi spoke to his youngest son about four Josephs: (i) Lehi's youngest son, Joseph; (ii) Lehi's ancestor, Joseph of Egypt, the son of Jacob and Rachel; (iii) Joseph's descendant, Joseph Smith Jr., a "choice seer"; and (iv) Joseph Smith's father – Joseph Smith Sr. Lehi teaches his own son, Joseph, about the prophecy of their ancestor, Joseph of Egypt, concerning his latter-day descendant, Joseph Smith, who will perform a great work that will bless the lives and bring salvation to many of their descendants. Ultimately, the four, inter-generational Josephs are not only connected by their family lineage, but also by their righteousness, their faithfulness, their good works, and the Book of Mormon, itself.

DISCOURSE: 2 Nephi 3[17]

KEY DOCTRINES

- **A Choice Seer**. Joseph of Egypt prophesies about the latter-day prophet, Joseph Smith.

- **Power of the Bible and Book of Mormon Together**. Writings of the descendants of Judah and the descendants of Joseph shall come together to confound false doctrines and provide knowledge of the Lord's covenants. The Book of Mormon will be instrumental in confirming and clarifying the teachings of the Bible.

COMMENTARY

Joseph of Egypt prophesied in detail about one of his descendants, a "choice seer," who the Lord would "raise up," to bless his posterity (2 Nephi 3:6). We believe this "choice seer" was the latter-day prophet, Joseph Smith, Jr.[18]

Joseph Smith: A Choice Seer

The following table includes prophecies from Joseph of Egypt, the son of Jacob and Rachel, and their application to the Prophet Joseph Smith, Jr.:

Prophesy	Application – Fulfillment
"A seer shall the Lord my God raise up, who shall be a choice seer unto the fruit of my loins" (2 Nephi 3:6).	Joseph Smith to "be called a seer, a translator, a prophet" (D&C 21:1). He was a seer to the descendants of Joseph – both through Lehi and Ephraim. The Lord Himself stated that Joseph Smith should "be called a seer" (D&C 21:1); and the "Prophet and Seer of the Lord" (D&C 135:3).
"He shall be esteemed highly among the fruit of thy loins" (2 Nephi 3:7).	There are millions of descendants of Joseph, whether through Lehi or Ephraim, who accept and revere Joseph Smith as a prophet.
"He shall do a work for the fruit of thy loins . . . , which shall be of great worth to them" (2 Nephi 3:7).	These descendants have been greatly blessed by the revelations, covenants and gospel restored by Joseph Smith, Jr.

---

[17] Compare JST Genesis 50:24-38 to 2 Nephi 3:4-22.
[18] Joseph Smith was a descendant of Joseph of Egypt through the latter's son, Ephraim. In the April 1952 general conference, Elder Eldred G. Smith, patriarch to the Church stated, "Joseph Smith, Senior, was a true descendant, through Ephraim, the younger son of Joseph." (Conf. Report, Apr. 1952).

"He shall do none other work, save the work which I shall command him" (2 Nephi 3:8).	There were several instances where the Lord instructed Joseph Smith to focus on a specific work, e.g., the translation of the Book of Mormon: "And you have a gift to translate the plates . . . and I have commanded that you should pretend to no other gift until my purpose is fulfilled in this; for I will grant unto you no other gift until it is finished" (D&C 5:4)
"He shall be great like unto Moses" (2 Nephi 3:9).	Moses gathered Israel from Egypt. Joseph Smith was given keys by Moses to gather Israel. (D&C 110:11). Both Moses and Joseph Smith gave the people God's commandments. Both Moses and Joseph Smith saw talked to God face-to-face. See also D&C 103:16.
"I give power to bring forth my word unto the seed of thy loins" (2 Nephi 3:11).	Joseph Smith received power from God to translate the Book of Mormon, and to receive other revelations from God. (D&C 3; 5; 10).
"The fruit of thy loins shall write; and the fruit of the loins of Judah shall write; and that which shall be written . . . shall grow together, unto the confounding of false doctrines" (2 Nephi 3:12).	The Book of Mormon and other modern revelations clarify many principles and doctrines contained in the Bible. (D&C 20:8-15; 42:12).
"And out of weakness he shall be made strong" (2 Nephi 3:13).	Joseph Smith had a humble background, was not classically educated, and often struggled financially, but was trained by the Lord. "He was ignorant of letters as the world has it, but the most profoundly learned and intelligent man that I have ever met in my life." (Taylor, Journal of Discourses, 21:155).
"They that seek to destroy him shall be confounded" (2 Nephi 3:14).	Joseph Smith was preserved until he accomplished his mission. (D&C 121:16-22). His assassination did not stop his work or the growth of the church he restored.
"His name shall be called after me; and it shall be after the name of his father" (2 Nephi 3:15).	Joseph Smith Jr. was the son of Joseph Smith Sr., and named after his father.
"For the thing which the Lord shall bring forth by his hand, by the power of the Lord shall bring my people unto salvation" (2 Nephi 3:15).	Joseph Smith restored gospel ordinances that lead to salvation.

Source: Book of Mormon Institute Manual, 2 Nephi 3:6-15

"The Prophet Joseph Smith fits in every detail with the prophecy made anciently by Joseph of Egypt. . . . In every respect Joseph Smith was God's . . . choice seer." (Hunter, Conf. Report, Oct. 1968). Elder Sterling W. Sill taught: "Joseph Smith fulfilled these prophecies [in 2 Nephi 3]. Joseph [of Egypt] had said, 'His name shall be called after me,' Joseph. 'And it shall be after the name of his father.' Joseph Smith's father's name was Joseph. Then the prophet [Joseph of Egypt] said, 'And he shall be like unto me.' Joseph, the son of Jacob, was sent before the face of the Egyptian famine to preserve life. And Joseph Smith was sent before the face of the spiritual famine spoken of by Amos (Amos 8:11-12), for exactly the same purpose, to unlock the granaries of spiritual truth, to dispel the darkness that covered the earth, and make possible that every living soul might have 'life everlasting' (Luke 18:30)." (Conf. Report, Apr. 1956).

The Lord told Joseph of Egypt that this seer would have "power to bring forth my word" (2 Nephi 3:11, 15). President Brigham Young testified: "It was decreed in the counsels of eternity, long before the foundations of the earth were laid, that he, Joseph Smith, should be the man, in the last dispensation of this world, to bring forth the word of God to the people. . . . He was foreordained in eternity to preside over this last dispensation." (Discourses of Brigham Young, 108). Several years before Joseph Smith was born, his paternal grandfather, Asael Smith, prophesied: "It has been borne in upon my soul that one of my descendants will promulgate a work to revolutionize the world of religious faith." (Reeve, Conf. Report, Oct. 1985).

A Choice Seer

Joseph Smith was both a prophet and a seer. (Mosiah 8:13-16). A seer can translate ancient records. A seer can use special instruments such as the Urim and Thummim (JS-H 1:35). A seer can know things past and future (Mosiah 8:13; 28:16). A seer reveals the word of the Lord obtained by translation and revelation. All of these attributes apply to the Prophet Joseph Smith. Elder Neal A. Maxwell taught: "Early in the restoration, by translation and revelation, numerous plain and precious truths appeared in fairly rapid succession. This occurred through Joseph Smith, the 'choice seer.'" (Conf. Report, Oct. 1985).

"The volume of resulting revelations and translations is enormous, underscoring the words 'choice seer.' But it isn't just the sheer volume of what Joseph received which is now being shared with mankind; it is also the existence of 'stunners' in the midst of such abundance. Through multiple revelations and translations, for example, came a description of a universe far exceeding the astrophysics of the 1830s, a cosmos containing 'worlds without number' . . . it is no surprise to us that scientists' latest estimate of the number of stars in the universe is approximately 70 sextillion – 'more stars in the sky,' scientists say, 'than there are grains of sand in every beach and desert on Earth.'" (Maxwell, Conf. Report, Oct. 2003).

Joseph Smith also fulfilled Joseph of Egypt's prophesy that "out of weakness he [the seer] will be made strong" (2 Nephi 3:13). "Overarching the Prophet Joseph's entire ministry were his comparative youth, his superficial formal education, and his incredibly rapid acquisition of knowledge and maturity. He was 14 at the First Vision and 17 at the first visit from the angel Moroni. He was 21 when he received the golden plates and just 23 when he finished translating the Book of Mormon (in less than 60 working days). . . . Because of the poverty of his family, he had little formal education and as a youth was compelled to work long hours to help put food on the family table. . . . He was almost continually on the edge of financial distress. . . . The Lord had advised him that 'in temporal labors thou shalt not have strength, for this is not thy calling.' (D&C 24:9)." (Oaks, Conf. Report, Apr. 1996).

"Joseph was, by the standards of the world, 'not learned.' . . . Emma Smith reportedly said that Joseph, at the time of translation of the Book of Mormon, could not compose a 'well-worded letter let alone dictate a book like the Book of Mormon.'. . . This obscure young man apparently paused while translating and dictating to Emma . . . concerning the 'wall of Jerusalem' and said, in effect, 'Emma, I didn't know there was a wall around Jerusalem.' But Joseph's keen mind was being awakened and expanded as the tutoring words of the Lord and of past prophets flowed through his quickened consciousness. In fact, he was the very seer foreseen anciently by the earlier Joseph in Egypt." (Maxwell, Conf. Report, Oct. 1983).

Although a "choice seer," Joseph Smith was not perfect. On one occasion, he said, "I never told you I was perfect – but there is no error in the revelations which I have taught." (Maxwell, Conf. Report, Oct. 2003, quoting The Words of Joseph Smith, 369). He was mortal, with human weaknesses. Joseph's humility, and candor about his own imperfections. is refreshing. Of his teenage years, Joseph recorded, "I frequently fell into many foolish errors, and displayed the weakness of youth, and the foibles of human nature; which, I am sorry to say, led me into divers temptations, offensive in the sight of God." Nevertheless, this behavior did not include "any great or malignant sins" since "a disposition to commit such was never in my nature" (JS-H 1:28). Later, the Prophet Joseph cautioned a group of Saints in Nauvoo to be patient with his imperfections. "He said he was but a man and they must not expect him to be perfect . . . but if they would bear with his infirmities and the infirmities of his brethren, he would likewise bear their infirmities." (Jesse, The Papers of Joseph Smith, Vol. 2, 1832-1842, p. 489).

Joseph Smith recorded several instances of his own human weaknesses in the revelations published in the Doctrine & Covenants. For example, after Joseph Smith allowed Martin Harris to take the first 116 manuscript pages of the Book of Mormon, the Lord chastised him for following the "persuasions of men" (D&C 3:6). Later, the Lord told Joseph to "repent and walk more uprightly" (D&C 5:21); and indicated that he had "sinned" (D&C 64:7; D&C 90:1). Joseph said, "The burdens which roll upon me are very great. My persecutors allow me no rest, and I find that in the midst of business and care the spirit is willing, but the flesh is weak. Although I was called of my Heavenly Father to lay the foundation of this great work and kingdom in this dispensation, and testify of His revealed will to scattered Israel, I am subject to like passions as other men, like the prophets of olden times." (History of the Church, 5:516). Although he was not perfect, and experienced temptations, severe opposition and persecution throughout his life, he never wavered from his divine appointment. Despite any mortal foibles, Joseph Smith was a model of virtue and righteousness, and lived and died fulfilling his calling as a true prophet of God.

Those who knew Joseph best testified as to his character, and sustained him as a prophet. President Wilford Woodruff, who knew Joseph Smith personally, and worked closely with him, testified that "I have felt to rejoice exceedingly in what I saw of brother Joseph, for in his public and private career he carried with him the Spirit of the Almighty, and he manifested a greatness of soul which I had never seen in any other man." (Woodruff, Journal of Discourses, 7:98).

John Taylor, who was with Joseph Smith when he was murdered, said: "I testify before God, angels, and men, that he was a good, honorable, virtuous man . . . that his private and public character was unimpeachable – and that he lived and died a man of God." (The Gospel Kingdom, p. 355). Brigham Young stated: "I do not think a man lives on the earth that knew [Joseph Smith] any better than I did; and I am bold to say that, Jesus Christ excepted, no better man ever lived or does live upon this earth." (Woodruff, Journal of Discourses, 9:332).

The Book of Mormon and the Bible Shall Grow Together

Joseph of Egypt prophesied that the Book of Mormon would be instrumental in supporting and clarifying the teachings of the Bible. Specifically, he wrote that the record written by the "fruit of the loins of Joseph," including Lehi's descendants, which is the Book of Mormon, would "grow together" with a sacred record written by "the fruit of the loins of Judah," or the Bible. (2 Nephi 3:12).

The fulfillment of the prophesy that these works of scriptures would "grow together" means that the records complement and support each other, gather together gospel truths, and serve as mutually supporting witnesses of Jesus Christ: "in the mouth of two or three witnesses every word may be established" (Matthew 18:16).[19]

Joseph prophesies that as the writings of his descendants and the writings of the descendants of Judah grow together, they shall confound false doctrines, lay down contentions, establish peace, and bring Joseph's (and Lehi's) descendants to the knowledge of the Lord's covenants with their fathers. (2 Nephi 3:12). After quoting this verse, Elder George Q. Cannon observed, "Now, here is a very remarkable prediction connected with the coming forth of this Book. It should have the effect, when united with the Bible – for it was the Bible that the Prophet was referring to as being the writings of the fruit of the loins of Judah; when these two Books should be united, it should have a remarkable effect – that is, their union should. They should confound false doctrine; they should lay down contentions, put an end to them and establish peace." (Journal of Discourses, 25:119).

The Book of Mormon and the Bible sustain each other, and the direct translation of the Book of Mormon through the gift and power of God clarifies certain teachings and doctrines that are not clear in the Bible. The books "grow together" to teach the true word of God, and to provide a comprehensive testament of Jesus Christ. In a sense, the Bible teaches the what, and the Book of Mormon teaches the why.

This is not only fulfillment of Joseph's prophesy cited by Lehi; it is also the fulfillment of Ezekiel's poetic prophesy about the coming together of the "stick of Judah" and the "stick of Joseph" (Ezekiel 37:15-20). "Thus saith the Lord God; Behold, I will take the stick of Joseph, which is in the hand of Ephraim . . . and will put them with him, even with the stick of Judah, and make them one stick, and they shall be one in mine hand" (Ezekiel 37:19).

(See "Scriptures - Bible" in Topical Index, 1 Nephi 13; see also Mormon 7; Moroni 10).

---

[19]Certain editions of these scriptures contain comprehensive cross-references. For example, in 1979, the King James version of the Bible was updated extensively with footnotes, indexes, and cross-references to the Book of Mormon, and other scriptures. (Packer, Conf. Report, Oct. 1982).

Discourse 5: Nephi, "Panoramic Vision of the Future" (1 Nephi 11-14)

Prophet	Key Doctrines	Scriptures	Audience	Date
Nephi	<ul><li>Pondering leads to Revelation</li><li>The Condescension of God</li><li>Panoramic Vision of the Future: Christ; Nephites & Lamanites; Gentiles; Bible and Book of Mormon; Restoration of the Gospel; Last Days</li></ul>	1 Nephi 11-14	Interview with an angel on a mountain, a vision written and shared in part with his brethren as well as the future readers of his record	600 – 592 B.C.

INTRODUCTION

Nephi is the author/editor of the first two books in the Book of Mormon. It is "I, Nephi," who begins the record. He first summarizes some of his father's teachings, and then records several events in connection with the exodus of Lehi's family to the promised land. We learn of Nephi's faithfulness ("I will go and do the things which the Lord has commanded," 1 Nephi 3:7); his tribulations with his brothers, who ultimately sought to kill him; and his humble acknowledgement of personal weakness ("My soul grieveth because of my iniquities. I am encompassed about, because of the temptations which do so easily beset me," 2 Nephi 4:17-18).

Nephi was a strong man, large in stature, who was a personal witness of Jesus Christ.[20] Nephi was chosen to be the leader of the righteous branch of Lehi's family, and recorded the spiritual and temporal history of his people. Nephi's writings include three lengthy discourses of his own, all directed to his people, the House of Israel, and future readers of his record. These discourses include selected teachings from the prophet Isaiah, and Nephi's own prophesies and instructions.

Nephi's first discourse appears chronologically after Lehi's vision of the tree of life. After listening to his father describe his vision, Nephi desires to know and understand the things Lehi saw. As Nephi "sat pondering in [his] heart," he is "caught away in the Spirit of the Lord" to "an exceedingly high mountain"[21] (1 Nephi 11:1). The Spirit conducts a brief interview with Nephi, and asks, "What desirest thou?"

---

[20] Nephi saw a vision of the Lord's birth and life, and later testified, "I have seen him." (2 Nephi 11:2-3).
[21] Compare Nephi's experience to Moses (Moses 1:1-2); Enoch (Moses 7:2-3); and Christ at the Mount of Transfiguration (Matt. 17:1-9). "The Lord often uses mountains to reveal his mysteries when there are no temples." (Nyman, I Nephi Wrote This Record, 137). See also Paul, 2 Cor. 12:2; John, Revelation 21:10.

Nephi's response is straightforward, "I desire to behold the things which my father saw" (1 Nephi 11:3). Thereafter, Nephi not only receives an interpretation of his father's vision of the tree of life, he also sees a panoramic vision of the future, including the birth and life of Christ, the scattering and gathering of the Jews, and future events in the land of promise.

Some of these events were evidently taught to Nephi and his family by Lehi. Nephi says that after his father "made an end of speaking the words of his dream, and also of exhorting them to all diligence, he spake unto them concerning the Jews" (1 Nephi 10:2). In the book of First Nephi, chapter ten, Nephi summarizes some of these teachings and prophesies of his father as a preamble to his own vision recorded in chapters eleven through fourteen (1 Nephi 10-14).

In First Nephi chapter ten, Nephi refers to some of Lehi's more comprehensive teachings that are not included in the Book of Mormon. For example, Nephi informs us that Lehi taught his family that Jerusalem will be destroyed and many Jews carried away captive into Babylon, but after a period of time, would return again (1 Nephi 10:3). Lehi prophesied that after the Jews return, indeed, specifically, 600 years after Lehi's family leaves Jerusalem, God would raise up a Messiah among the Jews, who will be a "Savior" and a "Redeemer of the world" (1 Nephi 10:4-5).

Lehi "*spake much*" about a prophet who shall come before the Messiah to prepare the way, and shall baptize the Messiah. Lehi further prophesied that the Messiah would be slain by the Jews, but would rise from the dead, and later manifest Himself to the Gentiles by the Holy Ghost. (1 Nephi 10:11). Lehi also "*spake much*" concerning the Gentiles, and that the house of Israel should be scattered throughout the earth, and then gathered again "after the Gentiles had received the fullness of the Gospel" (1 Nephi 10:12, *emphasis added*).

Nephi says that there were "*many* more things" that Lehi prophesied and taught "which I do not write in this book" (1 Nephi 10:15). Although we don't have the full record of Lehi's teachings at this time, we do know from Nephi's summary that Lehi taught his family about the coming of Christ, and the importance of the Gentiles in the gathering of the House of Israel.

Though Nephi does not provide details about these teachings of his father, they evidently served as the foundation for his detailed vision recorded in chapters 11-14, which extend beyond an interpretation of Lehi's dream of the tree of life to include the life and ministry of the Savior, the scattering and gathering of the Jews, and the restoration of the Gospel through the Gentiles. Nephi's desire to "see, and hear, and know" the things taught by his father led to a comprehensive and panoramic vision of Christ, the House of Israel, and future inhabitants of the promised land.

DISCOURSE: 1 Nephi 11 – 14

KEY DOCTRINES

- **Pondering the Word of God Can Lead to Revelation.** Nephi's righteous desires and faithfulness, coupled with pondering the words of his father, led to a marvelous vision.

- **Condescension of God**. The condescension and love of God are demonstrated through the life and mission of Jesus Christ, and His birth to a mortal mother.

- **Divine Attributes of Mary**. Mary demonstrates many of the divine attributes of her Son.

COMMENTARY

Pondering Leads to Revelation

Nephi *desired* to know the things his father, Lehi, saw in vision.[22] We are also told that Nephi had *faith* the Lord was able to make these things known unto him, and that he spent time "*pondering*" his father's teachings. (1 Nephi 11:1). Through this formula of desire, faith, and pondering, Nephi receives a marvelous vision. "Because of his believing heart and his diligent efforts, Nephi was blessed with a marvelous experience. He received a witness of the forthcoming birth, life, and Crucifixion of the Savior Jesus Christ; he saw the coming forth of the Book of Mormon and the Restoration of the gospel in the last days – all as a result of his desire to know for himself." (Christensen, Conf. Report, Oct. 2014).

It was Nephi's desire coupled with faith, and "pondering in his heart" about the words of his father, which opened the door for revelation from the Spirit of the Lord. Similar to Nephi's experience, there are several other recorded instances where pondering about the scriptures, coupled with faithful prayer, have led to visions and revelation. Some examples include:

- Joseph Smith and Sidney Rigdon's vision of the Savior. "While we *meditated* upon these things [John 5:29] . . . the eyes of our understanding were opened . . . and we beheld the glory of the Son on the right hand of the Father" (D&C 76:19-23).
- Joseph F. Smith's vision of the spirit world. "I sat in my room *pondering* over the scriptures [1 Peter 3, 4]; . . . As I *pondered* over these things, the eyes of my understanding were opened . . . and I saw the hosts of the dead, both small and great" (D&C 138:1-2, 11).
- Nephi, the son of Helaman, hears the voice of God. As Nephi was "*pondering* upon the things the Lord had shown him . . . behold a voice came unto him" (Hel. 10:2-4, 5-11).
- Joseph Smith's first vision. "I *reflected* . . . again and again [about James 1:5] . . . . I came to the conclusion that I must . . . *ask of God* . . . I began to offer up the *desires* of my heart to God. . . . I saw two Personages, whose brightness and glory defy all description, standing above me in the air" (JS-H 1:8, 12, 15, 17).

Pondering the word of God can be a path to personal revelation for each of us. "Ponder" means to weigh mentally, think deeply about, deliberate, and meditate. Elder D. Todd Christofferson counseled, "Study the scriptures carefully, deliberately. Ponder and pray over them. Scriptures are revelation, and they will bring added revelation." ("The Blessing of Scripture," *Ensign*, May 2010). "By pondering, we give the Spirit an opportunity to impress and direct." (Ashton, Conf. Report, Oct. 1987). President David O. McKay taught, "I should like to emphasize the need . . . for more meditation. . . . Meditation is one of the most secret, most sacred doors through which we pass into the presence of the Lord." (Conf. Report, Apr. 1967). The Lord, Himself, instructed the Nephites, and all of us, to "ponder upon the things which I have said" (3 Nephi 17:3). (See discussion, "Feasting on the Word of Christ" in 2 Nephi 32). See also, D&C 8:2-3 ("I will tell you in your mind and in your heart . . . this is the spirit of revelation").

---

[22] "I, Nephi, was *desirous* also that I might see, and hear, and know of these things" (1 Nephi 10:17, *emphasis added*). "[A]fter I had desired to know the things that my father had see, and believing that the Lord was able to make them known unto me . . . ." (1 Nephi 11:1, *emphasis added*).

Interview with an Angel

Nephi was blessed to receive direct instruction from both the "Spirit of the Lord" and by an "angel of the Lord" (1 Nephi 11:1,14).[23] The Spirit rewards Nephi for his faithful inquiry with a vision of the tree of life, and asks Nephi, "What desirest thou?" (1 Nephi 11:10). After Nephi responds, "To know the interpretation thereof" (1 Nephi 11:11), the Spirit departs, and an angel "came down and stood before [Nephi]" (1 Nephi 11:14), and provides a panoramic vision of the future of the world.[24]

In his vision and interview with the angel, Nephi receives an interpretation of Lehi's dream, and:

- Nephi sees the birth, ministry, and crucifixion of Christ (1 Nephi 11).
- Nephi sees a vision of the growth and the eventual destruction of his people (1 Nephi 12).
- Nephi sees the kingdoms of the Gentiles, and a "church" that fights the saints; the Gentiles in the promised land; records written by the Jews and Gentiles (1 Nephi 13).
- Nephi sees the latter-day conflict between good and evil, and the end of the world (1 Nephi 14).

President Spencer W. Kimball stated: "In his vision [Nephi] saw the birth, life, and ministry of the Christ, his coming to the Western Hemisphere and organizing his Church here. He saw three generations of righteousness and then centuries of unrighteousness, with battles culminating in the destruction of millions, followed by centuries of degradation, scattering, persecution, and suffering. He saw nations grow out of the Eastern empires, and the kingdoms of the Gentiles arise. He saw Columbus and other explorers cross the deep, and the puritans and pilgrims settle a new country. He envisioned the Revolutionary War, the total subjugation of the descendants of Lehi, the coming of the Bible, the restoration of the gospel, the organization of the Church, the coming forth of the Book of Mormon." (Conf. Report, Apr. 1949).

---

[23] Elder James E. Talmage suggests that the Spirit may have been the Holy Ghost. "The Holy Ghost [is also known by] synonyms, Spirit of God, Spirit of the Lord, or simply, Spirit . . . . That the Spirit of the Lord is capable of manifesting Himself in the form and figure of man, is indicated by the wonderful interview between the Spirit and Nephi, in which He revealed Himself to the prophet, questioned him concerning his desires and belief, instructed him in the things of God, speaking face to face with the man." (Talmage, Articles of Faith, 158-159).

[24] Nephi says that he was visited by an "angel of the Lord" (1 Nephi 11:14; 14:29). We do not know whether this is the same "angel from God" who declared "glad tidings of great joy," including the birth of Christ, to King Benjamin. (Mosiah 3:2-3). Or, whether this was the "angel of the Lord" who brought "glad tidings," and taught Samuel the Lamanite about the coming of Christ. (Hel. 13:6-7). Or, whether this was the angel that told Jacob that the name of the "Holy One of Israel" shall be Christ. (Jacob 10:3). Whether these angelic announcements concerning the coming of Christ were delivered by one, or several different heavenly messengers, is not revealed in the record.

The angel guides Nephi through the vision by alternately commanding Nephi to "Look," providing instruction, and asking questions. The angel asks at least seven questions during the vision/interview to focus Nephi's thinking and emphasize certain doctrines.[25] These questions include specific inquiries to Nephi: "what do you see?" and "what do you know?

Effective teaching through inquiries from heavenly beings dates back to the time of Adam. The Lord asks certain questions of Adam and Eve in the Garden of Eden both for instruction and to give an opportunity to confess transgression (Moses 4:15, 17, 19). Later, after the expulsion from the Garden, an angel visits Adam to ask/teach, "Why dost thou offer sacrifice unto the Lord?" (Moses 4:6). Divine questioning provides the mortal listener the opportunity to learn and grow.

The Lord Jesus Christ also taught through the use of questions. One example of this is the Savior's interaction with a "certain lawyer" in Luke 10:25-37. When the lawyer inquired, "what shall I do to inherit eternal life?" the Lord answered the question with a question, "What is written in the law? How readest thou?" (Luke 10:38). The inquiry, "what is written in the law," referred the lawyer back to the scriptures, and the deeper question, "how readest thou," probed for his understanding. The lawyer replied that the law teaches us to love God, and "thy neighbor as thyself," but then inquired, seeking some self-justification, "and who is my neighbor?" The Savior used this opportunity to expound His doctrine, and teach the parable of the Good Samaritan to demonstrate that we show our love of God by serving others. Like the Master Teacher, the angel used questions and scriptural references to increase mortal understanding.

Vision of Christ: The Condescension of God

In the portion of his vision recorded in chapter 11, Nephi witnesses the Savior descending to earth as a mortal: His birth to Mary, His baptism, His ministry, His miracles, His crucifixion, and His resurrection. Nephi learns that the key to his father's vision is the tree of life, which the angel identifies as the love of God, through the gift of the "Lamb of God," the "Son of the Eternal Father" (1 Nephi 11:21, 22). This love of God manifests itself in what the angel calls the "condescension of God" (1 Nephi 11:16, 26).

Condescension here means to descend, a voluntary descent from one's rank or dignity, where an entity of a superior status does something beneath its rank for the benefit of others. "Here was Jesus – a member of the Godhead, the Firstborn of the Father, the Creator, Jehovah of the Old Testament – now leaving His divine and holy station; divesting Himself of all that glory and majesty and entering the body of a tiny infant; helpless, completely dependent on His mother and earthly [step]-father. That He should not come to the finest of earthly palaces and be . . . showered with jewels but should come to a lowly stable is astonishing. Little wonder that the angel should say to Nephi, 'Behold the condescension of God!'" (Lund, Jesus Christ, Key to the Plan of Salvation, 16). President Gordon B. Hinckley affirmed: "Well did an angel ask a prophet . . . 'Knowest thou the condescension of God?' (1 Nephi 11:16). I suppose none of us can fully understand that – how the great Jehovah should come among men, his birth in a manger, among a hated people, in a vassal state." (Conf. Report, Apr. 1978).

---

[25] The angel's questions include: What beholdest thou? (1 Nephi 11:14; 1 Nephi 13:2). Knowest thou the condescension of God? (1 Nephi 11:16). Knowest thou the meaning of the tree which thy father saw? (1 Nephi 11:21). Thou rememberest the twelve apostles of the Lamb? (1 Nephi 12:9). Knowest thou the meaning of the book? (1 Nephi 13:21). Rememberest thou the covenants of the Father? (1 Nephi 14:8).

"Jesus Christ condescended to be tempted, tried, mocked, judged, and crucified, even though he had power and authority to prevent such actions. President John Taylor described the condescension of Christ in these beautiful words: 'It was further necessary that He should descend below all things, in order that He might raise others above all things; for if He could not raise Himself and be exalted through those principles brought about by the atonement, He could not raise others; He could not do for others what He could not do for Himself.' (The Mediation and Atonement, 144). Christ's suffering in the Garden of Gethsemane epitomizes the most magnificent of all the attributes of Christ, His perfect love." (Tingey, Conf. Report, Apr. 2006). The willingness of the Savior to live a mortal life under such circumstances – and undertake the Atonement so that we may be saved, demonstrates the perfect love of both the Father and the Son for us, and is symbolized in the beauty of the tree.

Mary, the Mother of Jesus Christ

At the very outset of his vision, Nephi beholds Mary, "a virgin, and she was exceedingly fair . . . A virgin most beautiful and fair above all other virgins" (1 Nephi 11:15). The angel asks: "Knowest thou the condescension of God?" (1 Nephi 11:16), and explains that "the virgin whom thou seest is the mother of the Son of God, after the manner of the flesh" (1 Nephi 11:18). Nephi then sees a vision of Mary "bearing a child in her arms" (1 Nephi 11:21), who the angel testifies is the "Lamb of God," the "Son of the Eternal Father" (1 Nephi 11:21). "Jesus Christ condescended to come to earth and be born as a helpless babe to Mary." (Tingey, Conf. Report, Apr. 2006). This was part of the condescension of the Lord – He agreed to be born to a mortal woman, and come to earth as a baby, and to inherit the limitations and challenges of mortality.

As to Mary, the scriptures are mostly - and respectfully - silent about the background and details of her life. Alma later identifies her by name, and describes her as a "precious and chosen vessel" (Alma 7:10; see also Mosiah 3:8). From the New Testament, we learn that Mary was of royal lineage, descended from King David,[26] and was a dutiful disciple of her Son, Jesus, and a faithful member of His church, after His death. She may have been a teenager at his birth,[27] and thus would have been in her late forties, at the time of his death and resurrection, 33 years later.

There are apocryphal accounts that Mary was raised in the temple, but there is no scriptural or doctrinal confirmation this was so. The story of Mary being presented at the temple as a child is recorded in the Protevanglium of James, an apocryphal book of the second century.[28] This writing was not canonized scripture, but evidently circulated in the early church. According to this account: "And the child [Mary] was three years old … and they [Mary and her parents, Joachim and Anna] went up to the Temple of the Lord, and the priest received her and kissed her and blessed her, saying, 'The Lord has magnified thy name in all generations. In thee, on the last

---

[26] "Matthew, in giving the genealogy of Jesus Christ, traces it back from his mother, through the lineage of the fathers, back to David." Snow, Journal of Discourses, 19:266. See Talmage, Jesus the Christ, 87. (Jesus inherited both from Mary, his mother, and from Joseph, his step-father, the blood of David and the right to David's throne.)

[27] Mary was "a young woman, one probably in the age range of those in our Young Women organization." (Holland, Conf. Report, Oct. 1995).

[28] "Verily, thus saith the Lord unto you concerning the Apocrypha – there are many things contained therein that are true, and it is mostly translated correctly; There are many things contained therein that are not true, which are interpolations by the hands of men" (D&C 91:1-2).

of the days, the Lord will manifest His redemption to the sons of Israel.' And he set her down upon the third step of the altar, and the Lord God sent grace upon her; and she danced with her feet and all the house of Israel loved her. And her parents went down marveling, and praising the Lord God because the child had not turned back. And Mary was in the Temple of the Lord as if she were a dove that dwelt there." (Protevangluim of James, v.7).

What we do know is that Mary was a pure and righteous young woman, worthy in every way to receive the unusual blessings coming to her. Although little of Mary's life is actually recorded, the scriptures reveal a pattern of righteousness; faithful obedience to the word of God; gratitude for God's mercy and blessings; and readiness to receive God's counsel and witness from His servants. (See Black, "Mary, His Mother," *Ensign*, Jan. 1991).

Righteousness. The angel Gabriel greeted her with the salutation, "Hail, thou that art highly favoured," and testified, "the Lord is with thee" (Luke 1:28), suggesting that Mary lived in a manner to be worthy of the Lord's companionship. D&C 121:45 reads "let virtue garnish thy thoughts unceasingly, then shall thy confidence wax strong in the presence of God . . . *[and] the Holy Ghost shall be thy constant companion.*" Mary was "highly favored" because she lived her life in a manner that allowed the Spirit of the Lord to be with her. (Luke 1:30).

Virtue. When told that she would conceive and bring forth a Son, this righteous and chaste woman responded with the honest inquiry, "How shall this be, seeing I know not a man?" (Luke 1:34). Mary's straightforward response to this heavenly being demonstrated her own obedience to the law of chastity. Her question was not an expression of doubt, but was a testimony of her virtue. Elder Talmage writes, "Not in the spirit of doubt such as had prompted Zacharias to ask for a sign, but through an earnest desire for information and explanation, Mary, conscious of her unmarried status and sure of her virgin condition, asked: 'How shall this be, seeing I know not a man?'" (Jesus the Christ, 88).

Obedience. After the angel told her that she would bear a child in miraculous fashion, and explained what the Lord wanted her to do, Mary replied with simple, faithful obedience: "Behold the handmaid of the Lord; be it unto me according to thy word" (Luke 1:38). Mary was willing to obey and to submit her will to the Lord, even if she did not fully understand the full ramifications. Mary, who used the term "handmaid," meaning "servant," was willing to submit entirely to the will of the Lord, in utter and complete obedience. This was a woman and mother who lived by the precept, "Thy will be done," perhaps serving as an example for her own son, Jesus, whose every action reflected the principle of "not my will, but thine, be done," and who, in turn, became the great exemplar for the world. It was Mary, who served as example and teacher for her son, Jesus, "who received not of the fullness at first, but received grace for grace" (D&C 93:12).

Humility. Mary was evidently a woman of great physical beauty (1 Nephi 11:15, "most beautiful and fair above all other virgins"), and had been told by an angel that she was "highly favored" of God. These conditions might lead to pride or vanity in some individuals. Nonetheless, Mary demonstrated great humility, acknowledging her "low estate" (Luke 1:48). "Mary, the mother of our Savior, was of most modest circumstances. . . Her strength was inward, not from outward material things." (Benson, Conf. Report, Oct. 1981). Mary's "acceptance of [her] sacred and historic role is a hallmark of humility." (Monson, Conf. Report, Oct. 1974).

Faith. Mary also displayed submissiveness, as well as great faith. "Submissiveness checks our tendency to demand advanced explanations of the Lord as [demonstrated by] a wondering but submissive Mary . . . Just as the capacity to defer gratification is a sign of real maturity, likewise the willingness to wait for deferred explanation is a sign of real faith and of trust spread over time." (Maxwell, Conf. Report, April 1985). "Mary . . . was the perfect example of complete submission to the will of God. She kept confidences. (Luke 2:19). In faith, she endured grief (John 20:11)." (Nelson, Conf. Report, Oct. 1989).

Rejoice in Righteousness. Luke records a later interaction between Mary and her cousin Elizabeth, where Mary states that her "soul doth magnify the Lord" (Luke 1:46). If we magnify the Lord, we enlarge His influence. Perhaps this quality helps others to understand and love Him. Who was it who first taught Jesus about His Father in Heaven, and the gospel? Jesus grew from "grace to grace," in a home and environment where His mother magnified the Lord.[29] In her daily life, Mary found joy in the Lord: "my spirit hath rejoiced in God" (Luke 1:47). Mary "knew her responsibility and took joy in it." (Benson, Conf. Report, Oct. 1981).

Gratitude. Mary expressed gratitude for the "great things" she received from God; and thankfulness for His "mercy" (Luke 1:49-50). She acknowledged his mighty works and blessings, "scattering the proud," "filling the hungry with good things," and "helping his servant, Israel" (Luke 1:51-54). Gratitude and acknowledgement of the Lord are hallmarks of true discipleship. "And in nothing doth man offend God . . . save those who confess not his hand in all things, and obey not his commandments" (D&C 59:21).

Sacrifice. Mary kept the religious ordinances of her day, offering sacrifice in the temple according to the laws of Moses. The scriptures state that "they [Mary and Joseph] had performed all things according to the law of the Lord" (Luke 2:22-25, 39). She was a diligent disciple: "[Mary and Joseph] went to Jerusalem *every year* at the feast of the Passover" (Luke 2:41, *emphasis added*). This was no easy journey, but a distance of 92 miles from the family home in Nazareth, by foot, or donkey or camel. **Every year**.[30]

Knowledge. Mary apparently studied the words of the prophets, and had been diligent as a young woman to learn the word of the Lord, for she alluded to His teachings and quoted scriptures, "as he [the Lord] spake to our fathers, to Abraham" (Luke 1:55). She knew the word of the Lord, and abided by its precepts.

This same Mary, who Nephi saw in vision, was a "precious and chosen vessel," an example of righteousness, virtue, obedience, humility, joy, gratitude, knowledge, sacrifice, and diligence. "Although Mary's calling was unique, all women [and men] can 'share her type of beauty. They are women who seek favor with God. . . . They are humble and live lives of chastity and virtue. . . . They have believing hearts and magnify the Lord. . . . They rejoice in the Savior and . . . recognize His gifts and mercies' (Wilcox, Daughters of God: Scriptural Portraits (1998), 179). (*quoted in* Jensen, Conf. Report, Oct. 2000).

---

[29] "And I, John, saw that he received not of the fullness at first, but received grace for grace" (D&C 93:12).
[30] A "grueling trip . . . very much uphill and downhill." "A Long, Cold Road to Bethlehem: Gospel accounts of Mary and Joseph's journey gloss over the arduous reality of life and travel in ancient Galilee," Los Angeles Times, Dec. 23, 1995.

In every way, Mary was worthy to serve as the mother of the Son of God. (See "Divine Attributes" in Topical Index, Alma 7).

Vision of the Nephites and Lamanites

The portion of Nephi's vision contained in chapter 12 summarizes Book of Mormon events. Nephi sees that his seed (the Nephites) and his brothers' seed (the Lamanites) become numerous, and conduct many wars. He beholds "wars, and rumors of wars, and great slaughters with the sword among my people" (1 Nephi 12:2). "Approximately eighty-five instances of armed conflict in varying degrees of intensity have been identified in the Book of Mormon. . . . Book of Mormon wars ranged from brief skirmishes and raids to campaigns lasting for years, including civil wars, coups, and guerilla warfare." (Largey, Book of Mormon Reference Companion, 783).

Nephi sees the resurrected Savior visit the people, and ordain twelve disciples to preside over His church. The people are righteous for four generations but then succumb to the temptations of the devil, symbolized by the mists of darkness; and they succumb to pride, symbolized by the large and spacious building (1 Nephi 12:17-18). They are ultimately destroyed by the people known as Lamanites, who then war among themselves, and gradually dwindle in unbelief.

This portion of the vision was devastating for Nephi. He later records that after the experience, he was "overcome because of my afflictions, for I considered that mine afflictions were great above all, because of the destruction of my people, for I had beheld their fall" (1 Nephi 15:5).

Vision of the Gentiles in America

In chapter 13, Nephi records a vision of the "nations and kingdoms of the Gentiles" (1 Nephi 13:3). The word "Gentiles" means "the nations," and refers to (i) those who are not of the House of Israel; (ii) those who do not believe in the God of Israel or who do not have the gospel, regardless of their lineage; and (iii) people who are not from or do not live in the land of Judah. In 1 Nephi 13, Nephi calls the people who come to the promised land from across the "many waters" Gentiles. (1 Nephi 13:12-17, 29, 30).

The angel shows Nephi the formation of a "great church" among the nations of the Gentiles, "which is most abominable above all other churches" (1 Nephi 13:4-5). Despite some speculation, this "great and abominable church" does not necessarily refer to a particular church, but is used symbolically to refer to any and all organizations that are designed to lead people away from God and His laws. Elder Bruce R. McConkie taught: "The titles *church of the devil* and *great and abominable church* are used to identify all . . . organizations of whatever name or nature – whether political, philosophical, educational, economic, social, fraternal, civic, or religious – which are designed to take men on a course that leads away from God and his laws and thus from salvation in the kingdom of God." (McConkie, Mormon Doctrine, 137-138).

"Actually, no single known historical church, denomination, or set of believers meets all the requirements for the great and abominable church . . . [or] fits the entire description. Rather the role of Babylon has been played by many different agencies, ideologies, and churches in many different times." (Robinson, "Warring against the Saints of God," *Ensign*, Jan. 1988).

The angel shows Nephi how these "great and abominable" organizations work to bring the "saints of God . . . down into captivity" (1 Nephi 13:5). They use "gold, and silver, and silks, and scarlets, and fine-twined linen, and all manner of precious clothing . . . [and] many harlots" (1 Nephi 13:7). These temptations are tools of destruction that focus the children of God on physical appetites, and distract them from the iron rod, and their path to the tree of life. Nephi tells us that these appetites are the "*desires*" of these organizations. (1 Nephi 13:8). The great and abominable church is, in many ways, similar to the great and spacious building, which was erected on false pride, love of riches, and lustful appetites.

Columbus and "Discovery" of America

In chapter 13, Nephi observes that the "Spirit of God" will be "wrought upon" certain Gentiles, who travel "upon many waters" to the land of promise. (1 Nephi 13:12-14). According to modern-day prophets, one of these Gentiles is Christopher Columbus. "This verse refers to Christopher Columbus, who was impelled by the Spirit of God to cross the ocean for the rediscovery of America, thus assisting in the furthering of God's purposes. Columbus himself, in a letter to the Spanish hierarchy wrote, 'Our Lord unlocked my mind, sent me upon the sea, and gave me fire for the deed. . . . who can doubt but that the Holy Ghost inspired me?'" (Tanner, Conf. Report, Apr. 1976).

"A host of critics have spoken out against [Columbus]. I do not dispute that there were others who came to this Western Hemisphere before him. But it was he who in faith lighted a lamp to look for a new way to China and who in the process discovered America. . . . In his reports to the sovereigns of Spain, Columbus repeatedly asserted that his voyage was for the glory of God and the spread of the Christian faith. Properly do we honor him for his unyielding strength in the face of uncertainty and danger." (Hinckley, Conf. Report, Oct. 1992).

Joseph Smith shared the following story about Columbus: "I break the ground; I lead the way like Columbus when he was invited to a banquet . . . . A shallow courtier present, who was jealous of him, abruptly asked him whether he thought that in case he had not discovered the Indies, there were not other men in Spain who would have been capable of the enterprise? Columbus made no reply, but took an egg and invited the company to make it stand on end. They all attempted it, but in vain; whereupon he struck it upon the table so as to break one end, and left it standing on the broken part, illustrating that when he had once shown the way to the new world nothing was easier than to follow it." (Words of Joseph Smith, 282).

The Revolutionary War

In his vision, Nephi saw other Gentiles who were led to the Promised Land. "Nephi saw in vision also the coming of the Pilgrims who came to escape religious persecution. He foresaw the coming to America of peoples from many nations, their wars and contentions. As Nephi said, they did humble themselves before the Lord and 'the power of God was with them, and also that the wrath of God was upon all those that were gathered together against them to battle. And I, Nephi, beheld that the Gentiles that had gone out of captivity were delivered by the power of God out of the hands of all other nations.' (1 Nephi 13:18-19)." (Tanner, Conf. Report, Apr. 1976).

"The Prophet Nephi was privileged to see a large part of the history of the establishment of this great nation. . . . And he saw that the Spirit of the Lord was here and that multitudes of people came to these shores and that God prospered them because they humbled themselves before him; that he was with them and that his power was here, and that during times of struggle and conflict – referring to the Revolutionary War – that the Lord was with them and sustained them and bore them off victorious." (Benson, Conf. Report, Apr. 1948).

"This great American nation the Almighty raised up that it might be possible in the latter days for the kingdom of God to be established on the earth. If the Lord had not prepared the way . . . it would have been impossible (under the stringent laws and bigotry of the monarchical governments of the world) to have laid the foundations for the coming of his kingdom." (Smith, Gospel Doctrine, 409). Benjamin Franklin described the crucial role of the power of God in the formation of the American nation: "In the beginning of the contest with Britain, when we were sensible of danger, we had daily prayer in this room for the divine protection. Our prayers, Sir, were heard – and they were graciously answered. All of us who were engaged in the struggle must have observed frequent instances of a superintending providence in our favor. . . I have lived a long time, and the longer I live, the more convincing proofs I see of this truth – that God governs in the affairs of men." (Franklin, Motion for Prayers in the Convention, 1138).

With respect to America, President Gordon B. Hinckley said: "Great are the promises concerning this land of America. We are told unequivocally that it 'is a choice land' (Ether 2:12; 2 Nephi 1:5)." (Conf. Report, Oct. 2001). The Lord promised that if the people should "serve him according to the commandments which he hath given, it shall be a land of liberty unto them; wherefore, they shall never be brought down into captivity; if so, it shall be because of iniquity; for if iniquity shall abound cursed shall be the land for their sakes, but unto the righteous it shall be blessed forever" (2 Nephi 1:7).

President Ezra Taft Benson declared: "I testify that America is a choice land. (2 Nephi 1:5). . . . America will be a blessed land unto the righteous forever and is the base from which God will continue to direct the worldwide latter-day operations of His kingdom." (Conf. Report, Oct. 1988). From the Americas, the blessings of the gospel will go to all people throughout the earth, benefiting all of God's children. Elder Eduardo Ayala of the Seventy said: "The conditions of peoples and of nations change due to progress in the world; nevertheless, in any such places . . . wherever members of our church are found, there will always be those who live these basic principles, and by so doing they bless the rest of the people." (Conf. Report, Apr. 1995).

Vision of the Restoration of the Gospel and the Latter Days

In chapter 14, Nephi learns that the latter days will be a time of wars and rumors of wars, during which, the Lord will work a "great and marvelous work"[31] that will separate the people – either "to the convincing of them unto peace and life eternal, or unto the deliverance of them to the hardness of their hearts and blindness of their minds" (1 Nephi 14:7). The "great and marvelous work" is the restoration of the Gospel of Jesus Christ. In this context, the word "great" means significant and meaningful. The word "marvelous" means wonderful and incomprehensible. "Work" refers to an act or accomplishment that is everlasting. "Now what is this marvelous work and a wonder prophesied about by . . . Nephi? The Prophet Nephi tells us in detail what this marvelous work is. First, he declared that in the latter days and on this land of promise the Savior would restore his gospel and establish his Church and kingdom." (Hunter, Conf. Report, Oct. 1958).

Nephi foresaw in the last days that the members of the church would be relatively "few," when compared with the population of the earth, but they would be "upon all the face of the earth" (1 Nephi 14:12). Elder Orson Pratt taught that the fulfillment of this prophesy is evidence of Joseph Smith's divine calling. "But what I wish to call your attention to at this time is one event which has been in a measure literally fulfilled. It is an event that no man, unless he were a Prophet inspired by the Most High God, could have had a heart big enough to prophesy of with the least expectation of its fulfillment; and that is, the Church of the Lamb of God that was to be raised up . . . should be among all nations and kingdoms of the Gentiles. (1 Nephi 14:14). This was uttered and printed before the Church of Latter-day Saints was in existence. How could a young man, inexperienced as Joseph Smith was, have had all this foreknowledge of future events, unless he was inspired of God? How did he know that any Church believing in the Book of Mormon would arise? He was then in the act of translating these records; the Church had not yet an existence; and he was young, inexperienced, and ignorant as regards the education and wisdom of this world. . . And how did he know that the dominions of this Church among all the nations and kingdoms of the Gentiles should be small? . . . Common sense tells us that this would be taking a stretch far beyond what any false prophet dare take, with any hope of fulfillment." (Journal of Discourses, 7:176).

Elder Pratt's statement was made in the mid-1800s, when the church was present in a just a few nations. Since that time, although church membership numbers are still very small compared to the total world population (approximately 16.3 million out of 7.5 billion, or 0.2%), the church has spread throughout the world, "upon all the face of the earth" (1 Nephi 14:12). In 2018, the church had congregations in 189 of the nations and territories of the world. "The number of members of the Church in the latter days would be relatively few, as Nephi prophesied, but they would be upon all the face of the earth, and the power and ordinances of the priesthood would be available to all who desired them." (Andersen, Conf. Report, Oct. 2016). President Joseph Fielding Smith said, "While it may be said . . . that we are but a handful in comparison with the world, yet we may be compared with the leaven of which the Savior spoke, which will eventually leaven the whole world." (Conf. Report, Oct. 1968). "We are few in number, just as Nephi foretold. But at the same time, you and I are eyewitnesses of Daniel's prophetic words: the 'stone . . . cut . . . without hands [is filling] the whole earth'" (Daniel 2:34-35). (Andersen, Conf. Report, Apr. 2013).

---

[31] See 2 Nephi 27:26; D&C 4:1; D&C 6:1; Isaiah 29:14.

The Bible and The Book of Mormon

In his vision of the Gentiles, Nephi sees a book, a record of the Jews, which was "carried forth among [the Gentiles]" (1 Nephi 13:20). The angel tells Nephi that the book was written by the Jews, and contains the covenants of the Lord made to the house of Israel. This is the Bible. Originally, the book contained "the fullness of the gospel," but certain "plain and precious" elements were removed. (1 Nephi 13:24-29). Elder Jeffrey R. Holland taught: "Elements . . . missing from the Bible were both 'plain and most precious.' They were plain in their simplicity and clarity, being easy to 'the understanding of . . . men': they were precious in their purity and profound worth, their saving significance and eternal importance to the children of God." (Holland, Christ and the New Covenant, 5). "The angel's words are plain and to the point: When the biblical records were originally written by Jewish prophets and apostles, they contained the fullness of the gospel. When these records went to the Gentiles, some valuable plain and precious things were taken out of them." (Nyman & Tate, eds., First Nephi, The Doctrinal Foundation, Matthews, "Establishing the Truth of the Bible," 204).

The angel then shows Nephi that the Lord will empower Gentiles in the promised land to bring forth other records that contain much of the "plain and precious" gospel (1 Nephi 13:34, 39-41). These records include the Book of Mormon. President Russell M. Nelson taught: "An angel . . . revealed that the writings in the Bible available in our day are not as complete as they were when originally written by prophets and apostles. He declared that the Book of Mormon shall restore plain and precious things taken away from the Bible. . . . and shall establish the truth of the Bible." (Conf. Report, Oct. 2007).

"We love and revere the Bible. . . . The Bible is the word of God. It is always identified first in our canon, our 'standard works.' . . . But . . . the Bible alone could not be the answer to all the religious questions. . . . Thus one of the great purposes of continuing revelation through living prophets is to declare to the world through additional witnesses that the Bible is true. 'This is written,' an ancient prophet said, speaking of the Book of Mormon, 'for the intent that ye may believe that,' speaking of the Bible. (Mormon 7:9). In one of the earliest revelations received by Joseph Smith, the Lord said, 'Behold, I do not bring [the Book of Mormon forth] to destroy [the Bible] but to build it up.' (D&C 10:52)." (Holland, Conf. Report, Apr. 2008).

"Scriptural witnesses authenticate each other. This concept was explained long ago when a prophet wrote that the Book of Mormon was 'written for the intent that ye may believe [the Bible]; and if ye believe [the Bible] ye will believe the [Book of Mormon] also.' (Mormon 7:9). Each book refers to the other. Each book stands as evidence that God lives and speaks to His children by revelation to His prophets. Love for the Book of Mormon expands one's love for the Bible and vice versa. Scriptures of the Restoration do not compete with the Bible; they complement the Bible." (Nelson, Conf. Report, Oct. 2007).

"It is not only desirable that the Book of Mormon should substantiate the Bible and supply certain missing parts, it is absolutely necessary for eternal justice. It appears that in the economy of God there must be more than one witness for the truths that are taught to mankind. Without a second or third witness, the law cannot be binding on the day of judgment. . . . Not just the truth of the Bible as history and as a cultural record, but to establish . . . and prove that the testimony of Jesus Christ contained in the scriptures is true and correct." (Nyman & Tate, First Nephi, The Doctrinal Foundation, Matthews, "Establishing the Truth of the Bible," 211-212). "In the mouth of two or three witnesses every word [is] established." (Matt. 18:16; see 2 Nephi 29:8).

The Book of Mormon supports, sustains, clarifies and augments doctrines from the Bible. President Ezra Taft Benson observed: "The Book of Mormon, the record of Joseph, verifies and clarifies the Bible. It removes stumbling blocks, it restores many plain and precious things. . . When used together, the Bible and the Book of Mormon confound false doctrines, lay down contentions, and establish peace." (Conf. Report, Oct. 1984). President Boyd K. Packer said: "The Old Testament and the New Testament . . . and the Book of Mormon . . . are now woven together in such a way that as you pore over one you are drawn to the other; as you learn from one you are enlightened by the other. They are indeed one in our hands." (Conf. Report, Oct. 1982).

The emphasis on the importance of possessing accurate, sacred records may have been particularly poignant for Nephi, who had obtained the brass plates for his family (and posterity) only through the shedding of Laban's blood, a thing which he "shrunk" away from doing "and would that [he] might not slay him" (1 Nephi 4:10).

Elder Jeffrey R. Holland provided the following insights about Nephi's experience with Laban: "Obedience *is* the first law of heaven, but in case you haven't noticed, some of these commandments are not easy, and we frequently may seem to be in for much more than we bargained for. . . . I speak of Nephi's obligation to slay Laban in order to preserve a record, save a people, and ultimately lead to the restoration of the gospel in the dispensation of the fullness of times. How much is hanging in the balance as Nephi stands over the drunken and adversarial Laban I cannot say, but it is a very great deal indeed. The only problem is that *we* know this, but Nephi does not. And regardless of how much is at stake, how can he do this thing? He is a good person, perhaps even a well-educated person. He has been taught from the very summit of Sinai 'Thou shalt not kill.' And he has made gospel covenants. 'I was constrained by the Spirit that I should kill Laban; but. . . I shrunk and would that I might not slay him' (1 Nephi 4:10). A bitter test? A desire to shrink? Sound familiar?"

"We don't know why those plates could not have been obtained some other way—perhaps accidentally left at the plate polishers one night or maybe falling out the back of Laban's chariot on a Sabbath afternoon. For that matter, why didn't Nephi just leave this story out of the book altogether? Why didn't he say something like, 'And after much effort and anguish of spirit, I did obtain the plates of Laban and did depart into the wilderness unto the tent of my father?' . . . But there it is, squarely in the beginning of the book—page 8—where even the most casual reader will see it *and must deal with it*. It is not intended that either Nephi *or* we be spared the struggle of this account."

"I believe that story was placed in the very opening verses of a 531-page book and then told in painfully specific detail in order to focus every reader of that record on the absolutely fundamental gospel issue of obedience and submission to the communicated will of the Lord. If Nephi cannot yield to this terribly painful command, if he cannot bring himself to obey, then it is entirely probable that he can never succeed *or* survive in the tasks that lie just ahead. 'I will go and do the things which the Lord hath commanded' (1 Nephi 3:7). I confess that I wince a little when I hear that promise quoted so casually among us. Jesus knew what that kind of commitment would entail, and so now does Nephi." ("The Will of the Father," BYU Speeches, Jan. 17, 1989).

As his vision winds down, Nephi sees a man dressed in a white robe. (1 Nephi 14:19). The angel tells Nephi that this man, whose name is John, is "one of the twelve apostles of the Lamb" and that he shall "write concerning the end of the world" (1 Nephi 14:20-22, 27). "John had the curtains of heaven withdrawn, and by vision looked through the dark vista of future ages, and contemplated events that should transpire throughout every subsequent period of time, until the final winding up scene." (Teachings of the Prophet Joseph Smith, 247). Nephi sees the things that John will see, but is forbidden to write them, "for the Lord hath ordained [John] that he should write them" (1 Nephi 14:25).

"While Nephi saw the remainder of the world's history, it was left to John the Apostle of Jesus to write. This undoubtedly referred to the Book of Revelation in the New Testament." (Nyman, I Nephi Wrote This Record, 195). Several other prophets have seen visions of the end of the world, including Adam, Enoch, the brother of Jared, Abraham, Moses, Joseph, Isaiah, Daniel, and Joseph Smith. "With the exception of John, however, the Lord instructed them to seal up their writings until the time of the end of the world." (Odgen and Skinner, Verse By Verse: The Book of Mormon, 1:66).

Nephi closes his panoramic vision of the future with his testimony, "I bear record that I saw the things which my father saw, and the angel of the Lord did make them known unto me . . . and if all the things which I saw are not written, the things which I have written are true" (1 Nephi 14:29-30).

Discourse 6: Nephi, "Hope in the Lord (Isaiah)" (1 Nephi 19-22)

Prophet	Key Doctrines	Scriptures	Audience	Date
Nephi	• Understanding Isaiah • Scattering and Gathering of Israel • Furnace of Affliction	1 Nephi 19:24 to 1 Nephi 22 (Isaiah 48-49)	To his "brethren" in the promised land, and the House of Israel.	588 B.C. – 570 B.C.

INTRODUCTION

Chronologically, this discourse was delivered after Lehi's family, together with Zoram, and the family of Ishmael, arrived in the promised land, but before Lehi dies and a group led by Nephi separates from a group led by his brothers, Laman and Lemuel. This is the last recorded sermon given by Nephi to the combined family of Lehi. It is also directed to the House of Israel and the future readers of his record. To this audience, the young prophet declares: "Hear ye the words of the prophet [Isaiah]" (1 Nephi 19:24). He then quotes Isaiah, and provides his own commentary to the scriptural passages, in answer to his brothers' question: "What meaneth these things which ye have read?" (1 Nephi 22:1).

Nephi's sermon begins in 1 Nephi 19:24: "Wherefore I spake unto them [Nephi's 'brethren'] saying: Hear ye the words of the prophet [Isaiah], ye who are a remnant of the house of Israel, a branch which have been broken off; hear ye the words of the prophet, which were written unto all the house of Israel, and liken them unto yourselves, that ye may have hope as well as your brethren from whom ye have been broken off; for after this manner has the prophet written." Nephi then quotes chapters 48 and 49 from the Book of Isaiah in their entirety.

Nephi states that he reads **scripture** to his people so that: (1) they might know concerning the doings of the Lord in other lands; and (2) they might more fully be persuaded to believe in the Lord. (1 Nephi 19:22-23). He then urges his family and future readers to "liken all scriptures unto us, that it might be for our profit and learning" (1 Nephi 19:23). President Ezra Taft Benson taught: "We urge you to study the Book of Mormon as individuals and then to do as the prophet Nephi counseled: liken the scriptures to yourselves so that it will be for your profit and learning. (See 1 Nephi 19:23-24)." (Conf. Report, Apr. 1984). (See 2 Nephi 32:3).

"Surely this is one of the greatest value of scripture," Elder Marion D. Hanks observed, "that we might learn them and liken them unto ourselves, apply the lessons and instructions of the revelations to our own lives. How can we do so unless we search, seek, ask, knock, invest ourselves earnestly, diligently in the effort to acquire and organize and share a knowledge of the gospel of Jesus Christ?" (Conf. Report, Oct. 1960). As we read and ponder, we should try to discern how a particular scripture or doctrine might apply to our individual circumstances, and why a particular event, concept or principle was included in the record. (See "Scriptures" in Topical Index; 2 Nephi 31 – "Feasting on the Words of Christ; Endure to the End").

DISCOURSE: 1 Nephi 19:24 – 1 Nephi 22

KEY DOCTRINES

- **Understanding the Words of Isaiah.** Isaiah's words predict the coming of Christ, contain the covenants of the Lord, and teach that "save Christ should come all men must perish." We should "liken them unto [us] and unto all men" (2 Nephi 11:4-8). Keys to understanding Isaiah:
    - understand the manner of prophesying among the Jews;
    - have the spirit of prophesy;
    - study other scriptures that reference and interpret Isaiah.

- **The Furnace of Affliction.** Israel will be refined in a "furnace of affliction."

- **Gathering of Israel**. The house of Israel shall be scattered, but shall not be forgotten, and ultimately Israel will be "nursed by the Gentiles" through the restoration of the gospel, and be gathered both temporally and spiritually. In the last days, the righteous need not fear. If we are obedient to the commandments, and endure to the end, we will be saved.

- **Satan Will Have No More Power**. In the last days, the "great and abominable church" will be destroyed, and Satan will have no power and be bound.

COMMENTARY

Delight in the Words of Isaiah

Elder Jeffrey R. Holland observed: "In an effort to persuade his rebellious brothers, the family of Lehi generally, and ultimately all of the house of Israel to 'remember the Lord their Redeemer' [1 Nephi 19:18], Nephi . . . taught from the great prophets recorded on the precious plates of brass. . . . [M]ost powerfully of all he taught them from the prophet Isaiah. To the future reader of his record, Nephi wrote, 'That I might more fully persuade them to believe in the Lord their Redeemer I did read unto them that which was written by the prophet Isaiah.'" (Holland, Christ and the New Covenant, 75). Nephi quotes Isaiah extensively in this discourse and throughout his record. He indicates in 1 Nephi 19:24 why he does this: "Hear ye the words of the prophet [Isaiah] . . . *that ye may have hope.*" (*Emphasis added*).

"Isaiah repeatedly warned about the consequences of wickedness and foretold the calamities that would fall upon the house of Israel as a result, including the scattering of Israel from the lands of their inheritance and the loss of the blessings of the covenant. He also testified repeatedly that Israel's only hope could come from redemption through the Messiah. Many of Isaiah's prophecies concern the coming of the Savior to the earth, both in the meridian of time and at the millennial day. Furthermore, he gave specific details concerning the latter-day gathering of Israel and the restoration of the gospel covenant." (LDS Institute, Book of Mormon Student Manual, 1 Nephi 19-21).

When the Savior visited the Nephites, he instructed: "ye have them [the words of Isaiah] before you, therefore search them" (3 Nephi 20:11). The Lord then quoted certain prophesies of Isaiah, and instructed: "I say unto you, that ye ought to search these things. Yea, a commandment I give unto you that ye search these things *diligently*; for great are the words of Isaiah" (3 Nephi 23:1, *emphasis added*). And, near the end of the Book of Mormon, Moroni instructs the generation living in the latter days: "Search the prophecies of Isaiah" (Mormon 8:23).

Understanding Isaiah is not easy. After recording several chapters of the Book of Isaiah from the brass plates (see, Isaiah 2-14 included in 2 Nephi 11-24), Nephi acknowledges that "Isaiah spake many things which were hard for many of my people to understand" (2 Nephi 25:1). President Boyd K. Packer shared his experience: "When I was about 10, I made my first attempt to read the Book of Mormon. The first part was easy-flowing New Testament language. Then I came to the writings of the Old Testament prophet Isaiah. I could not understand them; I found them difficult to read. I laid the book aside." (Conf. Report, Oct. 2001). It was not until several years later, when on a troop ship heading for the war in the Pacific that President Packer "read and reread the book. That was a life-changing event. After that, I never set the book aside [again]." Id.

Understanding Isaiah: A Primer

Although Isaiah is one of the most difficult prophets to understand, his words are among the most important for us to know. Nephi provides the following keys to understanding Isaiah's writings: (1) understand "the manner of prophesying among the Jews"; (2) be "filled with the spirit of prophesy" and (3) study the words of other prophets who quote and interpret the words of Isaiah (2 Nephi 25:1,4,7-8). "Applying one or more of these approaches will help us in searching the words of Isaiah, and we can thereby gain understanding – although it will probably come 'line upon line' and 'precept upon precept,' as Isaiah defined the process of receiving revelation (see Isa. 28:10)." (Nyman, Great are the Words of Isaiah, 8).[32]

Understand the Manner of Prophesying Among the Jews

One key to understand Isaiah is to understand the "manner of prophesying among the Jews" (2 Nephi 25:1). "A major difficulty in understanding the book of Isaiah is his extensive use of symbolism, as well as his prophetic foresight and literary style; these take many local themes (which begin in his own day) and extend them to a latter-day fulfillment or application." (Bible Dictionary, "Isaiah"). "We can become acquainted with the manner of writing among the Jews, coming to understand their literary mechanisms for better comprehension. Isaiah in particular wrote with sophisticated artistry; over 90 percent of his writings is in poetic form. . . . Types, figures, and symbols usually have a surface meaning but also a deeper, underlying meaning. Coming to understand the form is important – for example, the similes, metaphors, personification, and parallelisms." (Ogden and Skinner, Verse by Verse: The Book of Mormon, 1:93).

---

[32] See also: Bruce R. McConkie, "Ten Keys to Understanding Isaiah," *Ensign,* Oct. 1973. Gary Poll, "Keys to Understanding Isaiah," *BYU Education Week Lecture,* August 2002. Mark Eastmond, "Images of Mercy in the Writings of Isaiah," *Covenants, Prophecies, and Hymns of the Old Testament: The 30th Annual Sidney B. Sperry Symposium,* 196-197. Michael Wilcox, "Finding Themes and Patterns in the Scriptures," *BYU Education Week Lecture,* August 2008. Michael L. King, "Isaiah's Vision of God's Plan to Fulfill His Covenant," *Covenants, Prophecies, and Hymns of the Old Testament: The 30th Annual Sidney B. Sperry Symposium,* 162-179. David J. Ridges, "Isaiah Made Easier," *BYU Education Week Lecture,* August 2002. Donald W. Parry, Jay A. Parry, Tina M. Peterson, *Understanding Isaiah,* 62-67.

Isaiah used allusions and shortcut – or signaling - language which his Jewish audience would immediately recognize. For example, the book of Isaiah begins with the language, "Hear O heavens," which is a quote from the song of Moses (Deut. 32:1). This language would have been immediately recognized by the Hebrews as a preface to certain, important messaging. Examples of shortcut language for an audience in the Church of Jesus Christ of Latter-day Saints include:

(1) "No success can compensate _____"
(2) "Choose the _____"
(3) "We thank thee O God, for a _____"

Most members of the Church of Jesus Christ of Latter-day Saints would immediately be able to complete those phrases with: (1) "for failure in the home"; (2) "Right"; and (3) "Prophet." Similarly, Isaiah used both religious and cultural language throughout his writings that were familiar to his Jewish audience.

Be Filled with the Spirit of Prophecy

The second interpretive key has to do with our individual spiritual preparation. Nephi said that the "words of Isaiah . . . are plain unto all those that are filled with the spirit of prophecy" (2 Nephi 25:4). Elder Bruce R. McConkie taught: "In the final analysis there is no way to understand any scripture except to have the same spirit of prophecy that rested upon the one who uttered the truth in its original form. Scripture comes from God by the power of the Holy Ghost. . . . To interpret it, we must be enlightened by the power of the Holy Spirit." (*Ensign,* October, 1973). We obtain the spirit by exercising faith, living righteously and keeping the commandments.

In the Book of Revelation, the apostle John taught that the "testimony of Jesus is the spirit of prophesy" (Rev. 19:10). As we learn about Jesus, and strengthen our testimony of the Lord, we will be able to better understand Isaiah's Messianic references that appear throughout his teachings. Having a testimony of Jesus Christ, and living a righteous life that invites the spirit of the Holy Ghost, will enable us to better understand the things of the spirit conveyed by Isaiah.

Study the Words of Other Prophets Who Interpret Isaiah

The third key to understanding Isaiah is found through other scriptures.

- **Book of Mormon.** There are 66 chapters of Isaiah with 1,292 verses in the Bible. Book of Mormon prophets quote 414 verses of Isaiah, and paraphrase another 34. In other words, about one-third of the book of Isaiah is quoted or paraphrased in the Book of Mormon. Book of Mormon prophets were quoting or interpreting Isaiah from the brass plates, dating just 100 years from Isaiah's ministry. As Elder Bruce R. McConkie taught, "The Book of Mormon is the world's greatest commentary on the book of Isaiah." (*Ensign*, Oct. 1973).
- **New Testament**. Isaiah is quoted at least 57 times in the New Testament. Some of the quotations are duplicates; but they can help us understand the nature of Isaiah's writings.
- **Doctrine and Covenants**. Modern scriptures interpret, approve, clarify and enlarge upon the writings of Isaiah. When Moroni appeared to Joseph Smith on Sept. 21, 1823, he "quoted the eleventh chapter of Isaiah, saying that it was about to be fulfilled" (JS-H 1:40). D&C 113 contains interpretations of verses in chapters 11 and 52 of Isaiah. D&C 101 is key to understanding Isaiah 65. D&C 133 helps us understand Isaiah chapters 35, 51, 63 and 64. There are about 100 instances from footnotes in the Doctrine and Covenants where Isaiah is quoted, interpreted or paraphrased.

Nephi writes "my soul delighteth" in the words of Isaiah (2 Nephi 11:2), and he includes hundreds of verses from Isaiah, particularly about Christ, in his own writings.[33] Elder Jeffrey R. Holland observed: "Certainly the words of [Isaiah] brought delight to Nephi's soul, for 352 of the Isaiah verses quoted in the Book of Mormon – more than 80 percent of the total number in the entire book – come from Nephi's two books!" (Holland, Christ and the New Covenant, 77).

The Furnace of Affliction

Isaiah described the House of Israel as stubborn and disobedient, a "transgressor from the womb" (1 Nephi 20:4-8). He prophesies that the people will be "confounded," "harden their hearts in disobedience" and be "hated of all men" (1 Nephi 22:4-5). Despite their disobedience, however, the Lord allows them to repent and return to Him: "I defer mine anger . . . I refrain from thee, that I cut thee not off" (1 Nephi 20:9). The path back to the Lord, however, will involve a refining process that Nephi calls "the furnace of affliction" (1 Nephi 20:10).

"The furnace of affliction helps purify even the very best of Saints by burning away the dross in their lives and leaving behind pure gold. Even very rich ore needs refining to remove impurities. . . . A pattern in the scriptures and in life shows that many times the darkest, most dangerous tests immediately precede remarkable events and tremendous growth. 'After much tribulation come the blessings.' (D&C 58:4). . . . The Apostle Paul taught, 'For our light affliction, which is but for a moment, worketh for us a far more exceeding and eternal weight of glory.' (2 Cor. 4:17). It is interesting that Paul uses the term 'light affliction.' This comes from a person who was beaten, stoned, shipwrecked, imprisoned, and who experienced many other trials (2 Cor. 11:23-28)." (Johnson, Conf. Report, Apr. 2011).

"Most of us experience some measure of what the scriptures call 'the furnace of affliction.' Some are submerged in service to a disadvantaged family member. Others suffer the death of a loved one or the loss or postponement of a righteous goal like marriage or childbearing. Still others struggle with personal impairments or with feelings of rejection, inadequacy, or depression. Through the justice and mercy of a loving Father in Heaven, the refinement and sanctification possible through such experiences can help us achieve what God desires us to become." (Oaks, Conf. Report, Oct. 2000). "Much of our affliction is not necessarily our fault. Unexpected events, contradicting or disappointing circumstances, interrupting illness, and even death surround us and penetrate our mortal experience. Additionally, we may suffer afflictions because of the acts of others." (Richards, "The Atonement Covers All Pain," *Ensign*, May 2011). "It is challenging but vital to remain firm and steadfast when we find ourselves being refined 'in the furnace of affliction,' something that comes soon or late to all of us in mortality." (Christofferson, Conf. Report, Oct. 2018).

When faced with afflictions and trials, we may feel that the Lord has forgotten us. One of the messages of hope from Isaiah is that the Lord will never forget us, in spite of our transgressions. This lesson is taught through a comparison to parental love: "But behold, Zion hath said: The Lord hath forsaken me, and my Lord hath forgotten me – but he will show that he hath not. For can a woman forget her sucking child that she should not have compassion on the son of her womb? Yea, they may forget, yet I will not forget thee, O house of Israel" (1 Nephi 21:14-15).

---

[33] See also, 2 Nephi 11:2-3; 3 Nephi 23:1-3 (the Lord declares, "great are the words of Isaiah").

Elder Holland wrote: "This poetic passage provides yet another reminder of Christ's saving role, that of protective, redeeming parent to Zion's children. He comforts his people and shows mercy when they are afflicted, as any loving father or mother would toward a child, but, as Nephi here reminds us through Isaiah, much more than any mortal father and mother could do. Although a mother may forget her sucking child (as unlikely as any parent might think that could be), Christ will not forget the children he has redeemed or the covenant he has made with them for salvation in Zion. The painful reminders of that care and covenant are the marks of the Roman nails graven upon the palms of his hands, a sign . . . that he is the Savior of the world and was wounded in the house of his friends." (Christ and the New Covenant, 84). Through Christ, "comfort replaces pain, peace replaces turmoil, and hope replaces sorrow. . . . He will convert trial into blessing and, in Isaiah's words, 'give beauty for ashes.' (Isaiah 61:3)." (Christoffersen, Conf. Report, Oct. 2018).

The Lord is ever patient. Despite multiple, repeated transgressions by the House of Israel, "his hand is stretched out still" (2 Nephi 19:12, 17, 21; 2 Nephi 20:4). The Lord promised: "I [will] not forget thee, O house of Israel. Behold, I have graven thee upon the palms of my hands" (1 Nephi 21:15-16). This promise likewise applies to all of us in our day. Nephi teaches that despite the disobedience of the Gentiles, the Lord will be merciful. "For notwithstanding I shall lengthen out mine arm to them from day to day, they [the Gentiles in the last days] will deny me; nevertheless, I will be merciful unto them . . . if they will repent and come unto me; for mine arm is lengthened out all the day long, saith the Lord God of Hosts" (2 Nephi 28:32).

Elder Jeffrey R. Holland taught: "There can and will be plenty of difficulties in life. Nevertheless, the soul that comes unto Christ, who knows His voice and strives to do as He did, finds a strength, as the hymn says, 'beyond [his] own.' ('Lord, I Would Follow Thee'). The Savior reminds us that He has 'graven [us] upon the palms of [His] hands.' (1 Nephi 21:16). Considering the incomprehensible cost of the Crucifixion and Atonement, I promise you He is not going to turn His back on us now." (Conf. Report, Apr. 2006).

The Gathering of Israel

Nephi explains that although the house of Israel will be scattered "upon all the face of the earth" and "among all nations" (1 Nephi 22:3), it will be gathered again. "The gathering of Israel consists of receiving the truth, gaining again a true knowledge of the Redeemer, and coming back into the true fold of the Good Shepherd. In the language of the Book of Mormon, it consists of being 'restored to the true church and fold of God,' and then being 'gathered' and 'established' in various 'lands of promise.' (2 Nephi 9:2). 'When they shall come to the knowledge of their Redeemer, they shall be gathered together again to the lands of their inheritance' (2 Nephi 6:11)." (McConkie, Conf. Report, Apr. 1977). "[A]fter the house of Israel should be scattered they should be gathered together again . . . the remnants of the house of Israel, should be grafted in, or come to the knowledge of the true Messiah, their Lord and their Redeemer" (1 Nephi 10:14).

Nephi explains that the Lord will raise up a Gentile nation to aid in the gathering of Israel back to Zion (1 Nephi 21:22-23; 1 Nephi 22:6-9). This gathering, and the related restoration of the gospel, is a "marvelous work among the Gentiles," which is of great worth, and "likened unto [the house of Israel] being nourished by the Gentiles and being carried in their arms and upon their shoulders" (1 Nephi 22:8). In the last days, the Gentiles will "nurse" and "nourish" the house of Israel, and they, and their posterity, will have the opportunity to hear the gospel, and participate in the saving ordinances of the temple.

During the challenging, but glorious, period in the last days, God will bless the earth, and "make bare his arm in the eyes of all the nations, bringing about his covenants and his gospel" to the house of Israel (1 Nephi 22:11; see Isaiah 52:10). The arm is a symbol of power, and this scripture means that God will show His power throughout the world, in actively gathering His people.

Today, the gathering does not require the Lord's people to travel long distances to a designated geographical location. The gathering is accomplished when those born or adopted into the House of Israel (i.e., all believing people) are "gathered" into stakes and congregations of the faithful. President Russell M. Nelson taught that "it is not a matter of physical location; it is a matter of individual commitment. People can be 'brought to the knowledge of the Lord' without leaving their homelands. True, in the early days of the Church, conversion often meant emigration as well. But now the gathering takes place in each nation. . . . 'Every nation is the gathering place for its own people.' (McConkie, Mexico City Area Conf., 1972). The place of gathering for Brazilian Saints is in Brazil; the place of gathering for Nigerian Saints is in Nigeria; the place of gathering for Korean Saints is in Korea; and so forth. . . . Zion is wherever righteous Saints are. . . . Publications, communications, and congregations are now such that nearly all members have access to the doctrines, keys, ordinances and blessings of the gospel, regardless of their location." (Nelson, Conf. Report, Oct. 2006).

Elder McConkie instructed: "Scattered Israel in every nation is called to gather to the fold of Christ, to the stakes of Zion, as such are established in their nations. . . . Israel shall be gathered one by one, family by family, unto the stakes of Zion established in all parts of the earth so that the whole earth shall be blessed with the fruits of the gospel." (Conf. Report, Apr. 1977). "Publication of the Book of Mormon was the signal that the gathering had begun. The Book of Mormon itself is the instrument of gathering and conversion." (Christofferson, Conf. Report, Apr. 2019).

President Russell M. Nelson taught: "This doctrine of the gathering is one of the important teachings of The Church of Jesus Christ of Latter-day Saints. . . We not only teach this doctrine, but we participate in it. We do so as we help to gather the elect of the Lord on both sides of the veil." (Conf. Report, Oct. 2006). The "'gathering is the most important thing taking place on the earth today. Nothing else compares in magnitude, nothing else compares in importance, nothing else compares in majesty. And if you choose to . . . you can be a big part of it.'" (Christofferson, Conf. Report, Apr. 2019, *quoting* President Russell M. Nelson).

The gathering is "both temporal and spiritual" (1 Nephi 22:3). As part of this gathering, Abrahamic covenants are taught, and temple covenants and ordinances are revealed. "As vital to the [gathering] is the great redemptive effort on behalf of our ancestors." (Christofferson, Conf. Report, Apr. 2019). In a sense, the Lord is also gathering His people to His temples throughout the world. Nephi – and Isaiah – teach us that as part of this gathering, the Lord is "bringing about his covenants" (1 Nephi 22:11), including sacred and essential covenants in His Holy Temples.[34]

---

[34] As of March 2019, there were 162 dedicated temples, 11 under construction, and 28 announced (not yet under construction), or 201 temples for the spiritual (and physical) gathering of the Saints worldwide.

Preservation of the Righteous

The gathering also provides protection for the righteous, those who are faithful to their covenants, and live in obedience to the word of God. Nephi teaches that the righteous need not fear the tribulations of the last days:

- "the righteous need not fear; for . . . they shall be saved, even . . . by fire" (1 Nephi 22:17);
- "the righteous shall not perish" (1 Nephi 22:19); and
- "the righteous need not fear, for they . . . shall not be confounded" (1 Nephi 22:22).

Elder Orson Pratt taught: "Nephi looked upon these things [in the latter days] and saw the condition that the people would be in, and therefore he said, 'You need not fear.' Do you hear it, Latter-day Saints? You need not fear, for the Lord will preserve his people, even if it must needs be that he sends down fire from heaven." (Journal of Discourses, 6:199). Elder Dallin H. Oaks testified, "I am grateful for the Book of Mormon promise to us of the last days that 'the righteous need not fear,' for the Lord 'will preserve the righteous by his power.' I am grateful for the protection promised to those who have kept their covenants and qualified for the blessings promised in sacred places." (Conf. Report, Oct. 1992).

"As His covenant people, we need not be paralyzed by fear because bad things might happen. Instead, we can move forward with faith, courage, determination, and trust in God as we approach the challenges and opportunities ahead. . . . 'The Lord will fight for you, and you shall hold your peace.' (Exodus 14:14). In the face of fear, let us find our courage, muster our faith, and have confidence in the promise that 'no weapon that is formed against thee shall prosper.' (Isaiah 54:17)." (Uchtdorf, Conf. Report, April 2017).

Elder Bruce R. McConkie declared: "We do not say that all of the Saints will be spared and saved from the coming day of desolation. But we do say there is no promise of safety and no promise of security except for those who love the Lord and who are seeking to do all that he commands." (Conf. Report, Apr. 1979). President Ezra Taft Benson taught: "[The Lord] has promised that the righteous will be preserved by His power. But we must keep the commandments of God. We must pay our tithes and offerings, keep the Sabbath day a holy day, stay morally clean, be honest in all our dealings, and have our family and personal prayers. We must live the gospel." (Conf. Report, Oct. 1979).

Satan Will Have No More Power

The righteousness of the people in the last days will ultimately bind Satan. Nephi taught that the time would come when Satan has "no more power" over the hearts of the people, "for they dwell in righteousness" (1 Nephi 22:15, 26). Elder Bruce R. McConkie explained: "Our revelation says: 'And in that day Satan shall not have power to tempt any man.' (D&C 101:28). Does this mean that power is withdrawn from Satan so that he can no longer entice men to do evil? Or does it mean that men no longer succumb to his enticements because their hearts are so set on righteousness that they refuse to forsake that which is good to follow him who is evil? Clearly it means the latter. . . . How, then, will Satan be bound during the Millennium? It will be by the righteousness of the people." (McConkie, The Millennial Messiah, 668).

Elder George Q. Cannon observed: "Satan will be bound because he will not have power over the hearts of the children of men. . . . In the Gospel of the Lord Jesus Christ as God has revealed it unto us, there are laws so perfect that when this people . . . shall obey them they will be so far lifted up above the power of Satan that he will have but little power to tempt them." (Journal of Discourses, 24:141).

President James E. Faust proclaimed: "'Resist the devil, and he will flee from you.' (James 4:7). He cannot know our thoughts unless we speak them. And Nephi states that 'he hath no power over the hearts' of people who are righteous. (1 Nephi 22:26). We have heard comedians and others justify or explain their misdeeds by saying, 'The devil made me do it.' I do not really think the devil can make us do anything. Certainly he can tempt and he can deceive, but he has no authority over us which we do not give him. The power to resist Satan may be stronger than we realize. The Prophet Joseph Smith taught: 'All beings who have bodies have power over those who have not. The devil has no power over us only as we permit him. The moment we revolt at anything which comes from God, the devil takes power.' (Teachings of the Prophet Joseph Smith, 181). He also stated, 'Wicked spirits have their bounds, limits, and laws by which they are governed.' (History of the Church, 4:576). So Satan and his angels are not all-powerful." (Conf. Report, Oct. 1987).

Elder ElRay L. Christiansen counseled that the devil "seeks to darken and mislead the minds of men. He seeks to minimize the seriousness of wrongdoing. Deception and falsehood are his tools. He is a skillful imitator. While he is subject to the will of God and can never overthrow nor overcome God, he continuously and relentlessly keeps his forces at work with individuals and with groups, causing them to pursue selfish ends and to stir up among them trouble and dissension and persuading them to disobey the decrees of the Lord." (Conf. Report, Apr. 1957).

"Satan is a subtle snake, sneaking into our minds and hearts when we have let our guard down, faced a disappointment, or lost hope. He entices us with flattery, a promise of ease, comfort, or a temporary high when we are low. He justifies pride, unkindness, dishonesty, discontent, and immorality." (Rasband, Conf. Report, April 2019).

"Satan is cunning. . . 'We do not lose our faith by a blowout – just by slow leaks.' . . . The adversary presents his principles and arguments in the most approved style, and in the most winning tone, attended with the most graceful attitudes. . . . He is active. He is powerful, even though his power is limited." (Christiansen, Conf. Report, Apr. 1958). Fortunately, although the devil can entice us to do evil, "because we have agency [t]he devil can't make us do anything we choose not to do." (Faust, Conf. Report, Apr. 2007).

(See "Satan" in Topical Index, 1 Nephi 22; see also, "False Doctrines" in 2 Nephi 28).

Nephi's discourse to his brethren and the House of Israel is a message of hope in the Lord. The words of Isaiah testify that despite the Jewish diaspora (and Lehi's travels to the New World), the Lord will gather the house of Israel again, both physically and spiritually. No matter their physical location or spiritual situation, the Lord of Mercy will not forget them, for he has "graven them upon his hands." The hopeful message of Isaiah is that scattered Israel will be gathered in stakes (and temples) throughout the world. In the last days, despite wars, conflicts and commotions, the righteous who are obedient need not fear, for they will be protected by the Lord. Nephi teaches that Christ, Himself, will lead a millennial period of temporal, and political peace, when mankind will live together under Christ the King. And, ultimately, because of the righteousness of the people, Satan will be bound.

Discourse 7: Nephi, "Press Forward in Christ" (2 Nephi 25-33)

Prophet	Key Doctrines	Scriptures	Audience	Date
Nephi	<ul><li>Rejoice in Christ; Talk of Christ; Preach of Christ</li><li>Doctrine of Inclusion</li><li>Nephi's Warnings about False Doctrines</li><li>Endure to the End</li></ul>	2 Nephi 25-33 (after quoting Isaiah 2-14)	To his "people" (beloved brethren) and "all those that shall receive hereafter these things which I write" (2 Nephi 25:3)	Between 559 and 545 B.C. After arrival in promised land and split with other groups

INTRODUCTION

Nephi's last recorded discourse is consistent thematically and structurally with his previous two discourses. It relies on the words of Isaiah. It is comprehensive in scope. It is addressed to his people, and to future readers of the record. It contains warnings about false doctrines and fundamental teachings about first principles of the Gospel. And, it is centered on Christ.

Many years have passed since Lehi's family, Zoram, and the family of Ishmael have arrived in the Promised Land. A faction led by Laman and Lemuel has separated from the followers of God and Christ led by Nephi. There have been conflicts, and "wars and contentions" (2 Nephi 5:34). Nephi is an old man. He writes "unto [his] people," and also "unto all those that shall receive hereafter these things which I write" (2 Nephi 25:3).

Nephi, himself, identifies the purpose of this sermon. His words are intended to:

- persuade his people to do good (2 Nephi 33:4);
- teach his people about their forefathers (2 Nephi 33:4);
- speak of Jesus Christ and persuade his people to believe in Him (2 Nephi 33:4)
- encourage his people to endure to the end (2 Nephi 33:4); and
- speak harshly against sin (2 Nephi 33:5).

This is Nephi's great testimony of Christ. He begins by quoting Isaiah, teaching his people about their forefathers, and recounting that prophet's witness of Christ. Nephi then shares his own witness of the Savior and instructs his people to follow Christ's example in all things, and to consider how He treats others, "inviting all" to come unto Him. He speaks harshly against sin and false doctrine, and provides specific warnings against the tactics of the devil. Nephi then concludes his discourse with what he calls the "doctrine of Christ," and encourages his people to follow the Lord's example in all things, and admonishes them to "endure to the end" in righteousness.

Elder Jeffrey R. Holland said: "If we were to identify general sections of scripture that are absolutely central to the mission of the Book of Mormon, I'm not sure that there are any more important pages in the book than those that start with 2 Nephi 25 and conclude with Nephi's testimony at the end of chapter 33. That's only about fifteen pages, and yet it is a strong, central statement giving significance to the purpose of the Book of Mormon: to declare that Jesus is the Christ. This is Nephi's closing testimony. It is, for all intents and purposes, the end of his life." ("That Our Children Might Know," BYU Speeches, Aug. 25, 1981).

DISCOURSE: 2 Nephi 25-33

Summary of Nephi's "Own Prophecy" in Chapters 25 - 30:

After quoting Isaiah's writings in 2 Nephi 12-24 (Isaiah 2 – 14), Nephi supplements the prophecies of Isaiah "with mine own prophecy" (2 Nephi 25:7), delivered in "plainness," in chapters 25 through 30. His prophetic teachings comprise three general categories: (i) he speaks of the Lord, and identifies Jesus Christ as the source of salvation; (ii) he "speaks harshly against sin," and warns about Satan's tactics in the last days; and (iii) he teaches his people about their forefathers, and about the restoration of the gospel and the coming forth of the Book of Mormon to bless their descendants. Some of these prophecies contain the same subject matter as the vision Nephi received and recorded in 1 Nephi 11-14.

2 Nephi 25: Jerusalem is destroyed and the Jews are carried away captive into Babylon. They return to the land of Jerusalem, and there are wars and rumors of wars. Christ is manifest to the Jews, but they reject him, and crucify him. Christ is resurrected, and thereafter Jerusalem is destroyed again, and the Jews are scattered among all nations, and persecuted for many generations, until they believe in Christ. At that time, they will be restored and be redeemed through the Atonement of Christ.

2 Nephi 26: At the death and resurrection of Christ, great signs and tempests shall appear in the New World. The descendants of Lehi will be visited with destruction, but Christ shall visit the righteous survivors, and they shall have peace for three generations. After the fourth generation, the people of Nephi will be destroyed due to wickedness, and the posterity of Lehi will dwindle in unbelief. The Gentiles shall come upon the land and smite the people. There will be many churches and secret combinations among the Gentiles.

2 Nephi 27: The Book of Mormon will come forth. Three witnesses will testify of the book. A learned man will say that he cannot read a sealed book. The Lord will perform a marvelous work and a wonder in reestablishing His church on the earth.

2 Nephi 28: In the last days, there will be many churches that contend with each other. False doctrines will circulate among the people, and they will deny the power of God. The devil will deceive many.

2 Nephi 29: Many Gentiles will reject the Book of Mormon and say they have no need for scripture other than the Bible. Despite the "marvelous" circumstances surrounding the Book of Mormon, many people will not accept it. The Lord speaks to many nations, and commands the people to record His words. Scriptures from all nations combine to show that the Lord is God.

2 Nephi 30: The Gentiles who repent will be numbered among the covenant people. Many of Lehi's descendants and Jews will be restored to the knowledge of Christ. In the last days, the wicked will be destroyed, and the righteous spared. Peace will reign, the earth will be filled with knowledge, and Satan will be bound. Millennial conditions will abound.

KEY DOCTRINES

Nephi's prophecies in these chapters are interwoven with doctrinal discussions, which include:

- **Rejoice in Christ.** "We talk of Christ, rejoice in Christ, preach of Christ, and prophesy of Christ" (2 Nephi 25:26).

- **Doctrine of Inclusion.** All are invited to partake of salvation thru Christ: black and white, bond and free, male and female, Jew and Gentile; all are alike unto God.(2 Nephi 26:33).

- **Warnings about False Doctrines.** False doctrines include: "Eat, drink and be merry"; "all is well in Zion"; "lie a little"; "no harm in a little sin"; "there is no devil"; "we have received the word of God, and need no more" (2 Nephi 28:7-12, 21-22, 29).

- **Doctrine of Christ.** Have faith in Christ, repent, be baptized, receive the Holy Ghost, press forward, feasting on the words of Christ, and endure to the end, to obtain eternal life.

COMMENTARY

Talk of Christ, Rejoice in Christ, Preach of Christ

After reviewing Isaiah's prophecies of the Messiah, Nephi testifies "there is none other name given under heaven save it be this Jesus Christ . . . whereby man can be saved" (2 Nephi 25:20; see Mosiah 3:17; Acts 4:12). "And we talk of Christ, we rejoice in Christ, we preach of Christ, we prophesy of Christ . . . that our children may know to what source they may look for a remission of their sins" (2 Nephi 25:26). In just twelve verses in Second Nephi 25, from verse nineteen, when Nephi declares that an angel reveals that the name of the Messiah should be Jesus Christ, through verse thirty, "Christ" is mentioned fifteen times.

"The central purpose of the Book of Mormon is its testimony of Jesus Christ. Of more than 6,000 verses in the Book of Mormon, far more than half refer directly to Him." (Packer, Conf. Report, Apr. 2005). "The Book of Mormon has been organized into 6,607 verses, of which 3,925 refer to Jesus Christ, employing more than 100 titles. Thus, some form of Christ's name is used on an average of one reference for every 1.7 verses." (Nelson, Conf. Report, Oct. 1999).

More than 2500 years ago, Jacob taught that "none of the prophets have written, nor prophesied, save they hae spoken concerning this Christ" (Jacob 7:11). Likewise, in our day, modern-day apostles, who are special witnesses of the Lord Jesus Christ, all "talk of Christ," and "preach of Christ." Elder Quentin L. Cook taught: "The message, ministry, and Atonement of Jesus Christ, our Savior, are our essential . . . curriculum. No scripture characterizes our faith better than 2 Nephi 25:26: 'we talk of Christ, we rejoice in Christ, we preach of Christ, we prophesy of Christ.'" (Conf. Report, Apr. 2012).

Jesus Christ "is the central figure in all human history. His life and teachings are the heart of . . . holy scripture. The Old Testament sets the stage for Christ's mortal ministry. The New Testament describes his mortal ministry. The Book of Mormon gives us a second witness of His mortal ministry. He came to earth to declare His gospel as a foundation for all mankind. . . . He then gave His life in order to be our Savior and Redeemer. . . . He is the central figure in all human history. Our eternal destiny is always in His hands. It is a glorious thing to believe in Him and accept Him as our Savior, our Lord, and our Master." (Perry, Conf. Report, Oct. 2011). President Russell M. Nelson testified: "Nothing in human history equals the wonder, the magnitude, or the fruits of the matchless life of the Son of God. He is our exemplar and the author of our faith. And one day He will again come to the earth to begin His promised millennial reign." (Conf. Report, Oct. 1993).

Elder Bruce R. McConkie proclaimed: "[Jesus Christ] is the Lord Jehovah, the Great I Am, the Creator of heaven and earth and all things which in them are. And thus we testify that he is the God of Israel, the promised Messiah, the Only Begotten, the Son of God. . . . [H]e came into the world to ransom men from the temporal and spiritual death brought upon them through the fall of Adam; that he was born of Mary, inheriting from her the power of mortality, which is the power to die; that he is literally the Son of God . . . and that he inherited from his Father the power of immorality, which is the power to live. . . . [H]e was able to work out the infinite and eternal atonement, whereby all men are raised in immortality . . . while those who believe and obey his laws are raised also unto eternal life. . . . We accept him as the Son of God, as the Savior and Redeemer of the world." (Conf. Report, Oct. 1970). "We claim scriptural authority for the assertion that Jesus Christ was and is God the Creator . . . the God of Abraham, Isaac and Jacob . . . the God of the Old Testament record . . . . We affirm that Jesus Christ was and is Jehovah." (Talmage, Jesus the Christ, 32).

President Gordon B. Hinckley testified: "Our faith, our knowledge [of Christ] comes of the witness of a prophet in this dispensation who saw before him the great God of the universe and His Beloved Son, the resurrected Lord Jesus Christ. They spoke to him. He spoke with Them. . . . It was a vision of the Almighty and of the Redeemer of the world, glorious beyond our understanding but certain and unequivocating in the knowledge which it brought. It is out of that knowledge, rooted deep in the soil of modern revelation, that we, in the words of Nephi, 'talk of Christ, we rejoice in Christ, we preach of Christ' . . . . I know that Jesus Christ is the Only Begotten Son, the Redeemer of the world, who gave His life that we might have eternal life and who rules and reigns with His Father." (Conf. Report, Apr. 2002).

Jesus Christ is central to every doctrine, every ordinance, and every principle of the Church. Nephi taught that the "right way is to believe in Christ and deny him not . . . wherefore ye must bow down before him and worship him with all your might, mind, and strength, and your whole soul" (2 Nephi 25:28, 29). When we are baptized, we take on his name, a covenant we renew each week through partaking of the sacrament, where we promise to always remember Him. "May we follow our Savior, Jesus Christ, and always remember Him in all that we do and all that we say and in all of the acts of charity given one to another, that we may know that these things are done in remembrance of Him." (Hales, Conf. Report, Oct. 1997). We talk of Christ, we rejoice in Christ, we preach of Christ, and we prophesy of Christ. (2 Nephi 25:26). (See "Christ" in Topical Index, and Appendix A: Another Testament of Jesus Christ).

Doctrine of Inclusion

Nephi taught that Jesus Christ performed His work of salvation "for the benefit of the world; for he loveth the world, even that he layeth down his own life that he may draw ***all*** men unto him. Wherefore he commanded ***none*** that they shall ***not*** partake of his salvation" (2 Nephi 26:24, *emphasis added*). Salvation is not an exclusive club; but is open to all who would follow the Savior. The entrance requirements for the kingdom of heaven are the same for all mankind. In that sense, salvation can be universal. "I rejoice in the great plan of salvation that is big enough for all of our Father in Heaven's children." (Cook, Conf. Report, Apr. 2009).

Nephi repeats this principle of inclusion in the next few verses, with the questions: Does Christ tell ***anyone*** to "depart from [him]"; or to "depart out of the synagogues or houses of worship"; or, to "not partake of his goodness"; or to "not partake of his salvation"? The answer is a clear and resounding, "No!" (2 Nephi 26:25-28). "Perhaps no other passage in the Book of Mormon conveys more plainly the breadth of Christ's gift for all people everywhere than those which Nephi recorded. The gift was given freely and would be denied to no one who came to partake of that mercy and salvation." (Holland, <u>Christ and the New Covenant</u>, 48).

Elder Jeffrey R. Holland affirmed: "I testify that no one of us is less treasured or cherished of God than another. I testify that He loves each of us – insecurities, anxieties, self-image, and all. He doesn't measure our talents or our looks; He doesn't measure our professions or our possessions. He cheers on every runner, calling out that the race is against sin, not against each other." (Conf. Report, Apr. 2002).

The Lord instructed his ancient prophet Samuel: "Look not on his countenance, or on the height of his stature . . . for the Lord seeth not as man seeth; for man looketh on the outward appearance, but the Lord looketh on the heart" (1 Samuel 16:7). President Uchtdorf said, "God does not look on the outward appearance. I believe that he doesn't care one bit if we live in a castle or a cottage, if we are handsome or homely, if we are famous or forgotten. Though we are incomplete, God loves us completely. Though we are imperfect, He loves us perfectly." (Conf. Report, Oct. 2009).

The Lord's love and mercies are extended to all. His gospel message is one of inclusion. This was evident both in His conduct during his earthly ministry, and, explicitly, in His instructions to his disciples after his resurrection. Of Christ's ministrations during His life, President Howard W. Hunter observed: "Out of the abundance of his heart, Jesus spoke to the poor, the downtrodden, the widows, the little children; to farmers and fishermen, and those who tended goats and sheep; to strangers and foreigners, the rich, the politically powerful, as well as the unfriendly Pharisees and scribes. He ministered to the poor, the hungry the deprived, the sick. He blessed . . . people with physical disabilities. . . All were recipients of his love. All were 'privileged the one like unto the other, and none [were] forbidden.' (2 Nephi 26:28)." (Conf. Report, Apr. 1992).

After his resurrection, the Lord commanded his disciples to take the gospel to all the world and "teach all nations" (Matt. 28:19). President Spencer W. Kimball taught that His Gospel was a message of inclusion that would be extended to all people: "The Lord would have eliminated bigotry and class distinction. . . . And though he personally [during his mortal ministry] came to the 'lost sheep of the house of Israel,' . . . yet he later sent Paul to bring the gospel to the Gentiles and revealed to Peter that the gospel was for all. (see Acts 10:11-18)." (Conf. Report, Apr. 1954).

Later when other Jews complained about extending the gospel to the Gentiles, who were "unclean" under Jewish traditions, Peter taught: "God, which knoweth the hearts, bare them witness, giving them the Holy Ghost, even as he did unto us; And put no difference between us and them" (Acts 15:8-9). Christ's gospel was for all, Peter testified, "Of, a truth I perceive that God is no respecter of persons; But in every nation he that feareth him, and worketh righteousness, is accepted with him" (Acts 10:34-35).

Paul, who was specifically called to bring the gospel to the Gentiles, taught: "There is neither Jew nor Greek, there is neither bond nor free, there is neither male nor female: for ye are all one in Christ Jesus" (Galatians 3:28). He later instructed the Romans: "there is no difference between the Jew and the Greek . . . For whosoever shall call upon the name of the Lord shall be saved" (Romans 10:12-13). President Brigham Young observed, "Jesus Christ sent His disciples to preach the gospel to every creature, to the king and the peasant, to the great and the small, to the rich and the poor, to the bond and the free, to the black and the white." (Journal of Discourses, 11:124).

Nephi affirmed that the Lord does not set racial, gender or cultural boundaries in his invitation to follow Him: "he inviteth them all to come unto him and partake of his goodness; and he denieth none that come unto him, black and white, bond and free, male and female . . . and all are alike unto God, both Jew and Gentile" (2 Nephi 26:33). All are alike unto God: it is not the outward appearance, but the inner character that matters to the Lord.[35]

In one of Dr. Suess' colorful children's stories, fanciful creatures called Sneetches learn to not judge others by their outward appearance. In the story, there are two kinds of Sneetches: those with stars on their bellies, and those without. Initially, Sneetches with stars on their bellies look down on the Sneetches without them. "Because they had stars, all the Star-Belly Sneetches would brag, 'We're the best kind of Sneetch on the beaches.' With their snoots in the air, they would sniff and they'd snort, 'We'll have nothing to do with the Plain-Belly sort!' And whenever they met some when they were out walking, they'd hike right on past them without even talking." (Dr. Suess, The Sneetches and Other Stories, 4). This state of affairs saddened the star-less variety of Sneetch, until a certain Professor McMonkey McBean appeared with a machine that would apply stars to Sneetch bellies. Once they had stars, the formerly plain-bellied Sneetches proclaimed their own superiority. Nonetheless, seeking to regain their place at the top of the pecking order, the original star-bellied variety besought Professor McBean to remove their stars, and declared that it was the Sneetch without the star who was the "best on the beach." Soon, Sneetches were running in and out of machines that applied and removed stars until they had completely exhausted their funds, and no one could tell from the outside "which Sneetch was what one and what one was which."

At this point, the Sneetches realize that belly stars, and one's outward appearance, are not that important, after all. "I'm quite happy to say that the Sneetches got really smart on that day. That day they decided that Sneetches are Sneetches, and no kind of Sneetch is the best on the beaches. That day, all the Sneetches forgot about stars, and whether they had one, or not, upon thars." (Dr. Suess, The Sneetches and Other Stories, 24).

---

[35] In his "I have a dream" speech on August 28, 1963 in Washington, D.C., Dr. Martin Luther King, Jr. said, "I have a dream that my four little children will one day live in a nation where they will not be judged by the color of their skin but by the content of their character."

Just as Dr. Suess teaches that Sneetches are Sneetches, whether or not they have stars on their bellies, Nephi proclaims that people are "all alike unto God," whether or not they are the same race, color, or nationality. (2 Nephi 26:33). President Howard W. Hunter remarked, "we wish that men and women everywhere could understand and find the joy and peace that come from the knowledge that all people are children of God and therefore brothers and sisters – literally, actually, and in fact, regardless of race, color, language or religious belief." (Conf. Report, Oct. 1981). We are all alike unto God.

Indeed, as humans, we are much more genetically alike than different, especially when compared to other species. "Penguins, for example, have twice as much genetic diversity as humans. Fruit flies have 10 times as much. . . . There's more genetic diversity within a group of chimps on a single hillside in Gomba [Tanzania] than in the entire human species. . . . The visual differences we are attuned to don't tell us anything about what's beneath the skin." (www.pbs.org, "Race-The Power of an Illusion: Human Diversity – Go Deeper.")

"People today look remarkably diverse on the outside. But how deep are these differences between human groups? First, compared with many other mammalian species, humans are genetically far less diverse – a counterintuitive finding, given our large population and worldwide distribution. . . . Early studies of human diversity showed that most genetic diversity was found between individuals rather than between populations or continents. . . . [there is] no reason to assume that 'races' represent any units of relevance for understanding human genetic history." (Smithsonian National Museum of History: Modern Human Diversity – Genetics).

"The fact that humans are relatively homogeneous at the DNA level, combined with the fact that between-population variation is modest, has significant social implications. Importantly, these patterns imply that the DNA differences between individuals, and between populations, are relatively scant and do not provide a biological basis for any form of discrimination." (Jorde, "Genetic Variation and Human Evolution," Univ. of Utah School of Medicine). We are much more alike than different.

The outward differences we do have can be embraced. Sister Chieko N. Okazaki taught: "God has given us many gifts, much diversity and many differences, but the essential thing is what we know about each other – that we are all his children." (Conf. Report, Apr. 1996). Elder Holland compared the church to a choir, rich with diversity. "I would ask us . . . to remember it is by divine design that not all the voices in God's choir are the same. It takes variety – sopranos and altos, baritones and basses – to make rich music. To borrow a line quoted in the cheery correspondence of two remarkable Latter-day Saint women, 'All God's critters got a place in the choir.' . . . There is room for the single, for the married, for large families, and for the childless. There is room for those who once had questions regarding their faith and room for those who still do. There is room for those with differing sexual attractions." (Conf. Report, April 2017).

Elder M. Russell Ballard proclaimed: "Nearly 25 years ago, the First Presidency declared: 'Our message . . . is one of special love and concern for the eternal welfare of all men and women, regardless of religious belief, race, or nationality, knowing that we are truly brothers and sisters because we are sons and daughters of the same Eternal Father' (First Presidency Statement, 15 Feb. 1978). That is our doctrine – a doctrine of inclusion. That is what we believe. That is what we have been taught. Of all the people on this earth, we should be the most loving, the kindest, and the most tolerant because of that doctrine." (Conf. Report, Oct. 2001).

The Lord – and the Lord's church – welcomes all, irrespective of race, gender or background, and in spite of our imperfections. It is not who we are, but what we do, that qualifies us for entry into the kingdom of heaven. Salvation is based on the content of our character, not the color of our skin. "[A]nd he inviteth them all to come unto him and partake of his goodness; and he denieth none that come unto him, black and white, bond and free, male and female . . . and all are alike unto God" (2 Nephi 26:33).[36]

Nephi's Warnings: False Doctrines

In 2 Nephi chapter 28, Nephi prophesies about conditions present in the last days, and warns about several false doctrines that will deceive the people. Nephi prophesies that there will be many churches that teach "false and vain and foolish doctrines" (2 Nephi 28:9). He observes that many of the people will have "gone astray" (2 Nephi 28:14). Even the "humble followers of Christ" will "err because they are taught by the precepts of men" (2 Nephi 28:14).

His warnings are applicable to all: both those inside and outside of the Lord's church. President Joseph Fielding Smith quoted Nephi's warnings, and taught: "Do not think that this was said of the world, or even the 'stranger . . . within our gates.' It is said of members of the Church." (Conf. Report, Apr. 1969).

Some of the warnings are similar to the warnings and list of 'woes' identified by Nephi's brother Jacob (see 2 Nephi 9:27-38). Just as Jacob warns that the learned who ignore God and the rich who are full of pride will "perish," Nephi warns that the "wise, and the learned and the rich that are puffed up in the pride of their hearts . . . shall be thrust down to hell!" (2 Nephi 28:15).

Like Jacob, Nephi also issues a warning about the pernicious influence of false doctrines in the last days. He identifies several of these fallacious teachings in chapter 28.

False Doctrine	Verse
"Eat, drink, and be merry . . . for tomorrow we die"	2 Nephi 28:7
"[God] will justify in committing a little sin . . . there is no harm in this"	2 Nephi 28:8
"[L]ie a little, take the advantage of one because of his words"	2 Nephi 28:8
"God will beat us with a few stripes" but we will be saved, anyway	2 Nephi 28:8
"[R]evile against that which is good, and say that it is of no worth"	2 Nephi 28:16
"There is no hell; and . . . no devil, for there is none"	2 Nephi 28:22
"We have received the word of God, and we need no more of the word of God"	2 Nephi 28:29

---

[36]Elder Dallin H. Oaks taught that "bond" includes those whose freedom is restricted by physical or emotional afflictions; those who are addicted or imprisoned by sin; and those confined in the boundaries of erroneous ideas. (Conf. Report, Apr. 2006). With respect to gender, President Boyd K. Packer taught: "There is nothing in the revelations which suggests that to be a man rather than to be a woman is preferred in the sight of God, or that he places a higher value on sons than on daughters." (Conf. Report, Oct. 1993).

"Eat, drink, and be merry"

"Many of God's children live life as though there were no tomorrow, no day of reckoning. They fill their lives with the pursuit of comfort, gain, and pleasure. Of such, Nephi said, 'Yea, and there shall be many which shall say: Eat, drink and be merry, for tomorrow we die and it shall be well with us' (2 Nephi 28:7). As a result of such erroneous thinking the world is filled with lurid and lascivious attractions." (Dunn, Conf. Report, Apr. 2003). "Is this prediction of Nephi coming to pass in our day? . . . Are there those of us who would yield to the enticement and the pressure of acquaintances and associates to 'eat, drink, and be merry,' on certain occasions? Would we, for instance, when in the company of certain others, forsake principles, propriety and decency in order to conform with and be accepted by the group?" (Christiansen, Conf. Report, Oct. 1959).

"Satan seeks to deceive us about right and wrong . . . This detour typically starts off with what seems to be only a small departure: 'Just try it once. One beer or one cigarette or one porno movie won't hurt.' What all of these departures have in common is that each of them is addictive. . . . If we choose the wrong road, we chose the wrong destination. . . . Nephi warns . . . 'there shall be many which shall say: Eat, drink and be merry, for tomorrow we die; and it shall be well with us.' . . . Surely you have seen and heard these arguments. They will come at you in classrooms and hallways, in what you read, and in what you see in popular entertainment. . . . Be not deceived. Heed the ancient and modern prophetic warnings against thievery, drunkenness, and all forms of sexual sin. . . . Beware of the slick package and the glitz of a good time. What the devil portrays as fun can be spiritually fatal." (Oaks, Conf. Report, Oct. 2004).

"God will justify in committing a little sin"

Elder Neal A. Maxwell warned: "God never can justify us 'in committing a little sin.' He is the God of the universe, not some night court judge with whom we can haggle and plea bargain! Of course God is forgiving. He knows the intents of our hearts. He also knows what good we might have done while AWOL. In any case, what others do is no excuse for the disciple from whom much is required. Besides, on the straight and narrow path, there are simply no corners to be cut." (Conf. Report, Oct. 1988). The Doctrine and Covenants is clear: "For I the Lord cannot look upon sin with the least degree of allowance; [n]evertheless, he that repents and does the commandments of the Lord shall be forgiven" (D&C 1:31-32).

"Lie a little"

"Seeing our day, Nephi prophesied that many would say, 'Lie a little, take the advantage of one because of his words, dig a pit for thy neighbor; there is no harm in this' (2 Nephi 28:8). We live in a world where many look on the marketplace as a ruthless arena where the buyer must beware, where no one is obligated to do more than the law requires, and where fraud isn't fraud unless you can prove it in court. Members of the Church of Jesus Christ have a higher standard. . . . We are commanded to live the Golden Rule." (Oaks, Conf. Report, Oct. 1986). Elder ElRay Christiansen asked: "could it be that any of us would lie a little, or take advantage of one because of his words, perhaps by misquoting or exaggerating what he said? Are there any of us who would figuratively dig a pit for his neighbor, hoping that he will fall into it? Perhaps by taking unfair advantage of him, by shrewd maneuvering, thinking that as long as one gets away with it that he is a trustworthy and honest man. 'Make of yourself an honest man,' said Carlyle, 'and then you may be sure that there is one rascal less in the world.'" (Conf. Report, Oct. 1959).

President Gordon B. Hinckley taught: "Be strong, my brethren, with the strength of simple honesty. How easy it is to 'lie a little'. . . . Nephi so describes the people of his day, as he also describes so many of our day. How easy it is for us to say, 'We believe in being honest, true, chaste, benevolent.' But how difficult for so many to resist the temptation to lie a little, cheat a little, steal a little, bear false witness in speaking gossipy words about others. Rise above it. . . . Be strong in the simple virtue of honesty." (Conf. Report, Oct. 1992)

"God will beat us with a few stripes."

In speaking about this verse, President James E. Faust taught: "[One deception] is what some erroneously call 'premeditated repentance.' There is no such doctrine . . . it is in fact pernicious and a false concept. Its objective is to persuade us that we can consciously and deliberately transgress with the forethought that quick repentance will permit us to enjoy the full blessings of the gospel. . . . This foolish doctrine was foreseen by Nephi: 'And there shall be many which shall say: . . . God will justify in committing a little sin . . . if it so be we are guilty, God will beat us with a few stripes, and at last we shall be saved." (Conf. Report, Oct. 2000).

"Revile (or anger) against that which is good."

Elder Marvin J. Ashton counseled: "It should come as no surprise that one of the adversary's tactics in the latter days is stirring up hatred among the children of men. He loves to see us criticize each other, make fun or take advantage of our neighbor's known flaws, and generally pick on each other. The Book of Mormon is clear from where all anger, malice, greed, and hate come from. . . . By the looks of what we constantly see depicted in the news media, it appears that Satan is doing a pretty good job. In the name of reporting the news, we are besieged with . . . insults between business, athletic, or political opponents." (Conf. Report, Apr. 1992).

"There is no hell"

President Marion G. Romney taught: "A corollary to the pernicious falsehood that God is dead is the equally pernicious doctrine that there is no devil. Satan himself is the father of both of these lies. . . . Satan . . . is a powerful personage of spirit, the archenemy of God, of man, and of righteousness. The reality of the existence of both God and the devil is conclusively established by the scriptures and by human experience." (Conf. Report, Apr. 1971).

After quoting 2 Nephi 28:20-21, President James E. Faust observed: "I have always been fascinated that people are led carefully down to hell. Alexander Pope expressed a similar thought concerning the acceptance of evil:

> *'Vice is a monster of so frightful mien*
> *As to be hated needs but to be seen;*
> *Yet seen too oft, familiar with her face,*
> *We first endure, then pity, then embrace.'*

(Essay on Man, epistle 3, lines 217-220)." (Conf. Report, Apr. 1989).

He counseled, "We are inclined to accept something morally wrong if it is only a shade more wrong than something we are already accepting." (Conf. Report, Apr. 1989).

"We have enough scripture"

Nephi teaches that when the Book of Mormon would go forth "many" would say "we need no more of the word of God, for we have enough!" (2 Nephi 28:29). Joseph Smith taught: "It is nowhere said in [the Bible] that [God] would not, after giving, what is there contained, speak again." (History of the Church, 2:18).

President James E. Faust asked: "Does God love us less than those led by the ancient [Biblical] prophets? Do we need his guidance and instruction less? Reason suggests that this cannot be? Does he not care? Has he lost his voice? Has he gone on a permanent vacation? Does he sleep? The unreasonableness of each of these proposals is self-evident." (Conf. Report, Apr. 1980).

"All is well . . ."

President Thomas S. Monson warned, "lest we become complacent, may I quote from 2 Nephi in the Book of Mormon: 'At that day shall [the devil] lull them away into carnal security'. . . . Someone has said that our complacency tree has many branches, and each spring more buds come into bloom. We cannot afford to be complacent. We live in perilous times; the signs are all around us. We are acutely aware of the negative influences in our society . . . . We . . . must stand up to the dangers which surround us." (Conf. Report, Apr. 2005). In speaking of carnal temptations prevalent in today's world, Bishop Richard C. Edgley taught: "Nephi describes [Satan's] sales techniques as pacifying, flattering, and lulling as he declares, 'All is well' (2 Nephi 28:21-22). Among other things Satan would have us [adopt] is immorality in all its forms, including pornography, language, dress, and behavior. But such evil deeds bring emotional distress, loss of spirituality, loss of self-respect, lost opportunity." (Conf. Report, Oct. 2000).

These false doctrines are particularly corrosive because they eviscerate accountability, consequences and responsibility, and thus eliminate the need for repentance, change, and a Redeemer. Several of these Satanic tactics attack the foundation of the Plan of Salvation: if there is no sin, men need no forgiveness and no repentance, and they cannot progress. The false doctrines are Satan's not-so-subtle method of attacking the saving mission of the Lord Jesus Christ. Ever jealous of our chosen, elder brother, Lucifer would try to convince us that there is no need for a Savior, as there is nothing to save us from. Individually, and in the aggregate, his false doctrines represent a clever, though pernicious, and patently false, position.

The Doctrine of Christ: First Principles

In chapter 31, Nephi states that he will now "make an end of my prophesying" (2 Nephi 31:1). He concludes his discourse with "a few words which [he] must speak concerning the doctrine of Christ" (2 Nephi 31:2). (See 2 Nephi 31:21; 32:6). He says that he will speak plainly . . . for "my soul delighteth in plainness" (2 Nephi 31:3). The doctrine of Christ he preaches is direct and succinct: follow Christ, repent, be baptized, receive the Holy Ghost, and endure to the end. Joseph Smith later identified the elements of this doctrine as the "first principles" of the gospel: "We believe that the first principles and ordinances of the gospel are: first, Faith in the Lord Jesus Christ; second, Repentance; third, Baptism by immersion for the remission of sins; fourth, Laying on of hands for the Gift of the Holy Ghost." (Articles of Faith, 1:4).

Elder Jeffrey R. Holland stated: "The 'doctrine of Christ' as taught by Nephi in his grand, summation discourse focuses on faith in the Lord Jesus Christ, repentance, baptism by immersion, receiving the gift of the Holy Ghost, and enduring to the end. . . . As used in the Book of Mormon, 'the doctrine of Christ' is simple and direct. It focuses on the first principles of the gospel exclusively, including an expression of encouragement to endure, to persist, to press on. Indeed, it is in the clarity and simplicity of 'the doctrine of Christ' that its impact is found. . . . The doctrine of Christ is not complicated. It is profoundly, beautifully, single-mindedly clear and complete." (Holland, Christ and the New Covenant, 49-50, 56).

Elder Holland explained further: "Although a phrase like 'the doctrine of Christ' could appropriately be used to describe any or all of the Master's teachings . . . [n]ote that the phrase Nephi used is distinctly singular. In Nephi's concluding testimony, and later in the Savior's own declaration to the Nephites at his appearance to them, the emphasis is on a precise, focused, singular sense of Christ's doctrine, specifically that which the Prophet Joseph Smith declared to be 'the first principles and ordinances of the gospel.'" (Ibid. 49).

Nephi addresses each of these principles and concludes this section of his discourse (chapter 31) with the words: "this is the way; and there is none other way nor name given under heaven whereby man can be saved in the kingdom of God. And now, behold, this is the doctrine of Christ" (2 Nephi 31:21).

First, faith in the Lord Jesus Christ. Faith begins by hearing the word of Christ. (See Alma 32). Upon hearing those words, we exercise faith by choosing to follow His teachings and His example. Nephi teaches that Jesus said, "Follow thou me" (2 Nephi 31:10). We should "follow the example of the Son of the living God ... with real intent . . . [and] do the things which . . . I have seen your Redeemer do" (2 Nephi 31:9-16). To have faith is to follow Christ. Nephi calls this "relying wholly on His merits" (2 Nephi 31:19). He teaches us that to rely on His merits is to believe that He did what was necessary to save us. Faith in Christ is faith in His Atonement, and conducting our lives striving to follow His example. When we understand and believe that we can follow Christ and rely on His "merits, mercy and grace" (2 Nephi 2:8), we are able to have "faith unto repentance" (Alma 34:15). (See "Faith" in Topical Index, Alma 32).

Second, repentance. "Repent ye, repent ye" (2 Nephi 31:11). To repent, we recognize our sins, feel remorse, confess our sins to God, and do everything we can to perform restitution for actions that may have harmed others. This process is not just for major sins, but for imperfections, weaknesses and inadequacies. It is continuing course correction that puts us on a path to be "true followers" of Christ (Moroni 7:48). (See "Repentance" in Topical Index; Alma 36).

Third, baptism. Nephi teaches that Christ provided the perfect example for us to follow. This included the ordinance of baptism. We should "follow your Lord and your Savior down into the water" and "witness unto the Father that ye are willing to keep my commandments by the baptism of water" (2 Nephi 31:13-14). The Savior himself was baptized as an example for us, despite his holiness. "And now, if the Lamb of God . . . should have need to be baptized . . . how much more need have we . . . to be baptized" (2 Nephi 31:5).

While we are baptized for the remission of sins, the Savior, who was holy and without sin, was baptized to demonstrate obedience and fulfill the commandments in righteousness. Elder Robert D. Hales explained: "Entering into the kingdom of God is so important that Jesus was baptized to show us 'the straitness of the path, and the narrowness of the gate, by which [we] should enter' (2 Nephi 31:9) . . . . Jesus was baptized to fulfill His Father's commandment that sons and daughters of God should be baptized. He set the example for all of us to humble ourselves before our Heavenly Father. . . . He was baptized to witness to His Father that He would be obedient in keeping His commandments. . . . (See 2 Nephi 31:4-9). As we follow the example of Jesus, we, too, demonstrate that we will repent and be obedient in keeping the commandments of our Father in Heaven." (Conf. Report, Oct. 2000).

The ordinance of baptism requires us to *follow* the Savior. Nephi taught, "I know that if ye shall *follow the Son*, with full purpose of heart, acting no hypocrisy and no deception before God, but with real intent, repenting of your sins, witnessing unto the Father that ye are willing to take upon you the name of Christ, by baptism – yea, by *following your Lord and your Savior down into the water*. . . ." (2 Nephi 31:13, *emphasis added*).

In the ordinance of baptism, we promise to keep the commandments of the Savior, take on His name, and always remember Him. In return, the Savior promises to forgive, or remit, our sins, and bless us with His Spirit. Through baptism, we are born again, and become a "new creature" (Mosiah 27:26; 2 Cor. 5:17), undertaking a transformative commitment to follow Christ throughout our life. (See "Baptism of Little Children" in Topical Index, Moroni 8).

Fourth, the Gift of the Holy Ghost. After we are baptized, we are promised the gift of the Holy Ghost, as a guide and comforter. "He that is baptized . . . to him will the Father give the Holy Ghost" (2 Nephi 31:12). This is described as a "baptism of fire," a cleansing that also serves as a "witness of the Father and the Son" (2 Nephi 31:14, 18). "

"The gift of the Holy Ghost is received by confirmation after we have received the ordinance of baptism. This gift is the right and opportunity to have the Holy Ghost as a constant companion. If we listen to and obey His still, small voice, He will keep us on the covenant path we entered through baptism, warn us when we are tempted to depart from it, and encourage us to repent and adjust as necessary. Our focus after baptism is to keep the Holy Ghost always with us so that we can continue progressing along the covenant path. The Holy Ghost can be with us only to the degree we keep our lives clean and free from sin. For this reason, the Lord has provided a way for us to continually refresh the purifying effect of our baptism through another ordinance – the sacrament . . . [through which] the Savior performs His cleansing miracle yet again and qualifies us to have the continuing influence of the Holy Ghost." (Pieper, Conf. Report, Oct. 2018). (See "Holy Ghost" in Topical Index, Moroni 10).

Endure to the End

By abiding the first principles of faith, repentance, baptism and the Gift of the Holy Ghost, we witness that we are obedient and have "entered by the gate" that puts us on the "strait and narrow path" (2 Nephi 31:18-19). "It is a strait path, and it is a narrow path without a great deal of latitude at some points, but it can be thrillingly, and successfully traveled." (Holland, Conf. Report, Apr. 2014).[37]

"Once we have entered the strait and narrow path by our faith in Jesus Christ, repentance, and the ordinances of baptism and confirmation [the gift of the Holy Ghost], we must exert every effort to stay on the path. We do so by continually exercising faith in Jesus Christ, repenting, making commitments, and following the Spirit. Once we have been forgiven of our sins, we should try every day to remain free from sin so that we can always have the Holy Ghost with us. . . . If we fall short, we must repent in order to retain the blessings of the covenant. . . . In the scriptures, this lifelong commitment is often called 'enduring to the end.'" (Preach My Gospel, 66).

Nephi declares: "Wherefore, ye must press forward with a steadfastness in Christ, having a perfect brightness of hope, and a love of God and of all men. Wherefore, if ye shall press forward, ***feasting upon the word of Christ***, and ***endure to the end***, behold, thus saith the Father: Ye shall have eternal life" (2 Nephi 31:20, *emphasis added*). Nephi's message is consistent with the message of Lehi's dream: one must "press forward" on the path, "continually holding fast" to the iron rod -- the word of God. (1 Nephi 8:30). To continually hold fast is to "feast" on the words of Christ, not nibble or snack.

President Russell M. Nelson taught: "'Feasting upon the word of Christ' suggests more than mere nibbling, or bolting down fast food. Feasting implies savoring a sumptuous meal. To feast means more than to taste. To feast means to savor. We savor the scriptures by studying them in a spirit of delightful discovery and faithful obedience. When we feast upon the words of Christ . . . [t]hey become an integral part of our nature." (Conf. Report, Oct. 2000). Elder Robert D. Hales explained: "If you and I are to feast upon the words of Christ, we must study the scriptures and absorb His words through pondering them and making them a part of every thought and action." (Conf. Report, Oct. 1998).

Nephi taught that we must not only "press forward feasting on the word of Christ," but must "come unto Christ" and "endure to the end, in following the example of the Son of the living God" toward perfection. (2 Nephi 31:16). Checkpoints along this path include the first principles of the gospel, or "doctrine of Christ." (2 Nephi 31:21). Elder David A. Bednar taught: "Coming unto Christ is not a single event with a fixed point of beginning or ending; rather it is a process that develops and deepens during a lifetime. . . . As we 'press forward' on the pathway of discipleship, we can draw near unto the Savior with the expectation that He will draw near unto us." (Bednar, *New Era*, Apr. 2006).

---

[37] "Strait" means narrow, strict, exacting, and allowing for no deviation. "Mark you, this word strait is spelled s-t-r-a-i-t, not s-t-r-a-i-g-h-t. While no doubt the path that leads into the presence of God is straight, it is also strait, which means narrow. They cannot take with them that which does not apply, or which does not belong to the kingdom of God. All such things must be left behind when we enter into this narrow way which leads in to the presence of God." (Smith, Doctrines of Salvation, 2:13-14.) "The course leading to eternal life is both strait and straight." (McConkie, Mormon Doctrine, 769).

"We may be perfected by repeatedly and iteratively . . . exercising faith in [Christ], repenting, partaking of the sacrament to renew the covenants and blessings of baptism, and receiving the Holy Ghost as a constant companion to a greater degree. As we do so, we become more like Christ and are able to ***endure to the end***, with all that that entails." (Renlund, Conf. Report, Apr. 2015, *emphasis added*).[38] "The disciplined endurance described in this verse [2 Nephi 31:20] is the result of spiritual understanding and vision, persistence, patience, and God's grace." (Bednar, Conf. Report, Apr. 2015).

President Dieter F. Uchtdorf said: "When I was a young boy, 'endure to the end' meant to me mainly that I had to try harder to stay awake until the end of our Church meetings. Later as a teenager I progressed only slightly in my understanding of this scriptural phrase. I linked it with youthful empathy to the efforts of our dear elderly members to hang in there until the end of their lives. . . . [However], enduring to the end is not just a matter of passively tolerating life's difficult circumstances or 'hanging in there.' Ours is an active religion, helping God's children along the strait and narrow path to develop their full potential during this life and return to Him one day. Viewed from this perspective, enduring to the end is exalting and glorious, not grim and gloomy. . . . Enduring to the end is a process filling every minute of our life . . . . It is accomplished through personal discipline following the commandments of God." (Conf. Report, Oct. 2007).

Elder Joseph B. Wirthlin taught that "Enduring to the end is the doctrine of continuing on the path leading to eternal life after one has entered into the path through faith, repentance, baptism, and receiving the Holy Ghost. . . . Enduring to the end means that we have planted our lives firmly on gospel soil, staying in the mainstream of the Church, humbly serving our fellowmen, living Christ like lives, and keeping our covenants. Those who endure are balanced, consistent, humble, constantly improving, and without guile. Their testimonies are not based on worldly reasons; they are based on truth, knowledge, experience, and the Spirit." (Conf. Report, Oct. 2004).

If we keep the commandments and endure to the end, we may receive the gift of eternal life, "the greatest of all the gifts of God" (D&C 14:7). "Eternal" is both quantitative – it lasts forever, and qualitative – it is the type of life that God lives. This supernal gift of eternal life is conditional. "***If*** you keep my commandments ***and*** endure to the end you shall have eternal life" (D&C 14:7, *emphasis added*). "Those qualifying conditions include faith in the Lord, repentance, baptism, receiving the Holy Ghost, and remaining faithful to the ordinances and covenants of the temple." (Nelson, Conf. Report, Apr. 2007). Once again, the doctrine of Christ.

Nephi teaches his readers that the words of Christ "will ***tell*** you all things what ye should do" (2 Nephi 32:3, *emphasis added*). Nephi also instructs us to "receive the Holy Ghost," as it is the Holy Ghost, who "will ***show*** unto you all things what ye should do" (2 Nephi 32:5). Perhaps this duality of "tell" and "show" is analogous to the relationship between "think" and "feel"; and "mind" and "heart." These parallelisms (tell/show; think/feel; mind/heart) occur through the divine dualism of studying the words of Christ in our minds, and "receiving" the witness of the Holy Ghost in our hearts.

---

[38]In addition to 2 Nephi 31:15-16, 20, there are at least 26 admonitions in the scriptures to "endure to the end" to obtain eternal life. Matt. 10:22; Matt. 24:13; Mark 13:13; 1 Nephi 13:37; 1 Nephi 22:31; 2 Nephi 9:24; 2 Nephi 33:4; Omni 1:26; Alma 32:13, 15; Alma 38:2; 2 Nephi 15:9; 3 Nephi 27:6, 16-17; Mormon 9:29; Moroni 8:26; D&C 10:69; D&C 14:7; D&C 18:22; D&C 20:25; D&C 20:29; D&C 53:7.

This is the key to revelation. "Yea, behold, I will tell you in your mind and in your heart, by the Holy Ghost, which shall come upon you and which shall dwell in your heart. Now, behold, this is the spirit of revelation" (D&C 8:2-3). Concurrently, Nephi encourages his brethren and all of us to "pray always" to the Father in the name of Christ. (2 Nephi 32:9). The powerful triad of prayer, scripture study and confirming witnesses through the Holy Ghost all combine to form a spiritual foundation upon which we can receive direct, personal revelation. (See "Pondering Leads to Revelation" in 1 Nephi 11; see "Revelation" in Topical Index, Moroni 10).

"As you read the scriptures and pray for direction, you may not actually see the answer in the form of printed words on the page, but as you read you will receive distinct impressions, and promptings, and, as promised, the Holy Ghost 'will show unto you all things what ye should do.'" (Condie, *Ensign*, May 2002).

Nephi concludes his final discourse, his closing recorded testimony in mortality, with a plea to have faith in Christ: "And now, my beloved brethren, and also Jew, and all ye ends of the earth, hearken unto these words and believe in Christ. . . . for Christ will show unto you, with power and great glory, that they are his words, at the last day; . . . And I pray the Father in the name of Christ that many of us, if not all, may be saved in his kingdom at that great and last day. And now . . . I speak unto you as the voice of one crying from the dust: Farewell until that great day shall come" (2 Nephi 33:10, 12, 13).

Discourse 8: Jacob, "The Infinite Atonement" (2 Nephi 6-10)

Prophet	Key Doctrines	Scripture	Audience	Date
Jacob	• Redemption of Israel (Isaiah 49-52) • The Infinite Atonement • Warnings to the Disobedient	2 Nephi 6-10	To "people of Nephi" (2 Nephi 6:1).	Between 559 and 545 B.C. After arrival in promised land and split with other groups

INTRODUCTION

The spiritual record chronicled by Nephi includes a two-day sermon delivered by his younger brother, Jacob. This first discourse by Jacob in Second Nephi, chapters 6 through 10, is to the "people of Nephi," the followers of Christ. He speaks to them as a covenant people in a manner analogous to a conference of the modern day church, quoting scripture, providing guidance, warnings and admonitions. During the first day of the sermon, Jacob "reads the words of Isaiah," quoting Isaiah chapters 49 through 52. These excerpts include prophesies about the Messiah and the scattering and gathering of Israel. (2 Nephi 6-8). Jacob then clarifies some of the Messianic teachings included in the Isaiah readings, and instructs his people about the "infinite atonement" (2 Nephi 9:7). He also warns his people about the consequences of sin, with specific admonitions to the proud, the rich, and the disobedient. (2 Nephi 9). On the second day of the sermon, Jacob summarizes his messages from the first day, and reviews some of the teachings of his father, Lehi. (2 Nephi 10).

Jacob was a man of affliction (2 Nephi 2:1-4), born in the wilderness, orphaned at a young age, divided from members of his family, a refugee and wanderer who lamented, "our lives passed away like as it were unto us a dream, we being a lonesome and solemn people, wanderers, cast out from Jerusalem, born in tribulation, in a wilderness, and hated of our brethren . . . wherefore, we did mourn out our days" (Jacob 7:26). Nonetheless, Jacob was also a man of great faith, whose days were spent in the service of God (2 Nephi 2:3). He was blessed with a personal witness of Christ,[39] keen spiritual understanding and an unshakeable testimony (Jacob 7:5).

Nephi, who recorded Jacob's first discourse, clearly recognized the spiritual maturity and aptitude of his younger brother. We are told that it is Jacob who Nephi "consecrated" to be a priest and teacher of the people. (2 Nephi 6:1; Jacob 1:18). It is Jacob who is later instructed to care for the smaller plates and to record key spiritual teachings. (Jacob 1:2-4). It is the posterity of Jacob, not Nephi, who will care for these plates for the next several hundred years. And, it is Jacob who is "diligent in his calling" and "magnifies his office" by testifying boldly of the Atonement of Christ. (2 Nephi 9; Jacob 1:19; 2:2-3).

---

[39] Nephi testified that "my brother, Jacob, also has seen [Christ] as I have seen him" (2 Nephi 11:3). Lehi stated that Jacob "beheld in [his] youth [Christ's] glory" (2 Nephi 2:4).

With respect to Jacob's discourse on the Atonement, President Joseph Fielding Smith declared: "One of the most enlightening discourses ever delivered in regard to the atonement is found in the ninth chapter of 2 Nephi in the Book of Mormon. It is the counsel given by Jacob, brother of Nephi. It should be carefully read by every person seeking salvation." (Smith, <u>Answers to Gospel Questions</u>, 4:57).[40]

DISCOURSE: 2 Nephi 6-10

KEY DOCTRINES

- **Redemption of the House of Israel**. The Israelites will be scattered, but gathered again, and the Lord's covenants with His people will be fulfilled. The Savior will redeem Israel.

- **The Infinite Atonement**. The power of the resurrection overcomes physical death for all people. The power of the atonement overcomes spiritual death, upon condition of repentance. All will be resurrected. Those who also have faith in Christ, repent and are baptized, obey the commandments, and endure to the end will also be saved in the Kingdom of God. In the final judgment, if we have not repented, we will have a perfect knowledge of all our guilt.

- **Warnings to the Disobedient**. "Wo unto" the learned who hearken not unto God; the rich who choose their riches over God and despise the poor; and, the disobedient and unrepentant.

COMMENTARY

Redemption of the House of Israel

Jacob begins his discourse by stating his authority, "I, Jacob, having been called of God, and ordained after the manner of his holy order" (2 Nephi 6:2). He tells the people that he has spoken to them about "exceedingly many things," but wants to speak to them "concerning things which are, and which are to come" from the prophecies of Isaiah. (2 Nephi 6:4). Jacob instructs the people that they should "liken" the words he reads from Isaiah to themselves "because ye are of the house of Israel" (2 Nephi 6:5).[41] His intent is that they "might know concerning the covenants of the Lord that he has covenanted with all the house of Israel" (2 Nephi 9:1).

At the beginning of his discourse, Jacob quotes several verses from Isaiah 49, and then recites Isaiah chapters 50 and 51 in their entirety. These prophecies relate to the scattering and gathering of the House of Israel, and demonstrate that "the Lord God will fulfil his covenants which he has made to his children" (2 Nephi 6:12). The House of Israel will be disobedient, and be "smitten" and "scattered," but the Lord will be "merciful" in the last days and "recover" and "gather" Israel. (2 Nephi 6:11, 14).

---

[40] Nephi informs us that Jacob's actual discourse was longer than he recorded: "And now, Jacob spake many more things to my people at that time; nevertheless only these things have I caused to be written, for the things which I have written sufficeth me" (2 Nephi 11:1).

[41] Compare 1 Nephi 19:23-24. Nephi's admonition to liken the words of the prophet (Isaiah) to the people.

Jacob prophesies that: (i) those who were at Jerusalem have been "slain and carried away captive" (2 Nephi 6:8); (ii) they will return again (2 Nephi 6:9); (iii) Christ will come among them, but they will reject and crucify Him (2 Nephi 6:9); (iv) the people in Jerusalem will be scattered again, and "driven to and fro" (2 Nephi 6:10-11); however, (v) the Lord will be merciful, fulfill his covenants, and "deliver his covenant people," and they will be "gathered together again to the lands of their inheritance" (2 Nephi 6:11-17). Ultimately, Israel will be redeemed, and the "redeemed of the Lord shall return, and come with singing unto Zion" (2 Nephi 8:11).

The Savior Will Redeem Israel

Jacob quotes teachings of Isaiah that include references to (i) Christ's ministry; (ii) His crucifixion and atonement; (iii) His preservation of the House of Israel in the last days; and (iv) His millennial reign. (2 Nephi 6-8).

Topic	Selected References
Christ's ministry	The Holy One of Israel will "manifest himself unto [the Jews in Jerusalem] in the flesh" (2 Nephi 6:9). "When I came, there was no man; when I called, yea, there was none to answer" (2 Nephi 7:2). "The Lord God hath given me the tongue of the learned" (2 Nephi 7:4).
Christ's crucifixion	They shall "scourge him and crucify him" (2 Nephi 6:9). "I gave my back to the smiter, and my cheeks to them that plucked off the hair. I hid not my face from shame and spitting" (2 Nephi 7:6)
Christ's preservation of the House of Israel	After the Jews at Jerusalem shall be smitten, afflicted, and scattered, they shall "come to the knowledge of their Redeemer, [and] they shall be gathered together again to the lands of their inheritance" (2 Nephi 6:11), and the "Lord God will fulfill his covenants" (2 Nephi 6:12) and "recover them" (2 Nephi 6:14). "The Lord shall comfort Zion . . . and he will make her wilderness like Eden, and her desert like the garden of the Lord" (2 Nephi 8:3). "[T]he redeemed of the Lord shall return, and come with singing unto Zion; and everlasting joy and holiness shall be upon their heads; and they shall obtain gladness and joy" (2 Nephi 8:11).
Christ's millennial reign	The Messiah will "manifest himself unto them in power and great glory" (2 Nephi 6:14). The wicked, and those who do not believe in the Messiah will be destroyed by fire, tempest, earthquakes, bloodsheds, pestilence and famine (2 Nephi 6:15). "The heavens shall vanish away like smoke, and the earth shall wax old like a garment" (2 Nephi 8:6). Millennial Jerusalem will be "the holy city; for henceforth there shall no more come into thee the uncircumcised and the unclean" (2 Nephi 8:24).

Jacob instructs: "for this cause the prophet [Isaiah] has written these things" (2 Nephi 6:12), that is, to show that the Lord will fulfill his covenants concerning the salvation of all mankind through the Holy Messiah.

The prophecies Jacob quotes from Isaiah all point to salvation through Christ; Isaiah's nouns and verbs focus on redemption and salvation: "redeem" (2 Nephi 7:2); "help" (2 Nephi 7:9); "justifieth" (2 Nephi 7:8); "comfort" (2 Nephi 8:3,12); "light" (2 Nephi 8:4); "salvation" (2 Nephi 8:5); "judge" (2 Nephi 8:5); "cover" [protect] (2 Nephi 8:16); and, "plead" (2 Nephi 8:22).

Jacob explains to his people why he has quoted the two chapters of Isaiah, and what their major message conveys: "I have read these things that ye might know concerning the covenants of the Lord that he has covenanted with all the house of Israel" (2 Nephi 9:1). He tells the people that he speaks "these things" that they "may rejoice, and lift up your heads forever, because of the blessings which the Lord God shall bestow" (2 Nephi 9:3).

Jacob then changes topics from a review of Isaiah's prophecies concerning the physical scattering, gathering and redemption of Israel, to the spiritual gathering and redemption of each individual through the resurrection and the atonement. "Verses 1-3 [in chapter nine] constitute a doctrinal bridge to verse 4 and the verses following. Jacob moved from talking about the scattering and gathering of Israel to a discussion of physical death, and then to resurrection, because they are parallel. Death is the *scattering* of elements, and resurrection is the *gathering* or restoration of those elements." (Ogden and Skinner, Verse by Verse: The Book of Mormon, 150, *emphasis in original*). (See "Gathering" in Topical Index, 1 Nephi 19-22; "Scriptures – Isaiah")

Jacob begins this portion of his discourse with what the people, who evidently searched the records themselves, already understand, and builds on that understanding to teach them new doctrine. Jacob says: "*I know that ye have searched much*, many of you, to know of things to come; wherefore *I know that ye know* that our flesh must waste away and die; nevertheless, in our bodies we shall see God. Yea, *I know that ye know* that in the body he shall show himself to those at Jerusalem . . . for it behooveth the great Creator that he suffereth himself to become subject to man in the flesh, and die for all men, that all men might be subject unto him" (2 Nephi 9:4-5, *emphasis added*).

The Infinite Atonement

Jacob's teachings about Christ's resurrection and "infinite atonement" (2 Nephi 9:7), are the primary subjects of the remainder of his discourse. (See "Plan of Salvation" in Topical Index, 2 Nephi 2). Jacob instructs his people that since death is universal and comes to all mankind, an Atonement is necessary to overcome "death and hell, which I call death of the body, and also death of the spirit" (2 Nephi 9:10).[42]

One aspect of the Atonement, the "merciful plan" of God to redeem mankind from the fall, transgression, and death, is the **resurrection**. (2 Nephi 9:6). President John Taylor taught: "Was it known that man would fall? Yes. We are clearly told that it was understood that man should fall [2 Nephi 2:22-25], and it was understood that the penalty of departing from the law would be death . . . And there was a provision made for that. Man was not able to make that provision himself, and hence we are told that it needed the atonement of a God to accomplish this purpose" (2 Nephi 9:6-7) (Journal of Discourses, 22:300).

---

[42] President Russell M. Nelson observed: "The fullness of the gospel . . . connotes a fuller comprehension of the Atonement. This we do not obtain from the Bible alone. The word *atonement* . . . is mentioned only once in . . . the New Testament. In the Book of Mormon, it appears 39 times. The Book of Mormon also contains more references [81] to the Resurrection than does the Bible [41]." (Conf. Report, Oct. 1999).

The resurrection is the critical physical component of the atonement. Jacob describes how through the resurrection, Christ overcomes physical death for **all** people. As Elder Dallin H. Oaks taught: "Resurrection will come to all mortals who have ever lived upon this earth." (Conf. Report, Apr. 2000). In physical death, our flesh must "rot . . . and crumble to its mother earth" in the grave (2 Nephi 9:7). However, through the resurrection, the grave "shall deliver up its dead . . . and the spirit and the body is restored to itself again, and **all men** become incorruptible, and immortal" (2 Nephi 9:12-13, *emphasis added*). Through the power of the resurrection, temporal death is overcome, and "the bodies and the spirits of men will be restored one to the other" (2 Nephi 9:12). All become "incorruptible, and immortal, and they are living souls" (2 Nephi 9:13).

President Howard W. Hunter taught: "In spite of the great importance we place upon the resurrection in our doctrine, perhaps many of us may not yet have fully glimpsed its spiritual significance and eternal grandeur. If we had, we would marvel at its beauty as did Jacob, the brother of Nephi, and we would shudder at the alternative we would have faced had we not received this divine gift. Jacob wrote: 'O the wisdom of God, his mercy and grace! For behold, if the flesh should rise no more our spirits must become subject to that angel who fell from before the presence of the Eternal God, and became the devil, to rise no more.'" (2 Nephi 9:8) (Conf. Report, Apr. 1988). (See "Resurrection" in Topical Index, Alma 11).

Instead of being subject to the devil and "rise no more," we become subject to Christ, and not only rise again, but have the opportunity to be saved in the kingdom of God. God raises mankind from (i) physical death by the "power of the resurrection" and from (ii) spiritual death by the "power of the atonement" (2 Nephi 10:25). The impact of Christ's sacrifice is two-fold: first, that the power of the resurrection might overcome physical death for all; and, second, that the power of the atonement might overcome spiritual death (or hell), upon condition of repentance. (2 Nephi 9: 22-25; 10:25).

In Jacob's words, "And he cometh into the world that he may save all men *if* they will harken unto his voice . . . And he commandeth all men that they must repent, and be baptized in his name, having perfect faith in [Christ], or they cannot be saved" (2 Nephi 9:21, 23, *emphasis added*). Elder Oaks taught, "Being subject to our Savior means that if our sins are to be forgiven through His Atonement, we must comply with the conditions He has prescribed, including faith, repentance, and baptism. The fulfillment of these conditions depends upon our desires, our choices and our actions." (Conf. Report, April 2006).

Christ, "the great Creator . . . suffereth himself to become subject unto man in the flesh, and die for all men, that all men might become subject unto him" (2 Nephi 9:5). Christ suffered the Atonement so that (i) "the *resurrection* might pass upon all men" *and* (ii) "that all might stand before him at the great and *judgment* day" (2 Nephi 9:22, *emphasis added*). Elder Dallin H. Oaks declared, "I testify that when the Savior suffered and died for all men, all men became subject unto him and to his commandment that all must repent and be baptized in his name, having faith in him, 'or they cannot be saved in the kingdom of God.'" (Conf. Report, Oct. 1988). By subjecting himself to the pains and suffering of "every living creature, both men, women, and children, who belong to the family of Adam" (2 Nephi 9:21), Christ would not only be able to understand and succor the sufferer, he would also be able to judge in a manner that is just, merciful, and eternal.

In essence, Jacob teaches that we are saved through the atonement of Christ by obedience to the laws and ordinances of the gospel. (See Articles of Faith, 1:3). President Marion G. Romney stated: "In about 550 B.C. [Jacob] treated this whole subject how through the Atonement of Christ all mankind may be saved . . . in a masterful fashion." (Conf. Report, Oct. 1974). "[F]ollowing the resurrection each person – then an immortal soul – will be arraigned before the bar of God's justice and receive a final judgment based on his performance during his mortal probation, that the verdict will turn on obedience or disobedience to the laws and ordinances of the gospel. If these laws and ordinances have been complied with during mortal life, the candidate will be cleansed from the stain of sin by the atoning blood of Jesus Christ and be saved in the celestial kingdom of God, there to enjoy with God eternal life. Those who have not complied with the laws and ordinances of the gospel will receive a lesser reward." (Conf. Report, Oct. 1974).

Jacob teaches that after the resurrection, all men must appear before the judgment seat of Christ (the Holy One of Israel) to be judged according to the "holy judgment of God" (2 Nephi 9:15). "After the Resurrection we will have the supreme blessing of being judged by our Savior, who said: 'I will draw all men unto me, that they may be judged according to their works. And it shall come to pass, that whoso repenteth and is baptized in my name shall be filled; and if he endureth to the end, behold, him will I hold guiltless before my Father at that day when I shall stand to judge the world.'" (Clayton, Conf. Report, April 2017).

Because "there was an eternal law of God violated, it needed an eternal, infinite sacrifice to atone therefore." (Taylor, Journal of Discourses, 22:300). President Russell M. Nelson taught: "According to eternal law, the atonement required a personal sacrifice by an immortal being not subject to death. Yet He must die and take up His own body again. The Savior was the only one who could accomplish this. From His mother He inherited power to die. From His Father He obtained power over death." (Conf. Report, Oct. 1993).

"In some manner which I cannot fully explain and which you cannot fully explain, there was a necessity for an infinite atonement, a God dying for a fallen world, and that had to be by the shedding of blood, and his blood only could be shed to restore again that life which had been taken away, and bring back again to man the power to live forever." (Smith, Conf. Report, Oct. 1947). "The atoning sacrifice of Jesus Christ . . . is the central message of all the prophets. It was prefigured by the animal sacrifices prescribed by the law of Moses." (Oaks, Conf. Report, Apr. 2012). Amulek declared that this is the "whole meaning of the law" with "every whit pointing to that great and last sacrifice [of] . . . the Son of God" (Alma 34:14).

This sacrifice was the primary mission of Christ, a mission which He had accepted from the foundation of the world. Elder Carlos Amado said: "The first and greatest purpose [in the mission of Christ] was the unrivaled and amazing assignment that He received from His Father: to carry out an infinite and eternal sacrifice for all humanity. As Heavenly Father's Only Begotten Son in the flesh, He inherited all of His Father's divine qualities, and from His earthly mother, Mary, he inherited mortal characteristics. Only His sacrifice could rescue us from our mortal and fallen state. He came to the world with the specific purpose to give His life, since only His life could give us eternal life. No other mortal being, in the past, present, or future of the existence of the earth, has lived or will live to carry out the Atonement for our sins." (Conf. Report, Apr. 2008).

The Atonement is "infinite" with respect to time because it is everlasting; and, it is "infinite" with respect to scope because it applies to all people. Elder Shayne M. Bowen observed: "His Atonement is infinite. It applies to everyone. . . . That is what infinite means – total, complete, all, forever. President Boyd K. Packer has taught: 'There is no habit, no addiction, no rebellion, no transgression, no apostasy, no crime exempted from the promise of complete forgiveness. That is the promise of the atonement of Christ.'" (Conf. Report, Oct. 2006).

President Russell M. Nelson explained: "His Atonement is infinite – without an end. It was also infinite in that all humankind would be saved from never-ending death. It was infinite in terms of His immense suffering. It was infinite in time . . . . It was infinite in scope – it was to be done once for all. And the mercy of the Atonement extends not only to an infinite number of people, but also to an infinite number of worlds created by Him. It was infinite beyond any human scale of measurement or mortal comprehension." (Conf. Report, Oct. 1996). "Our Savior's Atonement is infinite and eternal. Each of us strays and falls short. We may, for a time, lose our way. God lovingly assures us, no matter where we are or what we have done, there is no point of no return." (Gong, Conf. Report, Oct. 2018). "[I]t is an infinite Atonement because it encompasses and circumscribes every sin and weakness, as well as every abuse or pain caused by others." (Callister, Conf. Report, Apr. 2019). The Atonement is infinite in time, scope, and application.

Elder Dallin H. Oaks asked: "Why is Christ the only way? How was it possible for him to take upon himself the sins of all mankind? Why was it necessary for his blood to be shed? And how can our soiled and sinful selves be cleansed by his blood? These are mysteries I do not understand. To me, as to President John Taylor, the miracle of the atonement of Jesus Christ is 'incomprehensible and inexplicable.' But the Holy Ghost has given me a witness of its truthfulness, and I rejoice that I can spend my life in proclaiming it." (Conf. Report, Oct. 1988).

The Savior is the Savior because in some way "incomprehensible and inexplicable" he bore the sins of all mankind. He can therefore intercede, and satisfy the demands of the law and justice on behalf of those who will believe in him, repent, be baptized, and obey his commandments. "And he commandeth all men that they must repent, and be baptized in his name, having perfect faith in [Him], or they cannot be saved in the kingdom of God" (2 Nephi 9:23-24).

The Atonement Covers Our Infirmities.

Elder Dallin H. Oaks taught: "Our Savior's Atonement does more than assure us of immortality by a universal resurrection and give us the opportunity to be cleansed from sin by repentance and baptism. His Atonement also provides the opportunity to call upon Him who has experienced all of our mortal infirmities to give us the strength to bear the burdens of mortality." (Conf. Report, Oct. 2015). (See "Christ Takes on Our Infirmities," Alma 7).

The purpose of the Atonement is "to make it possible for us to return to God's presence, become more like Him, and have a fullness of joy. This was done by overcoming four obstacles: Physical death; Spiritual death caused by Adam and our sins; Our afflictions and infirmities; [and] Our weaknesses and imperfections." (Callister, Conf. Report, Apr. 2019). Thus, the Atonement not only heals us from sin, it provides a balm for every affliction and infirmity we may suffer. Elder Jeffrey R. Holland declared: "I testify that the Savior's Atonement lifts from us not only the burden of our sins but also the burden of our disappointments and sorrows, our heartaches and our despair (See Alma 7:11-12)." (Conf. Report, Apr. 2006).

"Christ walked the path every mortal is called to walk so that he would know how to succor and strengthen us in our most difficult times. He knows the deepest and most personal burdens we carry. He knows the most public and poignant pains we bear. He descended below all such grief in order that he might lift us above it. There is no anguish or sorrow or sadness in life that he has not suffered in our behalf and borne away upon his own valiant and compassionate shoulders." (Holland, Christ and the New Covenant, 223-24).

Christ is a "merciful . . . high priest" (Hebrews 2:17) who understands us completely and compassionately. He knows our temptations, "for in that he himself hath suffered being tempted, he is able to succor them that are tempted" (Hebrews 2:18). Elder Dallin H. Oaks taught: "Our Savior experienced and suffered the fullness of all mortal challenges 'according to the flesh' so He could know 'according to the flesh' how to 'succor [which means to give relief or aid to] his people according to their infirmities.' He therefore knows our struggles, our heartaches, our temptations, and our suffering, for He willingly experienced them all as an essential part of His Atonement. And because of this, His Atonement empowers him to succor us – to give us strength to bear it all." (Conf. Report, Oct. 2015).

As Paul taught, "we have not an high priest which cannot be touched with the feeling of our infirmities" (Hebrews 4:15). "In the garden and on the cross, Jesus saw each of us and not only bore our sins, but also experienced our deepest feelings so that he would know how to comfort and strengthen us. . . . The Savior's atonement in the garden and on the cross is intimate as well as infinite. Infinite in that it spans the eternities. Intimate in that the Savior felt each person's pains, sufferings and sicknesses." (Bateman, Conf. Report, Apr. 1995).

"The Atonement not only benefits the sinner," taught President James E. Faust, "but also benefits those sinned against – that is, the victims. By forgiving 'those who trespass against us' the Atonement brings a measure of peace and comfort to those who have been innocently victimized by the sins of others." (Conf. Report, Oct. 2001). Elder C. Scott Grow stated, "Through His Atonement, He heals not only the transgressor, but He also heals the innocent who suffer because of those transgressions." (Conf. Report, Apr. 2011). (See Hafen, "Beauty for Ashes: The Atonement of Jesus Christ," *Ensign*, Apr. 1990).

"Some injuries are so hurtful and deep that they cannot be healed without help from a higher power and hope for perfect justice and restitution in the next life. Since the Savior has suffered anything and everything that we could ever feel or experience . . . He understands our pain and will walk with us even in our darkest hours." (Faust, Conf. Report, Oct. 2001).

The Savior is able to help us with any type of challenge we may face: "Many carry heavy burdens. Some have lost a loved one to death or care for one who is disabled. Some have been wounded by divorce. Others yearn for an eternal marriage. Some are caught in the grip of addictive substances or practices like alcohol, tobacco, drugs, or pornography. Others have crippling physical or mental impairments . . . Some have terrible feelings of depression or inadequacy. . . . The healing power of the Lord Jesus Christ – whether it removes our burdens or strengthens us to endure and live with them – is available for every affliction in mortality." (Oaks, Conf. Report, Oct. 2006).

Mortality comes with pains, afflictions and struggles. At one time or another, we may suffer:

- Sickness or the sickness of those we love
- Pain from injuries, or from physical or mental difficulties
- Grief in connection with the death of a loved one
- Failure in personal responsibilities, family relationships, occupations
- Rejection of the gospel by a spouse or child
- The infirmity of depression

- Racial or ethnic prejudices
- Unemployment, or other reverses in our career aspirations – rejection, failure to obtain promotion, etc. Financial difficulties.
- Physical or mental disabilities – suffering by those afflicted and their care-givers
- Burdens of loneliness, childlessness

"Our wounds may come from a natural disaster or an unfortunate accident. They may come from an unfaithful husband or wife, turning life upside down for a righteous spouse and children. The wounds may come from the darkness and gloom of depression, from an unanticipated illness, from the suffering or premature death of someone we love, from the sadness of a family member dismissing his or her faith, from the loneliness when circumstances do not bring an eternal companion, or from a hundred other heart-wrenching, painful '[sorrows] that the eye can't see.'" (Andersen, Conf. Report, Oct. 2018).

While Christ does not - and should not - always remove the infirmity, He can help us bear our burden(s) in faith and hope. As we ask in faith and rely on Him whose merits are mighty unto salvation, He can provide a spiritual salve to heal our wounds, and even the heaviest burdens can be made lighter. "Sometimes His power heals an infirmity, but the scriptures and our experiences teach that sometimes He succors or helps by giving us the strength or patience to endure our infirmities." (Oaks, Conf. Report, Oct. 2015.) "Sometimes He removes the affliction, sometimes He strengthens us to endure, and sometimes He gives us an eternal perspective to better understand their temporary nature." (Callister, Conf. Report, Apr. 2019). This is the healing power of the Atonement.

Jacob's Warnings: "Wo Unto the Disobedient . . ."

In order to face the inevitable judgment in a state of righteousness, Jacob warns his people not to transgress the law, and not to waste the days of their probation. (2 Nephi 9:27). He says, "it must needs be expedient that I teach you the consequences of sin" (2 Nephi 9:48). Verses 27 through 38 contain a litany of warnings,[43] with consequences for the disobedient and unrepentant.

(See "Wickedness – Warnings" in Topical Index, 2 Nephi 28).

Warning: "Wo unto . . . _____"	Consequence
Those who transgress the commandments (v. 27)	Awful is their state
The learned who ignore the counsel of God (v. 28)	Their wisdom is useless, they perish
The rich whose hearts are set on their treasures (v. 30)	Their treasure will perish with them
The deaf who will not hear (v. 31)	They shall perish
The blind who will not see (v. 32)	They shall perish
The uncircumcised of heart (disobedient) (v. 33)	Knowledge of their iniquities smite them
The liar (v. 34)	They shall be thrust down to hell
The murderer (v. 35)	They shall die
Those who commit whoredoms (v. 36)	They shall be thrust down to hell

---

[43] The style echoes the "woe oracle" of Isaiah, and was familiar to the Jews. See Isa. 3:11 ("woe unto the wicked); Isa. 5:8, 11, 18, 20, 21, 22 ("woe" for various acts); Isa. 10:1 ("woe" for unrighteous decrees); Isa. 29:15); Isa. 30:1; Isa. 33:1; Isa. 45:9, 10.

The Learned: Education

One of the first warnings is to those who are learned, but "hearken not" and "set aside" the counsels of God because they "think they are wise" and suppose "they know of themselves" (2 Nephi 9:28). It is a warning against pride – "vainness" and "foolishness"- in focusing on one's own learning and knowledge and ignoring the counsel of God. Indeed, those puffed up because of learning and riches are "despised by the Lord," unless they "cast these things away" and come down to the depths of humility. (2 Nephi 9:42). Isaiah warned: "Woe unto them that are wise in their own eyes" (Isaiah 5:21). This is a dangerous state.

Nonetheless, Jacob teaches, "to be learned is good," if one "hearken[s] unto God" (2 Nephi 9:29). The sacred and the secular are not mutually exclusive. Jacob counsels to always couple secular learning and knowledge with obedience to the teachings of the Lord. We should recognize that any wisdom gained, whether secular or religious, is through the grace and gift of God.

Indeed, the Lord Himself instructs us to seek wisdom from the best books, and to become acquainted with languages, tongues, and people. (D&C 88:118; 90:15). Elder Robert D. Hales observed: "Education prepares you for better employment opportunities. It puts you in a better position to serve and to bless those around you . . . it will strengthen you to fight against ignorance and error. As Joseph Smith taught: 'Knowledge does away with darkness, suspense and doubt. . . . In knowledge there is power.' 'To be learned is good if they hearken unto the counsels of God.'" (Conf. Report, Oct. 2015). "We must balance our secular learning with spiritual learning. . . . President J. Reuben Clark, Jr. spoke of the desired balance in these words: 'There is spiritual learning just as there is material learning, and the one without the other is not complete.'" (Benson, Conf. Report, Oct. 1986).

Elder Neal A. Maxwell taught: "[T]he cadence of the divine commitment to education and the quest for truth echo, like a drum roll, through the corridors of dispensational history – Abraham, a man of God and a brilliant astronomer, who pondered the planets and considered the cosmos in the loneliness of the desert; Jesus, the Master, who while yet a youth taught his elders in the seat of learning, having prepared himself intellectually and spiritually. . . . Those who possess absolute truths need fear no ancillary truth but should pursue learning vigorously." (Conf. Report, Oct. 1970).

Jacob's warning is to not let secular education or intellectual pursuits undermine our spiritual foundation. Just as faith without works is dead, so knowledge without faith is incomplete. The Lord has instructed us to "seek learning . . . by study *and* also by faith" (D&C 109:7). Elder Dallin H. Oaks advised: "We seek learning by studying the accumulated wisdom of various disciplines and by using the powers of reasoning placed in us by our Creator. We should also seek learning by faith in God, the giver of revelation. . . . Seekers who have paid the price in perspiration have been magnified by inspiration." (Conf. Report, Apr. 1989). Scholarship and reason are insufficient to know God and the doctrines of his gospel. Spiritual knowledge requires study and faith.

<u>The Rich</u>

Jacob chastises the rich whose hearts are set upon their worldly treasures rather than the things of God. (2 Nephi 9:30). Paul echoed this teaching in the familiar scripture, "the love of money is the root of all evil" (1 Timothy 6:10). Less familiar is the rest of the verse, which teaches that setting one's heart on riches can lead us to "err from the faith" and be "pierced through with many sorrows."

It is the attitude of those with riches that bothers Jacob. It is not the money, but the love of money that causes problems. It is not the content of the wallet, but the intent of the heart that concerns Jacob. He chastises those whose "hearts are upon their treasures; wherefore their treasure is their god" (2 Nephi 9:30). Jacob warns the rich, who prefer their riches to the things of God, to "not spend money for that which is of no worth" (2 Nephi 9:51), that "their treasure will perish with them" (2 Nephi 9:30). Their riches have cankered their souls, twisted their affections, and "because they are rich they despise the poor, and they persecute the meek" (2 Nephi 9:30).

President Gordon B. Hinckley taught, "We all need money to supply our needs. But it is the love of it which hurts us, which warps our values, which leads us away from spiritual things and fosters selfishness and greed." (Conf. Report, Apr. 1997). It is one's attitude toward riches rather than one's possession of riches that is the real problem. Jacob later delivers a longer and more comprehensive sermon about the love of riches, and how to handle wealth in Jacob 2:13-20.

(See "<u>Riches</u>" in Topical Index, Jacob 2).

<u>The Disobedient</u>

Jacob then warns the people that those who will not hear, see, or feel the truth shall "perish." His warning extends to those who know the law, but violate the Ten Commandments:

Jacob's warning	Ten Commandments
"Wo unto the liar"	#9 - "Thou shalt not bear false witness"
"Wo unto the murderer"	#6 – "Thou shalt not kill"
"Wo unto them who commit whoredoms"	#7 – "Thou shalt not commit adultery"
"Wo unto those that worship idols"	#2 – "Thou shalt not make any graven image"

(See "Obedience" in Topical Index, Mosiah 2-4).

"Jacob apparently had the Decalogue of Deuteronomy 5 or Exodus 20 in mind when he wrote [2 Nephi 9:27-38]. The prohibitions against worshiping images, committing murder or adultery, and bearing false witness (see Exodus 20:4-6, 13-14, 16) are clearly present in Jacob's sixth through ninth woes. Jacob's summary in these ten 'woes' is much more than a thoughtless copy of the biblical ideals. Whereas the Decalogue gave the law, Jacob goes one step further by stressing the consequences of breaking the law. Furthermore, Jacob's principles have been tailored as revelation to his people and to their needs." (Welch, "Jacob's Ten Commandments," 69-70).

Jacob concludes his 'woes' with the warning, "to be carnally-minded is death, and to be spiritually-minded is life eternal." (2 Nephi 9:39; see Romans 8:6). This core principle applies to nearly every commandment in the Decalogue.

President Gordon B. Hinckley taught: "Mental control must be stronger than physical appetites or desires of the flesh. As thoughts are brought into complete harmony with revealed truth, actions will then become appropriate. . . . Each of us, with discipline and effort, has the capacity to control his thoughts and his actions. This is part of the process of developing spiritual . . . maturity." (Conf. Report, Apr. 1987). As we "let virtue garnish [our] thoughts unceasingly . . . then shall [our] confidence wax strong in the presence of God" (D&C 121:45). Jacob's warnings help identify the basic criteria to develop this confidence and spiritual strength.

Evidently, Jacob's discourse was quite lengthy, and there was a necessary interruption, because at the end of chapter nine, Jacob says, "I would speak unto you more; but on the morrow I will declare unto you the remainder of my words" (2 Nephi 9:54).

Jacob's Summary

It was an eventful evening. Jacob records that "last night" an angel visited him and confirmed the name of the Holy One of Israel should be "Christ" (Jacob 10:3). Jacob then repeats some of the major themes that he previously taught from the words of Isaiah: Christ will come among the Jews and be rejected and crucified. (2 Nephi 10:3-4). The Jews will be "scattered among all nations" (2 Nephi 10:6). Nonetheless, they shall ultimately "be restored in the flesh, upon the earth, unto the lands of their inheritance" (2 Nephi 10:7). And, "the nations of the Gentiles shall be great in the eyes of me, saith God, in carrying them forth to the lands of their inheritance" (2 Nephi 9:8).[44]

Echoing Isaiah, and the teachings of his brother, Nephi, Jacob affirms: "The kings of the Gentiles shall be nursing fathers [unto the House of Israel] and their queens shall become nursing mothers" (2 Nephi 10:9). Jacob also teaches: "Wherefore *the Gentiles shall be blessed and numbered among the house of Israel*" (2 Nephi 10:18, *emphasis added*). In this scripture, Jacob confirms that the blessings and promises to the House of Israel may be extended to righteous Gentiles.

The remaining topics Jacob addresses in chapter 10 mirror themes from Lehi's final sermons to his children. Jacob was an apt student. After reviewing Isaiah's prophesies about the gathering of the House of Israel, Jacob repeats and reinforces the teachings of his father.

Doctrine	Lehi	Jacob
The promised land is a "choice land," a "land of promise," a "land of liberty," "consecrated" to the seed of Lehi.	Lehi prophesied that the promised land "shall be a land of liberty." (2 Nephi 1:6-7).	Jacob refers to this prophesy when he declares: "And this land shall be a land of liberty unto the Gentiles." (2 Nephi 10:11).
The Gift of Agency	Lehi taught Jacob that man is free to act and to choose (2 Nephi 2:16, 27).	Jacob reminds the people of Nephi that "ye are free to act for yourselves – to choose the way of death or the way of eternal life." (2 Nephi 10:23).

---

[44] Whether this prophesy relates to the return of the Jews to the Holy Land and the formation of the State of Israel in 1948 largely through the support of Western European, Gentile, nations, is not clear. But it is interesting that the Book of Mormon, published in 1830, includes such a prophesy.

Jacob concludes by both encouraging and warning his people: "And now, my beloved brethren, seeing that our merciful God has given us so great knowledge concerning these things, let us remember him, and lay aside our sins, and not hang down our heads, for we have not been cast off. . . . Therefore, cheer up your hearts, and remember that ye are free to act for yourselves – to choose the way of everlasting death or the way of eternal life. Wherefore my beloved brethren, reconcile yourselves to the will of God, and not to the will of the devil and the flesh; and remember, after ye are reconciled unto God, that *it is only in and through the grace of God that ye are saved*" (2 Nephi 2:20-24, *emphasis added*).

Jacob's discourse is rich with doctrine. He expounds on the teachings of his father, Lehi, on the Atonement contained in 2 Nephi chapter two, and provides additional explanation about the distinction between spiritual and physical death, and the importance of being spiritually-minded. He introduces the concepts of the resurrection of an incorruptible body; perfect knowledge of guilt or righteousness; the universal judgment of Christ; the first principles of the gospel; and concludes with a statement and promise concerning the dual application of the Atonement: "Wherefore, may God raise you from [physical] death by the power of the resurrection, and also from everlasting [spiritual] death by the power of the atonement, that ye may be received into the eternal kingdom of God . . . Amen" (2 Nephi 10:25). It is the Atonement of Christ that "puts all things right." (Christofferson, Conf. Report, Apr. 2019).

Elder D. Todd Christofferson taught: "The former Anglican Bishop of Durham, Dr. N. T. Wright, has aptly described the significance of Christ's Atonement, Resurrection, and Judgment in overcoming injustice and putting all things right. He said: . . . The facts about Jesus of Nazareth, and especially about his resurrection from the dead, are the foundation of the assurance that the world is not random. It is not ultimately a chaos; that when we do justice in the present we are not whistling in the dark, trying to shore up a building that will ultimately collapse, or to fix a car which is actually bound for the scrap-heap. When God raised Jesus from the dead, that was the microcosmic event in which the ultimate macrocosmic act of judgment was contained in a nutshell, [the] seed . . . of the ultimate hope. . . . [Jesus] himself underwent cruel and unjust judgment . . . to bear that chaos, that darkness, that cruelty, that injustice, in himself." (Conf. Report, Apr. 2019). The Atonement allows mercy to satisfy the justice that must exist in order to prevent chaos; otherwise, as Lehi taught Jacob, without justice and the law, there is no righteousness nor happiness, and "there is no God" (2 Nephi 2:13). (See "Justice and Mercy" in Topical Index, Alma 42).

Discourse 9: Jacob, "A Warning about Sin" (Jacob 2-3)

Prophet	Key Doctrines	Scriptures	Audience	Date
Jacob	• Warning about Riches and Pride • Warning about Immorality	Jacob 2-3	To the "people of Nephi" (Jacob 2:1) at "the temple" (Jacob 2:2; Jacob 1:17)	About 544 B.C. After the death of Nephi and separation of the family of Lehi into "Nephites" and "Lamanites"

INTRODUCTION

Jacob observes that after the death of Nephi, the people of Nephi began to "grow hard in their hearts, and indulge themselves somewhat in wicked practices" (Jacob 1:15). They become focused on worldly riches, and "began to be lifted up somewhat in pride" (Jacob 1:16). Therefore, Jacob, who had been consecrated as a priest and teacher of the people, was instructed by the Lord to go to the temple and preach "the word" that he has been given. The word of the Lord "came . . . unto me, saying: Jacob, get thou up into the temple on the morrow, and declare the word which I shall give thee unto this people" (Jacob 2:11). We are not told why the people would be gathered at the temple; perhaps it was in connection with a festival, or another regular time for the congregation to gather.

Jacob began his sermon by telling the people that "as yet, [they had] been obedient unto the word of the Lord" (Jacob 2:4). However, he then told them that he knew their thoughts, and that they were "beginning to labor in sin" (Jacob 2:5). He observed that the people had begun to be lifted up "*somewhat*" in pride. (Jacob 1:16); and begun to indulge "*somewhat*" in "wicked practices" (Jacob 1:15). Some of the people were already guilty of sinful acts, but the main focus of his discourse was not with sinful acts completed, but with sinful acts contemplated. "I must testify unto you concerning the wickedness of your hearts" (Jacob 2:6). He was issuing a warning about sinful behavior and its consequences to encourage his people to return to the right path before it was too late.

DISCOURSE: Jacob 2-3

KEY DOCTRINES

- **A Warning about Riches**. Prosperity can turn people away from the Lord. We should seek the kingdom of God before we seek riches.

- **A Warning about Immorality**. The Lord delights in chastity.

COMMENTARY

As a spiritual leader, Jacob had a divine responsibility to warn the people to refrain from sin. President Harold B. Lee taught: "I remember a remark that Elder Charles Callis made to me one day . . . He remarked, 'you know, I think that probably the most important thing we as General Authorities ought to be preaching is not only repentance from sin, but even more important than that, to teach the . . . entire Church generally, the awfulness of sin.'" (Conf. Rep. April 1956).

In his last recorded discourse, Jacob specifically warns about two kinds of sins: (i) pride that can result from the acquisition of riches (Jacob 2:12-20); and (ii) immorality (Jacob 2:23-24, 27-29). These two sins afflicted the Nephites in Jacob's day, the Israelites through the ages, and they continue to plague mankind today.

Riches and Pride

Jacob had previously warned the people about setting their hearts on riches – or coveting wealth - and the consequences that would follow. "[W]o unto the rich . . . [whose] hearts are upon their treasures; wherefore their treasure is their god" (2 Nephi 9:30). In this discourse, Jacob expounds on the hazards of accumulating wealth, and warns that the acquisition of riches has caused many of the people to be "lifted up in the pride of [their] hearts" and consider themselves "better than" their brethren. (Jacob 2:13).[45]

Elder Dean L. Larsen identified the dual dangers of wealth: "The *coveting* of wealth so often has resulted in avarice, dishonesty, and greed. The *acquisition* of wealth has frequently produced pride, self-satisfaction, and arrogance." (Conf. Report, Apr. 1991, *emphasis added*). Hearts set on one's riches lead to hearts full of pride, which lead to inequalities, and persecution of others: "[you] persecute your brethren because ye suppose that ye are better than they" (Jacob 2:13). Elder L. Tom Perry observed: "Those who are more prosperous can become filled with pride, and they look down on their brothers and sisters who have less, thinking them inferior." (Conf. Report, Apr. 1987). Pride follows riches like indigestion follows over-eating. Jacob identifies a vicious cycle of obtaining riches, becoming prideful, and then persecuting those who are not rich.

President Dieter F. Uchtdorf taught: "At its core, pride is a sin of comparison, for though it usually begins with 'Look how wonderful I am and what great things I have done,' it always seems to end with 'Therefore, I am better than you.' . . . This is the sin of 'Thank God I am more special than you.' At its core is the desire to be admired or envied. It is the sin of self-glorification." (Conf. Report, Oct. 2010). Considering ourselves "better than" others is anathema to God: it is "abominable unto him who created all flesh" since "the one being is as precious in his sight as the other" (Jacob 2:21).

Jacob warns to not let "this pride of your hearts destroy your souls" (Jacob 2:16). Pride can lead us away from God. Pride can make us more susceptible to temptation. "[B]eware of pride, lest thou shouldst enter into temptation" (D&C 23:1).

---

[45] Jacob preaches extensively about the danger of riches. Is it possible he was influenced by the impact of riches on his older brothers, Laman and Lemuel, who murmured about leaving their riches in Jerusalem? "[T]hese many years we have suffered in the wilderness, which time we might have enjoyed our possessions and the land of our inheritance" (1 Nephi 17:21).

"Pride is short-tempered, unkind, and envious. Pride exaggerates its own strength and ignores the virtues of others. Pride is selfish and easily provoked. Pride assumes evil intent where there is none and hides its own weaknesses behind clever excuses. Pride is cynical, pessimistic, angry, and impatient." (Uchtdorf, Conf. Report, Apr. 2016). "Pride is concerned with who is right. Humility is concerned with what is right." (Condie, Conf. Report, Oct. 1993).

"Pride is the great sin of self-elevation. It . . . justifies envy, greed, and vanity. In a sense, pride is the original sin, for before the foundations of this earth, pride felled Lucifer, a son of the morning 'who was in authority in the presence of God.' (D&C 76:25). If pride can corrupt one as capable and promising as this, should we not examine our own souls as well?" (Uchtdorf, "Pride and the Priesthood," Ensign, Nov. 2010). "Indeed, if charity is the pure love of Christ, then pride is the defining characteristic of Satan." (Uchtdorf, Conf. Report, Apr. 2016).

Full of pride, Lucifer sought to place himself above God. "Behold, here am I, send me, I will be thy son, and I will redeem all mankind, that not one soul shall not be lost, and surely I will do it; wherefore give me thine honor" (Moses 4:1). "Note the ego dripping from only three lines: two *me's* and four *I's*. Those vertical pronouns are usually accompanied by unbending knees." (Maxwell, Conf. Report, Oct. 1987). Ultimately, Lucifer's pride led to anger, and then rebellion, whereby he lost his position, and was cast down, becoming Satan, the "father of all lies" (Moses 4:4) and "miserable forever" (2 Nephi 2:18).

Riches: How to Handle Wealth; Prioritization Matters

Jacob did not teach that wealth was inherently evil, but that it was the prioritization of wealth over the things of God that would corrupt the hearts of his people. Jacob admonished: "***before*** ye seek for riches, seek ye for the kingdom of God." (Jacob 2:18, *emphasis added*). **Prioritization matters**. Elder L. Tom Perry observed: "So often it is the order of things that is fundamental in the Lord's instructions to us . . . we need to take Jacob's counsel to heart. . . . His words should cause us to ask soul-searching questions of ourselves. Is the order of things right in our own lives? Are we investing, first and foremost, in the things that are eternal in nature? Do we have an eternal perspective? Or have we fallen into the trap of investing in the things of this world first and then forgetting the Lord?" (Conf. Report, Apr. 1987). [46]

"The Lord is not telling us that we should not be prosperous. . . But He is telling us that we should seek prosperity only after we have sought and found Him. Then, because our hearts are right, because we love Him first and foremost, we will choose to invest the riches we obtain in building His kingdom. . . . We can tell whether or not we put the kingdom of God first by looking at how we treat our brothers and sisters. . . . Is there an absence of envy and backbiting? Do we rejoice in the success of a brother or sister as much as in our own? Do we share our substance so that all may be rich like unto us? Ultimately, are we our brothers' and sisters' keepers?" (Perry, Conf. Report, Apr. 1987). When our hearts are right, and we put the kingdom of God first, we will not aggrandize ourselves over others, and will treat each other with love and respect.

---

[46] "Although Jacob does not say it, this process can also work the other way. Those who are less fortunate begin to feel deprived. They become consumed by what they do not have, blaming others for their predicament and blaming the Lord. . . . The important point is that the Lord condemns both the preoccupation with worldly possessions and the lack of occupation with building His kingdom, whether it is a consequence of having too much or too little." (Perry, Conf. Report, Apr. 1987).

Elder Henry D. Taylor taught: "The possession of wealth and things of this world are not objectionable if used for righteous purposes." (Conf. Report, Oct. 1963). President Boyd K. Packer cautioned, however: "It is possible to be both rich . . . and at the same time have success spiritually. But the Lord warned of the difficulty of it when He talked of camels and needles (see Matthew 19:24)." (Conf. Report, Oct. 1980).

Elder Dallin H. Oaks taught: "The possession of wealth or significant income is not a mark of heavenly favor, and their absence is not evidence of heavenly disfavor. When Jesus told a faithful follower that he could inherit eternal life if he would only give all that he had to the poor (Mark 10:17-24), He was not identifying an evil in the *possession* of riches but an evil in that follower's *attitude* toward them. As we are all aware, Jesus praised the good Samaritan, who used the same coinage to serve his fellow man that Judas used to betray his Savior. The root of all evil is not money but the love of money." (Conf. Report, Apr. 2015, *emphasis in original*).

When our wealth becomes our priority, our passion, and our primary focus; when our "hearts are set on riches," we are more likely to turn away from the Lord. President Spencer W. Kimball taught: "The possession of riches does not necessarily constitute sin. But sin may arise in the acquisition and use of wealth. . . . Book of Mormon history eloquently reveals the corrosive effect of the passion for wealth. . . . Had the people used their wealth for good purposes they could have enjoyed a continuing prosperity. But they seemed unable for a sustained period to be simultaneously wealthy and righteous." (Kimball, Miracle of Forgiveness, 47-48).

Elder Dean L. Larsen observed: "[Jacob] felt there was nothing inherently wrong in acquiring wealth. The danger lay in its obscuring the need for acknowledging the Lord's hand in these blessings, and in failing to use the abundance to bless others and to accomplish the Lord's purposes." (Conf. Report, Apr. 1991). "The critical difference," Elder Oaks taught in an earlier address, "is the degree of spirituality we exercise in . . . managing the things of this world. If allowed to become an object of worship or priority, money can make us selfish and prideful. . . . In contrast, if used for fulfilling our legal obligations and for paying our tithes and offerings, money can demonstrate integrity and develop unselfishness." (Conf. Report, Oct. 1985).

Jacob teaches his people to share their riches, to use them to "do good" and help others. Jacob provided the following general guidelines for proper wealth accumulation and management (see Jacob 2:13-20):

1. Seek first for the kingdom of God (v.18)
2. Seek riches for the intent to do good (v. 19)
3. If you obtain riches, be "free with your substance" (v.17)
    - Clothe the naked (v.19)
    - Feed the hungry (v.19)
    - Liberate the captive (v.19)
    - Administer relief to the sick and afflicted (v.19)
4. Do not suppose you are better than those who don't possess similar wealth (v.13); think of others as your equals (v.17)
5. Do not persecute others who may have less than you do (v.13, 20)
6. Be humble – remember that man is nothing compared to God ("with one glance of his eye he can smite you to the dust," v.15)
7. Hearken to the commandments (v.16)

8. Remember that all blessings, including worldly riches, come from God (people obtained their riches through the "hand of providence," v.12-13)

President N. Eldon Tanner concluded: "The foundation and perspective then are these: We must first seek the kingdom, work and plan and spend wisely . . . and use what wealth we are blessed with to help build that kingdom. When guided by this eternal perspective and by building on this firm foundation, we can pursue with confidence our daily tasks and our life's work." (Conf. Report, Oct. 1979). President Tanner provided further guidelines on how to wisely manage earthly riches, with what he called "five principles of economic constancy": (1) pay an honest tithing; (2) live on less than you earn; (3) learn to distinguish between needs and wants; (4) develop and live within a budget; and, (5) be honest in all your financial affairs. (Conf. Report, Oct. 1979).

The Sin of Immorality

Jacob continues his sermon with the following words: "And now I make an end of speaking unto you concerning this pride. And were it not that I must speak unto you concerning a grosser crime, my heart would rejoice exceedingly because of you" (Jacob 2:22). Evidently, some of the people of Nephi were engaging in immoral behavior, seeking multiple wives and concubines. Jacob sternly warned that such things were an "abomination" to God, who "delights in the chastity of women" (Jacob 2:28). He condemns the people for their "whoredoms" and tells them that they have "broken the hearts of [their] tender wives, and lost the confidence of [their] children, because of [their] bad examples before them" (Jacob 2:35). (See "Chastity" in Topical Index; Alma 39).

Some of the people of Nephi apparently attempted to justify their lustful actions by "excusing themselves in committing whoredoms, because of the things which were written concerning David; and Solomon his son" with respect to multiple wives and concubines. (Jacob 2:23). This, however, was an unacceptable practice, and considered "an abomination before me; thus saith the Lord of Hosts" (Jacob 2:28)

In very rare instances, the Lord has commanded his people to practice plural marriage. This was the case in certain Old Testament times, with Abraham and his grandson, Jacob. (Genesis 16:1-3; D&C 132:34-35). Polygamy was also practiced during the early days of the restoration of the Church by certain individuals, including Joseph Smith and Brigham Young. (D&C 132:32-33). Nonetheless, Jacob taught the people of Nephi that they were not to engage in any form of plural marriage, and not to rely on the practices of the ancient prophets to justify such behavior. The Lord's commandment is to have one wife, except under the rare circumstances where the Lord explicitly commands otherwise to "raise up seed unto me" (Jacob 2:30). Monogamy is the rule; polygamy is the exception.

Early church leaders taught that the Lord may command the practice of polygamy for a time when He deems it necessary to "raise up seed" – to bring more children into the world who will be born in the covenant and be raised under gospel standards. "The Book of Mormon . . . condemns plurality of wives as being a practice exceedingly abominable before God. But even that sacred book makes an exception in substance as follows – 'Except I the Lord command my people.' (Jacob 2:30)." (Pratt, "Polygamy," Journal of Discourses, 6:351). See also, Snow, Journal of Discourses, 24:158. This commandment is not currently in effect.

President Gordon B. Hinckley declared: "I wish to state categorically that this Church has nothing whatever to do with those practicing polygamy. They are not members of this Church. Most of them have never been members. They are in violation of the civil law. . . . If any of our members are found to be practicing plural marriage, they are excommunicated, the most serious penalty the Church can impose. . . . More than a century ago God clearly revealed unto His prophet Wilford Woodruff that the practice of plural marriage should be discontinued, which means that it is now against the law of God." (Conf. Report, Oct. 1998).

Jacob is teaching from a temple. Published teachings from modern apostles make it clear that the two major sins Jacob addresses in his temple sermon would violate covenants that are made in the temple today, and are in direct opposition to counsel we receive from the Lord in that holy place. Elder James E. Talmage taught: "The ordinances of the endowment embody certain obligations on the part of the individual, such as a covenant and promise to observe the law of strict virtue and chastity . . . [and] to devote both talent and material means [riches] to the spread of truth." (Talmage, House of the Lord, 100). The opposite of immorality is, in the words of Elder Talmage, the "covenant and promise" of "strict virtue and chastity." The opposite of setting our hearts on riches is, as Elder Talmage puts it, our covenant "to devote material means to the spread of truth." (See also, Packer, The Holy Temple). Thus, by following the law of chastity, and by using any riches we may be blessed with to further the Lord's purposes, we are not only obeying the Lord's commandments as taught by Jacob, we are also fulfilling temple covenants.

Discourse 10: King Benjamin, "Service and Salvation" (Mosiah 2-4)

Prophet	Key Doctrines	Scriptures	Audience	Date
	• Service to Others and Our Debt to God • Salvation Only through Christ • Retain a Remission of Sins	Mosiah 2:9 to Mosiah 4	From a tower to the assembled people of Zarahemla who pitched tents around the temple (also written)	About 124 B.C.

INTRODUCTION

King Benjamin, a "holy man," led the people of Zarahemla for many years "in righteousness" (Words of Mormon 1:17). As King Benjamin "waxed old, and . . . saw that he must very soon go the way of all the earth" (Mosiah 1:9), he gathered the people together to confirm the appointment of his son, Mosiah, as the new king, and to give the people "a name that never [would] be blotted out, except it be through transgression" (Mosiah 1:12).

King Benjamin begins his sermon by reminding his people that he has served them with all his "might, mind and strength," without seeking gold or silver or any manner of riches. (Mosiah 2:12). The servant-king humbly disclaims any superior status for himself. He is "a mortal man" (Mosiah 2:10), who faces the typical challenges of mortality, "like as yourselves, subject to all manner of infirmities in body and mind" (Mosiah 2:11). This is a uniquely humble confession from royalty. Rather than imposing burdensome taxes and living off the bounty of the people, he has labored with "mine own hands that I might serve you" (Mosiah 2:14). King Benjamin teaches the people that they should follow his example of service and serve God by serving each other.

One scholar has observed that King Benjamin's discourse is organized thematically into three topics. "In the first section, Benjamin spoke as a king reporting his royal stewardship, recalling how he had provided them temporal and spiritual peace. For his second topic, he spoke as a prophet, once again teaching his people how to avoid spiritual chaos and unrest. In this phase of his speech he spoke the words of an angel, words which emphasized Christ's service to others, including a portrayal of Christ's atoning sacrifice. For his third and final topic, the prophet Benjamin spoke of how service can extend the knowledge of the glory, truth, and justice of God. . . . The common element in each section was the hope-filled message of service to God through service to humanity. The first two messages were examples of service from Benjamin's and Christ's lives. The third message was a discourse on how the people could retain a remission of their sins by implementing these examples of service." (Black, "King Benjamin: In the Service of Your God," in Nyman and Tate, eds., <u>The Book of Mormon: Mosiah, Salvation Only through Christ,</u> 1991).

King Benjamin's three key messages are: (i) we can serve God by serving our fellow man; (ii) we can obtain salvation only through Christ; and (iii) we can retain a remission of our sins through obedience, putting off the "natural man," and obtaining divine attributes.

Elder Milton R. Hunter said, "perhaps no other teacher except the Master has given a more beautiful, humble sermon." (Conf. Report, Oct. 1955). Elder Neal A. Maxwell called the speech "a sparkling doctrinal diamond that can be approached and appreciated in so many different ways." (Maxwell, "King Benjamin's Sermon: A Manual for Discipleship," in Welch and Ricks, eds., <u>King Benjamin's Speech: That Ye May Learn Wisdom</u> 1998, 1-22).

"The enduring value of Benjamin's classic speech in Nephite history can be confirmed in many ways by . . . subsequent texts in the Book of Mormon that remember and draw on his words. . . . The fact that each family was given a copy of this speech must have facilitated its far-reaching impact. Shortly after Benjamin's death, his son Mosiah sent Ammon and fifteen other emissaries to the land of Nephi, [where] Ammon 'rehearsed unto them the last words which King Benjamin had taught.' (Mosiah 8:3). . . . Almost a century later, Helaman spoke to his sons Nephi and Lehi, admonishing them to 'remember, my sons, the words which king Benjamin spake unto his people' (Helaman 5:9). . . . Benjamin's monumental speech also became a type of constitutional document in Nephite culture and specific influences are found in later Nephite law and society." (Welch, "Benjamin's Speech: A Masterful Oration" in Welch and Ricks, eds., <u>King Benjamin's Speech: That Ye May Learn Wisdom</u> 1998).

DISCOURSE: Mosiah 2:9 – Mosiah 3:27; Mosiah 4:11-30

KEY DOCTRINES

- **Service**. "When ye are in the service of your fellow beings ye are only in the service of your God" (Mos. 2:17).

- **Salvation**. Salvation comes through repentance and faith in Jesus Christ (Mosiah 3:12).

- **Retain a Remission of Sins.** The natural man is an enemy to God. We must become like a child, submissive, meek, humble, patient, full of love, and willing to submit to the Lord to receive a remission of our sins. (Mos. 3:19, 21). We can *retain* a remission of our sins through humility, prayer, faith, fulfillment of family duties and service to our fellow man.

COMMENTARY

Service

The over-arching theme of King Benjamin's discourse is service: "when ye are in the service of your fellow beings ye are only in the service of your God" (Mosiah 2:17). King Benjamin identifies three aspects of service (Mos. 2:17; Mos. 2:21; Mos. 5:13): (i) serving each other; (ii) servicing our debt to God by keeping His commandments; and (iii) coming to know God through service.

First, he teaches that when we serve our fellow man we serve God (Mosiah 2:17). And, through service to our fellow man, we are able to become more like Him. "In the end, Benjamin's point is this: The purpose of service is not to release us from our indebtedness to God but to increase our personal knowledge of him and his goodness." (Welch, "Benjamin's Speech: A Masterful Oration").

The apostle James taught that service is the hallmark of true religion: "Pure religion and undefiled before God and the Father is this, to visit the fatherless and the widows in their affliction, and to keep himself unspotted from the world" (James 1:27). "In short, James tells us that true religion is a devotion to God, demonstrated by love and compassion for fellow men. . . . Restated it may be said that true religion consists not only in refraining from evil (that is, remaining unspotted), but in deliberately and purposefully doing acts of kindness and service to others." (Hunter, Conf. Report, Oct. 1978).

Opportunities for Service. President Thomas S. Monson declared: "My brothers and sisters, we are surrounded by those in need of our attention, our encouragement, our support, our comfort, our kindness – be they family members, friends, acquaintances, or strangers. . . . You may lament: I can barely make it through each day, doing all that I need to do. How can I provide service for others? What can I possibly do? . . . Find someone who is having a hard time or is ill or lonely, and do something for him or her. . . . the needs of others are ever present, and each of us can do something to help someone." (Conf. Report, Oct. 2009). "Each day we have the opportunity to give help and service – doing the right thing at the right time, without delay. Think of the many people who have a difficult time obtaining a job or who are ill, who feel lonely, who even think that they have lost everything." (Alonso, Conf. Report, Oct. 2011).

Despite the best of intentions, it can be difficult to serve. Daily duties consume our attention; busy-ness obscures service opportunities. We may believe we lack time for service; or, we may fail to see the opportunity. President Thomas S. Monson observed: "I am confident it is the *intention* of each member of the Church to serve. . . . How often have you *intended* to be the one to help? And yet how often has day-to-day living interfered? . . . We become so caught up in the busyness of our lives. Were we to step back, however, and take a good look at what we are doing, we may find that we have immersed ourselves in the 'thick of thin things.' In other words, too often we spend most of our time taking care of the things which do not really matter . . . neglecting those more important causes." (Conf. Report, Oct. 2009).

We should pro-actively seek occasions to serve; otherwise, we may "find ourselves in the unenviable position of Jacob Marley's ghost . . . in Dickens' immortal A Christmas Carol. Marley sadly spoke of opportunities lost. Said he, 'no space of regret can make amends for one life's opportunities misused. . . . Why did I walk through the crowds of fellow-beings with my eyes turned down?' On the other hand, if we but look . . . the privilege to render service to others can come to each of us." (Monson, Conf. Report, Oct. 1965).

One reason the Lord organized a church is to provide a means and structure for us to serve each other. Elder Henry D. Taylor observed: "There is a joy that comes from working and rendering service in the Church and in being a servant to our fellow men. . . . To every faithful member of the Church will come opportunities to serve in some capacity . . . in missionary work, temples, home teaching, instructing classes, choirs and musical groups, work on welfare projects, administrative positions, and many other activities. . . . [We should] readily and humbly accept the callings that come and become servants in the house of the Lord. . . . Then we may rest assured that if we do our best, the Lord will do the rest." (Conf. Report, Oct. 1963).

In the Church of Jesus Christ, it is service, not status, that counts.

President Howard W. Hunter taught: "Our focus should be on righteousness, not recognition; on service, not status. The faithful visiting teacher, who quietly goes about her work month after month, is just as important to the work of the Lord as those who occupy what some see as more prominent positions in the Church. Visibility does not equate to value." ("To the Women of the Church," *Ensign*, Nov. 1992). The purpose of service is not to achieve earthly recognition or to obtain more chits on a heavenly tote board, but to selflessly lift others, change our nature, develop Christ-like attributes, and become more like our Father in Heaven.

President Marion G. Romney taught: "By serving and lifting others . . . we experience the only true and lasting happiness. Service is not something we endure on this earth so we can earn the right to live in the celestial kingdom. Service is the very fiber of which an exalted life in the celestial kingdom is made. . . . Oh, for the glorious day when these things all come naturally because of the purity of our hearts. In that day there will be no need for a commandment because we will have experienced for ourselves that we are truly happy only when we are engaged in unselfish service." (Conf. Report, Oct. 1982). "Those who lose themselves in service to others grow and flourish – and in effect save their lives." (Monson, Conf. Report, Oct. 2009).

"Rescuing" others through service was a recurring theme in President Monson's teachings. He said: "Let us remember the counsel of King Benjamin: 'When ye are in the service of your fellow beings ye are only in the service of your God.' Reach out to rescue those who need your help. Lift such to the higher road and the better way." (Conf. Report, Oct. 1999). Elder Dallin H. Oaks, among others, has observed: "As we know, President Thomas S. Monson has given great emphasis . . . in his memorable example and teachings about rescuing our fellow men and women." (See, Swinton, To the Rescue: The Biography of Thomas S. Monson, 149-161).

President Monson's modern day discourses are filled with calls to rescue our fellow men, and include many personal examples of service.

- "May we reach out and rescue those who have fallen by the wayside." (Conf. Report, Apr. 2003).
- "Through righteous living and by extending the helping hand and the understanding heart, you can rescue, you can save." (Conf. Report, Oct. 1992).
- "Let us reach out to rescue those who need our help and lift them to the higher road and the better way." (Conf. Report, Apr. 2005).

(See: "To the Rescue," Conf. Report, Apr. 2001; "Search and Rescue," Conf. Report, Apr. 1993).

Reasons We Serve. Why do we serve? What are the proper motivations to provide Christ-like service? Elder Dallin H. Oaks observed, "it is necessary to consider not only how we serve, but also why we serve. People serve one another for different reasons, and some reasons are better than others. . . . Since we are imperfect beings, most of us probably serve for a combination of reasons, and the combinations may be different from time to time as we grow spiritually." (Conf. Report, Oct. 1984).

Elder Oaks suggests six reasons we may be motivated to serve, in order generally ascending from the lowest to the highest:

(1) For an earthly reward – for money or perceived status;

(2) For the opportunity to "obtain good companionship" – favorable social interactions;

(3) Out of fear of punishment – if we don't serve, we will lose privileges or be punished;

(4) Out of a sense of duty, or out of loyalty to friends and family;

(5) Out of faith in God, and hope for an eternal reward for "being good"; and

(6) For the love of God and His children, on the basis of charity - the pure love of Christ.

"This principle – that our service should be for the love of God and the love of fellowmen rather than for personal advantage or any other lesser motive – is admittedly a high standard"; however, God will help us "so that we may serve one another for the highest and best reason, the pure love of Christ." (Conf. Report, Oct. 1984). (See "Charity" in Topical Index, Moroni 7).

Sometimes, the act of service can elevate our motivations. In other words, as we perform acts of kindness and service for less lofty reasons, love for those we serve can blossom. "Sometimes we may initially serve from a sense of duty or obligation, but even that service can lead us to draw on something higher within us, leading us to serve in 'a more excellent way' – as in President Nelson's invitation to 'a newer, holier approach to caring for and ministering to others.'" (Jones, Conf. Report, Oct. 2018). As we serve, we increase our love for those we serve; and, as our love grows, our motivations evolve from being based on fear, or duty – or another lesser motive - to being based on love and charity.

As we serve others, we need to maintain a proper balance, and serve with "wisdom and order" (Mosiah 4:27). Immediately following his charge to care for the needy, King Benjamin counseled, "it is not requisite that a man should run faster than he has strength" (Mosiah 4:27). "Running faster than we have strength is not requisite. Doing things diligently but 'in wisdom and order' is, in fact, necessary. . . . This balance between pace and diligence is a high and demanding exercise in the use of our time, talent, and agency. . . . It takes, however, real wisdom, discipline and judgment to do things in order."(Maxwell, Notwithstanding My Weakness, 6).

Elder Jeffrey R. Holland warned: "For caregivers, in your devoted effort to assist with another's health, do not destroy your own. In all these things be wise. Do not run faster than you have strength. Whatever else you may or may not be able to provide, you can offer your prayers and you can give 'love unfeigned.'" (Conf. Report, Oct. 2013). (See D&C 10:4). "When expectations overwhelm us, we can step back and ask Heavenly Father what to let go of. Part of our life experience is learning what not to do." (Eubank, Conf. Report, Apr. 2019). We must seek balance and wisdom in all things, including acts of service, particularly as long-term caregivers.

Gratitude and Obedience

King Benjamin taught the importance of gratitude as we serve: even if we "should serve [God] with all [our] whole souls [we] would be unprofitable servants" (Mosiah 2:21). This means that our debt to God is completely beyond our ability to repay. No matter what we do, we are unable to balance the ledger of blessings received from God. "We are told that we are unprofitable servants, and so we are, if we think of trying to pay our Savior back for what he has done for us, for that we can never do; and we cannot by any number of acts or a full life of faithful service, place our Savior in our debt." (Smith, Doctrines of Salvation, 1:15).

To make this point, King Benjamin asked his people to consider some examples of blessings received from God. "[I]n the first place, he has created [us], and granted unto [us our] lives" (Mosiah 2:23). Second, He has "kept and preserved" us; and supported us from "day to day" (Mosiah 2:21). Third, King Benjamin reminds the people, He has allowed us to live and to move, to exercise free will, and even to breathe. (Mosiah 2:21). "Even the air we breathe is a loving loan from him." (Nelson, Conf. Report, Oct. 1986).

President Joseph F. Smith declared: "All that we have comes from [God]. . . . Life, intelligence, wisdom, judgment, power to reason, all are the gifts of God to the children of men. He gives us our physical strength as well as our mental powers." (Conf. Report, Oct. 1899). Joseph Smith observed that "Men not unfrequently forget that they are dependent upon heaven for every blessing which they are permitted to enjoy." (Teachings of the Prophet Joseph Smith, 68).

Elder Joseph B. Wirthlin instructed: "How can we ever repay the debt we owe to the Savior? He paid a debt He did not owe to free us from a debt we can never pay. Because of Him we will live forever. Because of His infinite Atonement, our sins can be swept away, allowing us to experience the greatest of all the gifts of God: eternal life. Can such a gift have a price? Can we ever make compensation for such a gift? The Book of Mormon prophet King Benjamin taught 'that if you should render all the thanks and praise which your whole soul has power to possess . . . [and] serve him with all your whole souls yet ye would be unprofitable servants.'" (Conf. Report, Apr. 2004).

For all these blessings, King Benjamin teaches, "all that he requires of you is to keep his commandments" (Mosiah 2:22). President Joseph Fielding Smith instructed: "The violation of any divine commandment is a most ungrateful act, considering all that has been accomplished for us through the atonement of our Savior. We will never be able to pay the debt. . . . Now, he has asked us to keep his commandments." (Doctrines of Salvation, 1:131-132).). "And in nothing doth man offend God . . . save those that confess not his hand in all things, and obey not his commandments" (D&C 59:21). As King Benjamin exclaimed, "O how you ought to thank your heavenly King!" (Mosiah 2:19).

Gratitude and obedience are mutually reinforcing principles. We show gratitude by obedience. The Lord is pleased when we express our heartfelt gratitude regularly. Gratitude demonstrates humility, and is a manifestation of our acknowledgement of a reliance on God for blessings received. God "awaits our expressions of gratefulness each morning and night in sincere, simple prayer from our hearts for our many blessings, gifts, and talents." (Hales, Conf. Report, Apr. 1992). King Benjamin's discourse is a treatise on how to know God and how to become more like Him. We do so through service. We do so through gratitude. We do so through obedience. Gratitude, coupled with obedience, transforms "unprofitable servants" into diligent disciples.

Obedience Leads to Happiness

Obedience to the commandments also leads to additional blessings, and happiness. King Benjamin taught: "I would desire that you consider on the blessed and *happy state* of those that keep the commandments of God. For behold, they are blessed in all things, both temporal and spiritual" (Mosiah 2:41, *emphasis added*). "Happiness," said the Prophet Joseph Smith, "is the object and design of our existence; and will be the end thereof, if we pursue the path that leads to it; and this path is virtue, uprightness, faithfulness, holiness, and *keeping all the commandments of God*." (Teachings of the Prophet Joseph Smith, 255-56, *emphasis added*). Joseph Smith taught that "in obedience there is joy and peace unspotted, unalloyed; and . . . [God] never will institute an ordinance or give a commandment to His people that is not calculated in its nature to promote that happiness which He has designed, and which will not end in the greatest amount of good and glory to those who become the recipients of his law and ordinances." (Ibid., 256-57).

This "happy state" is part of the "abundant life" that can be ours through following the Lord Jesus Christ: "I am come that they might have life, and that they might have it more abundantly" (John 10:10). The Lord wants us to live life abundantly, and obtain happiness in this life while we prepare to return to His presence. By analogy, living an abundant life is like flying "first class."

After extensive business travel in satisfaction of airline requirements (i.e., obedience), I obtained enough airline miles to receive frequent, free upgrades to the first class section of the airplanes I flew. This was a new experience, with several blessings. We received much better food. We received wonderful service. And, we were closer to the Captain. When we live in obedience to the commandments, we receive wonderful spiritual food. We receive service from – and serve – others striving to obey. And, we are closer to the Lord.

This does not mean that an abundant life, or first class travel, is perfect. First class travelers still experience flight delays, and periods of severe air turbulence. And, even though we are traveling in first class, neither we nor our fellow travelers are perfect: the person in seat 3A may need a shower. Additionally, sometimes, especially if we constantly fly first class or have done so for a long period of time, we may not fully recognize or always appreciate how blessed we are to do so. The Lord reminds us that it is possible, for example, to be "baptized with fire and with the Holy Ghost, and [know] it not" (3 Nephi 9:20). It is a great blessing to live in obedience, and live striving to be obedient, to the Lord. We may not be free from life's challenges and problems, but the life we do live is more abundant, and happier, than it would otherwise be.

King Benjamin juxtaposed the "blessed and happy state of those that keep the commandments" with the "awful situation of those that have fallen into transgression" (Mosiah 2:40-41). As President Russell M. Nelson taught: "Keeping divine commandments brings blessings, every time. Breaking divine commandments brings a loss of blessings, every time." (Conf. Report, Apr. 2014). "In our day we face a . . . choice. We can foolishly ignore the prophets of God, depend on our own strength, and ultimately reap the consequences. Or we can wisely draw near to the Lord and partake of His blessings. King Benjamin described both paths and both consequences. He said that those who forsake the Lord will be 'consigned to an awful view of their own guilt and abominations, which doth cause them to shrink from the presence of the Lord into a state of misery and endless torment.' (Mosiah 3:25). But those who journey to a higher ground and keep the commandments of God 'are blessed in all things, both temporal and spiritual.'" (Wirthlin, Conf. Report, Oct. 2005).

"Happiness is the object and design of our existence; and will be the end thereof, if we pursue the path that leads to it; and this path is virtue, uprightness, faithfulness, holiness, and keeping all of the commandments of God." (Joseph Smith, History of the Church, 5:134-35). For those who have not known the ways of God, or who have strayed from them, it is not too late to change. Faith and repentance can lead to obedience, blessings, happiness, and ultimately to salvation, through the Atonement of Jesus Christ. As set forth in the Third Article of Faith, "We believe that through the Atonement of Christ, all mankind may be saved, by obedience to the laws and ordinances of the Gospel." And, because of his love for mankind, and his sacrifice, the Lord, and only the Lord Jesus Christ, can provide each of us with the means to obtain salvation. This is the next doctrine addressed by King Benjamin.

Glad Tidings: The Ministry and Mission of Jesus

King Benjamin tells the people that he has more to speak to them; "I have things to tell you concerning that which is to come" (Mosiah 3:1). He then shares with them a message of Christ's earthly ministry and divine mission, and a brief summary of the Lord's role in the Plan of Salvation. Indeed, King Benjamin has been instructed by an "angel from God" who declared unto him "glad tidings of great joy" (Mosiah 3:3). Mosiah chapter 3 contains the message to King Benjamin from the angel, who testifies they are "the words which the Lord God hath commanded me" (Mosiah 3:23).

King Benjamin shares the joyful message with his people, and quoting the angel, prophesies: "For behold, the time cometh, and is not far distant, that with power, the Lord Omnipotent who reigneth, who was, and is from all eternity to all eternity, shall come down from heaven among the children of men, and shall dwell in a tabernacle of clay, and shall go forth amongst men, working mighty miracles, such as healing the sick, raising the dead, causing the lame to walk, the blind to receive their sight, and the deaf to hear, and curing all manner of diseases" (Mosiah 3:5).

"And lo, he cometh unto his own, that salvation might come unto the children of men even through faith on his name; and even after all this they shall consider him a man, and say that he hath a devil, and shall scourge him, and shall crucify him. And he shall rise the third day from the dead; and behold, he standeth to judge the world; and behold, all these things are done that a righteous judgment might come upon the children of men. For behold, and also his blood atoneth for the sins of those who have fallen by the transgression of Adam" (Mosiah 3:9-11).

"And lo, he shall suffer temptations, and pain of body, hunger, thirst, and fatigue, even more than man can suffer, except it be unto death; for behold, blood cometh from every pore, so great shall be his anguish for the wickedness and the abominations of his people" (Mosiah 3:7; see D&C 19:18). "The apogee of Benjamin's address is the atonement. Benjamin's foretelling of Jesus' ministry revealed that Christ would bleed at every pore, 'so great shall be his anguish for the wickedness . . . of his people.' (Mosiah 3:7)." (Maxwell, "King Benjamin's Sermon: A Manual for Discipleship" in Welch and Ricks, eds., King Benjamin's Speech: That Ye May Learn Wisdom 1998, 1-22).

The angel says: "And he shall be called Jesus Christ, the Son of God, the Father of heaven and earth, the Creator of all things from the beginning; and his mother shall be called Mary" (Mosiah 3:7-8). The name-titles in verse eight represent various aspects of the mission of Christ. "Each of these titles has as its purpose to teach some singular truth. . . . *Jesus* [Hebrew = Joshua] is a given name; it means 'Jehovah saves.' *Christ* is a title meaning 'anointed' or 'anointed one.' *Son of God* denominates the reality of Jesus' divine nature. He is in reality God's Son. *Father of heaven and earth* denotes Christ's role in the creation. The title *Creator of all things* expands his creative role to embrace all that lives, dies, and is resurrected in and through his atoning sacrifice." (McConkie, Doctrinal Commentary, 2:147, *italics in original*).[47]

The Name of Jesus Christ

The angel teaches King Benjamin: "there shall be no other name given nor any other way nor means whereby salvation can come unto the children of men, only in and through the name of Christ, the Lord Omnipotent" (Mosiah 3:17). "From the beginning, God has declared the preeminence of the name of Jesus Christ . . . . An angel taught our first father, Adam, 'Thou shalt do all that thou doest in the name of the Son, and thou shalt repent and call upon God in the name of the Son forevermore' (Moses 5:8)." (Pieper, Conf. Report, Oct. 2018). Throughout the ages, the Lord has directed that "whatsoever ye shall do, ye shall do it in my name" (3 Nephi 27:7).

We pray in the name of Christ; we are baptized in the name of Christ; and we covenant that we "are willing" to take his name upon us in the renewing sacramental ordinance each week. Elder L. Edward Brown said: "When we use these sacred words, 'in the name of Jesus Christ' . . . [w]e are on holy ground. . . . We are using a name most sublime, most holy and most wonderful – the very name of the Son of God. We are now able to come unto the Father through His Beloved Son." (Conf. Report Apr. 1997).

King Benjamin later teaches the people that "there is no other name given whereby salvation cometh; therefore I would that ye should take upon you the name of Christ, all you that have entered into the covenant with God that ye should be obedient unto the end of your lives. And it shall come to pass that whosoever doeth this shall be found at the right hand of God, for he shall know the name by which he is called; for he shall be called by the name of Christ. . . . And I would that ye should remember also, that this is the name that I said I should give unto you that never should be blotted out, except it be through transgression; therefore, take heed that ye do not transgress, that the name be not blotted out of your hearts. I say unto you, I would that ye should remember to retain the name written always in your hearts" (Mosiah 5:8-12).

"Behold, Jesus Christ is the name which is given of the Father, and there is none other name given whereby man can be saved" (D&C 18:23; see Acts 4:12). "The Savior's name has singular and essential power. It is the only name by which salvation is possible." (Pieper, Conf. Report, Oct. 2018).

How do we take on the name of Christ? To access the power of the Savior's name, we must act. "Wherefore all men must *take* upon them the name which is given of the Father" (D&C 18:24, *emphasis added*). "The word take is not passive. It is an action word with multiple definitions. Likewise, our commitment to take upon us the name of Jesus Christ requires action and has multiple dimensions." (Pieper, Conf. Report, Oct. 2018).

---

[47] Similar to the angel's instruction to Nephi (1 Nephi 11:18), the angel teaches King Benjamin that the mother of Christ shall be a mortal woman, with the added specificity that her name shall be called Mary. See "Mary" in Topical Index, 1 Nephi 11.

Elder Dallin H. Oaks taught that our willingness to take on the name of Christ has several different meanings:

- We renew the baptismal covenant to take upon us his name and serve him.
- We take upon us his name as we fulfill our obligations as members of his church.
- Our willingness to take upon us his name "signifies our willingness to take upon us the authority of Jesus Christ in the sacred ordinances of the temple."
- Our willingness to take upon us his name "affirms our commitment to do all that we can to be counted among those whom he will choose to stand at his right hand and be called by his name at the last day." (Conf. Report, Apr. 1985).

Elder Oaks also observed that miracles are performed in the name of Christ: "At the conclusion of his ministry, the risen Lord identified signs that would follow those that believed (Mark 16:17-18): '*In my name* they shall do many wonderful works.' . . . When the names of God the Father and his Son, Jesus Christ, are used with reverence and authority, they invoke a power beyond what mortal man can comprehend. It should be obvious to every believer that these mighty names – by which miracles are wrought, by which the world was formed, through which man was created, and by which we can be saved – are holy and must be treated with the utmost reverence." (Conf. Report, Apr. 1986, *emphasis added*).

"In order to access the saving power that comes only through the name of Christ, we must . . . '[be] willing *to take upon [us] the name of Jesus Christ*' (D&C 20:37)'" through baptism. "The word *take* is not passive. It is an action word with multiple definitions . . . and has multiple dimensions. . . . By taking upon ourselves the name of Christ, we commit to take His teachings, His characteristics, and ultimately His love deep into our beings. . . . When we take upon us the name of Christ, we accept Him as our Savior and continually embrace His teachings. . . . [w]e *take* His gospel to be true and obediently live it with all of our heart, might, mind, and strength. . . . [w]e advocate His cause, and we 'stand as witnesses of [Him] at all times and in all things, and in all places that [we] may be in.'" (Pieper, Conf. Report, Oct. 2018, *emphasis in original*).

The Natural Man

The angel teaches King Benjamin that, in contrast to those who take upon themselves the name of Christ, "the **natural man** is an enemy to God"– and it is only through "putting off the natural man" and "becoming a saint through the atonement of Christ" can we be saved. (Mosiah 3:19). As we "put off the natural man" and develop divine qualities, we can become saints, men and women of Christ. "The change from being a natural man to a devoted disciple is a mighty one" (Nelson, Conf. Report, Oct. 2009). So, how do we conquer the "natural man"?

"To some degree, the natural man described by King Benjamin is alive and well in each of us. The natural man or woman is unrepentant, is carnal and sensual, is indulgent and excessive, and is prideful and selfish. . . . In contrast, the man or woman of Christ is spiritual and bridles all passions, is temperate and restrained, and is benevolent and selfless. Men and women of Christ lay hold upon the word of God, deny themselves and take up His cross, and press forward along a strait and narrow course of faithfulness, obedience, and devotion to the Savior and His gospel." (Bednar, Conf. Report, Apr. 2013). President Spencer W. Kimball taught, "The natural man is the 'earthy man' who has allowed rude animal passions to overshadow his spiritual inclinations." (Conf. Report, Oct. 1974).

Elder Neal A. Maxwell provides a comparison between the natural man and "the men and women of Christ": "Whereas the natural man says 'Worship me' and 'Give me thine power,' the men and women of Christ seek to exercise power by long-suffering and unfeigned love. Whereas the natural man vents his anger, the men and women of Christ are 'not easily provoked.' (1 Cor. 13:5). Whereas the natural man is filled with greed, the men and women of Christ 'seeketh not [their own].' Whereas the natural man seldom denies himself worldly pleasures, the men and women of Christ seek to bridle all their passions. (Alma 38:12)." (Conf. Report, Oct. 1990).

President Henry B. Eyring taught: "King Benjamin makes it clear how we can . . . have our natures changed through the Atonement of Jesus Christ. . . . It is this: that we can, and we must, become as a child – a little child. For some that will not be easy to understand or to accept. Most of us want to be strong. We may well see being like a child as being weak. . . . But King Benjamin, who understood as well as any mortal what it meant to be a man of strength and courage, makes it clear that to be like a child is not to be childish. . . . [We will] become as a child in our capacity to love and obey . . . We will become as a little child, obedient to God and more loving. . . . We obey and resist temptation by following the promptings of the Holy Ghost." (Conf. Report, Apr. 2006).

After the people hear the words of the angel quoted by King Benjamin, they fall to the earth, and ask for mercy and forgiveness through the "atoning blood of Christ" (Mosiah 4:1-3). Upon hearing King Benjamin's words, the multitude began to exercise faith in a Savior. The listening and responsive multitude received, because of their faith, a remission of their sins. The Spirit of the Lord comes upon the multitude, and King Benjamin continues to instruct them. He warns them to "be diligent in keeping the commandments" and reminds them that salvation and a remission of sins comes only through Christ. (Mosiah 4:6-8).

In Mosiah chapter 4, King Benjamin provides his people with a formula to avoid the natural man and develop the attributes of "men and women of Christ." This formula applies equally today as it did more than two thousand years ago. Elder Dallin H. Oaks taught: "In the Church of Jesus Christ of Latter-day Saints, we follow the formula prescribed by the prophet-king Benjamin. He taught that those who receive a remission of sins through the atonement of Christ are filled with the love of God and the knowledge of that which is just and true." (Conf. Report, Apr. 1990).

King Benjamin instructs his people to develop the following divine attributes of humility, prayer, perseverance, peace, and charity. (See "Divine Attributes" in Topical Index, Alma 7).

Attribute	Admonition
Humility (See "Humility")	"Humble yourselves in the depth of humility. Remember "the greatness of God," "his goodness and long-suffering" and "your own nothingness" (Mosiah 4:11) "All progress in spiritual things is conditioned upon the prior attainment of humility." (McConkie, Mormon Doctrine, 370). "Humility has been described as having the 'desire to submit to the Lord,' the 'desire to seek the Lord's will and glory,' and the 'desire to remove pride.' May we each develop our humility by submitting to the will of the Lord in all things so that we may retain a remission of sins." (Crockett, Conf. Report, Oct. 2000).

Prayer (See "Prayer")	"Call upon the name of the Lord daily" (Mosiah 4:11). "Prayer is one of the greatest blessings we have while here on earth. . . . Our daily prayers influence our thoughts, our words, and our actions. In order to retain a remission of our sins, it is essential that we ask our Heavenly Father each day for strength to stay in the straight and narrow way." (Crockett, Conf. Report, Oct. 2000).
Perseverance	Stand "steadfastly in the faith of that which is to come" (Mos. 4:11). "King Benjamin taught that his people were to stand steadfast 'in the faith of that which [was] to come.' . . . Today we can stand steadfast in the testimony of 'The Living Christ,' as given by living Apostles: 'We testify that He will someday return to earth. . . . He will rule as King of Kings and reign as Lord of Lords.'" (Crockett, Conf. Report, Oct. 2000).
Live in Peace	Do not "have a mind to injure one another," but live "peaceably with all people" (Mosiah 4:13). Those "who receive a remission of sins . . . are filled with the love of God and a knowledge of that which is just and true. That kind of person . . . lives peaceably with all people. That is our method, and . . . peace for all mankind is our goal." (Oaks, Conf. Report, Apr. 1990).
Fulfill Family Duties (See "Family")	Teach children in love and righteousness, and provide for their physical and spiritual needs. Teach them to love one another and to observe the commandments. (Mosiah 4:14). "Parents are responsible to provide for their children. . . . We are to look after their physical, their spiritual, and their emotional needs. . . . Nothing compares to a father who is responsible and in turn teaches his children responsibility. Nothing compares with a mother who is present with them to comfort them and give them assurance. Love, protection and tenderness are all of consummate worth." (Packer, Conf. Report, Apr. 2002). (See D&C 83:4; 93:40).
Help Those In Need	Provide relief to those in need, and do what we can to "not suffer that the beggar putteth up his petition to you in vain." (Mosiah 4:16). Elder Jeffrey R. Holland taught: "King Benjamin says that . . . we retain a remission of our sins by compassionately responding to the poor who plead to us." Elder Holland counsels that while we may not be able to do everything, "we should do what we can," and refers to the example of Mother Theresa caring for the poor: "What we do is nothing but a drop in the ocean. But if we didn't do it, the ocean would be one drop less [than it is]." (Holland, Conf. Report, Oct. 2014).

Retaining a Remission of Sins

King Benjamin instructs the people that he has spoken of "these things [including the divine attributes] . . . for the sake of retaining a remission of your sins from day to day that ye may walk guiltless before God" (Mosiah 4:26). Elder Neal A. Maxwell stated: "Retention [of remission of our sins] clearly depends on the regularity of our repentance." (Maxwell, "King Benjamin's Sermon: A Manual for Discipleship"). We obtain remission of our sins through regular repentance and incremental steps to obtain divine attributes.

"In his spiritually stirring farewell sermon to the people he had served and loved, King Benjamin described the importance of knowing the glory of God and tasting of His love, of receiving a remission of sins, of always remembering the greatness of God, and of praying daily and standing steadfastly in the faith. (Mosiah 4:11). He also promised that by doing these things, 'ye shall always rejoice, and be filled with the love of God, and *always retain a remission of your sins.*' (Mosiah 4:12)." (Bednar, Conf. Report, Apr. 2016, *emphasis in original*).

Elder David A. Bednar teaches about the essential requirement of ordinances in retaining a remission of sins. "To comprehend more fully the process whereby we may obtain and always retain a remission of our sins, we need first to understand the inseparable relationship among three sacred ordinances that provide access to the powers of heaven: baptism by immersion, laying on of hands for the gift of the Holy Ghost, and the sacrament. . . . Holy ordinances are central in the Savior's gospel and in the process of coming unto Him and seeking spiritual rebirth. Ordinances are sacred acts that have spiritual purpose, eternal significance, and are related to God's laws and statutes. . . . Therefore in the ordinances thereof, the power of godliness is manifest. And without the ordinances thereof, and the authority of the priesthood, the power of godliness is not manifest unto men in the flesh" (D&C 84:20-21). (Conf. Report, Apr. 2016).

Baptism is the gate, the introductory ordinance that provides the initial cleansing from sin. It is the preparatory step to obtain the gift and reception of the Holy Ghost. Baptism is the "channel and key by which the Holy Ghost will be administered." (Joseph Smith, Teachings, 95-96). "Receiving the sanctifying power of the Holy Ghost in our lives creates the possibility of an *ongoing cleansing* of our soul from sin." (Bednar, Conf. Report, Apr. 2016). Thus, baptism provides the initial cleansing and the Holy Ghost provides the opportunity for ongoing cleansing. The ordinance of the sacrament helps us to repent sincerely and be renewed spiritually. If we participate in this ordinance with a broken heart and contrite spirit, we can have the Spirit of the Lord to be with us. "And by the sanctifying power of the Holy Ghost . . . we can always retain a remission of our sins." (Bednar, Conf. Report, Apr. 2016).

(See "Repentance"; "Baptism," "Holy Ghost" in Topical Index).

King Benjamin teaches that "if ye do this [put off the natural man and attain Christ-like attributes] ye shall always rejoice, and be filled with the love of God, *and always retain a remission of your sins*" (Mosiah 4:12, emphasis added).

King Benjamin's Warning: Watch Yourselves

After reviewing the importance of charity and gratitude, King Benjamin concludes his discourse with a final warning and admonition: "And finally, I cannot tell you all the things whereby ye may commit sin, for there are diverse ways and means, even so many that I cannot number them. But this much I can tell you, that if ye do not watch yourselves, and your thoughts, and your words, and your deeds, and observe the commandments of God, and continue in the faith of what ye have heard concerning the coming of our Lord, even unto the end of your lives, ye must perish. And now, O man, remember, and perish not" (Mosiah 4:29-30).

President Henry B. Eyring observed: "King Benjamin taught that we are responsible for the determined effort necessary to resist temptation [and retain a remission of our sins]. He warned his people about specific temptations. But after giving those warnings, he put the obligation on them. . . . With the help of the Holy Ghost, we can watch over ourselves. We can pray to recognize and reject the first thoughts of sin." (Conf. Report, Apr. 2006).

President James E. Faust cautioned that we must stay vigilant and "watch ourselves" to "even unto the end of your lives" (Mos. 4:30). "We seem to be living in a time foreseen by King Benjamin. . . . I would like to say a word to you brethren who are a little older. President J. Reuben Clark . . . used to say from this pulpit, 'Brethren, I hope I can remain faithful to the end.' At that time, President Clark was in his 80s. As a young man, I could not understand how this wise, learned, experienced, righteous Apostle . . . could have any concern for his own spiritual well-being. . . . I now understand. . . . Over my lifetime, I have seen some of the most choice, capable, and righteous of men stumble and fall. They have been true and faithful for many years and then get caught in a web of stupidity and foolishness. . . . All of us, young and old, must constantly guard against the enticements of Satan. . . . We must choose wisely the books and magazines we read, the movies we see, and how we use modern technology, such as the Internet." (Conf. Report, Oct. 1997).

Echoing King Benjamin's warning to watch our thoughts, words and deeds, Elder Carlos E. Asay counseled: "I would offer these simple guidelines . . . :

> If it is not clean, do not think it;
>
> if it is not true, do not speak it;
>
> if it is not good, do not do it."

(Conf. Report, Apr. 1980); See Marcus Aurelius, <u>The Meditations of Marcus Aurelius</u>, 211 ("if it is not right, do not do it; if it is not true, do not say it").

Discourse 11: Abinadi, "Redemption through Christ" (Mosiah 13-16)

Prophet	Key Doctrines	Scriptures	Audience	Date
Abinadi	- Redemption through Christ - Christ as Father and Son	Mosiah 13 - 16	To King Noah and priests in land of Shilom / Lehi-Nephi (recorded by Alma the Elder). Zeniff's colony	About 148 B.C.

INTRODUCTION

Chapters 9 to 24 in the Book of Mosiah include the history of a Nephite colony led by a man named Zeniff, who left Zarahemla and traveled to the land of Lehi-Nephi in approximately 200 B.C. In about 121 B.C., the members of Zeniff's colony were re-united with the Nephites in Zarahemla. During the 80-year period of separation, three kings, Mosiah I, Benjamin, and Mosiah II, ruled in Zarahemla; and, three kings, Zeniff, Noah, and Limhi, reigned in Lehi-Nephi. During the reign of King Noah in Lehi-Nehi, the prophet Abinadi was sent by the Lord to warn the people to repent.

We don't know much about Abinadi, but believe that he came from among the people, not from outside their society.[48] He was a righteous, courageous man, who was called to warn the people that if they did not repent, destruction would follow. The Lord told him: "Abinadi, go and prophesy unto this people, for they have hardened their hearts against my words; they have repented not of their evil doings; therefore I will visit them in my anger . . . [and] in their iniquities and abominations" (Mosiah 12:1).

Abinadi prophesied that the people would be "brought into bondage," and be smitten with "afflictions," "famine," and a "great pestilence" (Mosiah 12:2,4,7); that "the life of king Noah shall be valued even as a garment in a hot furnace" (Mosiah 12:2-3); and "except they [the people of King Noah] repent [the Lord] will utterly destroy them from off the face of the earth" (Mosiah 12:8). The people were angry with Abinadi, and brought him before King Noah, but Abinadi would not recant, and rebuked the king and his priests for their "whoredoms" and "iniquities" (Mosiah 12:29,31).

Abinadi "preached boldly and courageously, knowing that he was putting his own life in jeopardy because of his words. Wicked King Noah angrily ordered his priests to kill Abinadi . . . . But when the priests tried to lay their hands on Abinadi, he withstood them saying: 'Touch me not, for God shall smite you if ye lay your hands upon me, for I have not delivered the message which the Lord sent me to deliver.' . . . The people of King Noah were afraid to touch Abinadi because the Spirit of the Lord was with him. 'His face shone with exceeding luster,' and he spoke 'with power and authority from God.' Abinadi declared that he would finish the message that God had sent him to deliver – and then it wouldn't matter what King Noah and the people did to him. (Mosiah 13:1-9). When Abinadi concluded his message, King Noah demanded that he deny the words he had spoken – or he would be put to death. But Abinadi refused." (Hales, Conf. Report, Apr. 1996).

---

[48] "There was a man among them whose name was Abinadi . . . ." (Mosiah 11:20).

Abinadi "continued his words" and finished his message (Mosiah 13:6 to Mosiah 16:15). In a powerful discourse, Abinadi prophesied of Christ, and explained that obedience to the law of Moses was necessary, but not sufficient, for salvation, and that the Mosaic "law of performances and of ordinances . . . were types of things to come" (Mosiah 13:30-31). He testified about the importance of the atonement, and that "there could not any man be saved except it were through the redemption of God" (Mosiah 13:32). Abinadi's doctrinal teachings clarified (i) the purpose of the law of Moses, (ii) the role of Christ as Redeemer, and (iii) the reality of the (future) resurrection.

"Abinadi infuriated wicked King Noah with his courageous testimony of Lord Jesus Christ. Eventually this great missionary offered the ultimate sacrifice for his witness and faith but not before his pure testimony touched one believing heart. . . . Many were converted to the gospel of Jesus Christ as a direct result of Abinadi's powerfully borne testimony of the Savior, believed by one soul – Alma." (Ballard, Conf. Report, Oct. 2004). "So far as we know, [Abinadi] converted but one man, yet that one man (Alma) became the progenitor of a posterity that kept the sacred records and served as the ecclesiastical leaders (and sometimes the political leaders) for the remainder of the Nephites' history, a period of well over four hundred years." (Matthews, "Abinadi," *Ensign*, Apr. 1992). Abinadi's bold testimony led to the conversion of the prophet Alma, but ultimately cost Abinadi his life.

DISCOURSE: Mosiah 13:6 – Mosiah 16

KEY DOCTRINES

- **Redemption**. Christ will come to earth to accomplish the resurrection and redeem his people. "[S]alvation doth not come by the law alone" but through the "atonement, which God himself shall make for the sins and iniquities of his people" (Mosiah 13:28).
    - Christ shall be crucified and slain, but will break the bands of death and become the first to be resurrected.
    - Christ shall take upon himself the iniquity and transgressions of those that hearken to the words of the prophets and believe in Him.
    - Christ shall have the power of judgment and the power to "make intercession for the children of men" (Mosiah 15:8).

- **Christ is the Son and the Father**. Christ is the literal Son of God, and also the "Father," in His roles as the father of our spiritual rebirth and salvation, and as the co-creator of "heaven and earth" (Mosiah 15:4).

COMMENTARY

The Law of Moses Is Fulfilled By Christ

Abinadi begins his message to King Noah and his priests with a strong rebuke for their failure to teach and keep the commandments of God. Abinadi says that he will "read unto you the remainder of the commandments of God, for I perceive that they are not written in your hearts" (Mosiah 13:11). He then proceeds to quote the Decalogue, as the Ten Commandments appear in Exodus.[49] (See "Obedience" in Topical Index, Mosiah 2-4).

10 Commandments in Mosiah	10 Commandments in Exodus
"Thou shalt have no other God before me." (Mosiah 12:35)	"Thou shalt have no other God before me." (Exodus 20:3)
"Thou shalt not make unto thee any graven image. . . ." (Mosiah 13:12-14)	"Thou shalt not make unto thee any graven image. . . ." (Exodus 20:4-6)
"Thou shalt not take the name of the Lord thy God in vain. . . ." (Mosiah 13:15)	"Thou shalt not take the name of the Lord thy God in vain. . . ." (Exodus 20:7)
"Remember the Sabbath day, to keep it holy. . . ." (Mosiah 13:16-19)	"Remember the Sabbath day, to keep it holy. . . ." (Exodus 20:8-11)
"Honor thy father and thy mother . . . ." (Mosiah 13:20)	"Honor thy father and thy mother . . . ." (Exodus 20:12)
"Thou shalt not kill." (Mosiah 13:21)	"Thou shalt not kill." (Exodus 20:13)
"Thou shalt not commit adultery." (Mosiah 13:22)	"Thou shalt not commit adultery." (Exodus 20:14)
"Thou shalt not steal." (Mosiah 13:22)	"Thou shalt not steal." (Exodus 20:15)
"Thou shalt not bear false witness against thy neighbor." (Mosiah 13:23)	"Thou shalt not bear false witness against thy neighbor." (Exodus 20:16)
"Thou shalt not covet thy neighbor's house . . . ." (Mosiah 13:24)	"Thou shalt not covet thy neighbor's house . . . ." (Exodus 20:17)

Elder Neal A. Maxwell observed, "most of the Ten Commandments are self-denying 'Thou shalt nots.' Heavenly Father loves his children perfectly, but he knows our tendencies perfectly, too. To lie, steal, murder, envy, to be sexually immoral, neglect parents, break the Sabbath, and to bear false witness – all occur because one mistakenly seeks to please himself for the moment regardless of divine standards or human consequences." (Conf. Report, April 1995). This was the situation in the court of King Noah. The wicked priests had sought to please themselves in iniquity, and utterly failed to obey the commandments or teach them to the people.

---

[49] It is likely that the source of the commandments were records that included the brass plates, which were available to the rulers in Zarahemla, as well. King Benjamin "taught [his sons] concerning the records which were engraven on the plates of brass . . . were it not for these plates, which contain these records and these commandments, we must have suffered in ignorance . . . [and] were it not for these things . . . that we might read and understand of [God's] mysteries, and have his commandments . . . our fathers would have dwindled in unbelief" (Mosiah 1:3-5).

Abinadi then explains that while "it is expedient that ye should keep [the commandments and] the law of Moses as yet . . . salvation does not come by the law alone; and were it not for the atonement, which God himself shall make for the sins and iniquities of the people, they must unavoidably perish, notwithstanding the law of Moses" (Mosiah 13:27-28).

Elder Dallin H. Oaks taught: "After all our obedience and good works, we cannot be saved from death or the effects of our individual sins without the grace extended by the atonement of Jesus Christ. The Book of Mormon makes this clear. It teaches that 'salvation does not come by the law alone' (Mosiah 13:28). In other words, salvation does not come simply by keeping the commandments." (Oaks, Ensign, Mar. 1994). "Salvation could not come to the world without the mediation of Jesus Christ." (Teachings of the Prophet Joseph Smith, 323).

Abinadi teaches that "Moses . . . and even all the prophets who have prophesied ever since the world began . . . said that God himself should come down among the children of men, and take upon him the form of man, and go forth in mighty power upon the face of the earth . . . [and] also that he should bring to pass the resurrection of the dead, and that he, himself should be oppressed and afflicted" (Mosiah 13:33-35).

Redemption through Christ: His Mission

Abinadi then quotes the messianic prophesy of Isaiah (see Isaiah 53), which describes, in poetic detail, the mission and sacrifice of the Savior, who:

- "has borne our grief and carried our sorrows" (Mosiah 14:4)
- "was wounded for our transgressions" and "bruised for our iniquities" (Mosiah 14:5)
- "made his grave with the wicked and with the rich in his death" (Mosiah 14:9)
- "made his soul an offering for sin" (Mosiah 14:10)
- "shall bear [our] iniquities" (Mosiah 14:11)
- "poured out his soul unto death; and he was numbered with the transgressors" (14:12)
- "bore the sins of many, and made intercession for the transgressors" (Mosiah 14:12)

Elder Jeffrey R. Holland observed: "Surely the most sublime, the lengthiest and most lyrical declaration of the life, death, and atoning sacrifice of the Lord Jesus Christ is that found in the 53rd chapter of Isaiah, quoted in its entirety in the Book of Mormon by Abinadi as he stood in chains before King Noah." (Holland, Christ and the New Covenant, 89). Gospel accounts from the New Testament demonstrate the remarkable accuracy of Isaiah's (and Abinadi's) prophesy.

PROPHECIES OF THE SAVIOR'S MORTAL MINISTRY FROM MOSIAH 14 (ISAIAH 53)	
Mosiah 14:2 (Isaiah 53:2): *"For he shall grow up before him as a tender plant, and as a root out of a dry ground: he hath no form nor comeliness; and when we shall see him, there is no beauty that we should desire him."*	When Isaiah spoke of the Savior as being a 'tender plant' without form and comeliness, he meant that Jesus was born as a small, helpless infant just as all people are. Despite his divine heritage, He grew as other people do. "Did not Christ grow up as a tender plant? There was nothing about him to cause people to single him out. In appearance, he was like a man; and so it is expressed here by the prophet that he had no form or comeliness, that is, he was not so distinctive, so different from others that people would recognize him [outwardly] as the Son of God. He appeared as a mortal man." (Smith, <u>Doctrines of Salvation</u>, 1:23). "Is this not Joseph's son?" (Luke 4:22). Bishop Victor L. Brown taught: "Unfortunately, artists and others have pictured him as effeminate, soft, and sad. If we analyze his life at all, we see a person who was masculine, strong, vigorous, interested in all that was going on about him, surely loving and kind, but at the same time one who could exhibit righteous anger. If this were not true, how could he have caused rough fishermen to follow him? (Matt. 4:19.) He spent his youth and young adulthood as a carpenter, a trade requiring strength and skill. Would he have dared drive the money changers from the temple had he not been a man of great strength and courage?" (Conf. Report, Oct. 1970).
Mosiah 14:3 (Isaiah 53:3): *"He is despised and rejected of men; a man of sorrows, and acquainted with grief: and we hid as it were our faces from him; he was despised, and we esteemed him not."*	Jesus experienced sorrow throughout His ministry. Members of his own family did not accept Him as the Messiah at first (John 7:5). People in his hometown sought to kill Him (Luke 4:16-30). His countrymen, the Jews, hid their faces from him, and "his own received him not" (John 1:11). One close friend betrayed Him; another denied Him (Luke 22:48, 54-62). In the end, "<u>all</u> the disciples forsook him, and fled" (Matt. 26:56), and His enemies demanded His crucifixion (Matt. 27:22). "No one's eyes were more penetrating than His, and much of what He saw pierced His heart. . . . . To a degree far more than we will ever understand, He was '*a man of sorrows, and acquainted with grief*' . . . . He was misunderstood or misrepresented, even hated from the beginning. No matter what He said or did, His statements were twisted, His actions suspected, His motives impugned. In the entire history of the world no one has ever loved so purely or served so selflessly— and been treated so diabolically for His effort." (Holland, Conf. Report, Oct. 1999, *emphasis added*).

Mosiah 14:4 (Isaiah 53:4): "Surely he hath borne our griefs, and carried our sorrows; yet we did esteem him stricken, smitten of God, and afflicted."	In the Garden of Gethsemane, the Savior began to take the sins of the world upon Himself (e.g., Mark 14:32-36; Luke 22:44; Matthew 26:28; D&C 19:16-19), or as Isaiah says, to bear our grief and carry our sorrows. Elder Talmage wrote: "Christ's agony in the garden is unfathomable by the finite mind, both as to intensity and cause…. He struggled and groaned under a burden such as no other being who has lived on earth might even conceive as possible. It was not physical pain, nor mental anguish alone, that caused Him to suffer such torture as to produce an extrusion of blood from every pore; but a spiritual agony of soul such as only God was capable of experiencing. . . . In that hour of anguish Christ met and overcame all the horrors that Satan could inflict…. In some manner, actual and terribly real though to man incomprehensible, the Savior took upon Himself the burden of the sins of mankind from Adam to the end of the world." (Talmage, Jesus the Christ, 613-614).
Mosiah 14:5 (Isaiah 53:5): "But he was wounded for our transgressions, he was bruised for our iniquities: the chastisement of our peace was upon him; and with his stripes we are healed."	The Savior was beaten, scourged with a whip, and crucified for men's transgressions. His suffering was for us and our salvation – and through His actions we are 'healed.' President Ezra Taft Benson taught: "Because He was God – even the Son of God – He could carry the weight and burden of other men's sins on Himself as Isaiah prophesied . . . In spite of that excruciating ordeal, He took the cup and drank. He suffered the pains of all men so we would not have to suffer. He endured the humiliation and insults of His persecutors without complaint or retaliation. He bore the flogging and then the ignominy of the brutal execution—the cross." (*Ensign*, Apr. 1991)
Mosiah 14:7 (Isaiah 53:7): "He was oppressed and he was afflicted, yet he opened not his mouth: he is brought as a lamb to the slaughter, and as a sheep before her shearers is dumb, so he opened not his mouth."	When Jesus stood before Pilate, the governor of Judea, "he was accused by the chief priests and elders, [but] he answered nothing" (Matt. 27:12). When Pilate questioned Him, Jesus held His peace and "answered him to never a word; insomuch that the governor marveled greatly" (Matt. 27:14). In fulfillment of Isaiah's prophesy, Jesus opened not his mouth before His accusers.
Mosiah 14:9 (Isaiah 53:9): "And he made his grave with the wicked, and with the rich in his death; because he had done no violence, neither was any deceit in his mouth."	At the time of crucifixion, Jesus' cross was placed between two thieves (John 19:18). After His death on the cross, Joseph of Arimathea, a rich man, went to Pilate and obtained permission to bury Jesus. This wealthy man, who could boldly go before the Roman governor, arranged for the body to be laid "in his own new tomb" (Matt 27:60).

Redemption through Christ: His Resurrection and Atonement

Abinadi then repeats the major theme of his discourse: "God himself shall come down among the children of men, and shall redeem his people" (Mosiah 15:1). In the five and one-half pages of his recorded sermon, the word "redeem" or "redemption" occurs eighteen times. Alma's key message is: Repent and be saved through the redemption of Christ, who will allow Himself to be "crucified and slain" through submission of His will to the "will of the Father" (Mosiah 15:7). "Having gained the victory over death," Christ receives "power to make intercession for the children of men" (Mosiah 15:8).

Elder D. Todd Christofferson taught: "Among the most significant of Jesus Christ's descriptive titles is Redeemer. . . . [T]he word *redeem* means to pay off an obligation or a debt. *Redeem* can also mean to rescue or set free as by paying a ransom. If someone commits a mistake and then corrects it or makes amends, we say he has redeemed himself. Each of these meanings suggests different facets of the great Redemption accomplished by Jesus Christ through His Atonement, which includes, in the words of the dictionary, 'to deliver from sin and its penalties, as by a sacrifice made for the sinner.'" (Conf. Report, April 2013).

As our mediator and intercessor, Christ stands between men or women and the fate they would otherwise receive through strict application of the law. "Having ascended into heaven . . . being filled with compassion towards the children of men; standing betwixt them and justice; having broken the bands of death, [and] taken upon himself their iniquity and their transgressions," He "satisfied the demands of justice" and "redeemed them" (Mosiah 15:9).

Echoing the teachings of Nephi, Jacob and Benjamin, Abinadi instructs the priests that salvation only comes through the mercy of God. Redemption is available to those who have:

- "heard the words of the prophets . . . concerning the coming of the Lord"
- "harkened unto their words"
- "believed the Lord would redeem his people"; and
- "looked forward . . . for a remission of their sins." (Mosiah 15:11).

"For these are they whose sins he has borne; these are they for whom he has died to redeem them from their transgressions" (Mosiah 15:12). The keys to redemption are faith (they who "believed"), repentance (they who "looked forward for a remission of sins"), and obedience (they who "heard and harkened" to the words of the prophets). Elder Dallin H. Oaks explained: "In these great scriptures from the Book of Mormon [Mosiah 15:11-12], we learn that those *who are qualified* by faith and repentance and compliance with the laws and ordinances of the gospel will have their sins borne by the Lord Jesus Christ." (Conf. Report, Apr. 1985).

Resurrection

Abinadi teaches that redemption through Jesus Christ includes not only a rescue from sin, but also from death. Christ "breaketh the bands of death, having gained the victory over death" (Mosiah 15:8). He "hath power over the dead; therefore he bringeth to pass the resurrection of the dead" (Mosiah 15:20). Jesus said: "I lay down my life, that I might take it again. No man taketh it from me, but I lay it down of myself. I have power to lay it down, and I have power to take it again" (John 10:17-18).

Abinadi teaches that there are differences how and when people are resurrected. He is the first Book of Mormon prophet to use the phrase "first resurrection" (Mosiah 15:26).

A summary of Abinadi's teachings on the resurrection include:

1. There is no resurrection without Christ. (Mosiah 16:7-8).
2. There is a first resurrection for the righteous who lived before the time of Christ. "All the prophets and all those that have believed in their words, or all those that have kept the commandments of God . . . are the first resurrection" (Mosiah 15:21).
3. Those that died before Christ "in their ignorance, not having salvation declared unto them" "have a part" in the first resurrection. (Mosiah 15:22). D&C 137:7 adds: "All who have died without a knowledge of this gospel, *who would have received it* if they had been permitted to tarry, shall be heirs of the celestial kingdom of God." (*Emphasis added.*)
4. "Little children," shall be part of the first resurrection. (Mosiah 15:25).
5. The unrepentant, who have known the commandments and would not keep them, who "willfully rebelled against God," have no part in the first resurrection. (Mosiah 15:26).
6. Judgment will come <u>after</u> the resurrection. (Mosiah 16:10).

Amulek and Alma the Younger later provide additional details on the doctrine of the resurrection, which have been further clarified through modern-day revelation. (See "Resurrection" in Topical Index; Alma 11).

In his teachings on the resurrection, as recorded, Abinadi does not specify the number of resurrections, or the status of the spirit between the time of death and the resurrection. These doctrinal gaps were later acknowledged by Alma the Younger. For example, with respect to timing of the resurrection, Alma the Younger said he did not know "whether there shall be one time, or a second time, or a third time, that men shall come forth from the dead" (Alma 40:5). Apparently, Alma didn't know, because Abinadi's discourse, which had been dutifully recorded by Alma the Elder, did not address this issue. Additionally, Alma the Younger explained, he had to "inquire diligently" of the Lord to know concerning the "space between the time of death and the resurrection" (Alma 40:9). Again, he had to ask the Lord because the doctrine had not been taught by Abinadi or earlier prophets.

Doctrines are often revealed precept by precept, which appears to be the case with the resurrection. There is consistency in what Abinadi did and did not teach, and what Alma the Younger was later able to refer to directly, and what he needed to supplement through his own, faithful inquiries and revelations on the subject. I find this consistency and correlation in the sequencing of the Book of Mormon revelations on resurrection to be a minor, but faith-promoting, piece of evidence supporting the truth of the overall record.

Christ as the Father and the Son

At the end of his sermon, Abinadi describes Christ with the phrase, "who is the very Eternal Father" (Mosiah 16:15). Similarly, one of the titles used by the prophet Isaiah to describe the Messiah is "the everlasting Father" (Isaiah 9:6). The concept that Christ is both the "Son" and the "Father" can be somewhat confusing, if taken out of context.

Earlier in his discourse, Abinadi states that Christ is called the Son because he is born of God to "dwell in the flesh" (Mosiah 15:2). And, He is called the "Father" because of (i) the power of God in Him (Mos. 15:3); (ii) His one-ness with the Father's purposes and role as creator of heaven and earth (Mos. 15:4); and (iii) His willingness to have his own will "swallowed up in the will of the Father" (Mosiah 15:7). Elder Jeffrey R. Holland observed: "As Abinadi taught, Christ was 'conceived by the power of God' and therefore has the powers of the Father within him. In addition to that divine lineal relationship, Christ also acts as the Father in that he is the Creator of heaven and earth, is the father of our spiritual rebirth and salvation, and is faithful in honoring – and therefore claiming the power of – the will of his Father above that of his own will." (Holland, Christ and the New Covenant, 183-184).

Elder M. Russell Ballard explained: "How can Jesus Christ be both the Father and the Son? It really isn't as complicated as it sounds. Though He is the Son of God, He is the head of the Church, which is the family of believers. When we are spiritually born again, we are adopted into His family. He becomes our Father or leader. . . . God, our Heavenly Father, is the Father of our spirits; we speak of God the Son as the Father of the righteous. He is regarded as the 'Father' because of the relationship between Him and those who accept His gospel." ("Building Bridges of Understanding," *Ensign*, June 1998). Abinadi teaches that the believers who qualify for redemption become the "seed" of Christ, and therefore Christ becomes their "Father" (Mosiah 15:10-13). "In spiritual and figurative terms [those who are qualified to have their sins borne by Christ] will become the sons and daughters of Christ, heirs to his kingdom." (Oaks, Conf. Report, Apr. 1985).

In 1916, the First Presidency issued a statement explaining how Jesus Christ is identified as both the "Son" and the "Father" in the scriptures:

1. **Jesus Christ the "Father" as Creator.** Within the context of creation of the heavens and the earth, "Jehovah, who is Jesus Christ the Son of Elohim, is called 'the Father,' and even 'the very Eternal Father of heaven and of earth.'" (Mosiah 16:15; Ether 4:7; Alma 11:38-39).
2. **Jesus Christ the "Father" of Those Who Accept the Gospel.** Another sense in which Jesus Christ is regarded as the 'Father' has reference to the relationship between Him and those who accept His gospel and thereby become heirs of eternal life. (D&C 50:41).
3. **Jesus Christ the "Father" by Divine Investiture of Authority.** Jesus the Son represents Elohim His Father in power and authority. Jesus spoke and ministered in and through the Father's name; and so far as authority and godship are concerned, His words and acts were and are those of the Father. ("The Father and The Son," *Ensign*, Apr. 2002).

Abinadi teaches that Christ came to earth to redeem mankind. He lived a perfect life, subjecting His will to that of His Father. He suffered and bore our sins that we might be redeemed from both death and hell. He is the first to be resurrected, and through His power, we will also be resurrected. He is both the Son of the Eternal Father, and the author and Father of our salvation.

Abinadi closes his discourse with the admonition: "And now, ought ye not to tremble and repent of your sins, and remember that only in and through Christ ye can be saved? Therefore, if ye teach the law of Moses, also teach that it is a shadow of those things which are to come – Teach them that redemption cometh through Christ the Lord" (Mosiah 16:13-15). After this witness, Abinadi was killed; however, his teachings lived on, inspiring a prophet and a people, and surviving for hundreds of years to provide the world today with key gospel doctrines and principles . . . and another testament of Jesus Christ.

The major themes of Abinadi's sermon are succinctly summarized in modern-day scripture: "Wherefore, the Almighty God gave his Only Begotten Son . . . . He suffered temptations but gave no heed unto them. He was crucified, died and rose again the third day; and ascended into heaven, to sit down on the right hand of the Father, to reign with almighty power, according to the will of the Father; that as many as would believe and be baptized in his holy name, and endure to the end, should be saved – Not only those who believed after he came in the meridian of time, in the flesh, but all those from the beginning, even as many as were before he came, who believed in the words of the holy prophets . . . who truly testified of him in all things, should have eternal life. As well as those who should come after, who should believe . . . by the Holy Ghost, which beareth record of the Father and of the Son. Which Father, Son and Holy Ghost are one God, infinite and eternal, without end, Amen" (D&C 20:21-28).

Discourse 12: Alma, "A Mighty Change of Heart" (Alma 5)

Prophet	Key Doctrines	Scriptures	Audience	Date
Alma	• Obtain a mighty change of heart (conversion) through faith in Christ, repentance, obedience. • A testimony is obtained through fasting, prayer, and the confirmation of the Spirit	Alma 5	To the people in the church in the city of Zarahemla Alma teaches through asking questions that help assess spiritual status.	About 83 B.C.

INTRODUCTION

Alma, called "Alma the Younger," was a son of a man named Alma who was among the priests of King Noah addressed by Abinadi. The elder Alma believed the words of Abinadi, and pleaded with King Noah to spare the prophet's life. The king was enraged and sought to kill Alma, who escaped, recorded the words of Abinadi and was converted. The elder Alma became the High Priest of the church, and a prophet-leader of the people.

His son, Alma the Younger, was born about 126 B.C., and lived primarily in the city of Zarahemla during the reign of King Mosiah, the son of King Benjamin. As a young man, Alma rebelled against his father, and, together with four sons of King Mosiah, actively persecuted members of the church. At this stage of his life, Alma was known as a "very wicked and idolatrous man. And he was a man of many words, and did speak much flattery to the people; therefore he led many of the people to do after the manner of his iniquities" (Mosiah 27:8). Alma later states, "I went about with the sons of Mosiah, seeking to destroy the church of God" (Alma 36:6).

After much fasting and prayer by his father and members of the church, Alma received a visit from an angel, who rebuked him for his actions. (Mosiah 27:11-19). Alma fell into an unconscious state for three days and three nights, suffering deep remorse and sorrow for his sinful behavior – "wading through much tribulation," tasting the "gall of bitterness," feeling the "bonds of iniquity," and "repenting nigh unto death" (Mosiah 27:29). During this process, the young man remembered his father's teachings about Jesus Christ, and sought forgiveness from the Lord. After humble, sincere prayer, pleading for mercy, Alma obtained forgiveness and felt the love of God. He soon received strength, and testified to the people that he had "repented of [his] sins, [had] been redeemed of the Lord" and "born of God" (Mosiah 27:24, 28).

From that time forward, Alma the Younger became a faithful disciple/servant of Jesus Christ, and immediately "traveled throughout all the land of Zarahemla . . . zealously striving to repair all the injuries which [he] had done to the church, confessing all [his] sins . . . . And thus [he was] an instrument in the hands of God in bringing many to the knowledge of the truth [and] their Redeemer" (Mosiah 27:35, 36). This Alma became a great missionary, leader and prophet, and spent the rest of his life serving the Lord and his people.

Subsequently, Alma became both the chief judge of the Nephite government, and the presiding high priest in the church. As he traveled among the people and "saw the wickedness of the church" and "great inequality among the people," he resigned from the office of chief judge and "confined himself wholly to the high priesthood" so that he "might go forth among his people . . . and preach the word of God unto them" (Alma 5:11, 12, 18-20). The first city he visited was Zarahemla where he delivered his first recorded discourse: "Alma began to deliver the word of God unto the people, first in the land of Zarahemla, and from thence throughout all the land. And these are the words which he spake to the people in the church which was established in the city of Zarahemla, according to his own record. . . . " (Alma 5:1, 2).

Throughout his address, Alma teaches by asking and answering questions. In the sixty-two verses of his sermon, he asks forty-one questions. President Ezra Taft Benson taught: "we all need to take a careful inventory of our performance. . . . Do we frequently review the crucial questions which Alma asks the members of the church in the fifth chapter of Alma in the Book of Mormon?" (Conf. Report, Apr. 1987). These questions – and our answers – can provide a spiritual barometer concerning our level of conversion and testimony.

DISCOURSE: Alma 5

KEY DOCTRINES

- **Conversion**. We can experience a mighty change of heart (conversion) through belief in the word of God, faith in Christ, repentance, obedience, and enduring to the end. Conversion generally is a process that occurs over time. Alma asks several questions to assess current spiritual status, including:
    - Are we sufficiently humble, and stripped of pride and envy? (Alma 5:28-29)
    - How would we feel if we were brought before God to be judged?

- **Testimony**. We can gain a firm testimony of the truth through study, fasting and prayer (Alma 5:46); the witness of the Holy Ghost is more powerful than the visitation of angels.

COMMENTARY

Conversion: A Mighty Change of Heart

At the beginning of his discourse, Alma reminds the members of the church in Zarahemla about the previous generation who had been delivered from both physical and spiritual bondage. He admonishes them to remember the "captivity of your fathers" and the Lord's "mercy and long-suffering towards them" (Alma 5:6). He testifies that their fathers experienced a "mighty change" in their hearts and were saved because they "humbled themselves," and "put their trust in God" (Alma 5:13). Alma then asks the people, "Have ye experienced this mighty change in your hearts?" (Alma 5:14). In essence, he is asking whether they have been truly converted.

"Conversion brings a mighty change of heart. . . . As true converts, we are motivated to do what the Lord wants us to do and to be who He wants us to be." (Nelson, Conf. Report, Oct. 2005). "Conversion is an enlarging, a deepening, and a broadening of the undergirding base of testimony. It is the result of revelation from God, accompanied by individual repentance, obedience, and diligence. Any honest seeker of truth can become converted by experiencing the mighty change of heart." (Bednar, Conf. Report, Oct. 2012).

"Conversion means 'to turn with.' Conversion is a turning from the ways of the world to, and staying with, the ways of the Lord." (Nelson, Conf. Report, Oct. 2005). "The verb convert means 'to turn from one belief or course to another,' conversion is 'a spiritual and moral change attending a change of belief with conviction.' As used in the scriptures, converted generally implies not merely mental acceptance of Jesus and his teachings, but also a motivating faith in him and in his gospel, a faith which works a transformation, an actual change in one's understanding of life's meaning and in one's allegiance to God – in interest, in thought, and in conduct. While conversion may be accomplished in stages, one is not really converted in the full sense of the term unless and until he is at heart a new person." (Romney, Conf. Report, Oct. 1975).

Elder D. Todd Christofferson taught: "How can you become converted? . . . Jeremiah spoke of the law of God, the gospel, being written in our hearts. He quotes the Lord speaking about us, His people in the latter days: 'I will put my law in their inward parts, and write it in their hearts. . . ' (Jer. 31:33). Ezekiel said conversion is like the Lord taking away our 'stony heart' and giving us a heart that loves Him and His gospel (Ezekiel 11:19-20)." (Conf. Report, Apr. 2004).

<u>A Change of Heart Generally Occurs over Time</u>

This process, the "mighty change of heart," does not usually happen in an instant. Elder Cecil O. Samuelson instructed: "while we believe fully in the mighty change of heart described in the scriptures, we must understand it often occurs gradually, rather than instantaneously or globally, and in response to specific questions, experiences, and concerns, as well as by our study and prayer." (Conf. Report, Apr. 2011).

"You may ask, Why doesn't this mighty change happen more quickly with me? You should remember that the remarkable examples of King Benjamin's people, Alma, and some others in scripture are just that – remarkable and not typical. For most of us, the changes are more gradual and occur over time . . . . more a process than an event." (Christofferson Conf. Report, Apr. 2008). Elder McConkie taught: "Except in . . . unusual circumstances, as with Alma, spiritual rebirth is a process. It does not occur instantaneously. It comes to pass by degrees." (<u>Doctrinal New Testament Commentary</u>, 3:401).

The process of conversion does not end at baptism. Elder M. Russell Ballard said: "We often think of conversion as applying only to investigators, but there are members who are not yet fully converted and who have yet to experience the mighty change of heart described in the scriptures." (Conf. Report, Oct. 2000). This is the question Alma was asking the members of the church . . . "Have ye experienced this mighty change in your hearts?" (Alma 5:14)

Alma's question was the first in a spiritual litmus test: Have you been converted? Are you like your faithful fathers, who experienced the "mighty change of heart" that turned them away from the world, and toward God? He teaches the people that they must exercise faith, perform works of righteousness, and have their sins forgiven to be truly converted. Elder Dallin H. Oaks taught: "We achieve this conversion by praying, by scripture reading, by serving, and by regularly partaking of the sacrament to always have his Spirit to be with us." (Conf. Report, Apr. 2015).

If You Have Experienced a Change of Heart, Can You Feel So Now?

Alma is preaching to members of the church. He knows that many of the people he is teaching had been "converted," or had previously "experienced a change of heart" (Alma 5:26), but have since distanced themselves from the Spirit and must repent. So his next question is not whether they have experienced the change of heart in the past, but, the "check-up" question: "if ye have experienced a change of heart, and if ye have felt to sing the song of redeeming love, I would ask, *can ye feel so now?*" (Alma 5:26, *emphasis added*).

This is a brilliant question. We may have been "converted" in the past. We may have enjoyed spiritual experiences while serving a mission, fulfilling a calling or during other periods in our lives. We may have felt joy from our Savior's love, and our love for others, at various times. But, the critical question is how we feel now. If we have previously experienced a mighty change of heart, and "felt to sing the song of redeeming love," do we feel so now? Is our conversion recommend current, or is it expired? Are we living so that we can feel the love of God in our life today? Not yesterday, not years ago, but today? His question could be re-cast: If you have been converted, do you feel converted now?

Conversion is not a one-time, past event. It must be current, continuous, and contemporary. Elder Marvin J. Ashton counseled, "Having a 'change of heart' at one time in our lives is insufficient to give us an understanding heart today. Helping and understanding a person years ago do not fill us with the love of God today. Christlike love must be continuous and contemporary." (Conf. Report, Oct. 1988).

Elder Dale G. Renlund explained that a "mighty change of our spiritual hearts is just the beginning . . . . To endure to the end, we need to be eager to please God and worship Him with fervor and passion. This means that we maintain faith in Jesus Christ by praying, studying the scriptures, partaking of the sacrament each week . . . . We need to actively help and serve others and share the gospel with them. We need to be perfectly upright and honest in all things, never compromising our covenants with God in our commitments to men, regardless of the circumstances. . . . We must identify temptations that easily beset us and put them out of reach – way out of reach. Finally, we need to frequently biopsy our mightily changed hearts and reverse any signs of early rejection." (Conf. Report, Oct. 2009).

Elder James B. Martino said, "I know some returned missionaries who have had undeniable spiritual experiences, but the *lack of certain spiritual habits* seem to have caused them to forget the times when God has spoken to them. To those returned missionaries and to all of us, if you 'have felt to sing the song of redeeming love, I would ask, can you feel so now?' (Alma 5:26). If you do not feel it now, you can feel it again. . . . Be obedient, remember the times when you have felt the Spirit in the past, and ask in faith. Your answer will come, and you will feel the love and peace of the Savior. It may not come as quickly or in the format you desire, but the answer will come. Do not give up! Never give up!" (Conf. Report, Oct. 2015, *emphasis added*).

"This question, 'Can you feel so now?' rings across the centuries. With all that we have received in this dispensation . . . Alma's challenge has never been more important. . . . It is not surprising that some in the Church believe they can't answer Alma's question with a resounding yes. They do not 'feel so now.' They feel they are in a spiritual drought . . . . [They] have not necessarily been involved in major sins or transgressions, but they have made *unwise choices*. Some are casual in their observance of sacred covenants. Others spend most of their time giving first-class devotion to lesser causes. Some allow intense cultural or political views to weaken their allegiance to the gospel of Jesus Christ. Some have immersed themselves in Internet materials that magnify, exaggerate, and in some cases, invent shortcomings of early Church leaders. Then they draw incorrect conclusions that can affect testimony. Any who have made these choices can repent and be spiritually renewed. . . . Alma emphasizes that through the Atonement of Christ, 'the arms of mercy are extended' to those who repent. (Alma 5:33)." (Cook, Conf. Report, Oct. 2012).

Whether from sins or "lack of certain spiritual habits," or "unwise choices," Alma exhorts those who are not currently converted to repent: "Behold, [the Lord God] sendeth an invitation to all men, for the arms of his mercy are extended towards them, and he saith: Repent and I will receive you" (Alma 5:33). As part of this process of spiritual renewal, Alma outlines several behavioral guidelines so that the people can feel the love and peace of the Savior, "walk blameless before God" and again "feel to sing the song of redeeming love" (Alma 5:26-27).

Avoid Pride, Envy, and Persecution

Specifically, Alma recommends three areas of behavior to retain conversion. Alma asks (i) if the people have been sufficiently humble; (ii) if they are stripped of pride and envy (iii) and whether they exhibit kindness toward their fellow men. (Alma 5:27-30). Elder Dale G. Renlund taught: "By honestly answering questions like these, we can correct early deviations from the strait and narrow path and keep our covenants with exactness." (Conf. Report, Oct. 2009).

These three requirements deal with how we consider ourselves, and how we treat our fellow man: be humble; don't envy; and love our neighbor. Just as King Benjamin taught that we serve God through service to others, Alma teaches that one barometer of our own conversion – and commitment to God – is how we treat each other. If we are truly converted, and have turned toward God with love, we will also turn toward our neighbor with love. Avoiding pride, eliminating envy, and treating others with kindness are three of the main verses in the "song of redeeming love."

1. *Are ye "sufficiently humble"? "Are ye stripped of pride?"*

Alma warns his "beloved brethren" about the dangers of being "puffed up in the pride of your hearts" and "setting your hearts upon the vain things of the world, upon your riches" (Alma 5:53). These admonitions are similar to the warnings given by both Jacob and Nephi about the evil of pride when one's heart is focused on riches. (see Jacob's warning in Jacob 2:12-22; and Nephi's observations about the "rich puffed up in the pride of their hearts" in the last days in 2 Nephi 28:12-15). Hearts puffed with pride are stiff and "stony" and less susceptible to turn toward God in a mighty change and feel redeeming love. (See "Humility" in Topical Index, Alma 32).

2. *"Are ye stripped of envy?"*

Alma warns that the envious are "not prepared" to meet God, and must repent. (Alma 5:29). "[We] must not look on [our] brethren and sisters and envy them that which they have. That is sinful, that is wrong, and the man or woman who indulges in it, indulges in a wrong spirit. God wants us to build each other up in righteousness. He wants us to love one another and to seek one another's benefit. This is the spirit of the Gospel of Jesus Christ." (Journal of Discourses 15:145).

One of the problems with envy is that it divides rather than unites. As President David O. McKay observed: "One of the first conditions that will bring about disunity . . . will be envy." (Conf. Report, Oct. 1967). "Hate, envy, jealousy, intolerance are all weapons used by Satan to thwart the purposes of God." (McKay, Conf. Report, Oct. 1947). "The unrighteous include . . . those whose hearts are so eaten out with envy that they become breeders of strife and dissensions." (Bowen, Conf. Report, Oct. 1949). Cain envied Abel. The sons of Jacob envied Joseph. The Jewish hierarchy envied Christ. Satan envies Our Heavenly Father and His Beloved Son.

Envy is "far-reaching – it can resent anything, including any virtue and talent, and it can be offended by everything, including every goodness and joy." (Holland, Conf. Report, Apr. 2002). We should not envy the good fortune of others. "We are not diminished when someone else is added upon." (Holland, Conf. Report, Apr. 2012). "Our very business in life is not to get ahead of others, but to get ahead of ourselves. To break our own records, to outstrip our yesterdays by our todays." (Monson, Conf. Report, Apr. 1973).

"It is easy to say those words, 'Love your neighbor as yourself,' but how hard it is to bring them right down to actual practice. . . . If we really could bring ourselves into full accord with that commandment, we should rejoice exultantly in the good fortunes that attend the efforts of our fellows, no matter in how great a degree they might eclipse us or how far they might excel us. You see, it requires that we root out envy . . . and that is the way we grow in the development of character and the cultivation of those perfections which God has directed that we strive to achieve. . . . If you want to overcome envy, you have to practice rejoicing in the good fortune and successes and attainments of your fellows . . . you have to practice generosity and contentment in seeing others prosper as you would like yourself to prosper." (Bowen, Conf. Report, Oct. 1951).

3. *"Is there one among you that doth make a mock of his brother, or that heapeth upon him persecutions? . . . Will ye persist in supposing ye are better one than another; yea will ye persist in the persecution of your brethren?"*

The corollary of envy, where one grinds one's teeth, narrows one's eyes, and covets what another has, is self-aggrandizement, where one raises one's nose in the air, and assumes a disdainful haughtiness, "supposing ye are better one than another" (Alma 5:54). This manifestation of pride, a snooty, self-importance, Alma warns, can lead to mocking and persecution of others rather than love and service. Elder Dallin H. Oaks observed that Alma provides "a potent reminder that neither riches or lineage nor any other privileges of birth should cause us to believe that we are 'better one than another.'" (Conf. Report, Apr. 2006).

Elder George Q. Cannon taught: "When wealth multiplies the people get lifted up in the pride of their hearts, and they look down on their poor brethren and despise them because they are better educated, have better manners, and speak better language – in a word because they have advantages which their poor brethren and sisters have not (Alma 5:53-56). There is sin in this, and God is angry with a people who take this course. He wants us to be equal in earthly things, as we are in heavenly." (Journal of Discourses, 15:145). "The love of Christ . . . requires that we neither mock our sisters and brothers nor persecute anyone." (Clyde, Conf. Report, Apr. 1995).

Alma teaches that conversion, the "mighty change of heart" occurs when we humble ourselves, put our trust in God, and strive to faithfully follow the savior. (Alma 5:6-12). We retain our conversion when we treat others without envy or malice and practice love and kindness to our fellow men. (Alma 5:53-55). The mighty change in heart is part of the conversion process, a process whereby we repent and accept the invitation from the Lord to change and "receive" Him. Alma taught that the Lord's invitation, "come unto me," is extended to all. (Alma 5:34-35). By coming unto Christ, and receiving Him in our own lives, we can experience a mighty change in our own hearts and become converted. By coming unto Christ, and emulating His treatment of others, we can retain and amplify our conversion, and continually "sing the song of redeeming love." (See "Inclusion" in Topical Index, 2 Nephi 26).

Alma's Testimony

Alma concludes his sermon about conversion and a "mighty change of heart" by bearing testimony of his own conversion. Alma testifies: "I know that Jesus Christ shall come, yea the Son, the Only Begotten of the Father, full of grace, and mercy, and truth . . . yea, the Son of God cometh in his glory, in his might, majesty, power and dominion" (Alma 5:48, 50). With respect to his teachings and testimony, Alma declares: "And how do ye suppose that I know of their surety? Behold, I say unto you they were made known unto me by the Holy Spirit of God. Behold, I have fasted and prayed many days that I might know these things of myself. And now I do know of myself that they are true, for the Lord God hath made them manifest unto me by his Holy Spirit; and this is the spirit of revelation which is in me" (Alma 5:45-46). (See "Testimony").

This is the same Alma who experienced a miraculous vision. He saw an angel. He heard a heavenly voice. He has a first rate "conversion story" to share – a literal miracle involving angels and voices that shook the earth. (Mosiah 27:10-32; Alma 36:6-23). However, when Alma explains his conversion, he focuses on his experience studying, fasting and praying for "many days." While not ignoring the impact of the angelic visitation, Alma became anchored in the gospel – and truly converted -- through study, fasting, prayer and a confirmation through the Holy Spirit, the "spirit of revelation." The same spirit of revelation, or spirit of conversion, is available to all who diligently seek it through the same methods: prayer, fasting, scripture study, and obedience.

"Although conversion is miraculous and life changing, it is a quiet miracle. Angelic visitations and other spectacular occurrences do not bring conversion. Even Alma, who saw an angel, became converted only after he 'fasted and prayed many days' for a witness of the truth (Alma 5:46)." (True to the Faith, 41).

Alma's closing witness to his brothers and sisters in Zarahemla is pure, simple, and straightforward: "I know that Jesus Christ shall come, yea, the Son, the Only Begotten of the Father, full of grace, and mercy, and truth. And behold, it is he that cometh to take away the sins of the world, yea, the sins of every man who steadfastly believeth on his name" (Alma 5:48).

Discourse 13: Alma, "Divine Attributes" (Alma 7)

Prophet	Key Doctrines	Scriptures	Audience	Date
Alma	• Christ Takes On Our Infirmities • Duty to God: Developing Divine Attributes	Alma 7	To the church in the city of Gideon	About 83 B.C.

INTRODUCTION

After teaching members of the church in Zarahemla, Alma visits the city of Gideon, which was located in the valley of Gideon, "being called after the man who was slain by the hand of Nehor with the sword" (Alma 6:7). Gideon was a righteous follower of Christ who had assisted in delivering the people of Limhi out of bondage. The people in Gideon were generally more faithful than the people of Zarahemla, and so Alma's message was more encouraging. He commends them for their righteousness, and teaches them based on their belief in the true and living God. (Alma 7:6).

In a broad-reaching testimony of Christ, Alma prophesies of His mortal ministry and teaches that the Savior would not only take upon Himself our sins, but also our pains, afflictions, sicknesses and infirmities, that He might be "filled with mercy" and know how to "succor his people," and give us strength to face the difficult challenges ("infirmities") of life. (Alma 7:11-12). Alma's discourse in Gideon is less a call to repentance, and more a sermon of encouragement, highlighting Christ's ability to strengthen His people, and teaching the faithful how to develop Christ-like attributes.

DISCOURSE: Alma 7

KEY DOCTRINES

- **Christ Takes On Our Infirmities**. Through the Atonement, Christ not only suffered to save us from death and sin, but also took on our infirmities.

- **Divine Attributes**. It is our duty to develop Christ-like attributes, such as humility, submissiveness, patience, temperance, diligence, faith, charity, and "abound in good works" (Alma 7:23).

COMMENTARY

Christ Takes on Our Infirmities (See "Atonement")

After Alma visited the church in Zarahemla, he went to the city of Gideon. He tells the people that of all things to come in the future, one thing is "of more importance than they all": the coming of Christ (Alma 7:7). Alma prophesies that the "kingdom of heaven is at hand, and the Son of God cometh upon the face of the earth" (Alma 7:9). He shall be "born of Mary" in the land of Jerusalem, and be the literal "Son of God" (Alma 7:10). (See "Mary" in Topical Index, 1 Nephi 11).

Alma teaches the members of the church in Gideon that Christ "hath power to do all things" (Alma 7:8). Part of this power is not only to save us from death and sin, but to "take upon him [our] infirmities" and provide us with strength to deal with life's challenges. (Alma 7:12). Alma echoes and expounds the teachings of Abinadi and Isaiah about the Savior's ministry and mission. He teaches that Christ will . . .

Take upon Him . . .	That He might . . .	Therefore the Atonement . . .
"Death"	"Loose the bands of death" (Alma 7:12)	Assures us of immortality through a universal resurrection.
"The sins of his people"	"Blot out their transgressions" (Alma 7: 13)	Gives us the opportunity to be cleansed from sin through repentance, baptism, and obedience.
"Our infirmities"	"Know according to the flesh how to succor his people according to their infirmities" (Alma 7:12)	Provides us with the strength to bear the burdens of mortality.

"The Savior has suffered not just for our sins and iniquities – but also for our physical pains and anguish, our weaknesses and shortcomings, our fears and frustrations, our disappointments and discouragement, our regrets and remorse, our despair and desperation, the injustices and iniquities we experience, and the emotional distresses that beset us. There is no physical pain, no spiritual wound, no anguish of soul or heartache, no infirmity or weakness you or I ever confront in mortality that the Savior did not experience first . . . the Son of God perfectly . . . understands, for He has felt and borne our individual burdens." (Bednar, Conf. Report, Apr. 2014).

The scriptures teach that Christ "suffereth the pains of every living creature" (2 Nephi 9:21); heals the brokenhearted (Luke 4:18); heals infirmities (Luke 5:15); heals those afflicted in any manner (3 Nephi 17:9); and bears our griefs and sorrows (Isaiah 53:4). He is a God of hope for each of us who may suffer. (See "Atonement" in Topical Index, 2 Nephi 9).

Developing Divine Attributes

After teaching the people of Gideon about the coming of Christ, and the comprehensive power of His Atonement, Alma commends them for their righteousness. (Alma 7:19). "And now because your faith is strong . . . concerning the things which I have spoken, great is my joy" (Alma 7:17). He says, "my soul doth exceedingly rejoice, because of the exceeding diligence and heed which ye have given to my word" (Alma 7:25). This is an obedient, righteous, congregation.

Therefore, rather than focus on their need to repent, he instructs them to fulfill their "duty to God" (Alma 7:22) by developing divine, Christ-like attributes. Alma provides a list of behavioral qualities and characteristics they should possess to "walk blamelessly before God": "And now I would that you should be ***humble***, and be ***submissive*** and ***gentle***; easy to be entreated; full of ***patience*** and ***long-suffering***; being ***temperate*** in all things; being ***diligent*** in keeping the commandments of God at all times; ***asking*** for whatsoever things ye stand in need, both spiritual and temporal; always ***returning thanks*** unto God for whatsoever things ye do receive. And see that ye have ***faith***, ***hope***, and ***charity***, and then ye will always abound in ***good works***" (Alma 7:23, *emphasis added*).

Alma's attributes are similar to the characteristics of a "divine nature" identified by Peter in the New Testament. (2 Peter 1:4-8). Peter implies that the attributes leading to a divine nature are additive. They are obtained in a step-by-step process, a self-reinforcing, sequential path leading from faith, to diligence, to virtue, to knowledge, to temperance, to patience, to godliness, to brotherly kindness, and finally, to charity. "The virtues outlined by Peter are part of the divine nature," President Ezra Taft Benson taught, "or the Savior's character. These are the virtues we are to emulate if we would be more like Him." (Conf. Report, Oct. 1986).

"The attributes of the Savior [in 2 Peter and D&C 4], as we perceive them, are not a script to be followed or list to be checked off. They are interwoven characteristics, added one to another, which develop in us in interactive ways. In other words, we cannot obtain one Christlike characteristic without also obtaining and influencing others. As one characteristic becomes strong, so do many more." (Hales, Conf. Report, April 2017). Elder Hales teaches, "as we earnestly strive to be true disciples of Jesus Christ, these characteristics will be interwoven, added upon, and interactively strengthened in us. . . . I testify that everyone can be a disciple of the Savior. Discipleship is not constrained by age, gender, ethnic origin, or calling." (Conf. Report, April 2017). Whether or not we agree with Peter's sequence, the acquisition of these "towering qualities" should be a goal for all who strive to follow the Lord.

We begin with **faith** as a foundation. "The first characteristic, to which all the others are added, is faith. Faith is the foundation upon which a godlike character is built. It is a prerequisite for all other virtues." (Benson, Conf. Report, Oct. 1986). Our initial faith is followed by diligent efforts to move forward in obedience, asking for assistance in prayer. We measure our faith by where it leads – diligent obedience. "Faith is a catalyst," Elder Hales teaches, "[w]ithout works . . . our faith is without power to activate discipleship." (Conf. Report, Apr. 2017). Thus, we are instructed to "give all **diligence**" to our faith; in Alma's words, we should "be diligent in keeping the commandments of God at all times" (Alma 7:23). Alma later teaches the Zoramites that we need to nourish our faith with "great diligence" (Alma 32:41). (See "Faith" in Topical Index, Alma 32).

Peter exhorts us to "add to your faith **virtue**" (2 Peter 1:5). President Ezra Taft Benson observed: "Peter goes on to say that we must add to our faith virtue. . . . Virtuous behavior implies that [one] has pure thoughts and clean actions. . . . Virtue is akin to holiness, an attribute of godliness. [We] should actively seek for that which is virtuous and lovely and not that which is debasing or sordid. . . . Whenever [one] departs from the path of virtue in any form or expression, he loses the Spirit and comes under Satan's power." (Conf. Report, Oct. 1986). "This virtue is more than sexual purity. It is cleanliness and holiness in mind and body. Virtue is also power. As we faithfully live the gospel, we will have power to be virtuous in every thought, feeling and action. Our minds become more receptive to the promptings of the Holy Ghost and the Light of Christ." (Hales, Conf. Report, Apr. 2017). In essence, virtue can result from faith and diligence. Faith is belief, and diligence is effort; but, virtue is power. True and virtuous principles fuel righteousness, and allow our confidence to wax strong as we follow Christ. (See "Chastity" in Topical Index, Alma 39).

With virtuous, pure thoughts, we are better able to comprehend and internalize gospel principles. Perhaps this is the reason Peter teaches that **knowledge** follows virtue. "By our virtuous living, we make the journey from 'I believe' to the glorious destination of 'I know.'" (Hales, Conf. Report, Apr. 2017). When we diligently obey the Lord in faith, and are living virtuous lives, the Holy Ghost becomes a welcome companion. He can quicken our minds, and our knowledge of Christ and His doctrine increases. "This knowledge is personal testimony born from personal experience. It is knowledge that transforms us." (Hales, Conf. Report, Apr. 2017). (See "Holy Ghost" in Topical Index, Moroni 10).

President Ezra Taft Benson observed: "The next step Peter describes in the growth process is to add knowledge to our faith and virtue. The Lord has told us that 'it is impossible for a man to be saved in ignorance.' (D&C 131:6). Every [person] should make learning a lifetime pursuit. While any study of truth is of value the truths of salvation are the most important truths any person can learn." (Conf. Report, Oct. 1986). (See "Education" in Topical Index, 2 Nephi 9).

The next aspect of the divine nature is **temperance**; or self-control, which includes the proper management of our time, talents, resources, and physical appetites. "As temperate disciples, we live the gospel in a balanced and steady way. We do not 'run faster than [we have] strength.'" (Hales, Conf. Report, Apr. 2017).

President Russell M. Nelson taught: "Temperance suggests sobriety and self-restraint in action. . . Repeatedly, scriptures teach that we should be 'temperate in all things' (1 Cor. 9:25; Alma 7:23; D&C 12:8). Temperance can protect each of us from the aftermath of excess." (Conf. Report, Oct. 1991). President Benson said: "[Temperance] means [one] is restrained in his emotions and verbal expressions. He does things in moderation and is not given to overindulgence. In a word, he has self-control. He is the master of his emotions, not the other way around. When temperance is born of faith, virtue and gospel knowledge, our ability to keep the first commandment preeminent is bolstered and enlivened." (Conf. Report, Oct. 1988).

"Being temperate in this way, we develop **patience** and trust in the Lord. We are able to rely on His design for our lives, even though we cannot see it with our own natural eyes. Therefore, we can 'be still and know that [He is] God (D&C 101:16)." (Hales, Conf. Report, Apr. 2017). We can accept the Lord's timetable. We are patient in our circumstances, and "move forward not only enduring all things but also enduring them patiently and well." (Ibid.).

Sometimes the Lord will "remove our burdens" and sometimes He will "strengthen us to endure and live with them." (Oaks, Conf. Report, Oct. 2006). "Patience," President Ezra Taft Benson taught, "is another form of self-control. It is the ability to postpone gratification and to bridle one's passions." (Conf. Report, Oct. 1986).

In his relationships with loved ones, a patient person does not engage in impetuous behavior that he or she will later regret. Patience is composure under stress. A patient person is understanding of others' faults. A patient person waits on the Lord. We sometimes read or hear of people who seek a blessing from the Lord, then grow impatient when it does not come swiftly. Part of the divine nature is to trust in the Lord enough to "be still and know that [he is] God" (D&C 101:16).

"This patience, Peter teaches, leads us to godliness. As the Father is patient with us, His children, we become patient with one another and ourselves. We delight in the agency of others and the opportunity it gives them to grow." (Hales, Conf. Report, Apr. 2017). As we develop patience, we become more like our Savior, who subjected His will to His Father. Thus, we add to patience **godliness**, and a reverence for holy things. Worship becomes more significant. We seek the blessings of the sacrament and temple participation, and we become more in tune with the needs of our brothers and sisters. Like the Savior, we will go about "doing good" (Acts 10:38).

The attribute of godliness, and putting God and our fellow man ahead of ourselves, helps us develop brotherly **kindness**, the hallmark of all true disciples. "One who is kind is sympathetic and gentle with others. He is considerate of others' feelings and courteous in his behavior. He has a helpful nature. Kindness pardons others' weaknesses and faults. Kindness is extended to all – to the aged and the young, to animals, to those low of station as well as the high." (Benson, Conf. Report, Oct. 1986). We begin to care more about others. We bless them that curse us. We do good to those who despitefully use us. (Matt. 5:44).

Each of these characteristics is added upon until we are now ready to progress to **charity**, which Peter puts at the apex of attributes, obtained after the perfecting influence of all the others. "And above all things have fervent charity among yourselves; for charity shall cover a multitude of sins" (1 Peter 4:8). Without charity, the other attributes may become self-serving, like "a sounding brass or tinkling cymbal" (1 Corinthians 13:1). Charity, or the pure love of Christ, is the defining characteristic of a disciple of Christ, and helps us emulate the life He led.

Mormon's later description of charity incorporates many of the divine attributes described by Alma and Peter: "Charity suffereth long [*patience*], and is kind [*kindness*], and envieth not, and is not puffed up [*humility*], seeketh not her own [*temperance*], is not easily provoked [*submissiveness*], thinketh no evil [*purity*], and rejoiceth not in iniquity [*godliness*] but rejoiceth in the truth [*knowledge*], beareth all things [*patience*], believeth all things [*faith*], hopeth all things, endureth all things [*patience*]" (Moroni 7:45; see 1 Cor. 13:4-7).

(See "Charity" in Topical Index, Moroni 7).

Elder Neal A. Maxwell observed: "Three . . . clusters of scriptures stress these towering qualities. (See Alma 7:23; Alma 13:28; D&C 121:41-42). Stunningly parallel, they form an almost seamless litany of attributes to be developed. . . . This repeated clustering is too striking to be random." (Conf. Report, Apr. 1985). Divine attributes are identified in several scriptural passages.

Alma's Divine Attributes – Scriptural Cross-Reference

Alma 7:23 Duty to God	2 Peter 1:4-8 Divine nature	Mosiah 4:11-16 Disciples	Alma 38:10-13 Teachers	Alma 13:28-29 Church members	Moroni 7:45 All/Charity
Humility	X	X	X	X	X
Submissiveness		X		X	X
Gentleness	X	X	X		
Patience	X		X	X	X
Long-suffering	X	X		X	X
Temperance	X		X		X
Diligence	X		X		
Obedience	X	X	X	X	
Prayer (Ask)	X	X	X	X	
Knowledge	X	X	X		X
Faith	X	X		X	X
Hope				X	X
Charity/Love	X	X	X	X	X
Purity/Virtue	X		X		X

These are also the qualities that "qualify" us to represent the Savior in missionary work. "And faith, hope, charity and love . . . qualify him for the work. Remember faith, virtue, knowledge, temperance, patience, brotherly kindness, godliness, charity, humility, diligence" (D&C 4:5-6). (See Monson, Conf. Report, Oct. 2007). And, they are the hallmarks of priesthood power. "No power or influence can or ought to be maintained by virtue of the priesthood, only by persuasion, by long-suffering, by gentleness and meekness, and by love unfeigned; By kindness, and pure knowledge . . . without hypocrisy, and without guile. . . . Let thy bowels also be full of charity towards all men . . . and let virtue garnish thy thoughts unceasingly; then shall thy confidence wax strong in the presence of God; and the doctrine of the priesthood shall distill upon thy soul as the dews from heaven" (D&C 121:41-42, 45).

These are the characteristics of Jesus Christ, who provided the pattern for all divine attributes. President Dieter F. Uchtdorf observed: "To follow Christ is to become more like Him. It is to learn from His character. As spirit children of our Heavenly Father, we do have the potential to incorporate Christlike attributes into our life and character. . . . The scriptures describe a number of Christlike attributes we need to develop during the course of our lives. They include knowledge and humility, charity and love, obedience and diligence, faith and hope." (Conf. Report, Oct. 2005).

President David O. McKay testified, "We need only to go to the Man of Nazareth and in him find embodied all virtues that go to make the perfect man. The virtues that combined to make this perfect character are truth, justice, wisdom, benevolence, and self-control. His every thought, word, and deed were in harmony and with divine law and, therefore, true. . . . Members of The Church of Jesus Christ of Latter-Day Saints are under obligation to make the sinless Son of Man their ideal – the One Perfect Being who ever walked the earth." (McKay, Conf. Report, Apr. 1968). "Disciples live so that the characteristics of Christ are woven into the fiber of their beings, as into a spiritual tapestry." (Hales, Conf. Report, April 2007).

As Peter put it, simply, the Lord "went about doing good" (Acts 10:38). The stated goal of Christ's teachings is that we also "do good." After his comprehensive review of the doctrine of Christ, Nephi says: "believe in these words, for they are the words of Christ . . . and they teach all men that they should do good" (2 Nephi 33:10, *emphasis added*).

The path to perfection requires change, as we shed proclivities of the natural man, and acquire Christlike attributes. "As we come unto Christ, we must surrender our worldly ways, our pride, and our selfishness." (Wood, Conf. Report, Apr. 1993). Elder David A. Bednar observed, "We are instructed to 'come unto Christ, and be perfected in him, and deny [ourselves] of all ungodliness' (Moroni 10:32), to become 'new creature[s] in Christ (2 Cor. 5:17), to put off 'the natural man' (Mosiah 3:19) . . . a fundamental change of what we feel and desire, what we think and do, and what we are." (Conf. Report, Apr. 2007). We can use the example and analogy of modifications in the attributes of micro-organisms through biotechnology to illustrate this change.

A Biotechnology Analogy: Developing Divine Attributes through Spiritual Engineering

In biotechnology, scientists modify the genes of an organism to highlight certain characteristics and achieve desired attributes, while purging others. Through genetic engineering, the organism is modified to produce useful products. One example is the modification of a base strain of microalgae to produce a structured fat that mimics the characteristics of cocoa butter. In this example, the genes in the base strain of the organism are either expressed (increased) or regressed (decreased) so that the attributes of the microalgae will be changed to match the "good" and "perfect" attributes of cocoa butter, and demonstrate the sought-after qualities of chocolate. These attributes include matching the flavor profile and controlling the melting point, which allows the product to remain in a solid form until it reaches a certain temperature, and then melt quickly – the "melt in your mouth" aspect of chocolate, symbolizing one characteristic of cocoa culinary "goodness."

For example, the original, microalgae base strain has certain characteristics. These are determined by the amount and proportion of fatty acids present, represented by the various lengths of the carbon chains in the base strain, compared to the ideal. For example, the initial microalgae may have a fatty acid profile of:

    25% comprised of C-16, palmitic acid

    5% comprised of C-18:0, stearic acid

    60% comprised of C-18:1, oleic acid

    10% comprised of C-18:2, linoleic acid

In order to achieve the ideal, a "perfect" structured fat target profile of cocoa butter, these percentages need to be altered to:

    30% comprised of C-16, palmitic acid

    35% comprised of C-18:0, stearic acid

    30% comprised of C-18:1, oleic acid

    5% comprised of C-18:2, linoleic acid

Base Strain Characteristic	Cocoa Butter – the "ideal"	Desired Result from Gene Modification
C-16 = 25%	C-16 = 30%	Express / Increase
C-18:0 = 5%	C-18:0 = 35%	Express / Increase
C-18:1 = 60%	C-18:1 = 30%	Regress / Decrease
C-18:2 = 10%	C-18:2 = 5%	Regress / Decrease

In this simplified example, the genes of the base strain are modified, either expressed or regressed, so the desired attributes and composition are attained. Certain attributes are increased, and certain attributes are decreased, so that the end result will be a "perfect" mimetic of cocoa butter – the ideal in this case. The microalgae has undergone a change that enables it to match the attributes of the "perfect" ideal.

Similarly, we all have certain attributes in our personal characters. We need to express (or increase/adopt/improve) the characteristics ("spiritual genes") that increase our Christ-like attributes such as charity, kindness, humility, knowledge, etc. And, we need to regress (or decrease/eliminate) the characteristics of the natural man: pride, selfishness, envy, anger, etc.

Characteristics	Modification
Kindness	Express/Increase
Charity	Express/Increase
Selfishness	Regress/Decrease
Pride	Regress/Decrease

Spiritual "genetic engineering" can thus transform characteristics of the natural man to attributes of the "man or woman of Christ." Our ultimate goal is to "match" the target, the perfect profile of our Lord, our Exemplar, Jesus Christ. And it is God, the master scientist, who knows perfectly which of our own personal proclivities need to be increased and which need to be decreased. "Know ye not that ye are in the hands of God" (Mormon 5:23).

This transformation may involve modifications not only to our preferences and proclivities, but also to our basic personalities. "Developing Christlike attributes can be a painful process. We need to be ready to accept direction and correction from the Lord and His servants." (Uchtdorf, Conf. Report, Oct. 2005). Elder Neal A. Maxwell may have been alluding to this type of change in his counsel to be submissive to the "shaping of the Lord" which changes what he calls our own "genetic endowment." He taught: "one's genetic endowment offers opportunity to be a careful steward. The submissive soul will be led aright . . . we need to break free of our old selves – the provincial, constraining, and complaining selves – and become susceptible to the shaping of the Lord." (Conf. Report, Apr. 1970).

This shaping, or character modification, can occur over time through the impact of various influences: "[O]ne's development need not be dramatic or tied to a single moment; it can occur steadily in seemingly ordinary, daily settings. If we are meek, a rich and needed insight can be contained in reproof. A new calling can beckon us away from comfortable routine and from competencies already acquired. One may be stripped of accustomed luxury in order that the malignant mole of materialism be removed. One may feel humiliated in order that pride be chipped away. The shaping goes on, and it is anything but merely cosmetic." (Maxwell, Conf. Report, Apr. 1970).

Our submissiveness to the Lord's shaping is a necessary element in this process. "It is a diligent, devoted effort on our part that calls forth his empowering and enabling grace, an effort that certainly includes submission to God's chastening hand and sincere, unqualified repentance." (Christofferson, Conf. Report, Apr. 2011).

"Any thought, activity or action that is compatible with the name, the life, or the teachings of Jesus Christ is acceptable. Any behavior that is not compatible with his name, his life, or his teachings is not acceptable and should be avoided." (Wood, Conf. Report, Apr. 1993). Elder Keith B. McMullin counseled: "Make a mental list of those things you know you ought not to be doing. Stop doing today at least one such thing, and replace it with what you ought to do." (Conf. Report, Apr. 1999). Although we are unlikely to achieve total spiritual and physical perfection in this life, we should strive to attain the divine attributes of perfection.

President David O. McKay taught that "the mission of the gospel of Jesus Christ [is] to make evil-minded men and women good, and to make good men and women better; in other words, to change men's lives, to change human nature. Beverly Nicols . . . author of The Fool Hath Said, writes impressively on changing human nature: 'You can change human nature. No man who has felt in him the Spirit of Christ, even for half a minute, can deny this truth, the one great truth. . . . You change human nature, your own human nature, if you surrender it to him.'" (Conf. Report, Oct. 1958). We change both through our own efforts, and the corrective guidance of the Lord. Over time, we can decrease the characteristics of the natural man, and increase the divine attributes of Christ. In Moroni's words, we need to "deny [our]selves of all ungodliness" and become "perfect in Christ" (Moroni 10:32).

Discourse 14: Amulek, "Resurrection" (Alma 10-11)

Prophet	Key Doctrines	Scriptures	Audience	Date
Amulek	• Resurrection: the spirit and body shall be reunited in its perfect form	Alma 10-11	To the people in the land of Ammonihah	About 82 B.C.

INTRODUCTION

After teaching the members of the church in Gideon "many things" (Alma 8:1), Alma returned to his home in Zarahemla. The following year, Alma taught the people in the land of Melek and "baptized [people] throughout all the land" (Alma 8:5). When he "finished in his work at Melek . . . he traveled three days' journey . . . to a city which was called Ammonihah" (Alma 8:5).[50]

Unfortunately, Alma's initial attempt to preach in the city of Ammonihah was unsuccessful. "Satan had gotten great hold upon the hearts of the people . . . therefore they would not hearken unto the words of Alma" (Alma 8:9). The people "reviled him, and spit upon him, and caused that he should be cast out of their city" (Alma 8:13). Alma leaves the city discouraged and "weighed down with sorrow" (Alma 8:14); however, an angel appears to him and instructs him to return. This is the same angel who first visited Alma and called him to repent. (Alma 8:15).

The angel blesses Alma for being faithful in keeping the commandments since that time, and tells him to "lift up thy head and rejoice" (Alma 8:15). Alma "returns speedily" to Ammonihah, and meets a man named Amulek, who welcomes Alma to his house. Alma stays "many days" with Amulek and teaches his family. Thereafter, Alma is commanded to take Amulek and preach again to the people. Alma "boldly testifies" of the wickedness of the people, and commands them to repent or they will be cut off from the Lord. The people contend with Alma, and are angry with him, but then Amulek begins to preach to them, and they are "astonished, seeing there was more than one witness who testified of the things whereof they were accused, and also of the things which were to come." (Alma 10:12).

The Book of Alma, chapters 10 and 11, contains Amulek's teachings. In his discourse, Amulek relates his conversion process, and tells how he has been taught and blessed by his missionary companion, the prophet Alma. Amulek was a popular man in Ammonihah, with "many kindreds and friends," and wealthy – he had "acquired much riches by the hand of my industry" (Alma 10:4). However, until he met Alma, he was not faithful in the church. He had been "called many times and would not hear" (Alma 10:6), and had "rebelled against God" until "an angel of the Lord" appeared to him, and told him to host "a prophet of the Lord" in his house. (Alma 10:7). Amulek met Alma and brought him to his home, where Alma taught and blessed Amulek's family. (Alma 10:11).

---

[50] There are no recorded discourses or other details about Alma's teachings in the land of Melek.

Amulek testifies to the people of Ammonihah about the truthfulness of Alma's words. He commands them to "repent, for the kingdom of heaven is at hand" (Alma 10:20). He is challenged by several Ammonihah lawyers, particularly by the lawyer, Zeezrom, who, perhaps knowing of Amulek's financial success in the past, offers him sums of money to deny the existence of God. Amulek refuses the payment, and testifies boldly of Christ. He instructs the people that salvation from sin only comes through Jesus Christ. He also teaches the people about the resurrection, that through the Atonement, <u>all</u> mankind will be resurrected and stand before God "to be judged according to their works" (Alma 11:44).

DISCOURSE: Alma 10:1-11; 17-27; Alma 11:22-46

KEY DOCTRINES

- **Resurrection**. The physical resurrection is universal: "all shall rise from the dead" (Alma 11:41). The spirit and the body shall be reunited again in its perfect form. (Alma 11:43-44). See: 2 Nephi 9; Mosiah 13-15; Alma 39-42.

COMMENTARY

Resurrection Is Universal

Amulek teaches the people of Ammonihah that because of Christ, all mankind "shall rise from the dead and stand before God and be judged according to their works" (Alma 11:41). The literal and universal nature of the resurrection is vividly described by Amulek: "Christ shall loose the bands of this temporal death, that ***all*** shall be raised from temporal death. . . . Now, this restoration shall come to all, both old and young, both bond and free, both male and female, both the wicked and righteous" (Alma 11:42-44, *emphasis added*).

Resurrection is a foundational doctrine in the restored gospel. "The Resurrection is at the core of our beliefs as Christians. Without it, our faith is meaningless. The Apostle Paul said, 'If Christ be not risen, then is our preaching vain, and [our] faith is also vain.'" (Wirthlin, Conf. Report, Oct. 2006). Joseph Smith declared: "The fundamental principles of our religion are the testimony of the Apostles and Prophets, concerning Jesus Christ, that He died, was buried, and rose again the third day, and ascended into heaven; and all other things which pertain to our religion are only appendages to it." (Teachings of the Prophet Joseph Smith, 121, *quoted in* Oaks, Conf. Report, Apr. 2000).

Resurrection is universal: "The Lamb of God hath brought to pass the resurrection, so that *all* shall rise from the dead." (Teachings of the Prophet Joseph Smith, 367). "As in Adam all die, even so in Christ shall *all* be made alive" (1 Cor. 15:22, *emphasis added*). Elder Milton R. Hunter said that the resurrection is Christ's gift to all: Jesus Christ "set into operation the law of resurrection and thereby gave as a free gift to every man, woman, and child, resurrection, or, in other words, immortality. Thus we will all, the wicked as well as the righteous, enjoy immortality." (Conf. Report, Apr. 1949). President James E. Faust testified: "He [Christ] was able to redeem from physical death the believers and the obedient as well as the unbelieving and disobedient. Every person born or yet to be born is the beneficiary of . . . the atonement of the Savior. . . . Through the grace of Jesus Christ, immortality comes to all men, just or unjust, righteous or wicked." (Conf. Report, Oct. 1988).

"The Savior's Redemption has two parts," taught Elder D. Todd Christofferson. "First, it atones for Adam's transgression and the consequent Fall of man by overcoming what could be called the direct effects of the fall – physical and spiritual death. Physical death is well understood . . . In the words of Paul, 'For as in Adam all die, even so in Christ shall all be made alive' (1 Cor. 15:22). This redemption from physical death is both universal and without condition." (Conf. Report, Apr. 2013). By the redemption of Christ, all overcome physical death and are resurrected to immortality, to come back before the Lord to be judged. "As I have been lifted up by men even so men be lifted up by the Father, to stand before me, to be judged of their works" (3 Nephi 27:14).

Resurrection Is a Restoration: Appearance and Attributes of a Resurrected Body

Amulek taught that in the resurrection, "the spirit and the body shall be reunited again in its perfect form; both limb and joint shall be restored to its proper frame . . . not so much as a hair of their heads be lost; but everything shall be restored to its perfect frame" (Alma 11:43-44). "Each of us has physical, mental, and emotional limitations and weaknesses. These challenges, some of which seem so intractable now, will eventually be resolved. None of these problems will plague us after we are resurrected." (Elder Paul V. Johnson, Conf. Report, Apr. 2016).

President Spencer W. Kimball taught: "I am sure that if we can imagine ourselves at our very best, physically, mentally, spiritually, that is the way we will come back. Can you imagine that? Life at our prime? Never sick, never in pain, never burdened by the ills that so often beset us in mortality" (*quoted in* Wirthlin, Conf. Report, Oct. 2006). Elder Sterling W. Still described a resurrected body as "beautiful beyond all comprehension, with quickened senses, amplified powers of perception, and vastly increased capacity for love, understanding, and happiness." (Conf. Report, Oct. 1976). Joseph Smith added that, "the glorious spirit gives [resurrected beings] the likeness of glory and bloom; [we] . . . will glory in beauty. No man can describe it to you – no man can write it." (Teachings of the Prophet Joseph Smith, 368).

On a lighter note, Elder Orson Pratt observed: "Many persons, when they advance in years, lose their hair and become baldheaded. Will they rise in the resurrection without hair, because they have been laid in the grave in that condition? No, that would be imperfection, and we have a statement in the Book of Mormon that not so much as one hair shall be lost." (Journal of Discourses, 16:326). A comforting thought for many of us.

President Joseph Fielding Smith explained: "There is no reason for any person to be concerned as to the appearance of individuals in the resurrection. Death is a purifying process as far as the body is concerned. We have reason to believe that the appearance of old age will disappear and the body will be restored with the full vigor of manhood and womanhood." (Smith, Answers to Gospel Questions, 4:185). "Deformity will be removed; defects will be eliminated, and men and women shall attain to the perfection of their spirits, to the perfection God designed in the beginning." (Smith, Gospel Doctrine, p. 23).

"What a comfort to know that all who have been disadvantaged in life from birth defects, from mortal injuries, from disease, or from the natural deterioration of old age will be resurrected in 'proper and perfect frame.'" (Oaks, Conf. Report, Apr. 2000). "Every fundamental part of every body will be restored to its proper place again in the resurrection, no matter what may become of the body in death. If it be burned by fire, eaten by sharks, no matter what. Every fundamental part of it will be restored to its *own proper place*." (Smith, Answers to Gospel Questions, 5:103).

President Joseph F. Smith taught that "there will be a restoration effected; every organ, every limb that has been maimed, every deformity caused by accident or in any other way, will be restored and put right. Every limb and joint shall be restored to its proper frame." (Journal of Discourses, 24:75). "The Resurrection is brought to pass by the Atonement of Jesus Christ and is pivotal to the great plan of salvation. . . . When we come to this earth life, our spirit is united with our body. We experience all the joys and challenges associated with mortal life. When a person dies, their spirit is separated from their body. Resurrection makes it possible for a person's spirit and body to be united again, only this time that body will be immortal and perfect – not subject to pain, disease, or other problems." (Johnson, Conf. Report, Apr. 2016).

Elder Dallin H. Oaks testified: "Many living witnesses can testify to the literal fulfillment of these scriptural assurances of the resurrection. Many, including some in my own extended family, have seen a departed loved one in vision or personal appearance and have witnessed their restoration in 'proper and perfect frame' in the prime of life. Whether these were manifestations of persons already resurrected or of righteous spirits awaiting an assured resurrection, the reality and nature of the resurrection of mortals is evident." (Conf. Report, Apr. 2000).

There appears to be one exception to a full restoration of the body to its perfect form. Elder Tad R. Callister explained, "In his resurrected state, Jesus retained the prints of nails in his hands and feet as a special manifestation to the world. Such marks, however, are only temporary. After all have confessed that he is the Christ, his resurrected body will, like those of all mankind, be restored to its 'proper and perfect frame.'" Encyclopedia of Mormonism, 2:734.

A resurrected body does not have blood.
President Russell M. Nelson taught: "Our physical frames, now subject to disease, death, and decay, will acquire immortal glory. Presently sustained by the blood of life, and ever aging, our bodies will be sustained by spirit and become changeless and beyond the bounds of death. A resurrection means to become immortal, without blood, yet with a body of flesh and bone." (Conf. Report, Oct. 1995).

President Brigham Young instructed: "when he [Christ] was resurrected, another element took the place of the blood. It will be so with every person who receives a resurrection: the blood will not be resurrected with the body, being designed only to sustain the life of the present organization." (Journal of Discourses, 7:160). "The resurrection will again unite the spirit with the body, and the body becomes a spiritual body, one of flesh and bones but quickened by the spirit instead of blood." (Hunter, Conf. Report, Apr. 1969). Joseph Smith taught: "As concerning the resurrection I will merely say that . . . all will be raised by the power of God, having spirit in their bodies, and not blood" (Teachings of the Prophet Joseph Smith, 199-200).

We don't know precisely how the resurrection will be accomplished. We don't know the details, the biology or the physical science of the resurrection. In discussing the miracle of the resurrection, President Nelson taught: "The miracle of the resurrection is matched only by the miracle of the creation. No one knows precisely how two gene cells unite to make one. Nor do we know how that resulting cell multiplies and divides to make others – some to become eyes that see, ears that hear or fingers that feel. . . . This process of regeneration and renewal is but prelude to the promised phenomenon and future fact of our resurrection." (Conf. Report, Apr. 1987).

Elder Orson Pratt said: "I do not believe that every particle [referring to 'familiar elements such as hydrogen, oxygen, carbon'] that is ever incorporated in the systems of human creatures will be resurrected with them, I have no such idea. But a sufficient amount of the particles which have once been incorporated in the system will be used by the Almighty in the resurrection to make perfect and complete tabernacles for celestial spirits to dwell in." (Journal of Discourses, 16:353). "The Lord who created us in the first place surely has power to do it again. The same necessary elements now in our bodies will still be available – at His command. The same unique genetic code now embedded in each of our living cells will still be available to format new ones then. The miracle of the resurrection [will be] wondrous." (Nelson, Conf. Report, Apr. 1992).

Capabilities of a resurrected body.

From the scriptural records, we know a resurrected body is tangible, comprised of elements, described as flesh and bone. We also know from the record of witnesses that the resurrected Christ was able to eat – at least fish and honey -- perhaps other things. We also learn that a resurrected body can operate outside of our current understanding of physical laws. After his resurrection, Jesus appeared to his disciples in a closed and locked room – moving freely through physical objects -- and visibly descended from and ascended into the sky. Evidently, there is a much greater ability to control the matter that comprises a resurrected body than the matter comprising our earthly bodies.

President Joseph Fielding Smith taught: "Resurrected bodies pass through solid objects. Resurrected bodies have control over the elements. … When the Angel Moroni appeared to Joseph Smith, the Prophet saw him apparently come down and ascend through the solid walls or ceiling of the building. … It was just as easy for the Angel Moroni to come to the Prophet Joseph Smith through the building as it was for our Savior to appear to his disciples after his resurrection in the room where they were assembled when the door was closed. … How could he do it? He had power over the elements." (Doctrines of Salvation, 2:288).

The scriptures affirm:

- A resurrected body can eat (broiled fish and honeycomb) (Luke 24: 42-43).
- A resurrected body can ascend into and descend from the sky (3 Nephi 11:8).
- A resurrected body can pass through solid objects (John 20:19; JSH 1:30, 43).
- The knowledge and intelligence we gain on earth "will rise with us in the resurrection" (D&C 130: 18-19).
- A resurrected body shall have a perfect knowledge (2 Nephi 9:14).
- Spirits of the dead look upon separation from the body as bondage (D&C 138: 12-17).
- Without the reuniting of our spirits and bodies in the resurrection, we cannot receive a "fullness of joy" (D&C 93:33-34).

Knowledge of the Resurrection Provides Comfort and Hope

The knowledge of a resurrection provides several blessings, including: (i) Hope to overcome physical and other deficiencies when we receive a perfected body; (ii) Incentive to keep the commandments in mortality since we will be accountable in the afterlife; (iii) Courage to face our own death; and (iv) Comfort in the face of a mortal separation from loved ones who have died.

Elder Dallin H. Oaks taught: "The assurance of resurrection gives us the strength and perspective to endure the mortal challenges faced by each of us and by those we love, such things as the physical, mental, or emotional deficiencies we bring with us at birth or acquire during mortal life. Because of the resurrection, we know that these mortal deficiencies are only temporary! The assurance of the resurrection also gives us a powerful incentive to keep the commandments of God during our mortal lives. . . . Our sure knowledge of a resurrection to immortality also gives us the courage to face our own death – even a death that we might call premature. . . . The assurance of immortality also helps us bear the mortal separations involved in the death of our loved ones. . . . [T]he assured resurrection makes our mortal separations temporary and gives us the hope and strength to carry on." (Conf. Report, Apr. 2000).

Elder Paul V. Johnson affirmed: "The reality of the Resurrection of the Savior overwhelms our heartbreak with hope. . . . We know that He can make us whole no matter what is broken in us. We know that He 'shall wipe away all tears from [our] eyes; and there shall be no more death, neither sorrow, nor crying, neither shall there be any more pain.' (Revelations 21:4)." (Conf. Report, Apr. 2016).

President Russell M. Nelson testified: "Gratefully and positively, I affirm that there is life after life, first in the spirit world and then in the Resurrection, for each and every one of us. I know that God lives and that Jesus the Christ is His Son. He is 'the resurrection and the life.' (John 11:25). He lives." (Conf. Report, Apr. 1987).

Discourse 15: Alma, "Probationary State; High Priesthood" (Alma 12-13)

Prophet	Key Doctrines	Scriptures	Audience	Date
Alma	• Life Is a Probationary State • Melchizedek Priesthood; Foreordination	Alma 12-13	To the people in the city of Ammonihah, particularly to Zeezrom and to Antoniah, a chief ruler.	About 82 B.C.

INTRODUCTION

Alma's discourse in the Book of Alma, chapters 12 and 13, is a continuation of Amulek's sermon in chapter 11. "Now Alma, seeing that the words of Amulek had silenced Zeezrom . . . he opened his mouth and began to speak unto him, and to establish the words of Amulek, and to explain things beyond, or to unfold the scriptures beyond that which Amulek had done. Now the words that Alma spake unto Zeezrom were heard by the people round about [in the city of Ammonihah]; for the multitude was great" (Alma 12:1-2).

After Amulek contended with Zeezrom, Alma began to "establish the words of Amulek . . . to unfold the scriptures beyond that which Amulek had done" (Alma 12:1). Alma taught the people of Ammonihah basic truths about the plan of salvation. He testified that our Heavenly Father, knowing that we would fall into transgression, prepared a way for us to be redeemed and live with Him forever. Alma explains that the plan includes not only the blessing of resurrection, but also "a space granted unto man in which he might repent; therefore this life became a probationary state; a time to prepare to meet God" (Alma 12:24).[51]

DISCOURSE: Alma 12-13

KEY DOCTRINES

- **Life Is a 'Probationary State'** a time to prepare to meet God. (Alma 12:24).
    - We will be held accountable before God for our thoughts, words, and actions. (Alma 12:14).
    - Do not procrastinate repentance. (Alma 13:27).

- **The High Priesthood.** High Priests are ordained after the order of the Son of God.
    - Melchizedek was an example of a great high priest.
    - Foreordination: many priesthood leaders were "called and prepared from the foundation of the world" (Alma 13:3).

---

[51] The term "probationary state" is a phrase used only by Alma in the Book of Mormon.

COMMENTARY

Life is a Probationary State

Alma teaches the people of Ammonihah that life is a "probationary state," during which God "gave commandments unto men," to allow them to demonstrate "according to their wills and pleasures whether to do evil or to do good" (Alma 12:31). During this time of probation, God told men: "If ye will repent, and harden not your hearts, then will I have mercy upon you, through mine only begotten Son; [t]herefore, whosoever repenteth and hardeneth not his heart, he shall have claim on mercy through mine Only Begotten Son unto a remission of his sins; and these shall enter into my rest" (Alma 12:33-34).

(See "Plan of Salvation" in Topical Index, 2 Nephi 2).

What God has done . . .	What we must do . . .
Granted time to repent in this life, as a "probationary state" (Alma 12:24)	Repent and prepare to meet God (Alma 12:24)
Provided for the resurrection of the dead that we might overcome temporal death (Alma 12:25)	Call on God; demonstrate faith, repentance and holy works (Alma 12:30)
Sent angels to teach men (Alma 12:29)	Do not harden our hearts (Alma 12:34)
Conversed with men, and taught them the plan of redemption (Alma 12:28, 30)	Choose to "do good" (Alma 12:31)
Gave commandments to men (Alma 12:32)	Keep the commandments of God (Alma 12:31)
Promised mercy, through His Son, to men [and women] who will repent and not harden their hearts (Alma 12:33)	Repent (Alma 12:33,34,37)

Note that God gave His children commandments "*after* having made known unto them the plan of redemption" (Alma 12:32). "The sequence in the teaching process from this verse is that our Heavenly Father first taught Adam and Eve the plan of redemption; then He gave them commandments. All commandments have their eternal importance in the context of the great plan of [redemption]. . . . If we can help people first understand the plan, they will find a deeper and more permanent motivation to keep the commandments. . . . When we understand the great plan of [redemption], we are gaining an eternal perspective, and the commandments, ordinances, covenants, and the experiences, trials, and tribulations can be seen in their true and eternal light." (Jensen, Conf. Report, Apr. 2000).

Elder Boyd K. Packer taught: "Young people wonder 'why?' – Why are we commanded to do some things, and why we are commanded not to do other things? A knowledge of the plan of happiness, even in outline form, can give your minds a 'why' . . . Most of the difficult questions we face in the Church right now . . . cannot be answered without some knowledge of the plan as a background. Alma said this, and this is, I think of late, my favorite scripture, although I change now and again: 'God gave unto them *commandments, after* having made known unto them the *plan of redemption*' (Alma 12:32) . . . If you are trying to give a 'why,' follow that pattern." ("The Great Plan of Happiness," CES, Aug. 10, 1993).

Judgment Based on What We Have Become

Alma declared that all men, women and children who come into the world will eventually be "brought before the bar of God, to be judged according to our works" (Alma 12:12). If we have lived wicked lives in mortality and not repented, in the final judgment, not only will our actions condemn us, but "our words will condemn us . . . and our thoughts will also condemn us" (Alma 12:14). This teaching echoes the warning of King Benjamin: "if ye do not watch yourselves, and your thoughts, and your words, and your deeds . . . even unto the end of your lives, ye must perish" (Mosiah 4:30); (See "Natural Man").

"Alma was preaching this doctrine [of resurrection and judgment] . . . to his people. He explained to them that every man, woman and child, 'both bond and free . . . both the wicked and the righteous' (11:44), would be resurrected and required to stand before the judgment seat of God. There they would be held accountable for the lives they lived in mortality, for every act they committed, for every word they spoke, and for every thought that they thought. . . . 'For our words will condemn us, yea, all our works will condemn us; we shall not be found spotless; and our thoughts will condemn us.' (Alma 12:14). (Hunter, Conf. Report, Apr. 1949).

(See "Judgment" in Topical Index, Alma 41-42).

Spiritual Death

The people in Ammonihah, however, were unrepentant, and had "hardened their hearts" against the Lord. Alma warned that if they did not repent, they would be condemned by their actions, words, and thoughts, and suffer a "spiritual death," which is a "second death." This spiritual death is the fate of the unrepentant, who receive great blessings, have knowledge of the truth, but reject such light and knowledge, and die in their sins. (Alma 9:19-23; 12:16).

"Alma explained that God would divide the people into two groups. He would look upon the members of one group and smile. They are the righteous. He would proclaim to them that they could enter into his presence. Great would be their joy. And then he would look upon those who composed the other group, and they would be so ashamed because of the lives they had lived in mortality that they would cry to the mountains to come down and hide them from the presence of God." (Hunter, Conf. Report, Apr. 1949). President Russell M. Nelson taught: "But there is another type of separation known in scripture as spiritual death. It 'is defined as a state of spiritual alienation from God.'" (Conf. Report, Apr. 1992).

Alma summarized the state of those who suffer spiritual death:

- Their state will be awful (Alma 12:13)
- They will not dare to look upon God, and would "be glad" if the "rocks and the mountains" could "fall upon us to hide us from his presence" (Alma 12:14)
- They must acknowledge the judgments of God are just (Alma 12:15)
- Their torment shall be "as a lake of fire and brimstone" (Alma 12:17)
- They will be subject to the power and captivity of Satan (Alma 12:17)
- They shall be as though there had been no redemption made (Alma 12:18)

In describing the judgment of the wicked, King Benjamin said that those who are evil will be "consigned to an awful view of their own guilt and abominations, which doth cause them to shrink from the presence of the Lord into a state of misery and endless torment" (Mosiah 3:25). Alma describes this torment "as a lake of fire and brimstone" (Alma 12:17). "The torment of disappointment in the mind of man is as exquisite as a lake burning with fire and brimstone.' That lake of fire and brimstone . . . is the description in the scriptures for hell." (Packer, Conf. Report, Apr. 2001).

Modern day prophets and revelations indicate that there may still be a possibility (although extremely difficult) to repent after death, and that an eternal spiritual death only occurs with the sons of perdition. (D&C 76:31-38). "But, thanks be to the Eternal Father, through the merciful provisions of the Gospel all mankind will have the opportunity of escape or deliverance from this spiritual death either in time or eternity," taught President Joseph F. Smith, through faith in Christ, "in connection with repentance and obedience to the ordinances of the Gospel." (Journal of Discourses, 23:169-170).

"All mankind will receive general salvation, excepting the sons of perdition. . . . These sons of perdition (perhaps only a few in number) will be resurrected but will not be redeemed from the power of Satan because they are still filthy; as the prophet Alma said of them: 'they shall be as though there had been no redemption made.'" (Conf. Report, Apr. 1972). This does not mean, however, that we should wait to repent after we die. "Although we are taught that some repentance can occur in the spirit world (see D&C 138:31, 33, 58), that is not as certain. Elder Marvin J. Ballard taught: 'It is much easier to overcome and serve the Lord when both flesh and spirit are combined as one. This is the time when men are more pliable and susceptible. . . . This life is the time to repent.'" (Oaks, Conf. Report, Apr. 2019).

Alma warns the people of Ammonihah, "with great anxiety . . . that ye would hearken unto my words, and cast off your sins, and not procrastinate the day of your repentance" (Alma 13:27). (See Alma 34:32-33). He admonishes them: Do not procrastinate until it is too late. Do not continue in wickedness and face judgment in a state of sin. "Our Savior has the power and stands ready to cleanse us from evil. Now is the time to seek His help to repent of our wicked or unseemly desires and thoughts." (Oaks, Conf. Report, Apr. 2019). Do not be resurrected, only to die a spiritual death. Repent now. (See "Procrastinate" in Topical Index, Alma 34).[52]

---

[52] "It is far more difficult to repent in the spirit world of sins which involve physical habits and actions." (Stapley, Conf. Report, Oct. 1977). "According to Oliver B. Huntington, the Prophet Joseph Smith said that 'a man can do as much in this life in one year as he can do in ten years in the spirit world without the body.'" (McConkie, Doctrinal Commentary, 3:256).

Melchizedek Priesthood

When Alma first taught the wicked inhabitants of the city of Ammonihah, they challenged his authority. (Alma 9:1-6). When he returns to teach them the discourse recorded in Alma 12-13, Alma affirms the authority of God, "the high priesthood of the holy order of God" (Alma 13:6). Elder Bruce R. McConkie observed: "The Nephites, who were faithful and true in keeping the law of Moses, had the Melchizedek Priesthood. . . . Some of our best information about the Melchizedek Priesthood is found in Alma 13." (McConkie, The Promised Messiah, 421).

Melchizedek, the Great High Priest

Alma first teaches the people of Ammonihah about the great high priest, Melchizedek, who "exercised mighty faith," and "did preach repentance unto his people" (Alma 13:18). Melchizedek established peace in the land; "therefore he was called the prince of peace" (Alma 13:18). And "none were greater" (Alma 13:19).

We don't know much about this great prophet and high priest. According to the LDS Bible Dictionary, Melchizedek was "a notable prophet and leader who lived about 2000 B.C. He is called the king of Salem (Jerusalem), king of peace, and 'priest of the most High God.'" We know that Abraham paid tithing to Melchizedek (Alma 13:15; Genesis 14:18); and that Melchizedek blessed Abraham (Hebrews 7:1-4; JST, Genesis 14:37, 40). We also understand that "Melchizedek was a man of faith, who wrought righteousness; and when a child he feared God, and stopped the mouths of lions, and quenched the violence of fire" (JST, Genesis 14:26). Perhaps Melchizedek is Paul's unnamed prophet who "wrought righteousness, obtained promises, stopped the mouths of lions, [and] quenched the violence of fire" (Hebrews 11:33-34).

Some have speculated that Shem, the son of Noah, who lived long enough to be a contemporary with the next ten generations, including Abraham, was also Melchizedek. "Many saints and gospel scholars have wondered whether these men were the same person. The truth is, we don't know the answer." (Gygi, "Is It Possible that Shem and Melchizedek are the Same Person?" *Ensign*, Nov. 1973).

What we do know is that "[b]ecause Melchizedek was such a great high priest," the high priesthood is called the Melchizedek priesthood. (D&C 107:2; Hebrews 7:17). Previously, it had been called "*the Holy Priesthood, after the Order of the Son of God*. But out of respect or reverence to the name of the Supreme Being, to avoid the too frequent repetition of his name, they, the church, in ancient days, called that priesthood after Melchizedek" (D&C 107:3, *emphasis added*).

Melchizedek, who called his people to repentance and saved them from the effects of sin, became a type and example of Christ. Alma describes Melchizedek with words and phrases that also describe Christ: *high priest, king, man of mighty faith, preacher of repentance, prince of peace, and a king who reigned under his father*. "Indeed, so exalted and high was the position of Melchizedek in the eyes of the Lord and of his people that he stood as a prototype of the Son of God himself." (McConkie, Mormon Doctrine, 475).

Foreordination

Alma explains that those called to the priesthood were "called and prepared from the foundation of the world according to the foreknowledge of God" (Alma 13:3). To Jeremiah, the Lord said: "Before I formed thee in the belly I knew thee; and before thou camest forth out of the womb I sanctified thee, and I ordained thee a prophet unto the nations" (Jeremiah 1:5). The Prophet Joseph Smith taught: "Every man who has a calling to minister to the inhabitants of the world was ordained to that very purpose in the Grand Council of heaven before the world was." (Teachings of the Prophet Joseph Smith, 365).

Abraham beheld a vision of the pre-mortal world and the host of intelligences organized before the world was: "[A]mong all these . . . were many of the noble and great ones," whom God described as being "good" (Abraham 3:22). "And God saw these souls that they were good, and he stood in the midst of them, and he said: These I will make my rulers . . . and he said unto me: Abraham, thou art one of them; thou wast chosen before thou wast born" (Abraham 3:23).

"As with Abraham," taught Elder Bruce R. McConkie, "so with all the prophets, and for that matter so, to one degree or another, with the whole house of Israel and with all the members of the Lord's earthly church – all are participants in the blessings of foreordination . . . . Our revelations, ancient and modern, abound in pronouncements relative to the law of foreordination . . . as it applies to specific individuals called according to the foreknowledge of God to special labors in mortality. . . . [The Lord] knows the end from the beginning. . . . And he – the Almighty – chooses the prophets and apostles who minister in his name and present his message to the world in every age and dispensation. He selects and foreordains his ministers; he sends them to earth at the times before appointed; he guides and directs their continuing mortal preparations; and he then calls them to those positions they were foreordained to receive from before the foundations of the earth. . . . And hence comes the doctrine of foreordination. When we come into mortality, we bring the talents, capabilities, and abilities acquired by obedience to law in our prior existence." (Conf. Report, Apr. 1974).

"In the premortal spirit world, God appointed certain spirits to fulfill specific missions during their mortal lives. This is called foreordination. Foreordination does not guarantee that individuals will receive certain callings or responsibilities. Such opportunities come in this life as a result of the righteous exercise of agency, just as foreordination came as a result of righteousness in the premortal existence." (True to the Faith, 69). President Spencer W. Kimball taught: "In the world before we came here, faithful women were given certain assignments while faithful men were foreordained to certain priesthood tasks. While we do not now remember the particulars, this does not alter the glorious reality of what we once agreed to." (Conf. Report, Oct. 1979). President J. Reuben Clark said: "I like to think that perhaps in that grand council something at least was said to us indicating what would be expected of us, and empowering us, subject to the re-confirmation here, to do certain things in building up the kingdom of God." (Conf. Report, Oct. 1950).

Elder Neal A. Maxwell observed: "Premortality is not a relaxing doctrine. For each of us, there are choices to be made, incessant and difficult chores to be done, ironies and adversities to be experienced, time to be well spent, talents and gifts to be well employed. Just because we were chosen 'there and then,' surely does not mean we can be indifferent 'here and now.' Whether foreordination for men, or foredesignation for women, those called and prepared must also prove 'chosen and faithful.' In fact, adequacy in the first estate may merely have ensured a stern, second estate with more duties and no immunities." (Conf. Report, Oct. 1985).

High Priesthood Sanctification

Alma teaches that mortal priesthood holders may become ***sanctified*** "through the blood of the Lamb" (Alma 13:11). To be sanctified, high priests must develop "exceeding faith," and must "[choose] to repent and work righteousness" (Alma 13:10). They cannot "look upon sin save it were with abhorrence" (Alma 13:12). They must be "pure and spotless before God" (Alma 13:11-12). Through the Atonement, faithful, righteous priesthood holders may qualify to "enter into the rest of the Lord their God" (Alma 13:12-13, 16). Alma teaches that there were "many, exceedingly great many" high priests who met these standards, who became "sanctified by the Holy Ghost" (Alma 13:12).

This does not mean that these high priests were perfect in mortality or that sanctification in mortality would provide freedom from earthly temptations. President Russell M. Nelson taught: "Alma said that 'there were many, exceedingly great many,' who were pure before the Lord. This does not mean that these people never made mistakes or never had need of correction." (Conf. Report, Oct. 1995). In modern revelation, the Lord warns: "Therefore let the church take heed and pray always, lest they fall into temptation; yea, and *even let those who are sanctified take heed also*" (D&C 20:33-34, *emphasis added*). The principles of agency still apply.

President Brigham Young taught: "I will put my own definition to the term sanctification, and say it consists in overcoming every sin and bringing all into subjection to the law of Christ. God has placed in us a pure spirit; when this reigns predominant . . . and triumphs over the flesh and rules and governs and controls . . . , this I call the blessing of sanctification. Will sin be perfectly destroyed? No, it will not. . . . Do not suppose that we shall ever in the flesh be free from temptations to sin. Some suppose that they can in the flesh be sanctified body and spirit and become so pure that they will never again feel the effects of the power of the adversary of truth. . . . I think we shall more or less feel the effects of sin so long as we live, and finally have to pass the ordeals of death." (Journal of Discourses, 10:170).

Discourse 16: Alma, "Nourish Faith with the Word of God" (Alma 32-33)

Prophet	Key Doctrines	Scriptures	Audience	Date
Alma	• Humility • Nourish Faith with the Word of God	Alma 32-33	To Zoramites in the land of Antionum (at the hill Onidah)	About 74 B.C.

INTRODUCTION

In approximately 74 B.C., Alma learned that a people known as Zoramites, who inhabited a land east of Zarahemla, called Antionum, "were perverting the ways of the Lord" (Alma 31:1). "And now, as the preaching of the word had a great tendency to lead the people to do that which was just – yea, it had had more powerful effect upon the minds of the people than the sword, or anything else – therefore Alma thought it was expedient that they should try the virtue of the word of God [with the Zoramites]. Therefore he took Ammon, and Aaron, and Omner [sons of King Mosiah] . . . and also Amulek and Zeezrom . . . and he also took two of his sons [Shiblon and Corianton]" (Alma 31:5-6). When they arrived in Antionum, Alma and his missionary companions were astonished to find that the Zoramites not only failed to "keep the commandments of God" (Alma 31:9), but "they did worship after a manner which Alma and his brethren had never beheld" (Alma 31:12; see Alma 31:12-23).

Alma found the Zoramites to be a "wicked and perverse people . . . [whose] hearts were lifted up unto great boasting, in their pride" (Alma 31:24-25). Alma and his missionary companions immediately "began to preach the word of God unto the people, entering into their synagogues, and into their houses; yea, and even . . . in their streets. And it came to pass that after much labor among them, they began to have success among the poor class of people" (Alma 32:1-2). At one point, while Alma was "teaching and speaking unto the people upon the hill Onidah, there came a great multitude unto him . . . [who] were poor in heart, because of their poverty" (Alma 31:4). They said to Alma, "[we] are despised of all men because of [our] poverty [and have been] cast out of our synagogues . . . behold, what shall we do?" (Alma 32:4-5). Alma perceived the readiness of these Zoramites to be taught, and he answered their question with a discourse on humility and faith. (See Alma 32:7 – Alma 33:23).

Elder Jeffrey R. Holland wrote: "In [the] brilliant discourse [of Alma 32-33], Alma moves the reader from a general commentary on faith in the seedlike word of God to a focused discourse on faith in Christ as the Word of God, grown to a fruit-bearing tree, a tree whose fruit is exactly that of Lehi's earlier perception of Christ's love. . . . Christ is the seed, the tree, and the fruit of eternal life." (Holland, Christ and the New Covenant, 169).

DISCOURSE: Alma 32-33

KEY DOCTRINES

- **Humility**. Blessed are they who humble themselves, without being compelled to be humble.

- **Faith.** If you have faith, you "hope for things which are not seen, which are true" (Alma 32:21). Belief in Christ is the foundation of faith. We should "plant the word" of faith in Christ – believing that he will redeem his people, atone for our sins, rise from the dead and judge us at the last day – and then "nourish the word" so that it becomes a tree springing up unto everlasting life. (Alma 33:22-23).

COMMENTARY

Humility

Alma identifies two categories of people: (i) those who are "compelled to be humble" (Alma 32:13); and (ii) those who humble themselves voluntarily "because of the word" (Alma 32:14). Alma observes that those who are <u>compelled</u> to be humble are "blessed" as they seek repentance; find mercy; and, endure to the end. (Alma 32:13). Those who <u>voluntarily</u> humble themselves are "much more blessed" (Alma 32:14) when their humility leads them to believe in the word of God, repent and be baptized "without stubbornness of heart" (Alma 32:16). "It is in nurturing humility and submissiveness that we . . . put ourselves in a frame of mind and heart to receive the promptings of the Spirit." (Wickman, Conf. Report, Oct. 2002).

Elder Carlos E. Asay taught: "Most of us seem to have the 'Nephite cycle' as part of our character. There is a point when we are teachable; our humility enables us to grow and to ride the crest of spirituality. Then there are other times when we begin to feel self-sufficient and puffed up with pride. . . . How much better it would be if we were humbled by the word of the Lord and strong enough in spirit to remember our God in whatsoever circumstances we find ourselves." (Asay, <u>Family Pecan Trees</u>, 193-194). Elder Neal A. Maxwell observed: "it is better if we are humbled 'because of the word' rather than being compelled by circumstances, yet the latter may do." (Conf. Report, Oct. 2000). "Blessed are they who humble themselves without being compelled to be humble" (Alma 32:16).

President Ezra Taft Benson put it succinctly: "Let us choose to be humble. We can do it. I know we can." (Conf. Report, Apr. 1989):

- "We can choose to humble ourselves by conquering enmity toward our brothers and sisters, esteeming them as ourselves, and lifting them as high or higher than we are.
- We can choose to be humble by receiving counsel and chastisement.
- We can choose to humble ourselves by forgiving those who have offended us.
- We can choose to be humble ourselves by rendering selfless service.
- We can choose to humble ourselves by going on missions and preaching the word.
- We can choose to humble ourselves by getting to the temple more frequently.
- We can choose to humble ourselves by confessing and forsaking our sins.
- We can choose to humble ourselves by loving God, submitting our will to His, and putting Him first in our lives." (Conf. Report, Apr. 1989).

"Pride is the universal sin, the great vice. . . the great stumbling block to Zion. . . . The antidote for pride is humility." (Benson, Conf. Report, Apr. 1989). (See "Pride" in Jacob 2).

President Spencer W. Kimball taught: "Humility is meekness. . . . (although one can be bold and meek at the same time). . . . Humility is not pretentious or proud . . . . Humility is teachableness – an ability to realize that all virtues and abilities are not concentrated in one's self. . . . Humility is gracious, quiet, serene . . . . It never struts or swaggers. . . Humility is never accusing nor contentious. . . . It is not boastful . . . . Humility is repentant and seeks not to justify its follies. It is forgiving of others in the realization that there may be errors of the same kind or worse chalked up against itself. . . . Humility makes no bid for popularity and notoriety; demands no honors. . . . [However,] It is not self-abasement – the hiding in the corner, the devaluation of everything he does or thinks or says; but it is the doing of one's best in every case and leaving one's acts, expressions, and accomplishments to largely speak for themselves." ("Humility," BYU Devotional, Jan. 16, 1963).

Faith: Hope for Things Which Are Not Seen, Which Are True

Humility prepares one to receive the word of God, and to develop faith. Alma teaches that "faith is not to have a perfect knowledge of things; therefore if ye have faith ye hope for things which are not seen, which are true" (Alma 32:21). In Paul's words: "Now faith is the substance of things hoped for, the evidence of things not seen" (Hebrews 11:1). (See also 2 Nephi 31-32, Mormon 8-9, Moroni 7).

Elder Boyd K. Packer wrote: "Faith, to be faith, must go beyond that for which there is confirming evidence. Faith, to be faith, must go into the unknown. Faith, to be faith, must walk to the edge of the light and then a few steps into the darkness. . . . In a world filled with skepticism and doubt, the expression 'seeing is believing' promotes the attitude, 'You show me, and I will believe.' We want all of the proof and all of the evidence first. . . . When will we learn that in spiritual things it works the other way about – that believing is seeing? Spiritual belief precedes spiritual knowledge. When we believe in things that are not seen but are nevertheless true, then we have faith." (Packer, Faith, 42-43). President Howard W. Hunter taught that "faith becomes the first step in any action and must be the first step in understanding the gospel." (Conf. Report, Apr. 1975).

How, then, to take that first step to obtain faith? Alma challenges the people to "experiment upon my words" (Alma 32:27). He acknowledges that they cannot know of their surety at first, but if they will just "exercise a particle of faith" and "desire to believe," that will be a beginning. "'If ye can no more than desire to believe,' Alma says, exercising just 'a particle of faith,' giving even a small place for the promises of God to find a home – that is enough to begin. Just believing, just having a 'molecule' of faith – simply hoping for things which are not yet seen in our lives . . . that simple step, when focused on the Lord Jesus Christ, has ever been and always will be the first principle of His eternal gospel." (Holland, Conf. Report, Apr. 2006).

President Dieter F. Uchtdorf taught, "wanting to believe is the necessary first step . . . it requires a little scientific curiosity – it requires an experiment upon the word of God – and the exercise of a 'particle of faith.' . . . It requires seeking in the full meaning of the word. . . . If we make no effort to believe, we are like the man who unplugs a spotlight and then blames the spotlight for not giving any light." (Conf. Report, Oct. 2015).

Elder L. Whitney Clayton observed: "Alma's call for us to desire to believe . . . reminds us that belief and faith require our personal choice and action. We must 'awake and arouse [our] faculties.' We ask before it is given unto us; we seek before we find; we knock before it is opened unto us." (Conf. Report, Apr. 2015).

To experiment denotes action. When we experiment with the word, we act in accordance with the Lord's teachings. This puts us on the path to faithfulness. First we do, then we know. Compare Alma's invitation to "experiment" with the Lord's admonition: "If any man will do his will, he shall know of the doctrine, whether it be of God" (John 7:17). In other words, as we make efforts to obey the word of God, or test by trying, we can learn it is true. The process is desire, then act, then know.

"Experiences with the Spirit follow naturally when a person is willing to experiment upon the word." (Ballard, Conf. Report, Oct. 2000). "As we experiment upon the words given to us by the scriptures and the living prophets – even if we only have a desire to believe – and do not resist the Spirit of the Lord, our souls will be enlarged and our understanding will be enlightened." (Uchtdorf, Conf. Report, Apr. 2005). Desire precipitates experimentation; and experimentation leads to faith.

Comparing the Word to a Seed: Planting and Nourishing Faith

Alma compares this process to planting and growing a seed: "Now we will compare the word unto a seed" (Alma 32:28). He likens the initial development of faith to a seed that is planted in the heart and then, through experimenting with the word, begins to "swell" and "sprout." The seed begins "to enlarge my soul," "to enlighten my understanding," and "to be delicious to me" (Alma 32:28).

This swelling of the heart, enlarging of the soul, and enlightening of the understanding all suggest a manifestation of feelings from the Holy Spirit, which can provide mental and spiritual enlightenment, and confirm the "truth of all things" (Moroni 10:5). As the metaphorical seed swells and sprouts, Alma teaches, we realize it is "good" (Alma 32:30). And, it is this realization that will begin to "strengthen [our] faith. . . for behold it sprouteth and beginneth to grow" (Alma 32:30). The growth of faith is like the growth of a seed.

Elder Craig C. Christensen reminded us: "This is often how a testimony begins: with sacred, enlightening, assuring feelings . . . . However, as wonderful as these feelings are, they are only the beginning. Your work to grow your testimony is not done – any more than the work of growing a redwood tree is done when the first tiny sprout pokes out of the ground." (Conf. Report, Oct. 2014). To grow further, the sprouting seed will need nourishment, care and cultivation.

<u>Nourishing the Word</u>. The next step is to "nourish" the sprouting seed of faith. "So a seed of faith is planted in your heart. You may even have felt some of the expansion of your heart promised in Alma. . . . But, like a growing plant, it must be nurtured or it will wither. Frequent and heartfelt prayers of faith are crucial and needed nutrients. Obedience to the truth you have received will keep the testimony alive and strengthen it. Obedience to the commandments is part of the nourishment you must provide." (Eyring, Conf. Report, Apr. 2011).

Elder Joseph B. Wirthlin observed that "with nurturing attention, a tiny seed of faith can grow into a vibrant, strong, fruitful tree of testimony. . . . If we study, ponder, and pray, our faith in the unseen but true things of God will grow." (Conf. Report, Oct. 1998). President James E. Faust taught: "We . . . need to prepare our own seedbeds of faith. To do this we need to plow the soil through daily humble prayer, asking for strength and forgiveness. We need to harrow the soil by overcoming our feelings of pride. We need to prepare the seedbed by keeping the commandments to the best of our ability." The seeds of faith need to be nourished and nurtured. Where does this process take place? President Faust continued: "There is no better place for the spiritual seeds of our faith to be nurtured than within the hallowed sanctuaries of our temples and in our homes." (Conf. Report, Oct. 1999).

"You must nourish the seed; in other words, you must nourish the testimony that you have that it is true, by living the teachings of the gospel. If you will do this, [Alma] tells us, the seed will grow into a tree and bring forth fruit. But if the tree is neglected, it will not take root; and when the heat of the sun comes and scorches it, it will wither and die. This is not because the seed or the word of God was not true nor because the fruit thereof would not be desirable, but it is because . . . the tree was not nourished, in which event one cannot have the fruit thereof that he otherwise would obtain." (Anderson, Conf. Report, Apr. 1972).

The image of the "heat of the sun" scorching the plant "because it has no root and withers away" in Alma's discourse (Alma 32:38), is similar to the image of the sun scorching the seed that fell on stony places and "had no root and withered away" in the Savior's parable of the sower. (Matt. 13:5-6). In that parable, we learn that those who receive the seed in stony places "heareth the word, and anon with joy receive it; Yet hath he not root in himself, but . . . when tribulation or persecution ariseth because of the word, by and by he is offended" (Matt. 13:21). Thus, trials and tribulations can terminate testimonies that lack roots.

On the other hand, Alma teaches, if we "nourish the word, yea, nourish the tree as it beginneth to grow, by your faith with great ***diligence***, and with ***patience*** . . . it shall take root; and behold it shall be a tree springing up unto everlasting life" (Alma 32:41, *emphasis added*). "In most cases, our testimonies will grow the same way a tree grows: gradually, almost imperceptibly, as a result of constant care and diligent efforts." (Christensen, Conf. Report, Oct. 2014). It takes work and time for faith to grow and to produce fruit.

Nourish the Word with Diligence and Patience
A seed does not grow into a tree at once; this process takes time. A young seedling cannot be forced to emerge immediately, but gradually appears and strengthens as it develops roots. President Dieter F. Uchtdorf observed: "Too often we approach the gospel like a farmer who places a seed in the ground in the morning and expects corn on the cob by the afternoon. When Alma compared the word of God to a seed, he explained that the seed grows into a fruit-bearing tree gradually, as a result of our 'faith, and [our] diligence, and patience, and long-suffering' (Alma 32:43). It's true that some blessings come right away: soon after we plant the seed in our hearts, it begins to swell and sprout and grow, and by this we know that the seed is good. . . . Knowing that the seed is good is not enough. We must 'nourish it with great care, that it may get root.' Only then can we partake of the fruit." (Conf. Report, Apr. 2009).

President Boyd K. Packer taught that we should have patience with the sprouting seed: "My experience has been that a testimony does not burst upon us suddenly. Rather, it grows, as Alma said, from a seed of faith. . . . Do not be disappointed if you have read and reread and yet have not received a powerful witness. You may be somewhat like the disciples spoken of in the Book of Mormon who were filled with the power of God . . . and they knew it not. [See 3 Nephi 9:20]" (Conf. Report, Apr. 2005).

Elder Neal A. Maxwell observed: "acquiring faith is not a one-time thing. . . . Jesus described the steady process as being one of 'line upon line, precept upon precept.' (D&C 98:12). But we're all at different points in this process . . . of desiring, experimenting, verifying and knowing." (Conf. Report, Apr. 1991).

President Dieter F. Uchtdorf acknowledges that we may have doubts in this process: "It's natural to have questions – the acorn of honest inquiry has often spouted and matured into a great oak of understanding. . . . One of the purposes of the Church is to nurture and cultivate the seed of faith – even in the sometimes sandy soil of doubt and uncertainty. Faith is to hope for things which are not seen but which are true. Therefore . . . please, first doubt your doubts before you doubt your faith." (Conf. Report, Oct. 2013). Elder Jeffrey R. Holland urged, "Hold fast to what you already know and stand strong until additional knowledge comes. . . . In this Church, what we know will always trump what we do not know." (Conf. Report, Apr. 2013). At times, we simply must choose to have faith.

Bishop Richard C. Edgley observed: "Alma's classic discussion on faith, as recorded in the 32nd chapter of Alma in the Book of Mormon, is a series of choices to ensure the development and the preservation of our faith. Alma gave us a directive to choose. His were words of action initiated by choosing. He used the words *awake, arouse, experiment, exercise, desire, work, and plant*. Then Alma explained that if we make these choices and do not cast the seed out by unbelief, then 'it will begin to swell within [our] breasts' (Alma 32:28). . . . Thus, we are responsible for our own faith. We are also responsible for our lack of faith." (Conf. Report, Oct. 2010).

- "If confusion and hopelessness weigh on your mind, choose to 'awake and arouse your faculties.' Humbly approaching the Lord with a broken heart and contrite spirit is the pathway to truth and the Lord's way of light, knowledge and peace.
- If your testimony is immature, untested, and insecure, choose to 'exercise [even] a particle of faith'; choose to 'experiment upon [His] words.' . . .
- When logic, reason, or personal intellect come into conflict with sacred teachings and doctrine, or conflicting messages assault your beliefs . . . choose to not cast the seed out of your heart by unbelief. Remember, we receive not a witness until after the trial of our faith (Ether 12:6).
- If your faith is proven and mature, choose to nurture it 'with great care.' As strong as our faith is, with all the mixed messages attacking it, it can also become very fragile. It needs constant nourishment through continued scripture study, prayer, and the application of His word." (Edgley, Conf. Report, Oct. 2010, *emphasis added*).

Elder Dallin H. Oaks taught: "Each of you needs to build a reservoir of faith so you can draw upon it when someone you love or respect betrays you, when some scientific discovery seems to cast doubt on a gospel principle, or when someone makes light of sacred things. . . . You need to draw on your reservoir of faith when you are weak or when someone else calls on you to strengthen them. You also need to draw on your reservoir of faith when some requirement of Church membership or service interferers with your personal preferences. You need the strength that comes from faith and trust in the Lord Jesus Christ." (Conf. Report, Apr. 1994).

Faith in the Lord, Jesus Christ

It is not just abstract faith, but faith in the Lord Jesus Christ that we must desire and nourish. As Alma summarizes his teachings on faith, he admonishes the people to "begin to believe in the Son of God" (Alma 33:22). He teaches that a belief in Christ is the object of faith – to believe, as the ancient prophets Moses, Zenos and Zenock testified, in the Savior, "that he will come to redeem his people, and that he shall suffer and die to atone for their sins; and that he shall rise again from the dead, which shall bring to pass the resurrection, that all men shall stand before him, to be judged at the last and judgment day, according to their works" (Alma 33:22). Alma says "ye shall plant *this word* in your hearts" (Alma 33:23, emphasis added). So, what is the word, the seed, we should plant? What is the object of our faith?

Specifically:

1. We believe that Christ came to earth to redeem his people. His Mission.
2. We believe that Christ suffered and died to atone for our sins. His Atonement.
3. We believe that Christ rose again from the dead. His Resurrection.
4. We believe that all men shall stand before Christ, to be judged at the last day. His judgment. (See Alma 33:22).

What Alma calls the "word" (Alma 33:23), therefore, comprises the core elements of faith in the Lord Jesus Christ – the fundamental things we believe about the Savior. Compare Alma's succinct list to the following statement by Joseph Smith: "The fundamental principles of our religion are the testimony of the Apostles and Prophets [the word] concerning Jesus Christ, that He died, was buried, and rose again the third day, and ascended into heaven; and all other things which pertain to our religion are only appendages to it." (Teachings of the Prophet Joseph Smith, 121). We nourish the seed of faith in Him, as we study His word, pray in His name and keep His commandments.

"Faith in the Lord Jesus Christ prepares you for whatever life brings. This kind of faith prepares you to deal with life's opportunities – to take advantage of those that are received and to persist through the disappointments of those that are lost. Most importantly, faith in the Lord Jesus Christ opens the door of salvation and exaltation." (Oaks, Conf. Report, Apr. 1994).

Alma teaches that as our faith in Christ grows, we can be blessed both in this life – to bear the burdens that may be placed upon us joyfully ("faith prepares you to deal with life's opportunities"); and in the life to come – to obtain everlasting life ("faith opens the door of salvation and exaltation"). (Oaks, Conf. Report, Apr. 1994). Alma concludes his message by encouraging the Zoramites to "plant *this word* [of Christ] in your hearts. . . . And behold, it will become a tree, springing up in you unto *everlasting life*. And then may God grant unto you *that your burdens may be light, through the joy of his Son*" (Alma 33:23). However, Alma reminds the people, it must be their choice – to choose faith: "And even all this can ye do *if ye will*. Amen" (Alma 33:23, *emphasis added*).

Discourse 17: Amulek, "Atonement, Prayer & Procrastination" (Alma 34)

Prophet	Key Doctrines	Scriptures	Audience	Date
Amulek	• The Atonement: the Great and Last Sacrifice • Prayer • Do Not Procrastinate Repentance	Alma 34	To Zoramites in the land of Antionum at the hill Onidah – to a multitude of the poorer people	About 74 B.C.

INTRODUCTION

Amulek's sermon in Alma chapter 34 follows Alma's discourse in Alma chapters 32 and 33 to the more humble Zoramites in the land of Antionum. After Alma taught the Zoramites, he "sat down upon the ground, and Amulek arose and began to teach them" (Alma 34:1). Amulek begins by continuing the message of Alma, and bearing his own testimony. He says: "And as ye have desired of my beloved brother [Alma] that he should make known unto you what ye should do . . . and he hath exhorted you unto faith and to patience . . . and we have beheld that the great question which is in your minds is whether the word be in the Son of God, or whether there shall be no Christ. And ye also beheld that my brother has proved unto you, in many instances, that the word is in Christ unto salvation . . . And now, behold I will testify unto you of myself that these things are true. Behold, I say unto you, that I do know that Christ shall come among the children of men, to take upon him the transgressions of his people, and that he shall atone for the sins of the world" (Alma 34:3-8). Elder Neal A. Maxwell said: "The Book of Mormon provides resounding and great answers to what Amulek designated as 'the great question'; namely, is there really a redeeming Christ? The Book of Mormon with clarity and with evidence says, 'Yes! Yes! Yes!'" (BYU Book of Mormon Symposium, Oct. 10, 1986).

Amulek preaches succinctly on three topics: the need for Christ's Atonement, the need to "exercise your faith unto repentance" through constant prayer (Alma 34:17), and the need to not "procrastinate the day of your repentance" (Alma 34:32).

DISCOURSE: Alma 34

KEY DOCTRINES

- **The Atonement**. The infinite atonement of Jesus Christ can satisfy the demands of justice and bring salvation to those who have "faith unto repentance" (Alma 34:15).

- **Prayer.** Pray unto God (i) in all places – in your fields, in your houses, in your closets and secret places, in your wilderness; (ii) at all times – morning, mid-day, and evening; and (iii) for all purposes – over your flocks, over your crops, over your household (families), against the power of your enemies and against the devil. (Alma 34:17-27).

- **Preparation**. "[T]his life is the time . . . to prepare to meet God . . . do not procrastinate the day of your repentance" (Alma 34:32-33).

COMMENTARY

The Atonement: The Great and Last Sacrifice

Amulek testifies that Christ "shall atone for the sins of the world" (Alma 34:8). "[F]or according to the great plan of the Eternal God there must be an atonement made, or else all mankind must unavoidably perish" (Alma 34:9). Amulek, who found salvation through the preaching of Alma (Alma 10:2-11), teaches that the atonement applies to *all* men. Unless an atonement is made, "*all* mankind must unavoidably perish," "*all* are hardened," and "*all* are lost" (Alma 34:9, *emphasis added*). (See "Atonement" in Topical Index, 2 Nephi 9).

The Atonement: An Infinite and Eternal Sacrifice

Amulek taught that the atonement must be an "infinite and eternal sacrifice" (Alma 34:10, 12, 14). This sacrifice could only be performed by one who is qualified and capable. Amulek explained that the Atonement had to be a "great and last sacrifice" by one who was more than human. (Alma 34:10). "According to eternal law, that atonement required a personal sacrifice by an immortal being not subject to death." (Nelson, Conf. Report, Oct. 1993). Only Christ, who inherited the ability to sacrifice his mortal body and suffer temporal death from his mortal mother, and who inherited the ability to not suffer death, but live forever, from His immortal Father, could accomplish an "infinite and eternal sacrifice."

Bishop Richard C. Edgley said: "The unfathomable extent of Christ's mercy and His Atonement are explained by Amulek in the 34th chapter of Alma in the Book of Mormon. Amulek explains that there must be a 'great and last sacrifice' (Alma 34:10). And then he clarifies that this cannot be a sacrifice of beast or fowl similar to those already known by [those who observed the law of Moses]. It had to be a sacrifice of a God – Jesus Christ." (Conf. Report, Apr. 2002).

Christ Performed the Atonement Because He Loves Us

Christ had both the ability and capability to perform the great atoning sacrifice. He was both willing and able to perform the Atonement for His brothers and sisters. President Ezra Taft Benson explained: "He [Christ] was *able* to accomplish [the Atonement] because He was the Son of God and He possessed the power of God. He was *willing* to accomplish His mission because He loves us. No mortal being had the power or capability to redeem all other mortals from their lost and fallen condition, nor could any other voluntarily forfeit his life and thereby bring to pass a universal resurrection of all other mortals. Only Jesus Christ was *able* and *willing* to accomplish such a redeeming act of love." (Conf. Report, Oct. 1983, *emphasis added*).

The scriptures describe Christ's love through symbolism and imagery. Amulek teaches that when Christ satisfies the demands of justice through the Atonement, it is as if He "encircles [us] in the arms of safety" (Alma 34:16), a vivid image. Any child knows the feeling to be held in the arms of a loving parent: safety, mercy, protection, warmth, love and peace. The scriptures refer to Christ's encircling arms as His "arms of mercy" (Mosiah 16:12; Alma 5:33); and "the arms of his love" (2 Nephi 1:15; D&C 6:20). Elder Jay E. Jensen taught: "Arms are tangible, and we use them to express affection and love. When I come home from the office, I am encircled in the tangible arms of my wife. I have experienced arms of love and safety throughout my service in Latin America by means of the common greeting, un *abrazo*, or hug." (Conf. Report, Oct. 2008).

Elder David A. Bednar explained: "because of His infinite and eternal sacrifice, [Christ] has perfect empathy and can extend to us His arm of mercy. He can reach out, touch, succor, heal, and strengthen us to be more than we could ever be and help us to do that which we could never do relying only upon our own power." (Conf. Report, Apr. 2014). Elder Neil L. Andersen observed: "The scriptures speak of His arms being open (Mormon 6:17), extended (Alma 19:36), stretched out (2 Kings 17:36), and encircling (2 Nephi 1:15). They are described as mighty (D&C 123:6), and holy (3 Nephi 20:35), arms of mercy (Alma 5:33), arms of safety (Alma 34:16), arms of love (D&C 6:20), 'lengthened out all the day long' (2 Nephi 28:32)." (Conf. Report, Oct. 2009).

Sister Bonnie D. Parkin taught: "When we allow ourselves to feel 'encircled eternally in the arms of his love' (2 Nephi 1:15), we feel safe, and we realize that we don't need to be immediately perfect." (Conf. Report, Oct. 2006).

As imperfect mortals, it is difficult, if not impossible, for us to understand Christ's perfect love. President Dieter F. Uchtdorf observed: "I marvel to think that the Son of God would condescend to save us, as imperfect, impure, mistake prone, and ungrateful as we often are. I have tried to understand the Savior's Atonement with my finite mind, and the only explanation I can come up with is this: God loves us deeply, perfectly, and everlastingly. I cannot even begin to estimate 'the breadth, and length, and depth, and height . . . [of] the love of Christ.' (Ephesians 3:18-19)" (Conf. Report, Apr. 2015). We cannot begin to fathom the extent of this love.

<u>The Atonement Allows Mercy to Satisfy Justice: Exercising "Faith Unto Repentance"</u>
Amulek explained that Christ's Atonement would allow mercy to "overpower" justice, and "satisfy the demands of justice" to "bring salvation to all those who shall believe on his name" (Alma 34:15-16). President John Taylor taught that "it was understood that the penalty of departing from the law would be death, death temporal. And there was a provision made for that. Man was not able to make that provision himself, and hence we are told that it needed the atonement of a God to accomplish this purpose; and the Son of God presented himself to carry out that object . . . [a]nd was accepted by his Father, just the same as any man who owes a debt, if he is not able to pay that obligation, and somebody steps forward and says, I will go security for him. If the persons to whom he is indebted are willing to take him as security they will receive the security's note or obligation to meet the debt. So Jesus offered himself. Now, man could not have done that. Man could do all that he is capable of doing. But there was an eternal law of God violated and it needed an eternal, infinite sacrifice to atone therefore; and Jesus offered himself as that sacrifice to atone for the sins of the world." (<u>Journal of Discourses</u>, 22:300). The atoning sacrifice had to be carried out by the sinless Son of God because fallen man could not atone for his own sins. (Alma 34:11). (See "<u>Justice & Mercy</u>" in Topical Index, Alma 42).

Amulek taught that in order to receive the full blessings of the atonement, we must "exercise faith unto repentance," a phrase he repeats four times in three verses. (Alma 34:15-17). Repentance is the necessary condition, and the grace of Christ is the necessary means by which "mercy can satisfy the demands of justice" (Alma 34:16).

Elder Robert E. Wells explained: "Just how much faith do I need for the atonement of Christ to work for me? In other words, how much faith do I need to receive salvation? In the book of Alma . . . we find the answer. The prophet Amulek taught this simple but grand principle: 'The Son of God bringeth about means unto men that they may have faith unto repentance.' . . . So the combination of faith in Christ plus faith unto repentance is vitally important. That concept is one of the greatest insights we have into the importance of simple, clear faith – faith sufficient to repent

... all that we need is just enough faith to recognize that we have sinned and to repent of our sins, to feel remorse for them, and to desire to sin no more but to please Christ the Lord. Then the greatest miracle of all, the Atonement, whereby Christ rescues us from our deserved punishment, is in effect in our behalf." (Van Orden & Top, Doctrines of the Book of Mormon: The 1991 Sperry Symposium, 6-7).

Elder Neal A. Maxwell observed: "No part of walking by faith is more difficult than walking the road of repentance. However, with 'faith unto repentance,' we can push roadblocks out of the way, moving forward to beg God for mercy." (Conf. Report, Oct. 1991). We must "return to the Lord" with faith unto repentance since "only unto him that has faith unto repentance is brought about the great and eternal plan of redemption" (Alma 34:16).

Amulek thus follows Alma's doctrinal explication of faith (Alma 32), the first principle of the gospel, with the doctrinal introduction of repentance, the second principle of the gospel. These principles are intertwined and sequential – faith precedes repentance; and, without faith, or belief, in Christ, repentance cannot occur. This was the experience of Amulek's missionary companion and mentor, Alma. (See Alma 36). The turning point in Alma's repentance was when he remembered what his father had taught him about Jesus Christ, and when he (Alma) sought mercy, in faith, from Christ.

When we choose to repent, we invite the Savior into our lives. The effect can be immediate. Amulek teaches the people to "come forth and harden not your hearts any longer; for behold now is the time and day of your salvation; and therefore, if ye will repent and harden not your hearts, ***immediately*** shall the great plan of redemption be brought about unto you" (Alma 34:31, *emphasis added*). As we feel godly sorrow and exercise faith unto repentance, we can immediately feel the joy of the Savior's love. (See "Repentance" in Topical Index, Alma 36).

Pray at All Times, in All Places, for All Things

Amulek teaches that the first step "to exercise your faith unto repentance" is to "begin to call upon his holy name" in prayer. (Alma 34:17). "Yea, cry unto him for mercy; for he is mighty to save" (Alma 34:18). Just as Alma responded to the Zoramites' question, "in what manner they should begin to exercise faith?" with a discussion of prayer, so Amulek teaches that the way to begin to exercise faith unto repentance is also through prayer. (Alma 33:1, 3).

Amulek teaches the people to pray at all times, in all places, and for all things.

1. At all times. Amulek teaches that we should pray "morning, mid-day, and evening" (Alma 34:21), "continually" (Alma 34:27).
2. In all places. Amulek teaches that we should pray "in [our] houses"; "in [our] fields" – or workplaces; "in [our] closets and secret places"; and "in [our] wilderness" (Alma 34:20, 21, 26).[53]

---

[53] "The mention of 'closets and secret places' is a clear reference to the . . . custom of the ancient Hebrew of having special shrines or prayer-rooms in their houses. . . . But what we wish especially to notice here is that 'your wilderness' is a normal and natural part of the Nephite scene, with people going into the wilderness on a regular basis, where they are admonished to pray as in other places." (Nibley, Approach to the Book of Mormon, 404).

3. <u>For all things</u>. Amulek teaches that we should pray about our work, "over all [our] flocks" and "over the crops of [your] fields, that they may increase"; about our families, "over all [our] household"; and for protection, "against the devil" and "against the power of [our] enemies. (Alma 34:20-25). He says that we should pray about our overall "welfare," which would include physical, mental, spiritual and emotional health, and the "welfare of those who are around [us]" (Alma 34:27).

President Ezra Taft Benson expounded on Amulek's teachings with specific guidelines to "improve our communication with our Heavenly Father" (Conf. Report, Apr. 1977):

"*We should pray frequently*. We should be alone with our Heavenly Father at least two or three times each day, 'morning, mid-day, and evening,' as the scriptures indicate (Alma 34:21). In addition . . . our hearts should be full, drawn out in prayer unto [our Heavenly Father] continually."

"*We should find an appropriate place where we can meditate and pray*. We are admonished that this should be 'in your closets and your secret places, and in your wilderness.' (Alma 34:26). That is, it should be free from distraction, in secret."

"*We should prepare ourselves for prayer*. If we don't feel like praying, then we should pray until we feel like praying. . . . (Alma 34:17-18)."

"*Our prayers should be meaningful and pertinent*. Do not use the same phrases at each prayer. Each of us would become disturbed if a friend said the same few words to us each day, treated the conversation as a chore, and could hardly wait to finish it in order to turn on the TV and forget us. . . . For what should we pray? We should pray about our work, against the power of our enemies and the devil, for our welfare and the welfare of those around us. (Alma 34: 20, 22-25, 27). We should counsel with the Lord pertaining to all our decisions and activities. We should be grateful enough to give thanks for all we have. We should confess his hand in all things. . . ."

"*After making a request through prayer, we have a responsibility to assist in its being granted*. We should listen. Perhaps while we are on our knees, the Lord wants to counsel us. 'Sincere praying implies that when we ask for any virtue or blessing we should work for the blessing and cultivate the virtue.' (*quoting* David O. McKay, True to the Faith, 208)."

(Conf. Report, Apr. 1977, *emphasis in original*).

We should pray as if it all depends on the Lord, and then act as if it all depends upon us. Elder Wilford W. Andersen shared the following story: "I heard a story about a father who noticed his young daughter kneeling beside her bed, praying that Heavenly Father would protect little birds from entering a bird trap her brother had built and placed in the backyard. Later that day, the father grew concerned. He knew the trap was a good one. He had helped his son build it."

"'I heard you praying this morning that Heavenly Father would protect the little birds from your brother's trap,' he said to his daughter. 'But sometimes sad things happen even when we pray that they won't.' She responded, 'I just know he won't catch any birds, Daddy.' 'I admire your faith, sweetheart,' the father said. 'But if he does catch some birds, I hope that won't hurt your faith.' 'He won't Daddy,' she said. 'I know he won't.' The father asked, 'How can you have such great faith?' 'Because after I said my prayers,' his daughter replied, 'I went out back and kicked his bird trap all to pieces.' It is good to pray for Heavenly Father's blessings. But after we say amen, we have to go to work." ("Developing the Faith to Reap," Ensign, Jan. 2019).

Amulek taught that our prayers should be comprehensive. He taught the humble Zoramites that no matter what other privileges had been denied them, they could always pray – in their fields, in their families, in their houses, and in their hearts. (Alma 34:20-26). "Amulek tells us we should pray about everything in our lives. He says, 'Pour out your souls [to God] in your closets, and your secret places, and in your wilderness.' (Alma 34:26). Your Heavenly Father wants you to pray about your hopes and fears, your friends and family, your school and work and the needs of those around you. Most of all, you should pray to be filled with the love of Christ." (Christofferson, Conf. Report, Apr. 2004).

Joseph Smith said: "Follow the directions of the Book of Mormon, and pray over, and for your families, your cattle, your flocks, your herds, your corn, and all things that you possess; ask the blessing of God upon all your labors, and everything that you engage in." (Teachings of the Prophet Joseph Smith, 247).

In his admonitions on prayer, Amulek first says that we should "call" upon the Lord (Alma 34:17). He then instructs us to "cry unto him," and repeats that phrase seven times (Alma 34:.18-25). Finally, he tells us to "pour out [our] souls" to the Lord (Alma 34:26). This progression from "call" to "cry" to "pour out your souls" suggests that all prayer is not the same. Even our perfect Savior "prayed more earnestly" at times (See Luke 22:44).

Amulek also taught that our prayers need to be accompanied by righteous acts of love and service. "You will remember the great sermon of Amulek on prayer, in which he tells the people to pray and tells them how often to pray – morning, night, and noon – and tells them where to pray and how to pray and what to pray for. He goes into great detail and then he says that 'after ye have done all these things, if ye turn away the needy, and the naked, and visit not the sick and afflicted, and impart of your substance, if ye have, to those who stand in need – I say unto you, if ye do not any of these things, behold your prayer is in vain, and availeth you nothing, and ye are as hypocrites who do deny the faith.' (See Alma 34:17-38)." (Romney, Conf. Report, Apr. 1978).

Do Not Procrastinate Repentance

After teaching about prayer, and the importance of accompanying petitions to our Heavenly Father with acts of charity to our fellow man, Amulek admonishes, "now, my brethren, I would that . . . ye come forth and bring fruit unto repentance" (Alma 34:30). He is saying to the assembled Zoramites: "Now is the time to change." Amulek uses phrases such as "*now* is the time and the day of your salvation," "repent . . . *immediately*," and "*this life* is the time to prepare to meet God" (Alma 34:31-32, *emphasis added*). He says: "I beseech of you that ye *do not procrastinate the day of your repentance*" (Alma 34:33, *emphasis added*).

President Henry B. Eyring observed: "'Now' can seem so difficult, and 'later' appear so much easier. The truth is that today is always a better day to repent than any tomorrow. First, sin has its debilitating effects on us. The very faith we need to repent is weakened by delay. . . . And second, even should we be forgiven at some later time, the Lord cannot restore the good effects our repentance today might have had on those we love and are to serve." (Conf. Report, Oct. 1999).

On several occasions, President Russell M. Nelson has urged us not to procrastinate: "Now is the time. . . Begin with repentance. . . . Now is the time to enroll our names among the people of God. . . . Now is the time to align our goals with God's goals. . . . Now is the time to prepare." (Conf. Report, Apr. 2005). He quotes the poet Henry Van Dyke, "The Sun-Dial at Wells College":

The shadow by my finger cast
Divides the future from the past:
Before it, sleeps the unborn hour,
In darkness, and beyond thy power:
Behind its unreturning line,
The vanished hour, no longer thine:
One hour alone is in thy hands –
The NOW on which the shadow stands.

President Nelson said: "Unfinished business is our worst business. Perpetual procrastination must yield to perceptive preparation." (Conf. Report, Apr. 1992). Procrastination is "an unwillingness to accept personal responsibilities now." (Nelson, Conf. Report, Apr. 2007). President Nelson's prophetic message is one of urgency, hastening the work: "do not procrastinate."

Amulek knew about procrastination in accepting the word of God. He told the people of Ammonihah that he "was called many times but would not hear" and "would not know" (Alma 10:6). He confessed that he had "[rebelled] against God in the wickedness of my heart" for many years. (Alma 10:6). Nonetheless, Amulek repented and became a great missionary companion, and friend, of Alma the prophet. It is perhaps because of Amulek's own experience that his teachings on procrastination and repentance carry such a sense of urgency.

President Harold B. Lee admonished: "Today is the day for us to begin to search our souls. Have you discovered which is the most important of all the commandments to you today? . . . Are you going to begin working on it today? Or are you going to wait until it is too late? The little boy says, 'Well, when I get to be a big boy, then I'm going to do so and so.' And what is that? When he gets to be a big boy . . . then he says, 'When I get married, then I'll do so and so.' And then after he gets married, it all changes, and 'Well, when I retire.' And then after he is retired, a cold wind sweeps down over him and suddenly he realizes too late that he has lost everything. And it is too late. And yet all his life he has had all the time that there was. He just hasn't taken advantage of it. Now, today, this is the day for us to begin to do something about it, before it is too late." (Ricks College, Mar. 3, 1962; Teachings of Presidents of the Church: Harold B. Lee, 24).

President Lee also taught: "Now, if you have made mistakes, make *today* the beginning of a change of your lives. Turn from the thing that you have been doing that is wrong. The most important of all the commandments of God is that one that you are having the most difficulty keeping today. If it is one of dishonesty, if it is one of unchastity, if it is one of falsifying, not telling the truth, *today is the day for you to work on that* until you have been able to conquer that weakness. . . . Put that aright and then you start on the next one that is most difficult for you to keep." (Teachings of Presidents of the Church: Harold B. Lee, 30, *emphasis added*).

Discourse 18: Alma, "Repentance; Small and Simple Things" (Alma 36)

Prophet	Key Doctrines	Scriptures	Audience	Date
Alma	• Alma's Repentance and Conversion • By small and simple things are great things brought to pass.	Alma 36-37	To his son, Helaman	About 74 B.C.

INTRODUCTION

After Alma returned from his mission to the Zoramites, he gave individual counsel to each of his three sons.[54] In Alma's discourse to his son, Helaman, comprising Alma chapters 36 and 37, Alma teaches Helaman about repentance through the example of his own conversion. Alma also emphasizes three key themes of the Book of Mormon: (i) keep the commandments and prosper in the land; (ii) the Lord delivers his people; and (iii) salvation – in this case the personal redemption of Alma – comes through Jesus Christ.

Alma provides three examples of his ancestors who were delivered by the Lord: (i) those led by Helaman's grandfather, Alma the Elder (Alma 36:2); (ii) those led by Moses who came out of Egypt (Alma 36:28); and (iii) those led by Lehi out of the land of Jerusalem (Alma 36:29). Importantly, he also testifies of the deliverance of "whosoever shall put their trust in God" (Alma 36:3).

Alma also encourages Helaman several times to follow his example in righteousness:

- "Ye should do as I have done" in remembering the deliverance of our fathers. (Alma 36:2).
- "Ye also ought to retain in remembrance, as I have done" the captivity and deliverance of our fathers. (Alma 36:29).
- "Ye ought to know as I do know" that inasmuch as you keep the commandments, you will prosper in the land. (Alma 36:30).

He then teaches Helaman about repentance, and his personal deliverance from the effects of sin. Elder Marion D. Hanks taught: "In chapter 36 of the book of Alma in the Book of Mormon is a remarkable lesson for every father, or for those who stand in place of a father. To his son Helaman, Alma bore a strong testimony of faith and repentance. Remember that Alma, in youthful rebelliousness, had made serious mistakes. He wanted his sons to avoid those mistakes and to find what he, Alma, had discovered of the tender mercies of God, without the terrible, painful experiences through which he had gone." (Conf. Report, Apr. 1974).

---

[54] Alma's home at one time was in the land of Zarahemla (see Alma 15:18), but the record does not reveal where he gave these instructions to his sons.

DISCOURSE: Alma 36-37

KEY DOCTRINES

- **Repentance**. Alma was racked with torment for past sins, but through the mercy of Christ was forgiven and filled with joy. (Alma 36:17-21).

- **Small and Simple Things**. "By small and simple things are great things brought to pass" (Alma 37:6-7). The words of Christ, although a simple thing, lead to eternal life.

COMMENTARY

Principles of Repentance

Most of the Book of Alma chapter 36 comprises the personal testimony of Alma with respect to his repentance and conversion. Alma knew personally the pain of sin and the joy of repentance. He had once lived a life of rebellion against the Lord's teachings, and disappointed his own father, Helaman's grandfather. For a period of time, Alma "went about seeking to destroy the church" (Alma 36:6). Finally, because of the prayers of Alma's father and others, an angel intervened. (Mosiah 27:14). "And behold, [the angel] spake unto us [Alma and the sons of Mosiah], as it were the voice of thunder, and the whole earth did tremble beneath our feet; and we all fell to the earth, for the fear of the Lord came upon us" (Alma 36:7). "And [the angel] said unto [Alma]: If thou wilt of thyself be destroyed, seek no more to destroy the church of God" (Alma 36:9).

Alma the Younger described his feelings when he saw and heard the angel. As he realized that he had rebelled against God and had "not kept his holy commandments," he was "tormented with the pains of hell," "racked with eternal torment" and "harrowed up to the greatest degree" (Alma 36:12-13). "Racked means 'tortured.' Anciently a rack was a framework on which the victim was laid with each ankle and wrist tied to a spindle which could then be turned to cause unbearable pain. A harrow is a frame with spikes through it. When pulled through the ground, it rips and tears into the soil. The scriptures frequently speak of souls and minds being 'harrowed up' with guilt. Torment means 'to twist,' a means of torture so painful that even the innocent would confess." (Packer, Conf. Report, Apr. 2001).

In his deepest anguish, after spending "three days and three nights . . . racked, even with the pains of a damned soul" (Alma 36:16), Alma turned to Christ. "And it came to pass that as I was thus racked with torment, while I was harrowed up by the memory of my many sins, behold, I remembered also to have heard my father prophesy unto the people concerning the coming of one Jesus Christ, a Son of God, to atone for the sins of the world. Now, as my mind caught hold upon this thought, I cried within my heart: O Jesus, thou Son of God, have mercy on me, who am in the gall of bitterness, and am encircled about by the . . . chains of death" (Alma 36:17-18).

Elder Jeffrey R. Holland taught: "Alma had been touched by the teaching of his father, but it is particularly important that the prophecy he remembered was one regarding 'the coming of one Jesus Christ, a Son of God, to atone for the sins of the world.' (Alma 36:17). That is the name and that is the message that every person must hear. Alma heard it, and he cried out from the anguish of a hell that kept burning and a conscience that wouldn't heal. 'O Jesus, thou Son of God, have mercy on me.'" (Holland, However Long and Hard the Road, 85).

Alma then testifies that as he sincerely sought Christ's mercy, he "could remember [his] pains no more . . . and [his] soul was filled with joy as exceeding as [his] pain" (Alma 36:19, 20). President Spencer W. Kimball wrote: "In Alma's account the sensitive reader can in a measure identify with him, feel his pains, experience his great sense of horror at the recognition of the depth of his sin. The reader can then share also in the great relief which Alma was to find. How did he gain this relief? In the same way every transgressor does – by partaking of the miracle of forgiveness through genuine repentance and by casting himself wholly on the mercies of Jesus Christ . . . . Now anguish was turned to joy, pain to calm, darkness to light. Only now could Alma have peace." (Kimball, The Miracle of Forgiveness, 365- 366).

Alma testified that after he cried out to Jesus for mercy, he "was harrowed up by the memory of [his] sins no more" (Alma 36:19). Alma may have still remembered his sins, but he no longer suffered for them. "Satan will try to make us believe that our sins are not forgiven because we can remember them. Satan is a liar; he tries to blur our vision and lead us away from the path of repentance and forgiveness. God did not promise that we would not remember our sins. Remembering will help us avoid making the same mistakes again. But if we stay true and faithful, the memory of our sins will be softened over time. . . . Alma testified that after he cried out to Jesus for mercy, he could still remember his sins, but the memory of his sins no longer distressed and tortured him, because he knew he had been forgiven. (Alma 36:17-18)." (Uchtdorf, Conf. Report, Apr. 2007).

Alma was filled with "joy" and "marvelous light" as he experienced forgiveness through the Atonement (Alma 36:20). President Marion G. Romney testified: "The joy and peace of conscience which comes to one who has received a remission of his sins is graphically portrayed in the account Alma gives to his son, Helaman, of his conversion." (Conf. Report, Oct. 1980). "His joy came because of contrite repentance . . . . Only by repentance and asking for forgiveness of the Lord was Alma able to put his pain behind him and receive of the joy and light of the gospel." (Hales, Conf. Report, Oct. 1998). As part of this process, Alma speaks of being both "born of God" and being "filled with the Holy Ghost" (Alma 36:23-24). Elder Dallin H. Oaks instructed: "The joy that follows the remission of sins comes from the Spirit of the Lord. It is a fulfillment of the Lord's promise that 'I will impart unto you of my Spirit . . . which shall fill your soul with joy.' (D&C 11:13)." (Conf. Report, Oct. 1991).

Alma's conversion story demonstrates several principles of repentance.

1. He **recognized** the sin: "I did remember all my sins . . . I saw that I had rebelled against God, and that I had not kept his holy commandments" (Alma 36:13).
2. He felt true **remorse** for his sins: "I was racked with eternal torment"; "my soul was harrowed up"; he experienced "inexpressible horror"; "for three days and for three nights [he] was racked, even with the pains of a damned soul" (Alma 36:12, 14, 16).
3. He **turned to Christ, in faith**, to help him, seeking forgiveness and mercy, in great humility. (Alma 36:18). The turning point of his repentance was when he remembered what his own father had taught about Christ and when he turned to the Savior for help.
4. He **confessed** to the Lord and to those he injured ("confessing all [his] sins" Mos. 27:35).
5. He performed **restitution**, as much as possible for leading people away from the church (Alma 36:6,14) by dedicating his life to bring people into the church: "from that time even until now, I have labored without ceasing, that I might bring souls unto repentance" (Alma

36:24). Alma (and the sons of Mosiah) went about "zealously striving to repair all the injuries which they had done to the church, confessing all their sins" (Mosiah 27:35).
6. He **abandoned his sins** and did the will of the Lord. He never did return to his former activities and behavior, and completely turned his life around to become a faithful servant, high priest and prophet of the Lord.

President Spencer W. Kimball taught: "Repentance seems to fall into five steps:

1. *Sorrow for sin*. To be sorry for our sin we must know something of its serious implications. When fully convicted, we condition our minds to follow such processes as will rid us of the effects of the sin. We are sorry. We are willing to make amends, pay penalties, to suffer even to excommunication if necessary.
2. *Abandonment of sin*. It is best when one discontinues his error because of his realization of the gravity of his sin and when he is willing to comply with the laws of God. . . . The discontinuance must be a permanent one. True repentance does not permit repetition. . . .
3. *Confession of sin*. The confession of sin is an important element in repentance. . . . As soon as one has an inner conviction of his sins, he should go to the Lord in 'mighty prayer' . . . and never cease his supplications until he shall, like Enos, receive the assurance that his sins have been forgiven by the Lord. . . . Next [in the case of serious sins], the offender should seek the forgiveness of the Church through his bishop. . . . The bishop is our best earthly friend. He will hear the problems, judge the seriousness, then determine the degree of repentance.
4. *Restitution for sin*. When one is humble in sorrow, has unconditionally abandoned the evil, and confessed to those assigned by the Lord, he should next restore insofar as possible that which was damaged. . . .
5. *Do the will of the Father*. . . . Attend to personal and family prayers . . . keep holy the Sabbath; live strictly the Word of Wisdom; attend to all family duties; and above all, keep your life clean and free from all unholy and impure thoughts and actions."

("President Kimball Speaks Out on Morality," Ensign, Nov. 1980, *emphasis in original*).

Elder Richard G. Scott reviewed these five steps and then added a sixth step, which Alma also demonstrated: "I would add a sixth step: Recognition of the Savior. Of all the necessary steps to repentance, I testify that the most critically important is for you to have a conviction that forgiveness comes because of the Redeemer. It is essential to know that only on His terms can you be forgiven. . . . Satan would have you believe that serious transgression cannot be entirely overcome. The Savior gave His life so that the effects of all transgression can be put behind us, save the shedding of innocent blood and the denial of the Holy Ghost." (Conf. Report, Apr. 1995).

Elder H. Burke Peterson taught: "The secret to cleansing our spirit of whatever the impurity is not very complicated. It begins with sincere, heartfelt prayer every morning and ends with prayer every night. This is the most important step I know in the cleansing process. It may simply be a prayer for strength to turn from bad habits, or a prayer that sin will be distasteful to you. Meanwhile, remember that not all prayers are answered the same day or even the next day. Sometimes it takes a long time. But with this step in place, I have seen hundreds of miracles take place. Without it, there is continued frustration, unhappiness and despair. . . .The second step in this plan of attack is to gain an added measure of spiritual strength through a daily study of the scriptures. Your study need not be long, but it should be every day. If I were you, I would read the scriptures tonight and never let a day pass without reading in them, even if only for a few minutes.

There is an added measure of inspiration promised to those who read the scriptures regularly. The scriptures will assist us to overpower darkness with light. The third step I would counsel is: when necessary, receive the blessing that comes in the confession process. . . . Stopping the activity and cleansing the spirit of impurities . . . will not be easy, and it will not be quick, but it can be sure." (Conf. Report, Oct. 1993).

President Uchtdorf taught: "Satan wants us to think that when we have sinned we have gone past a 'point of no return' – that it is too late to change our course. . . . To make us lose hope, feel miserable like himself, and believe that we are beyond forgiveness, Satan might . . . imply that there is no mercy. . . . [but] Christ came to save us. If we have taken a wrong course, the Atonement of Jesus Christ can give us the assurance that sin is *not* a point of no return. A safe return is possible if we will follow God's plan for our salvation." (Conf. Report, Apr. 2007). "Our Savior's Atonement is infinite and eternal. Each of us strays and falls short. We may, for a time, lose our way. God lovingly assures us, no matter where we are or what we have done, there is no point of no return. He waits ready to embrace us." (Gong, Conf. Report, Apr. 2018). Through repentance and the Atonement, through the mercy of Christ, we can be completely forgiven.

President Boyd K. Packer testified: "Nowhere is the generosity and mercy of God more manifest than in repentance. Our physical bodies, when harmed, are able to repair themselves, sometimes with the help of a physician. If the damage is extensive, however, often a scar will remain as a reminder of the injury. With our spiritual bodies it is another matter. Our spirits are damaged when we make mistakes and commit sins. But unlike the case of our mortal bodies, when the repentance process is complete, *no scars remain because of the Atonement of Jesus Christ*. The promise is: 'Behold, he who has repented of his sins, the same is forgiven, and I, the Lord, remember them no more.' (D&C 58:42). . . . The Atonement, which can reclaim each one of us, bears no scars. That means that *no matter what we have done or where we have been or how something happened, if we truly repent, He has promised that He would atone. And when He atoned, that settled that.* . . . I am so grateful for the blessings of . . . the Atonement which can wash clean every stain no matter how difficult or how long or how many times repeated. The Atonement can put you free again to move forward, cleanly and worthily, to pursue that path that you have chosen in life." (Conf. Report, Apr. 2015, *emphasis added*).

"Repentance means a change of mind and heart – we stop doing things that are wrong, and we start doing things that are right." (Uchtdorf, Conf. Report, Apr. 2007). The Prophet Ezekiel said, "if he turn from his sin, and do that which is lawful and right . . . he shall surely live, he shall not die. None of his sins that he hath committed shall be mentioned unto him" (Ezekiel 33:14-16). In true repentance, we literally and symbolically turn toward the Lord. And the Lord will turn to us with forgiveness and mercy.

The word repent implies a course correction: we turn away from sin, and turn toward God. Elder Dale G. Renlund taught, "In Swedish, the word [for repentance] is *omvand*, which simply means 'to turn around.' The Christian writer C. S. Lewis . . . noted that repentance involves 'being put back on the right road. A wrong sum can be put right,' he said, 'but only by going back till you find the error and working it afresh from that point, never by simply going on.' Changing our behavior and returning to the 'right road' are part of repentance, but only part. Real repentance also includes a turning of our heart and will to God and renunciation of sin." (Conf. Report, Oct. 2016).

The Hebrew word used for repentance in the Old Testament is *shub*, which means to "turn back" or "return." (See, Burton, "The Meaning of Repentance," *Ensign*, Nov. 1988). Regarding *shub*, the *Theological Wordbook of the OT* states, "The Bible is rich in idioms describing man's responsibility in the process of repentance. . . . All these expressions of man's penitential activity, however, are subsumed and summarized by this one verb *shub*. Far better than any other verb it combines in itself the two requisites of repentance: to turn from evil and to turn to the good . . . the fact that people are called 'to turn' either 'to' or 'away from' implies that sin is not an ineradicable stain, but by turning, a God-given power, a sinner can redirect his destiny."

Elder Neil L. Andersen instructed: "When we sin, we turn away from God. When we repent, we turn back toward God. The invitation to repent is rarely a voice of chastisement but rather a loving appeal to turn around and to 're-turn' toward God. It is the beckoning of a loving Father and His Only Begotten Son to be more than we are, to reach up to a higher way of life, to change, and to feel the happiness of keeping the commandments." (Conf. Report, Oct. 2009). "Repentance is not an event; it is a process. It is the key to happiness and peace of mind. . . . Too many people consider repentance as punishment – something to be avoided except in the most serious of circumstances. But this feeling of being penalized is engendered by Satan. He tries to block us from looking to Jesus Christ, who stands ready to heal, forgive, cleanse, strengthen, purify, and sanctify us." (Nelson, Conf. Report, Apr. 2019).

President Harold B. Lee said, "When you have done all within your power to overcome your mistakes, and have determined in your heart that you will never repeat them again, then . . . peace of conscience [can come to you] by which you will know that your sins have been forgiven." (*quoted* in Uchtdorf, Conf. Report, Apr. 2007). President Gordon B. Hinckley said, "Brothers and sisters, all the Lord expects of us it to try, but you have to really try." (*quoted in* Cornish, Conf. Report, Oct. 2016). "You are going to make it as long as you keep repenting and do not rationalize or rebel. The God of heaven is not a heartless referee looking for any excuse to throw us out of the game. He is our perfectly loving Father, who yearns more than anything else to have all of His children come back home and live with Him. . . . He truly gave His Only Begotten Son that we might not perish but have everlasting life." (Cornish, Conf. Report, Oct. 2016).

"All of us have made wrong turns along the way. I believe the kind and merciful God, whose children we are, will judge us as lightly as He can for the wrongs that we have done and give us maximum blessings for the good that we do. . . . As President Kimball reminds us: 'The principle of repentance – of rising again whenever we fall, brushing ourselves off, and setting off again on that upward trail – is the basis for our hope.'" (Faust, Conf. Report, Oct. 1996).

"President J. Reuben Clark Jr. contributed this valuable insight when he said: 'I feel that [the Savior] will give that punishment which is the very least that our transgression will justify. I believe that he will bring into his justice all of the infinite love and blessing and mercy and kindness and understanding which he has. . . . And on the other hand, I believe that when it comes to making the rewards for our good conduct, he will give us the maximum that it is possible to give." (Faust, Conf. Report, Oct. 2001.

"The Atonement can wash clean every stain no matter how difficult or how long or how many times repeated. . . . What it fixes is fixed. . . . It just heals, and what it heals stays healed." (Packer, Conf. Report, Apr. 2015). The Atonement enables the miracle of forgiveness.

Small and Simple Things

In Chapter 37, Alma commands Helaman to take possession of the scriptural records, including the plates of brass, and keep a record of the people on the plates of Nephi. (Alma 37:1-3). He teaches his son that the scriptures are designed to enlarge our memory, convince us of the error of our ways, and bring us to a knowledge of God and His plan of salvation. (Alma 37:8-9). Elder Neal A. Maxwell observed: "By searching the holy scriptures, we access a vast, divine data bank, a reservoir of remembrance. In this way, the scriptures can, as the Book of Mormon says, enlarge the memory." (Conf. Report, Apr. 1991).

Elder D. Todd Christofferson taught: "The scriptures enlarge our memory by helping us always to remember the Lord and our relationship to Him and the Father. They remind us of what we know in our premortal life. And they expand our memory in another sense by teaching us about epochs, people, and events that we did not experience personally. . . The scriptures also enlarge our memory by helping us not forget what we and earlier generations have learned." (Conf. Report, Apr. 2010).

The scriptures may appear to be a "small and simple thing," Alma taught; however, "by small and simple things are great things brought to pass" (Alma 37:6). Elder M. Russell Ballard stated: "We observe vast, sweeping world events; however, we must remember that the purposes of the Lord in our personal lives generally are fulfilled through the small and simple things, and not the momentous and spectacular. . . . Like weak fibers that form a yarn, then a strand, and finally a rope . . . small things combined together can become too strong to be broken. We must ever be aware of the power that the small and simple things can have in building spirituality." (Conf. Report, Apr. 1990). He then identifies some of the small and simple things that can build spirituality: family and personal prayers; scripture study, particularly the Book of Mormon; family home evenings; and thoughtfulness, kindness, and gentleness in family interactions. "Through these and other similar small and simple things, we have the promise that our lives will be filled with peace and joy." (Ballard, Conf. Report, Apr. 1990).

Elder David A. Bednar said: "Each family prayer, each episode of family scripture study, and each family home evening is a brushstroke on the canvas of our souls. No one event may appear to be very impressive or memorable. But just as the yellow and gold and brown strokes of paint complement each other and produce an impressive masterpiece, so our consistency in doing seemingly small things can lead to significant spiritual results" ("More Diligent and Concerned at Home," *Ensign,* Nov. 2009, 19–20). President Gordon B. Hinckley warned: "It is so likewise with evil things. Small acts of dishonesty, small acts of an immoral nature, small outbursts of anger can grow into great and terrible things." (Conf. Report, Apr. 1984).

Liahona as a Type: The Words of Christ Point the Way

Alma used the workings of the Liahona as an example of small and simple things that bring great things to come to pass. "To assist Lehi's colony in journeying through the great Arabian Desert and across the great seas, the Lord prepared a . . . *Liahona*, which means 'compass' – the equivalent of an early twenty-first century global positioning system. But instead of functioning through electrical power, it operated on faith and obedience." (Ogden and Skinner, Verse by Verse: The Book of Mormon, 2:31). Noting that the Liahona worked by faith, Alma said, "Nevertheless, because those miracles were worked by small means . . . [the people] were slothful and forgot to exercise their faith and diligence and then those marvelous works ceased, and they did not progress in their journey" (Alma 37:41).

"In addition to its literal function, [the Liahona] had – like most gospel concepts – a symbolic function. It was a real object that typified an underlying reality. The Liahona was a type and shadow of Christ, who points the way all of us should go in life." (Ogden and Skinner, Verse by Verse: The Book of Mormon, 2:31). Elder W. Rolfe Kerr instructed: "So we see, brethren and sisters, that the words of Christ can be a personal Liahona for each of us, showing us the way. Let us not be slothful because of the easiness of the way. Let us in faith take the words of Christ into our minds and into our hearts as they are recorded in sacred scripture. . . . Let us with faith and diligence feast upon the words of Christ, for the words of Christ will be our spiritual Liahona telling us all things what we should do." (Conf. Report, Apr. 2004). The words of Christ serve as a spiritual compass leading to eternal life.

Elder M. Russell Ballard observed: "Is our journey sometimes impeded when we forget the importance of small things? Do we realize that small events and choices determine the direction of our lives just as small helms determine the direction of great ships? (James 3:4)." (Conf. Report, April 1990). "The gospel of Jesus Christ is simple, no matter how much we try to make it complicated. We should strive to keep our lives similarly simple, unencumbered by extraneous influences. . . What are the precious, simple things of the gospel that bring clarity and purpose to our lives? . . . I believe there is one simple but profound – even sublime – principle that encompasses the entirety of the gospel of Jesus Christ. . . . The Savior spoke of this principle when He answered the Pharisee who asked, 'Master, which is the great commandment in the law? Jesus said unto him, Thou shat love the Lord thy God with all thy heart, and with all thy soul, and with all thy mind. This is the first and great commandment. And the second is like unto it, Thou shalt love thy neighbor as thyself.' (Matthew 22:36-40). . . . President Spencer W. Kimball said: . . . 'So often, our acts of service consist of simple encouragement or of giving . . . help with mundane tasks, but what glorious consequences can flow . . . from small but deliberate deeds.' . . . Great things are wrought through simple and small things . . . our small and simple acts of kindness and service will accumulate into a life filled with love for Heavenly Father, devotion to the work of the Lord Jesus Christ, and a sense of peace and joy each time we reach out to one another." (Ballard, Conf. Report, Apr. 2011).

Small choices can prepare us to face great challenges.

The Lord said: "Out of small things proceedeth that which is great" (D&C 64:33). If we consistently perform the small and simple acts of spiritual and temporal preparation, we will be better positioned to face life's challenges and opportunities. Our small choices determine our destiny, whether in response to an unforeseen crisis or as the sum total of decisions made in a lifetime. The principle has both spiritual and secular applications. The concept of creating great things from small and simple means is implicit in the Hawaiian proverb, "he puko'a kani'aina," which roughly translated means: a small coral reef can grow into a large island.

A person can accomplish great things through small acts of preparation. One example of this was demonstrated by a U.S. Airways pilot who faced a crisis on a cold January day in New York in 2009.

Miracle on the Hudson

On January 15, 2009, U.S. Airways Flight 1549, piloted by Captain Chesley B. Sullenburger, took off from runway four at LaGuardia Airport in New York City. The plane, an Airbus A320, with 150 passengers and five crew, was heading to Charlotte, North Carolina.

About three minutes into the flight, the plane ran into a flock of Canadian geese, with more than 100 large birds. The windshield went dark, and passengers heard several loud thuds in both engines, which soon burst flames from their exhaust, and then went silent. The crew radioed air traffic controllers at New York Terminal Radar Approach Control with the message: "Hit birds. Lost thrust in both engines, turning back to LaGuardia." The event, known as a "bird strike,"[55] caused both engines to lose power. At the time, the plane was at 3,000 feet and climbing rapidly.

Captain Sullenberger (or "Captain Sully" as he was known) asked air traffic control if the plane could be cleared for an emergency landing, but then immediately radioed – "We can't do that. I'm going to have to bring the plane down due to lack of altitude." Air traffic control at La Guardia reported seeing the aircraft pass just a couple hundred feet above the George Washington Bridge, and, avoiding the heavily populated city buildings in Manhattan, Captain Sully brought the plane down in the middle of the Hudson River as close as possible to a ferry station that had watercraft that could respond quickly in the frigid weather.

The crew immediately began evacuating the 150 passengers onto the wings and to an inflatable slide that doubled as a life raft. The impact from the landing had ripped a hole in the underside of the plane, and twisted the fuselage, causing the cargo doors to pop open and start to fill the plane with water from the rear. The partially submerged plane began to slowly sink into the frigid waters of the river and drift downstream.

As the plane filled with water, Captain Sully twice traversed the length of the cabin to confirm that no one remained inside, and was the last person out of the plane. All 155 occupants, the passengers and crew, successfully evacuated from the plane as it sank into the river, and were rescued by nearby watercraft. Several passengers suffered injuries, but only one required hospitalization overnight. The incident came to be known as the "Miracle on the Hudson."

The entire crew was awarded the Master's Medal of the Guild of Air Pilots and Navigators, with a citation that read: "this emergency evacuation, with the loss of no lives, is a heroic and unique aviation achievement, the most successful [of its kind] in aviation history." Captain Sully later said: "Even though this was an unanticipated event for which we have never specifically trained, I was confident that I could quickly synthesize a lifetime of training and experience, adapt it in a new way to solve a problem I had never seen before and get it right the first time, and so that's what I did." (*Newsweek*, July 11, 2015).

Captain Sullenburger later received a letter that read: "It is clear that many choices in your life prepared you for that moment when the engines failed. I hope your story encourages those who toil and prepare in obscurity to know that their reward is simple – they will be ready if the test comes. I hope your story of preparation encourages others to imitation." (Zaslow, "What We Can Learn from Sully's Journey," Wall Street Journal, Oct. 14, 2009).

---

[55] It is somewhat troubling that such instances occur frequently enough that the aviation industry has an official term for when an aircraft collides with a bird in flight.

It is our choices about the small and simple things that can prepare us for moments of crisis – when the metaphorical engines fail; or when we need strength to face temptation; or when we are presented with a unique or critical opportunity, what John Adams described as an "animating occasion."[56] It is the small and simple things – the preparation, the practice, toiling away in obscurity – that shape our characters and allow us to fulfill our destinies.

"In the Savior's work, it is often by small and simple means that 'great things [are] brought to pass.' We know that it requires repetitive practice to become good at anything. Whether it's playing the clarinet, kicking a ball into a net, repairing a car, or even flying an airplane, it is through practicing that we may become better and better." (Uchtdorf, Conf. Report, Oct. 2018).

Look to God and Live

Alma concludes his discourse to his son Helaman with the admonition: "Yea, see that ye look to God and live" (Alma 37:47). This phrase refers to the incident where the ancient Israelites were bitten by poisonous serpents. (Numbers 21:6-9). The children of Israel beseeched Moses to save them from the serpents, and the Lord instructed Moses to create a brass serpent and set it on a pole, with the promise that everyone who looked upon the raised serpent would be healed. As Alma observed, "because of the hardness of their hearts," the Israelites did not understand the symbolic meaning of the brass serpent. While "many did look and live," others did not believe, and would not follow Moses' instruction to look to be healed.

The brass serpent was a type or symbol of Christ. Just as the ancient Israelites were physically healed by merely looking at the brass serpent, we can be spiritually healed by simply looking to Christ. The Lord Himself taught: "As Moses lifted up the serpent in the wilderness, even so must the Son of man be lifted up: that whosoever believeth in him should not perish, but have eternal life" (John 3:14-15). The reason many of the Israelites did not look to the serpent was that they did not believe doing so would heal them.

Alma used the example of the brass serpent to teach his son that the people could be spiritually healed by "merely casting about [their] eyes" on Christ, and believing on Him. President Thomas S. Monson taught: "Look to God and live. No problem is too small for His attention nor so large that He cannot answer the prayer of faith." (Conf. Report, Apr. 1999). Whether it be small and simple things, or momentous events, we are counseled to look to our Father in Heaven.

President Marion G. Romney observed: "Six thousand years of human history attests to Alma's wisdom. Every chapter thereof teaches that the uninspired wisdom of men cannot build a lasting stable civilization or bring peace and happiness to individual men. All the evidence teaches that if man would live abundantly and preserve his civilization, he must look to God. . . . The need for us to look to God . . . in order to live is inherent in the very nature of man and his environment. . . . Happiness, joy, peace, salvation, and every other component of the abundant life for men and peace among nations, are attained by obedience to the laws upon which they are predicated." (Conf. Report, Oct. 1962).

---

[56] John Adams wrote: "I shall never shine until some animating occasion calls forth all my powers." (Quoted in Congressional Record, June 25, 2001, v. 147, pt. 8, 11758).

Discourse 19: Alma, "Effective Teaching" (Alma 38)

Prophet	Key Doctrines	Scriptures	Audience	Date
Alma	• Attributes of an Effective Teacher	Alma 38	To his son, Shiblon	About 74 B.C.

INTRODUCTION

Shiblon served as a missionary with his father, Alma, among the Zoramites. After this mission, Alma recognized Shiblon's faithfulness and steadiness in preaching the gospel. Elder Michael T. Ringwood observed: "Shiblon was one of the sons of Alma the Younger. We are more familiar with his brothers Helaman, who would follow his father as the keeper of the records and the prophet of God, and Corianton, who gained some notoriety as a missionary who needed some counsel from his father. . . . To Shiblon, his middle son, Alma wrote a mere 15 verses. Yet his words in those 15 verses are powerful and instructive." (Conf. Report, Apr. 2015).

Alma said to Shiblon: "I trust that I shall have great joy in you, because of your steadiness and your faithfulness unto God. . . . I have great joy in thee already, because of your faithfulness and thy diligence, and thy patience and thy long-suffering among the people" (Alma 38:2-3). Alma also spoke of Shiblon's righteousness to his brother, Corianton: "Have ye not observed the steadiness of thy brother, his faithfulness, and his diligence in keeping the commandments of God? Behold, has he not set a good example for thee?" (Alma 39:1).[57]

"It appears Shiblon was a son who wanted to please his father and went about doing what was right for right's sake rather than for praise, position, power, accolades, or authority. Helaman must have known and respected this about his brother, for he gave Shiblon custody of the sacred records he had received from his father. . . . '[Shiblon] was a just man, and he did walk uprightly before God; and he did observe to do good continually, to keep the commandments of the Lord his God' (Alma 63:2). . . . Shiblon was truly good and without guile. He was a person who sacrificed his time, talents, and effort to help and lift others because of a love of God and his fellowmen. He is described perfectly by the words of President Spencer W. Kimball: 'Great women and men are always more anxious to serve than to have dominion.'" (Ringwood, Conf. Report, Apr. 2015).

DISCOURSE: Alma 38

---

[57] We know that when he says "thy brother," Alma is talking about Shiblon, because Alma only took two of his sons to go teach the Zoramites. (See Alma 31:6-7; 39:2). "Now the eldest of his sons he took not with him, and his name was Helaman; but the names of those whom he took with him [to preach to the Zoramites] were Shiblon and Corianton" (Alma 31:7).

KEY DOCTRINES

- **Attributes of Effective Teaching** (as a missionary or gospel teacher) include: Be diligent and temperate; do not boast of wisdom or strength; be bold not overbearing; bridle passions; refrain from idleness; acknowledge unworthiness before God; and be sober. (Alma 38:10-14).

COMMENTARY

Attributes of an Effective Teacher

Alma praised his son, Shiblon for his "steadiness and faithfulness unto God" (Alma 38:2), and provided counsel that would help him "continue to teach" (Alma 38:10) the word of the Lord. Elder D. Todd Christofferson stated, "I am reminded of our mothers' counsel: 'Eat your vegetables; it will do you good.' Our mothers are right, and in the context of steadfastness in the faith, 'eating your vegetables' is to pray constantly, to feast on the scriptures daily, to serve and worship in the Church, to worthily take the sacrament each week, to love your neighbor, and to take up your cross in obedience to God each day." (Conf. Report, Oct. 2018).

Alma provided the following instructions: "And now, as ye have begun to teach the word even so I would that ye should continue to teach; and I would that ye would be **diligent** and **temperate** in all things. See that ye are not lifted up unto **pride**; yea, see that ye **do not boast** in your own wisdom, nor of your much strength. Use **boldness**, but not overbearance; and also see that ye **bridle all your passions**, that ye may be filled with love; see that ye **refrain from idleness** . . . acknowledge your unworthiness before God at all times. . . . Now go, my son, and teach the word unto this people. **Be sober**" (Alma 38:10-12, 15 *emphasis added*).

These qualities are similar to the attributes that "qualify" those that "embark in the service of God" (see D&C 4:6): faith, virtue, knowledge, temperance, patience, brotherly kindness, godliness, charity, humility, and diligence. Alma had previously taught the righteous members of the church in Gideon to seek similar characteristics, attributes that would allow them to "walk blameless before [God], that [they] may walk after the holy order of God" (Alma 7:22). "And now I would that ye should be humble, and be submissive and gentle; easy to be entreated; full of patience and long-suffering; being temperate in all things; being diligent in keeping the commandments of God. . . ." (Alma 7:23).

(See "Divine Attributes in Topical Index, Alma 7).

"Be diligent and temperate in all things." (Alma 38:10).

Diligence is consistent, careful, and conscientious effort. To be **temperate** is to use moderation. Elder Kent D. Watson taught: "Being temperate means to carefully examine our expectations and desires, to be diligent and patient in seeking righteous goals. . . . a temperate soul – one who is humble and full of love – is also a person of increased spiritual strength. With increased spiritual strength, we are able to develop self-mastery and to live with moderation. We learn to control, or temper, our anger, vanity, and pride" (Conf. Report, Oct. 2009). A teacher is under control, and does not let his or her emotions influence perception about his or her students, or delivery of the message. (See "Temperance," Alma 7).

"See that ye are not lifted up unto pride; . . . do not boast." (Alma 38:11).

One aspect of **pride** is putting greater trust in oneself than in God. Pride is also evident when a person thinks he or she is superior to or more important than others. "True disciples speak with quiet confidence, not boastful pride." (Hales, Conf. Report, Oct. 2008). President Ezra Taft Benson taught: "The proud make every man their adversary by pitting their intellects, opinions, works, wealth, talents, or any other worldly measuring device against others. In the words of C. S. Lewis: 'Pride gets no pleasure out of having something, only out of having more of it than the next man. . . . It is the comparison that makes you proud: the pleasure of being above the rest.'" (Conf. Report, Apr. 1989). A teacher is a servant, and does not teach for the honors of men, but to benefit the student, and to share the word of God. A teacher avoids self-serving performances and vain discussions. (See "Humility" in Topical Index, Alma 32).

"Use boldness, but not overbearance." (Alma 38:12).

"To be ***bold*** means to be confident that God is with us and can help us act without fear in His service. To be ***overbearing*** can mean to push our beliefs or attitudes on others without being sensitive to their needs and feelings." (Book of Mormon Study Guide for Home-Study Seminary Students, Unit 19: Alma 38, *emphasis added*). Elder Robert D. Hales taught: "Yet even as we feel to speak the word of God with boldness, we must pray to be filled with the Holy Ghost. We should never confuse boldness with Satan's counterfeit: overbearance. True disciples speak with quiet confidence, not boastful pride." (Conf. Report, Oct. 2008).

Elder Gene R. Cook instructed, "you can stand up for the truth wherever you are, at all times, and in all places. Sometimes our members are fearful to speak up for the truth in clubs, associations, or even, at times, among members of the church. As the Lord has said, it should be done with boldness but not overbearance." (Conf. Report, Apr. 1976). The Prophet Joseph Smith counseled missionaries: "Let the Elders be exceedingly careful about unnecessarily disturbing and harrowing up the feelings of the people. Remember that your business is to preach the gospel in all humility and meekness, and warn sinners to repent and come to Christ." (Teachings of the Prophet Joseph Smith, 43).

"Bridle all your passions." (Alma 38:12).

To **bridle** means to restrain, guide or control. President Boyd K. Packer said: "A bridle is used to guide, to direct, to restrain. Our passion is to be controlled." (Conf. Report, Apr. 2015). Elder Bruce C. Hafen explained that a bridle was meant to direct, not destroy, desires and passions. "Is self-denial wise because something is wrong with our passions, or because something is right with our passions? Alma taught his son: 'See that ye bridle all your passions, *that ye may be filled with love.*' (Alma 38:12). He did not say eliminate or even suppress your passions, but *bridle* them – harness, channel, and focus them. Why? Because discipline makes possible a richer, deeper love." (Hafen, The Belonging Heart, 302, *emphasis in original*).

"Bridling increases strength, increases power, increases love. . . . Alma never said kill your passions. The implication is not that passions are evil, that we shouldn't have them. On the contrary, we bridle something we love, something whose power we respect." (Dunn, Conf. Report, Oct. 1981). Alma counseled his son Shiblon to "bridle all [of his] passions, that [he] may be filled with love" (Alma 38:12).

"Significantly, disciplining the natural man in each of us makes possible a richer, a deeper, and a more enduring love of God and of His children. Love increases through righteous restraint and decreases through impulsive indulgence." (Bednar, Conf. Report, Apr. 2013). President Russell C. Taylor observed: "That is an interesting paradox – true love comes when you bridle your passions, when you use self-control." (Conf. Report, Apr. 1989).

Bridling one's passions to obtain true love is similar to the paradox that brakes enable a car to go fast. Indeed, without brakes, a car would be idle, never being able to go, since it would not be able to stop. Brakes enable speed. Similarly, and paradoxically, through bridling one's passions, one can experience greater passionate fulfillment in true love. Bridling one's passions, however, is not always easy.

Elder Burton observed: "I admit that except for the Savior no person alone can completely harness his appetites and passions. I do say, however, that with the help of God we can all learn to control those appetites and passions. As we practice righteousness and approach ever closer to God, the easier it becomes to resist temptation." (Conf. Report, Apr. 1981).

President Thomas S. Monson said: "Most of you are familiar with the play Camelot. I'd like to share with you one of my favorite lines from this production. As the difficulties among King Arthur, Sir Lancelot, and Queen Guinevere deepen, King Arthur cautions, 'We must not let our passions destroy our dreams.' This plea I would leave with you tonight. Do not let your passions destroy your dreams." (Conf. Report, Apr. 2005). (See "Chastity" in Topical Index, Alma 39).

"Refrain from idleness." (Alma 38:12).

Elder Henry D. Taylor taught: "**Idleness** is an offense against the gospel and has received the Lord's severe condemnation . . . 'Thou shalt not be idle; for he that is idle shall not eat the bread nor wear the garments of the laborer.' (D&C 42:42). 'For the idler shall be had in remembrance before the Lord.' (D&C 68:30)" (Conf. Report, Apr. 1961).

Elder Alvin R. Dyer instructed: "When a man shuns effort, he is in no position to resist temptation. So, through all the ages, idleness has been known as the parent of all the vices. . . . The dry rot of ennui, the vague self-disgust of those who cannot 'deal with time,' is the natural result of idleness.'" (Conf. Report, Oct. 1971, *quoting* Jordan, The Strength of Being Clean, 18-19).

In ancient times, the prophet Ezekiel defined one of the iniquities of Sodom as an "abundance of idleness" (Ezekiel 16:49). In our day, President Gordon B. Hinckley admonished: "I am suggesting that we spend a little less time in idleness, in the fruitless pursuit of watching some inane and empty television programs. Time so utilized can be put to better advantage, and the consequences will be wonderful." (Conf. Report, Apr. 1995).

Elder J. Richard Clarke observed: "Idleness gives room for doubts and fears. If disappointments come, keep right on working. If sorrow overwhelms you . . . work. . . . When faith falters and reason fails, just work. . . . Work is the greatest remedy available for both mental and physical afflictions." (Conf. Report, Apr. 1982). A teacher puts in the time, studies, ponders, works and prepares.

"Be sober." (Alma 38:15).

Being **sober** means being earnest and serious in assessing your circumstances and careful and circumspect in weighing the consequences of your actions. Soberness therefore yields good judgment, as well as measured conduct. Alma counseled each of his sons – Helaman, Shiblon, and Corianton – to "be sober" (Alma 37:47; Alma 38:15; Alma 42:31). Paul also exhorted young men to be "sober minded" (Titus 2:6; see Romans 12:3). Mormon observed that Helaman's 2,000 stripling warriors were effective in battle because of their courage, strength, trustworthiness, and their "soberness" (Alma 53:20-21). A teacher is earnest and serious, perhaps using humor judiciously, but avoiding levity for levity's sake.

All of these righteous attributes prepare us to teach and serve others. Throughout the ages, prophets and apostles have echoed Alma's instruction to his son, Shiblon, on the importance of effective teaching. During the meridian of time, Paul placed the priority of teachers next to apostles and prophets: "And God hath set some in the church, first apostles, secondarily prophets, thirdly teachers" (1 Cor. 12:28). And, in the early 1900's, President David O. McKay, then an apostle, said: "No greater responsibility can rest upon any man, than to be a teacher of God's children." (Conf. Report, Oct. 1916). More recently, Elder Harold G. Hillam observed: "We are in essence a church of teachers. Regardless of life's circumstances or the nature of one's calling, all members of the Church have the opportunity to teach and to testify." (Conf. Report, Oct. 1997).

President Spencer W. Kimball taught: "Please take a particular interest in strengthening and improving the quality of teaching in the Church. . . . I fear at times that all too often many of our members come to church, sit through a class or meeting, and then return home having been largely uninformed. . . . We all need to be touched and nurtured by the Spirit, and effective teaching is one of the most important ways this can happen. " (Conf. Report, Apr. 1981). President Gordon B. Hinckley said: "Effective teaching is the very essence of leadership in the church. Eternal life will come only as men and women are taught with such effectiveness that they change and discipline their lives. They cannot be coerced into righteousness or into heaven. They must be led, and that means teaching." (*quoted* by Holland, Conf. Report, Apr. 1998).

Elder M. Russell Ballard provided additional guidelines for teachers in the church: "I believe there is no greater call in the Church than to be an effective teacher. . . . In each teaching setting, whether it is a family home evening, a class, a sacrament meeting, or a general or stake conference, the teacher should strive to create a heartfelt desire in his students to live worthy of eternal life with our Heavenly Father. . . . My plea to the teachers of the Church is to study, ponder, and pray for guidance in your preparation. Use the scriptures and the approved curriculum materials, teaching with the objective to bless and inspire the lives of those assigned to you." (Conf. Report, Apr. 1983).

"The goal of gospel teaching . . . is not to pour information into the minds of class members. . . . The aim is to inspire the individual to think about, feel about, and then do something about living gospel principles." (Monson, Conf. Report, Oct. 1970). "Elder David A. Bednar shared these three simple elements of effective teaching in a training meeting: (1) key doctrines, (2) invitation to action, and (3) promised blessings." (Osguthorpe, Conf. Report, Oct. 2009). Elder Jeffrey R. Holland provided additional counsel for effective teaching: "Never sow seeds of doubt. Avoid self-serving performance and vanity. Prepare lessons well. Give scripturally based sermons. Teach the revealed doctrine. Bear heartfelt testimony. Pray and practice and try to improve." (Conf. Report, Apr. 1998). "The best teacher is a good role model." (Soares, Conf. Report, Apr. 2019).

Elder Gene R. Cook outlined what he called: "Spiritual Guides for Teachers of Righteousness." These "Guides" include the attributes identified by Alma – Alma's language is included in brackets where applicable within the quoted material below. Elder Cook said, "I would like to suggest eight standards against which a person can measure his own teaching of the gospel as well as the doctrines taught by others . . .

1. "Not only will the teacher teach the truth, but the Spirit of the Lord will accompany the truth and the teacher. . . . The teacher will not teach without authority nor speak independently for himself . . . [*teach the word*]
2. "The teacher will be in accord with the General Authorities as a group and with his local leaders, knowing they are guides to safety. . . . He will not complain, criticize, or speak evilly of the Lord's anointed. . . .
3. "The teacher of righteousness will teach from the holy scriptures and will teach that which is taught and confirmed by the Holy Ghost. He will not 'teach for doctrines the commandments of men.' (JS-H 1:19). He will not mingle the history and opinions of men with the scriptures nor spend religious instruction time teaching speculation or the philosophies of the world. . . . [*teach the word*]
4. "The teacher will teach in simplicity, according to the true needs of the people, basic gospel doctrines like faith, repentance, and prayer, which all men – all men – can apply. He will not look beyond the mark by exaggerating, by teaching in the fringe areas, by expanding on the scriptures, or by teaching exotic extremes in any principle, like excessively lengthy prayers, false doctrines about the Savior or about Adam, or extremes in diet, or politics, or investments. . . . He knows of . . . 'temperance in all things.' (D&C 12:8). [*be temperate*]
5. "The teacher will speak in the light of day. He will not speak of secret doctrines, of special groups 'in the know,' or of secret ordinations. [*do not boast in your own wisdom*]
6. "The teacher will treat all those being taught as like unto himself, not esteeming himself above his brethren. He will seek excellence before the Lord, but not to excel over his companions in the work. . . . [*see that ye are not lifted up unto pride*]
7. "The teacher of righteousness will be anxious to glorify the Lord. He will refuse to assume any glory unto himself. He will not practice priestcrafts – that is, preaching and holding himself up as a light to the world for gain or for the honor of men. . . . [*see that ye are not lifted up unto pride and do not boast in your own wisdom or strength*]
8. "The teacher himself will be in the process of continual personal repentance. He will be an example of meekness, charity, pure motives, dependence on the Lord. He will not just be teaching the doctrine, but also applying it. All in all, it will be evident whom he represents [*be filled with love*]."(Conf. Report, Apr. 1982).

The primary exemplar of effective teaching was the Master, Jesus Christ. As Elder Holland observed: "When Nicodemus came to Jesus early in the Savior's ministry, he spoke for all of us when he said, 'Rabbi, we know that thou art a teacher come from God.' (John 3:2)." (Conf. Report, Apr. 1998). Alma's attributes of an effective teacher in Alma 38:10-15 mirror the divine characteristics of Christ set forth in Alma 7:23. This is not surprising since Christ, Himself, was the Master teacher. Elder Ballard reinforced Alma's counsel to Shiblon on the importance of teaching in his statement of gratitude to the Lord: "To the master teacher, the Lord Jesus Christ . . . I say: I thank thee, oh Lord, for teaching us that there is no greater call than to be an effective teacher." (Conf. Report, Apr. 1983).

Discourse 20: Alma, "Chastity, Justice & Mercy" (Alma 39-42)

Prophet	Key Doctrines	Scriptures	Audience	Date
Alma	• Chastity (ch. 39) • Restoration (ch. 40) • Restoration: Wickedness is Not Happiness (ch. 41) • Justice & Mercy (ch. 42)	Alma 39-42	To his son, Corianton	About 74 B.C.

INTRODUCTION

Alma's third son, Corianton, was called to serve a mission to the Zoramites, but failed to live the standards of a missionary. He deserted his ministry and went to the land of Siron, to pursue the harlot, Isabel. (Alma 39:3). Corianton violated the law of chastity, which Alma told him was "most abominable above all sins save it be the shedding of innocent blood or denying the Holy Ghost" (Alma 39:5). Alma "commanded" his son to "repent and forsake" his sins (Alma 39:9), and lamented about the collateral damage of Corianton's actions, and the impact it had on others: "for when they saw your conduct they would not believe in my words" (Alma 39:11).

After a sharp, severe rebuke, Alma began to teach his son. The pattern demonstrated by Alma in dealing with his disobedient son, Corianton, demonstrates the proper exercise of priesthood power by a loving father. Alma's discourse to his son, Corianton, is an example of exercising righteous priesthood authority: "Reproving betimes with sharpness . . . then showing forth afterwards an increase of love" (D&C 121:41-44). First, as "moved upon by the Holy Ghost" (D&C 121:43; Alma 39:12), Alma reproved Corianton with sharpness. Then, after patiently teaching fundamental gospel principles, Alma showed forth an increase of love, and seeing that his son was humble and repentant, Alma helped him lift the burden of his guilt.

President Boyd K. Packer observed: "Alma knew personally the pain of punishment and the joy of repentance. He himself had once greatly disappointed his own father, Corianton's grandfather. He rebelled and went about 'seeking to destroy the church' (Alma 36:6)" (Conf. Report, Apr. 2006). Now, Alma, in turn, was the father pleading with his son Corianton to repent.

President Packer remarked: "In agony and shame, Corianton was brought 'down to the dust in humility' (Alma 42:30). Alma, who was Corianton's father and also his priesthood leader was now satisfied with Corianton's repentance. He lifted the terrible burden of guilt his son carried and sent him back to the mission field: 'And now, O my son, ye are called of God to preach the word unto this people. . . . Go thy way, declare the word with truth and soberness. . . And may God grant unto you even according to my words' (Alma 42:31). Corianton joined his brothers, Helaman and Shiblon, who were among the priesthood leaders. Twenty years later in the land northward, he [Corianton] was still faithfully laboring in the gospel." (Conf. Report, Apr. 2006).

President James E. Faust observed: "One of the tender stories of the Book of Mormon takes place when Alma speaks to his son Corianton, who has fallen into transgression while on a mission to the Zoramites. As he counsels him to forsake his sin and turn again to the Lord, he learns that Corianton is worried about what will happen to him in the Resurrection. There follows a detailed treatment of the probationary state of this life, of justice versus mercy, and God's plan for our happiness in the hereafter, culminating in this verse: 'And mercy claimeth the penitent, and mercy cometh because of the atonement; and the atonement bringeth to pass the resurrection of the dead; and the resurrection of the dead bringeth back men into the presence of God; and thus they are restored into his presence, to be judged according to their works, according to the law and justice.' (Alma 42:23)." (Conf. Report, Oct. 1996).

Elder Richard G. Scott concluded: "You will be helped by studying the magnificent explanation of the need for repentance and how it can be obtained, as Alma counseled his wayward son, Corianton, in the Book of Mormon. Through trust in the plan of happiness and the capacity of the Savior to realize His promises, the darkness of sin can be swept away and the joy of a worthy life returned with the trust of loved ones, when earned the Lord's way." (Conf. Report, Oct. 2002).

"The account of this loving father and a wayward son, drawn from the Book of Mormon . . . is a type, a pattern, an example. Each of us has a loving Father in Heaven. Through the Father's redeeming plan, those who may stumble and fall 'are not cast off forever.' . . . 'The Lord cannot look upon sin with the least degree of allowance; nevertheless' (D&C 1:31-32), the Lord said, 'he who has repented of his sins, the same is forgiven, and I, the Lord, remember them no more.' (D&C 58:42). Could there be any more sweeter or more consoling words, more filled with hope, than those words from the scriptures? 'I, the Lord, remember [their sins] no more.' That is the testimony of the Book of Mormon." (Packer, Conf. Report, Apr. 2006).

DISCOURSE: Alma 39-42

KEY DOCTRINES

- **Importance of Chastity.** Sexual sin is an abomination to the Lord. (Alma 39:5). Steps in repentance include: forsake sins, sin no more, and keep the commandments. (Alma 39:9,13)

- **Resurrection.** Resurrection is a restoration of the spirit to the body in its proper and perfect frame. (Alma 40:23).

- **Restoration.** Restoration is good to good and evil to evil (Alma 41:3-5); we can't be restored from sin to happiness, as **"wickedness never was happiness"** (Alma 41:10).

- **Justice and Mercy.** Under the plan of redemption, if we repent, mercy can overcome justice. (Alma 42:13,22,24). The atonement was necessary for **mercy** to appease the demands of **justice,** as well as bring to pass the resurrection (Alma 42:15, 23).

COMMENTARY

The Importance of Chastity

Corianton's path to immorality evidently began with pride, and likely the corresponding belief that behavioral restrictions and rules did not apply to him. Sister Julie B. Beck taught: "Corianton was supposed to be serving a faithful mission, but he thought he was strong enough and smart enough to handle risky situations and bad company, and he got himself into big trouble and big sin when he started going to the wrong places, with the wrong people, doing the wrong things." (Conf. Report, Apr. 2007). Corianton's "boasting" in his "strength" and "wisdom" (Alma 39:2) was a precursor to his committing sexual sins. At some point, Corianton's reliance on the "arm of flesh" led him to succumb to temptations of the flesh.

Corianton then abandoned his ministry, and committed sexual sin, which is "an abomination in the sight of the Lord; yea, most abominable above all sins save it be the shedding of innocent blood or denying the Holy Ghost" (Alma 39:5).

Why is sexual immorality such a grievous sin? Modern-day prophets and apostles have consistently warned: "The plaguing sin of this generation is sexual immorality." (President Ezra Taft Benson *quoted in* Wirthlin, Conf. Report, Oct. 1994). President Boyd K. Packer taught: "If we pollute our fountains of life or lead others to transgress, there will be penalties more 'exquisite' and 'hard to bear' (D&C 19:15) than all the physical pleasure could ever be worth. . . . The only legitimate, authorized expression of the powers of procreation is between husband and wife, a man and a woman, who have been legally and lawfully married. Anything other than this violates the commandments of God." (Conf. Report, Apr. 2015).

Elder Jeffrey R. Holland observed: "What is there . . . that prompts Alma to warn his son Corianton that sexual transgression is 'an abomination'? . . . By assigning such seriousness to a physical appetite so universally bestowed, what is God trying to tell us about its place in His plan for all men and women? I submit to you He is doing precisely that – commenting about the very plan of life itself. Clearly among His greatest concerns regarding mortality are how one gets into this world and how one gets out of it. He has set very strict limits in these matters." (Conf. Report, Oct. 1998).

"The plan of happiness requires the righteous union of male and female, man and woman, husband and wife." (Packer, Conf. Report, Oct. 1993). "There was provided in our bodies – and this is sacred – a power of creation, a light, so to speak, that has the power to kindle other lights. This gift was to be used only within the sacred bonds of marriage. Through the exercise of this power of creation, a mortal body may be conceived, a spirit enter into it, and a new soul born into this life. This power is good. It can create and sustain family life. The power of creation . . . is essential to the [plan of happiness]. . . The misuse of it may disrupt the plan." (Packer, Conf. Report, Apr. 1972).

Elder Dallin H. Oaks declared: "Some who do not know the plan of salvation behave like promiscuous animals, but Latter-day Saints – especially those who are under sacred covenants – have no such latitude. We are solemnly responsible to God for the destruction or misuse of the creative powers he has placed within us." (Conf. Report, Oct. 1993).

Ancient and modern day prophets suggest several reasons to be morally clean:

1. **Demonstrate love of God**. Obeying the law of chastity will please our Heavenly Father, for the Lord "delights" in chastity. (Jacob 2:28).
2. **Obtain a reward of confidence and strength**. Through chaste thoughts and actions, we will grow in confidence and strength. If we "let virtue garnish [our] thoughts unceasingly; then shall [our] confidence wax strong in the presence of God" (D&C 121:45). President Gordon B. Hinckley taught, "I have thought, what a wonderful thing, what a marvelous thing it would be to stand with confidence – unafraid and unashamed and unembarrassed – in the presence of God. This is the promise held out to every virtuous man and woman." Quoting Tennyson's poem about Sir Galahad, the prophet affirmed: "My strength is as the strength of ten, because my heart is pure." (Hinckley, Conf. Report, Oct. 1970).
3. **Sustain family relationships**. Obeying the law of chastity will strengthen marital and family relationships. Jacob teaches that through immorality the people have "broken the hearts of your tender wives and lost the confidence of your children" (Jacob 2:35). Immorality destroys trust, "and it takes a long time to rebuild that trust when it is lost." (Holland, Conf. Report, Apr. 2010).
4. **Preserve our agency**. Immorality can take away our power to exercise agency. Immorality is addictive behavior, and negatively impacts our ability to makes choices. "Addiction surrenders later freedom to choose." (Nelson, Conf. Report, Oct. 1988)
5. **Properly use a sacred power**. The power of creation is a sacred, God-given right. To mis-use that power is to abuse that power.
6. **Control appetites**. Obeying the law of chastity allows us to control our physical appetites, and increases the power of our spiritual selves over our physical selves. If we are "faithful over a few things, [He will make us a] ruler over many things" (Matt. 25:21). One of the ways we progress toward godliness is to control the body we have been given in this life, so that we can be trusted with greater power in the future.
7. **Obey the commandments**. Chastity is a commandment – "Thou shalt not commit adultery" (Exodus 20:14; D&C 42:24) or "anything like unto it" (D&C 59:6). We should trust in the Lord to obey his commandments, which are given for our benefit – whether or not they are consistent with societal norms, or even whether we completely understand the supporting rationale. When Adam was asked why he was following the commandment to perform sacrifices, he responded, "I know not, save the Lord commanded me" (Moses 5:6). That alone is sufficient reason.

Despite lax morals in society, "[t]he Lord's standard regarding sexual purity is clear and unchanging. Do not have any sexual relations before marriage, and be completely faithful to your spouse after marriage." (For the Strength of Youth, 35). Elder Richard G. Scott declared: "Any sexual intimacy outside the bonds of marriage . . . is a sin and is forbidden by God . . . those intimate acts are forbidden by the Lord outside the enduring commitment of marriage because they undermine His purposes. . . . They cause serious emotional and spiritual harm. . . . Sexual immorality creates a barrier to the influence of the Holy Spirit. . . . It causes powerful physical and emotional stimulation. In time that creates an unquenchable appetite that drives the offender to ever more serious sin." (Conf. Report, Oct. 1994).

Elder Jeffrey R. Holland provided several practical recommendations to avoid and overcome temptations to violate the law of chastity. (Conf. Report, Apr. 2010):

- Avoid the neighborhood. Separate from people, materials and circumstances that will harm you. "Like Joseph in the presence of Potiphar's wife, just run."
- Seek help. Counsel with a bishop. Find suitable professional help. Pray without ceasing.
- Self-control. In addition to filters on computers, "[e]xercise more control over even the marginal moments that confront you. If a TV show is indecent, turn it off. If a movie is crude, walk out. If an improper relationship is developing, sever it."
- Drive away improper thoughts. "Replace lewd thoughts with hopeful images and joyful memories; picture the faces of those who love you and would be shattered if you let them down."
- Create spiritual sanctuaries. Welcome appropriate art, music and literature into your home. Attend the temple as often as circumstances allow. "And when you leave the temple, remember the symbols you take with you, never to be set aside or forgotten."

"May the joy of our fidelity to the highest and best within us be ours as we keep our love and our marriages, our society and our souls, as pure as they were meant to be." (Holland, Conf. Report, Apr. 2010).

"In matters of human intimacy, you must wait! You must wait until you can give everything, and you cannot give everything until you are legally and lawfully married. . . . If you persist in pursuing physical satisfaction without the sanction of heaven, you run the terrible risk of such spiritual, psychic damage that you may undermine both your longing for physical intimacy and your ability to give wholehearted devotion to a later, truer love. You may come to that truer moment of ordained love, of real union, only to discover to your horror that what you should have saved you have spent." (Holland, Conf. Report, Oct. 1998).

President Boyd K. Packer taught: "Much of the happiness that may come to you in this life will depend on how you use this sacred power of creation. . . . If [Satan] can entice you to use this power prematurely, to use it too soon, or to misuse it in any way, you may well lose your opportunities for eternal progression. . . . Protect and guard your gift. Your actual happiness is at stake. . . . Heavenly Father has bestowed this choicest gift of all upon you – the power of creation. It is the very key to happiness." (Conf. Report, Apr. 1972).

Thus, we see that: (i) the power of creation is essential to the plan of happiness; (ii) we must use that power in the proper, authorized ways; (iii) misuse of the power may undermine true love. Sexual purity leads to happiness, while sexual immorality leads to misery.

President Ezra Taft Benson warned: "The plaguing sin of this generation is sexual immorality. This, the Prophet Joseph said, would be the source of more temptations, more buffetings, and more difficulties for the elders of Israel than any other. (See Journal of Discourses, 8:55). President Joseph F. Smith said that sexual impurity would be one of the . . . dangers that would threaten the Church within – and so it does. It permeates our society." (Conf. Report, Apr. 1986). President Benson also taught: "No sin is causing the loss of the Spirit of the Lord among our people more today than sexual promiscuity. It is causing our people to stumble, damning their growth, darkening their spiritual powers, and making them subject to other sins." (Conf. Report, Oct. 1964).

And, Elder Milton R. Hunter instructed: "I firmly believe that there is no sin that human beings commit that causes a loss of happiness, that causes the people to be degraded more completely, that breaks up homes more thoroughly, that ruins love more permanently, that drives out the Spirit of God and causes apostasy from the true Church more definitely than does the sin of sex immorality." (Conf. Report, Oct. 1947).

Knowing the importance of the law of chastity, Alma, both father and priesthood leader, admonishes his son, Corianton, to repent, and teaches him how he may be forgiven through the blessings of the Atonement. Alma commands Corianton to "forsake your sins, and go no more after the lusts of your eyes, but cross yourself in all these things" (Alma 39:9).

The phrase "cross yourself" is not as familiar today, but means to "erase, to cancel, to counteract, to stop, to preclude" (Webster's First Edition of an American Dictionary of the English Language, 1828). It involves self-mastery, and refers here to avoiding sexual immorality. President Benson cautioned: "Consider carefully the words of the prophet Alma to his errant son, Corianton, 'Forsake your sins, and go no more after the lusts of your eyes.' (Alma 39:9). 'The lusts of your eyes.' In our day, what does that expression mean? Movies, television programs, and video recordings that are both suggestive and lewd. Magazines and books that are obscene and pornographic. We counsel you . . . not to pollute your minds with such degrading matter, for the mind through which this filth passes is never the same afterwards." (Conf. Report, Apr. 1986).

In order to repent, he taught Corianton (i) to "forsake" his sins; (ii) to not follow the "lusts of [his] eyes"; (iii) to "counsel with [his] elder brothers"; (iv) to "acknowledge [his] faults"; (v) to withstand the temptations of the devil; and, finally, (vi) to "turn to the Lord with all [his] mind, might and strength" (Alma 39:9-13). These basic principles of repentance include confessing and forsaking sins, following the counsel of priesthood leaders, and replacing unclean activities with service to the Lord.

Elder Richard G. Scott explained what one must do to be forgiven of serious sins, such as sexual immorality: "For a moment I speak to anyone who has succumbed to serious temptation. Please stop now. You can do it with the help from an understanding parent, bishop, or stake president. Serious transgression such as immorality requires the help of one who holds keys of authority, such as a bishop or stake president, to quietly work out the repentance process to make sure that it is complete and appropriately done. Do not make the mistake to believe that because you have confessed a serious transgression, that you have repented of it. That is an essential step, but it is not all that is required. . . . You personally must make sure that the bishop or stake president understands those details so that he can help you properly through the process of repentance for full forgiveness." (Conf. Report, Oct. 1998).

In teaching that forgiveness for sexual immorality is possible, although not easy, Elder Jeffrey R. Holland said: "To you is extended the peace and renewal of repentance available through the atoning sacrifice of the Lord Jesus Christ. In such serious matters the path of repentance is not easily begun or painlessly traveled. But the Savior of the world will walk that essential journey with you. He will strengthen you when you waver. He will be your light when it seems most dark. He will take your hand and be your hope when hope seems all you have left. His compassion and mercy, with all their cleansing and healing power, are freely given to all who truly wish complete forgiveness and will take the steps that lead to it." (Conf. Report, Oct. 1998).

While forgiveness is available, the preferred course is to completely avoid sexual sin, and properly use the gift of the power of creation. David O. McKay taught: "Man is endowed with appetites and passions for the preservation of his life and the perpetuation of his kind. These, when held under proper subjection, contribute to his happiness and comfort; but when used for mere gratification, lead to misery and moral degradation. . . . I appeal to you to keep your soul unmarred and unsullied from this sin, the consequence of which will smite and haunt you intimately until your conscience is seared and your character sordid. A chaste, not a profligate life is the source of virile manhood, the crown of beautiful womanhood, the contributing source of harmony and happiness in family life, and the source of strength and perpetuity of the race." (Conf. Report, Oct. 1951).

Sexual purity brings its own reward, both in this life and the life to come. President Heber J. Grant observed: "How glorious is he who lives the chaste life. He walks unfearful in the full glare of the noonday sun, for he is without moral infirmity. He can be reached by no shafts of base calumny, for his armor is without flaw. His virtue cannot be challenged by any just accuser, for he lives above reproach. His cheek is never blotched with shame, for he is without hidden sin. He is honored and respected by all mankind, for he is beyond their censure. He is loved by the Lord, for he stands without blemish. The exaltations of eternities await his coming." (Conf. Report, Oct. 1942 – "Message of the First Presidency").

Restoration & Resurrection; Between Death and Resurrection

To help Corianton repent, Alma realized that he needs to review with his son several elements of the plan of salvation. He begins with Christ. As Alma began to teach Corianton about the mission of Christ, who would "come to take away the sins of the world" (Alma 39:15), he perceives that Corianton was confused about certain doctrines, and "worried concerning the resurrection of the dead" (Alma 40:1). (See "Resurrection" in Topical Index, Alma 11).

"Alma was a model of a perceptive father who is trying to counsel with and bless his son, and, through the inspiration available to all parents, he began to zero in on Corianton's real issue – a profound doctrinal question. Why was Corianton 'worried concerning the resurrection of the dead'? Because if a person claimed that there is no life after this one and no resurrection to live forever, that reasoning could be used to further justify sinning: Live it up here in mortality; go after whatever your body wants here in this life because there's nothing afterwards. It was important for Alma to resolve his son's doubt." (Ogden & Skinner, Verse by Verse: The Book of Mormon, 2:40).

Elder Carlos E. Asay taught: "Those who believe that the grave is man's final destiny live without a hope of a better world and are inclined to embrace that fatalistic approach, 'Eat, drink and be merry, for tomorrow we die' (2 Nephi 28:7). This approach often leads to wanton experimentation, immoral conduct, and all the other behaviors that reap misery and remorse of conscience. Whereas those who believe in a life after death are much more inclined to lead purposeful lies. Belief in a resurrection and related truths encourages one to obey the commandments, repent of sins, serve others, and do the other things that bring joy and happiness both here and hereafter." (Conf. Report, Apr. 1994).

Alma had "inquired diligently" of God about the resurrection (see Alma 11), and was able to teach his son several basic doctrines.

1. There is no resurrection until after the coming of Christ. (Alma 40:2).
2. There is a time appointed that <u>all</u> shall come forth from the dead. (Alma 40:4).
3. No one knows the time of an individual's resurrection, but God. (Alma 40:4).
4. There will be a period of time between death and the resurrection. (Alma 40:6).
5. In the resurrection, the spirit and body are reunited, and every limb and joint shall be restored to their "proper and perfect frame" (Alma 40:23).

Alma teaches: "there is a time appointed that all shall come forth from the dead. Now when this time cometh no one knows; but God knoweth the time which is appointed" (Alma 40:4). Since there would be a time appointed for people to rise from the dead, "there must be a space betwixt the time of death and the time of the resurrection" (Alma 40:6). Alma tells Corianton that he, himself, had wondered as to this period of time between death and resurrection, and "what becometh of the souls of men from this time of death to the time appointed for the resurrection?" (Alma 40:7). With respect to the time of resurrection, Alma says that he had "inquired diligently of the Lord to know" what happens to spirits that leave the mortal body when it dies (Alma 40:9).

Elder Charles W. Penrose explained: "The Prophet Alma, touching on this subject [the separation of the spirit from the body], explained to the people in his day what an angel of God made known unto him. . . . He wanted to know something of the condition of man between death and the resurrection, and he says an angel of God made known unto him that there is a space between death and resurrection." (Journal of Discourses, 21:220). Alma learned that, upon the death of the body, the spirits of mankind go to either "paradise" or "outer darkness," which is also called spirit "prison."[58] Paradise is a state of rest, a state of peace, a state of happiness. (Alma 40:12). It is a place where spirits "rest from all their troubles and from all care, and sorrow" (Alma 40:12). On the other hand, spirit prison is a state of misery, a state of fear, a state of darkness, with "weeping, and wailing, and gnashing of teeth" (Alma 40: 13, 14).

"The spirits of the wicked are in a state of unrest, having a knowledge of all their wickedness, and a remembrance of all their transgressions; they are in a state of fear, looking for the wrath and indignation of God, not knowing what their punishment will be; while on the other hand, the spirits of the righteous enter into a state of rest. They have a perfect knowledge of all that God has done for them, and all their acts of righteousness, and they await in peace for the time when their bodies shall be brought forth from the dust to stand in the presence of their God to receive their crown." (Penrose, Journal of Discourses, 21:220).

Elder Orson Pratt taught: "the spirits of all men, as soon as they depart from this mortal body, return home again to that God who gave them life, and then shall it come to pass that the spirits of the righteous shall enter into a state of rest, peace and happiness, called Paradise, where they shall rest from all their labors. And then shall it come to pass that the spirits of the wicked . . . shall depart into outer darkness, where there is weeping and wailing and gnashing of teeth; and in these two states or conditions the children of men shall be placed until the time of the resurrection." (Journal of Discourses, 17:181).

---

[58] See Isaiah 24:22; 1 Peter 3:19; D&C 38:5; D&C 138:22, 30.

In 1918, President Joseph F. Smith received a revelation about the state of spirits between death and resurrection. (See D&C 138). In vision, the prophet saw the Savior among the spirits in paradise: "the Son of God appeared, declaring liberty to the captives who had been faithful; [a]nd there he preached to them the everlasting gospel . . . But unto the wicked he did not go . . . . Where these were, darkness reigned, but among the righteous there was peace" (D&C 138:18-22).

Although the Savior didn't personally preach to the spirits in prison, his representatives were sent. "But behold, from among the righteous, [the Lord] organized his forces and appointed messengers" to go and "carry the light of the gospel to them that were in darkness, even to all the spirits of men; and thus was the gospel preached to the dead" (D&C 138:30).

President Joseph F. Smith learned that those in spirit prison will have the opportunity to hear the gospel and to repent before the final judgment. (D&C 138:29-34, 57-59). He learned that those who "repent will be redeemed, through obedience . . . and after they have paid the penalty of their transgressions, and are washed clean, shall receive a reward according to their works" (D&C 138:58-59). Elder George Q. Cannon stated: "Joseph [Smith] taught in later years, this doctrine: that there was a space between death and the resurrection, and during that space the children of men who had not had an opportunity of hearing the Gospel in this life, could hear it proclaimed by men who had authority in the spirit world." (Journal of Discourses, 24:368).

Restoration of the Spirit to the Body

The righteous remain in a state of happiness, and the wicked remain in a state of misery, unless and until they repent, until the time of the resurrection and final judgment. Alma states that he did ***not*** know all things about the resurrection and its times and sequencing. (Alma 40:5, 8, 19-21). He can still testify, however, about what he does know. It is not necessary to understand every detail about a doctrine to be able to testify of its truthfulness. Although he admittedly does not have perfect knowledge concerning all aspects of the resurrection, Alma is able to testify about basic truths: "But this much I say, that there is a space between death and the resurrection of the body, and a state of the soul in happiness or in misery until the time which is appointed of God that the dead shall come forth, and be reunited, both soul and body, and be brought to stand before God, and be judged according to their works" (Alma 40:21).

At the resurrection, Alma teaches: "The soul shall be restored to the body, and the body to the soul; yea, and every limb and joint shall be restored to its body; yea even a hair of the head shall not be lost; but all things shall be restored to their proper and perfect frame" (Alma 40:23). (See Alma 11:43). Elder Charles W. Penrose explained that "at the resurrection, the body and the spirit shall be brought up and restored to each other, and not only the body and spirit but every part and particle belonging to the body; not a hair of the head shall be lost; every joint and muscle and fiber and sinew, and every part and particle necessary to make up a perfect physical body for the spirit to dwell in, shall be restored to that spirit in the resurrection. That is the doctrine laid down by the Prophet Alma, as taught to him by an angel." (Journal of Discourses, 21:220).

(See "Resurrection" in Topical Index, Alma 11).

From time to time in the Book of Mormon, doctrinal nuggets are embedded in the discussion of other principles. In Alma's discussion of the resurrection, and review of his inquiry about the time between death and resurrection, he observed that "all is as one day with God, and time only is measured unto men" (Alma 40:8). This is an amazing observation, and is a difficult principle for us to understand in our temporal state. Simply put, God's "time" differs from mortal man's "time," and God is not bound by "time" as we understand it. From a modern scriptural passage that would have intrigued Einstein, we learn that there is evidently a distinction between "God's time, angel's time, prophet's time, and man's time" depending on location in the universe. (D&C 130:4). With respect to God's "time," the scriptures reveal that "all things . . . are manifest, past, present, and future, and are continually before the Lord" D&C 130:7. The Lord told Moses: "all things are present with me, for I know them all" (Moses 1:6) (Cf., Jacob 9:20, "[God] knoweth all things, and there is not anything save he knows it"). Unfortunately, Alma does not discuss the concept of God's time further, but returns to his teaching on the resurrection and restoration.

Restoration: Wickedness Never Was Happiness

<u>Restoration of the Spirit: Good to Good; Evil to Evil</u>

Corianton does not fully understand the restoration that will take place in the resurrection. Alma perceives that his son's "mind has been worried . . . concerning this thing" (Alma 41:1), and so he teaches Corianton about the restoration, that there would be both a physical and spiritual restoration. In the physical restoration, "the soul of man should be restored to its body, and that every part of the body should be restored to itself" (Alma 41:2). In the spiritual restoration, good works and desires will "be restored unto that which is good" (Alma 41:3). On the other hand, "if their works are evil they shall be restored unto them for evil" (Alma 41:4). "The one raised to . . . happiness according to his desires of happiness; and the other to evil according to his desires of evil" (Alma 41:5). The restoration will bring all things to their "proper order" (Alma 41:2, 4).

Corianton apparently thought that one could live a life of evil, but be restored to an afterlife of good. This is not restoration. Alma is clear: "Do not suppose, because it has been spoken concerning restoration, that ye shall be restored from sin to happiness. Behold, I say unto you, wickedness never was happiness" (Alma 41:10).[59] President Ezra Taft Benson warned, "You cannot do wrong and feel right. . . . 'When I do good I feel good,' said Abraham Lincoln, 'and when I do bad I feel bad.' Sin pulls a man down into despondency and despair. While a man may take some temporary pleasure in sin, the end result is unhappiness." (Conf. Report, Oct. 1974). "Evil never was happiness. Sin never was happiness. Happiness lies in the power and the love and the sweet simplicity of the gospel of Jesus Christ." (Hinckley, Conf. Report, Apr. 1997).

President Joseph F. Smith taught: "Bad habits are easily formed, but not so easily broken. Are we yielding to our evil habits, thinking they are only trifles after all, and we will get rid of them in the grave? Do we expect that our bodies will be cleansed in the grave, and we shall come forth with perfect and sanctified bodies in the resurrection? There are some among us who teach such things and excuse themselves for their practices, saying they will be cleansed in the grave. Alma taught a very different doctrine. He said to Corianton: 'Do not suppose . . . that ye shall be restored from sin to happiness.' (Alma 41:10, 15)." (Conf. Report, Apr. 1969).

---

[59] See the description of the Nephites just a few years before the birth of the Savior: They "sought . . . for that which [they] could not obtain; . . . for happiness in doing iniquity, which thing is contrary to the nature of that righteousness which is in our great and Eternal Head" (Helaman 13:38).

Elder Richard G. Scott taught: "Truly the statement of Alma, an inspired prophet and compassionate father, is borne out . . . 'wickedness never was happiness.' If you are ever tempted to experiment with the alluring offerings of Lucifer, first calmly analyze the inevitable consequences of such choices, and your life will not be shattered. You cannot ever sample those things that are forbidden of God as destructive of happiness and corrosive to spiritual guidance without tragic results." (Conf. Report, Apr. 2004).

"Vast sums of money are spent each year to package and disguise sin and evil to make them appear enticing, attractive, even harmless. However, regardless of appearances, 'wickedness never was happiness' (Alma 41:10) and never will be. . . . You are free to choose . . . and are permitted to act, but you are not free to choose the consequences. With absolute certainty, choices of good and right lead to happiness and peace, while choices of sin and evil eventually lead to unhappiness, sorrow, and misery." (Wirthlin, Conf. Report, Oct. 1989).President Brigham Young observed: "When people do right, they rest upon their beds, sleep sweetly, and rejoice in righteousness in their secret moments. When they do evil, it brings sorrow and deep pain to them in their private reflections." (Journal of Discourses, 9:101).

There is a difference between lasting happiness and transitory pleasure. Elder James E. Talmage taught: "*Happiness* is true food, wholesome, nutritious and sweet; it builds up the body and generates energy for action, physical, mental and spiritual; *pleasure* is but a deceiving stimulant which, like spirituous drink, makes one think he is strong when in reality enfeebled; makes him fancy he is well when in fact stricken with deadly malady. *Happiness* leaves no bad after-taste, it is followed by no depressing reaction; it calls for no repentance, brings no regret, entails no remorse; *pleasure* too often makes necessary repentance, contrition, and suffering; and, if indulged to the extreme, it brings degradation and destruction. True *happiness* is lived over and over again in memory, always with a renewal of the original good; a moment of unholy *pleasure* may leave a barbed sting, which, like a thorn in the flesh, is an ever-present source of anguish." (*Improvement Era*, 17, 173, *quoted* by Hansen, in Conf. Report, Oct. 1993, *emphasis added*).

President Russell M. Nelson quoted one of Shakespeare's characters who was contemplating the difference in pleasure and happiness:

> *What win I, if I gain the thing I seek?*
> *A dream, a breath, a froth of fleeting joy.*
> *Who buys a minute's mirth to wail a week?*
> *Or sells eternity to get a toy?*
> *For one sweet grape who will the vine destroy?*
> ('Lucrece,' lines 211-215)

"Remember to be carnally-minded is death, and to be spiritually-minded is life eternal.' (2 Nephi 9:39)." (Conf. Report, Oct. 1985).

(See "Happiness" in Topical Index, Mosiah 4.)

Judgment

"The judgment most commonly described in the scriptures is the Final Judgment that follows the resurrection (2 Nephi 9:15). Many scriptures state that 'we shall all stand before the judgment seat of Christ' (Romans 14:10; Mosiah 27:13) 'to be judged according to the deeds [that] have been done in the mortal body' (Alma 5:15; Alma 41:3). All will be judged 'according to their works' (3 Nephi 27:15) and 'according to the desire[s] of their hearts' (D&C 137:9; Alma 41:6)." (Oaks, Conf. Report, Apr. 2019).

The purpose of the Final Judgment is to determine whether we "have become new creatures, with 'no more disposition to do evil, but to do good continually' (Mosiah 5:2). The judge of this is our Savior, Jesus Christ (see John 5:22; 2 Nephi 9:41). After His judgment, we will all confess 'that his judgments are just' (Mosiah 16:1), because His omniscience (see 2 Nephi 9:15, 20) has given Him a perfect knowledge of all of our acts and desires, both those righteous or repented and those unrepented or unchanged." (Oaks, Conf. Report, Apr. 2019). "To assure that we will be clean before God, we must repent *before* the Final Judgment." (Oaks, Conf. Report, Apr. 2019, *emphasis in original*).

Alma teaches that the justice of God requires that "all things should be restored to their proper order" (Alma 41:2). "We know from the Book of Mormon that the resurrection is a restoration that brings back 'carnal for carnal' and 'good for that which is good.' (Alma 41:13) . . . . The principle of restoration also means that persons who are not righteous in mortal life will not rise up righteous in the resurrection. Moreover, unless our mortal sins have been cleansed and blotted out by repentance and forgiveness, we will be resurrected with a 'bright recollection' and a 'perfect knowledge of all our guilt and our uncleanliness.' (2 Nephi 9:14)." (Oaks, Conf. Report, Apr. 2000).

The "righteous shall have a perfect knowledge of their enjoyment, and their righteousness, being clothed with purity," however, the unrighteous shall have a "perfect knowledge of all of our guilt, and our uncleanliness, and our nakedness" (2 Nephi 9:14). The prophet Amulek later taught that after the resurrection, "we shall be brought to stand before God, knowing even as we know now, and have a bright recollection of all our guilt" (Alma 11:43).

We will face "things as they really are about ourselves and have 'a perfect knowledge' of all our rationalizations, pretenses, and self-deceptions." (Bednar, Conf. Report, Apr. 2015). "From such teachings we conclude that the Final Judgment is not just an evaluation of a sum total of good and evil acts – what we have *done*. It is an acknowledgement of the final effect of our words and thoughts – what we have *become*. It is not enough for anyone just to go through the motions. The commandments, ordinances, and covenants of the gospel are not a list of deposits required to be made in some heavenly account. The gospel of Jesus Christ is a plan that shows us how to become what our Heavenly Father desires us to become." (Oaks, Conf. Report, Oct. 2000).

All will be restored to "their works" and "the desires of their hearts" – in the Lord's merciful way and time. (Alma 41:3; D&C 137:9). If "the desires of their hearts were good . . . they should also, at the last day, be restored unto that which is good" (Alma 41:3). "Words such as . . . *restored* and *desire* imply that happiness is a consequence, not a reward. We are *restored* to a state of happiness when we have chosen to live according the plan of happiness. Our joy in God's kingdom will be a natural extension of the happiness we cultivate in this life." (Goaslind, Conf. Report, Apr. 1986).

Our desires are recorded in our lives and characters. Elder Bruce R. McConkie wrote: "In a real though figurative sense, the book of life is the record of the acts of men as such record is written in their own bodies. . . That is, every thought, word, and deed has an [effect] on the human body; all these leave their marks, marks which can be read by Him who is Eternal as easily as the words in a book can be read." (McConkie, Mormon Doctrine, 97).

An analogy in the digital world is Internet tracking. Elder Randall L. Ridd said: "The Internet also records your desires, expressed in the form of searches and clicks. There are legions waiting to fill those desires. As you surf the Internet, you leave tracks – what you communicate, where you have been, how long you have been there, and the kinds of things that interest you. In this way, the Internet creates a cyber profile for you – in a sense, your 'cyber book of life.' As in life, the Internet will give you more and more of what you seek. If your desires are pure, the Internet can magnify them, making it ever easier to engage in worthy pursuits. But the opposite is also true." (Conf. Report, Apr. 2014). In life, our thoughts and desires leave tracks on our characters, our faith, and our works.

Justice & Mercy

In chapter 42, Alma continues: "I perceive there is somewhat more which doth worry your mind, which ye cannot understand – which is concerning the justice of God in the punishment of the sinner; for ye do try to suppose that it is injustice that the sinner should be consigned to a state of misery. Now behold, my son, I will explain this thing unto thee" (Alma 42:7). "Alma's son Corianton needed help understanding some basic doctrine . . . 'concerning the justice of God . . .' He questioned, by way of justification of his sinning: Is it right that God would punish his own children if he loved them? Alma would certainly have already taught this principle to his son, but he had to teach it again because sin without repentance causes one to lose knowledge." (Odgen and Skinner, Verse by Verse: The Book of Mormon, 2:48).

It was important for Alma to review with Corianton some basic truths about resurrection, restoration, and now, justice and mercy. Evidently, Corianton had not internalized several key gospel principles. President Boyd K. Packer has said, "True doctrine, understood, changes attitudes and behavior. The study of the doctrines of the gospel will improve behavior quicker than a study of behavior will improve behavior." (Conf. Report, Oct. 1986).

Alma reviewed the plan of salvation with Corianton. He discussed the Fall of Adam and Eve. He explained why death is necessary, and taught Corianton about the Atonement, justice and mercy. Alma taught Corianton that through the Fall, man had become separated from God, and "had become carnal, sensual, and devilish, by nature" and "this preparatory state became a state for them to prepare" to return to God. (Alma 42:10). Mortal life became a test to see whether we would follow our temporal, carnal natures, or follow our eternal, spiritual predispositions. (See "Plan of Salvation," Topical Guide, 2 Nephi 2).

Unfortunately, none of us is able to perfectly follow our spiritual predispositions. All of us make mistakes in this life. "For all have sinned and come short of the glory of God" (Romans 3:23). Alma teaches that we have all transgressed divine law in some respect, making us all subject to the demands of justice. (Alma 42:14, 18). None is exempt. (D&C 107:84). "[I]f it were not for the plan of redemption (laying it aside)" we would be "cut off from the presence of the Lord" (Alma 42:11).

"And thus we see that all mankind were fallen, and they were in the grasp of justice" (Alma 42:14). And justice requires a "punishment" for sin against the law (Alma 42:17). Justice requires consistency not arbitrariness, order not chaos, and consequences for sin. "Now there was a punishment affixed, and a just law given, which brought remorse of conscience unto man" (Alma 42:18). This remorse, without repentance, is part of the punishment.

"The punishment may, for the most part, consist of the torment we inflict upon ourselves. It may be the loss of privilege or progress. . . . We are punished by our sins, if not for them." (Packer, Conf. Report, Oct. 1995). Joseph Smith taught: "A man is his own tormentor and his own condemner. Hence the saying, they shall go into the lake that burns with fire and brimstone (Rev. 21:8). The torment of disappointment in the mind of man is as exquisite as a lake burning with fire and brimstone. I say, so is the torment of man." (Joseph Smith, Journal of Discourses 6:1). "Those who have done wrong always have that wrong gnawing them." (DHC, 6:366). Isaiah wrote: "the wicked are like the troubled sea, when it cannot rest, whose waters cast up mire and dirt. There is no peace, saith my God, to the wicked" (Isaiah 57:20, 21).

On the other hand, "remorse of conscience" (Alma 42:18) can lead to repentance and forgiveness, and thus consists of appropriate guilt: "For godly sorrow worketh repentance to salvation" (2 Cor. 7:10). President Boyd K. Packer explained: "All of us sometime, and some of us much of the time, suffer remorse of conscience from things we did wrong or things left undone. That feeling of guilt is to the spirit what pain is to the physical body. . . . Justice requires that there be a punishment. Guilt is not erased without pain. There are laws to obey and ordinances to receive, and there are penalties to pay. Physical pain requires treatment and a change in lifestyle. So it is with spiritual pain. There must be repentance and discipline." (Conf. Report, Apr. 2001).

Alma then explains to Corianton how through our repentance and Christ's Atonement, mercy can satisfy justice, and we can be redeemed. "But there is . . . a repentance granted; which repentance, mercy claimeth; otherwise, justice claimeth the creature and executeth the law, and the law inflicteth the punishment" (Alma 42:22). And "mercy claimeth the penitent, and mercy cometh because of the atonement" (Alma 42:23). "And now, the plan of mercy could not be brought about except an atonement should be made; therefore God himself atoneth for the sins of the world, to bring about the plan of mercy, to appease the demands of justice, that God might be a perfect, just God, and a merciful God also" (Alma 42:15). Elder Richard G. Scott declared: "I testify that except for the Atonement of the Holy Redeemer, the demands of justice would prevent every soul born on earth from returning to the presence of God . . . for all make mistakes for which we cannot personally appease justice." (Conf. Report, Apr. 1997).

"Through the Atonement of Jesus Christ and His grace, our failures to live the celestial law perfectly and consistently in mortality can be erased . . . . Justice demands, however, that none of this happen without our willing agreement and participation. . . . Justice is an essential attribute of God. . . But as a consequence of being perfectly just, there are some things God cannot do. . . .He cannot allow mercy to rob justice. . . . It is because He is just that He devised the means for mercy to play its indispensable role in our eternal destiny. So now, 'justice exerciseth all his demands, and also mercy claimeth all which is her own' (Alma 42:24). . . . Even so, 'according to justice, the plan of redemption could not be brought about, only on conditions of repentance.' (Alma 42:13). It is the requirement of and the opportunity for repentance that permits mercy to perform its labor without trampling justice. Christ died not to save indiscriminately but to offer repentance." (Christofferson, Conf. Report, Oct. 2014).

"The Redeemer can settle your individual account with justice and grant forgiveness through the merciful path of repentance. Full repentance is absolutely essential for the Atonement to work its complete miracle in your life. By understanding the Atonement, you will see that God is not a jealous being who delights in persecuting those who misstep. . . . He so loves each of us that He was willing to have His perfect, sinless, absolutely obedient, totally righteous Son experience indescribable agony and pain and give Himself in sacrifice for all. Through that atonement we can live in a world where absolute justice reigns in its sphere so the world will have order. But that justice is tempered through mercy attainable by obedience to the teachings of Jesus Christ." (Scott, Conf. Report, Apr. 1995).

President Packer said: "We all make mistakes. Sometimes we harm ourselves and seriously injure others in ways that we alone cannot repair. We break things that we alone cannot fix. It is then in our nature to feel guilt and humiliation and suffering, which we alone cannot cure. That is when the healing power of the Atonement will help. . . . If Christ had not made His Atonement, the penalties for mistakes would be added one on the other. Life would be hopeless. But He willingly sacrificed in order that we may be redeemed." (Conf. Report, Apr. 2001). "The joyful news for anyone who desires to be rid of consequences of past poor choices is that the Lord sees weaknesses differently than He does rebellion. Whereas the Lord warns that un-repented rebellion will bring punishment, when the Lord speaks of weaknesses, it is always with mercy." (Scott, Conf. Report, Oct. 2013).[60]

"That Day of Judgment will be a day of mercy and love – a day when broken hearts are healed, when tears of grief are replaced with tears of gratitude, when all will be made right. Yes, there will be deep sorrow because of sin. Yes, there will be regrets and even anguish because of our mistakes, our foolishness, and our stubbornness that caused us to miss opportunities for a much greater future. But I have confidence that we will not only be satisfied with the judgment of God; we will also be astonished and overwhelmed by His infinite grace, mercy, generosity, and love for us, His children. If our desires and works are good, if we have faith in a living God, then we can look forward to what Moroni called, 'the pleasing bar of the great Jehovah, the Eternal Judge.'" (Uchtdorf, Conf. Report, Oct. 2016).

"If it is true that our bad unspoken thoughts are recorded against us, will it not be just as true that all our good thoughts unspoken, the kindness, tenderness, sympathy, pity, love, beauty, and charity that . . . cause the heart to throb with silent good, find remembrance in the presence of God, also? Yes, I firmly believe that all of our good impulses and thoughts will find remembrance with the Lord just as much as will the evil that we have thought, said, or done; and certainly since God is our loving Father, he will remember the good with a greater degree of satisfaction and joy than he will the evil." (Hunter, Conf. Report, Oct. 1946).

"President J. Reuben Clark Jr. contributed this valuable insight when he said: 'I feel that [the Savior] will give that punishment which is the very least that our transgression will justify. I believe that he will bring into his justice all of the infinite love and blessing and mercy and kindness and understanding which he has. . . . And on the other hand, I believe that when it comes to making the rewards for our good conduct, he will give us the maximum that it is possible to give, having

---

[60] See Proverbs 28:13; 1 Cor. 2:3; 15:43; 2 Cor. 13:4; James 3:17; Jacob 4:7; Alma 34:17; 3 Nephi 22:8; Ether 12:26-28; D&C 24:11; 35:17; 38:14; 62:1.

in mind the offense which we have committed.' As Isaiah wrote, if we will return unto the Lord, 'he will abundantly pardon.' (Isaiah 55:7)." (Faust, Conf. Report, Oct. 2001).

Earlier, President James E. Faust taught: "All of us have made wrong turns along the way. I believe the kind and merciful God, whose children we are, will judge us as lightly as He can for the wrongs that we have done and give us maximum blessings for the good that we do. . . . Of vital importance is resolving transgression, experiencing the healing process which comes of repentance. As President Kimball reminds us: 'The principle of repentance – of rising again whenever we fall, brushing ourselves off, and setting off again on that upward trail – is the basis for our hope.'" (Conf. Report, Oct. 1996).

"When we repent, we have the Lord's assurance that our sins, including our acts and desires, will be cleansed and our merciful final judge will 'remember them no more' (D&C 58:42; see also Isaiah 1:18; Jeremiah 31:24; Hebrews 8:12; Alma 41:6; Helaman 14:18-19). Cleansed by repentance, we can qualify for eternal life." (Oaks, Conf. Report, Apr. 2019). The Savior has the power and stands ready to cleanse us. President Oaks testified: "Now is the time to seek His help to repent . . . [and] to be clean and prepared to stand before God at the Final Judgment. . . . Because of God's plan and the Atonement of Jesus Christ, I testify with a 'perfect brightness of hope' that God loves us and we can be cleansed by the process of repentance." (Conf. Report, Apr. 2019).

Elder Earl C. Tingey testified: "Through the Atonement, God has provided a means whereby we can both overcome our sins and become completely clean again. This is made possible by the eternal law of mercy. Mercy satisfies the claims of justice through our repentance and the power of the Atonement. Without the power of the Atonement and our complete repentance, we are subject to the law of justice." (Conf. Report, Apr. 2006).

President Packer's Parable on Justice and Mercy

In his seminal address on justice and mercy ("The Mediator," Conf. Report, April 1977), President Packer taught: "I commend to you the reading of the 42nd chapter of Alma. It reveals the place of justice and should confirm that the poet spoke the truth when he said, 'In the course of justice [only], none of us should see salvation.' (Shakespeare, *Merchant of Venice*, IV. i. 199-200). Let me tell you a story – a parable.

"There once was a man who wanted something very much. It seemed more important than anything else in his life. In order for him to have his desire, he incurred a great debt. He had been warned about going into that much debt, and particularly about his creditor. But it seemed so important for him to do what he wanted to do and to have what he wanted right now. He was sure he could pay for it later. So he signed a contract. He would pay it off some time along the way. He didn't worry too much about it, for the due date seemed such a long time away. He had what he wanted now, and that was what seemed important. The creditor was always somewhere in the back of his mind, and he made token payments now and again, thinking somehow that the day of reckoning really would never come.

"But as it always does, the day came, and the contract fell due. The debt had not been fully paid. His creditor appeared and demanded payment in full. Only then did he realize that his creditor not only had the power to repossess all that he owned, but the power to cast him into prison as well. 'I cannot pay you, for I have not the power to do so,' he confessed. 'Then,' said the creditor, 'we will exercise the contract, take your possessions and you shall go to prison. You agreed to that. It was your choice. You signed the contract, and now it must be enforced.'

"'Can you not extend the time or forgive the debt?' the debtor begged. 'Arrange some way for me to keep what I have and not go to prison. Surely you believe in mercy? Will you not show mercy?' The creditor replied, 'Mercy is always so one-sided. It would serve only you. If I show mercy to you, it will leave me unpaid. It is justice I demand. Do you believe in justice?'

"'I believed in justice when I signed the contract,' the debtor said. 'It was on my side then, for I thought it would protect me. I did not need mercy then, nor think I should need it ever. Justice, I thought, would serve both of us equally as well.' 'It is justice that demands that you pay the contract or suffer the penalty,' the creditor replied. 'That is the law. You have agreed to it and that is the way it must be. Mercy cannot rob justice.' (see Alma 42:25). "There they were: One meting out justice; the other pleading for mercy. . . . Both laws, it seemed could not be served. They are two eternal ideals that appear to contradict one another. Is there no way for justice to be fully served, and mercy also?

"There is a way! The law of justice can be fully satisfied and mercy can be fully extended – but it takes someone else. And so it happened this time. The debtor had a friend. He came to help. He knew the debtor well. He knew him to be shortsighted. . . . Nevertheless, he wanted to help because he loved him. He stepped between them, faced the creditor, and made this offer. 'I will pay the debt if you will free the debtor from his contract so that he may keep his possessions and not go to prison.' As the creditor was pondering the offer, the mediator added, 'You demanded justice. Though he cannot pay you, I will do so. You will have been justly dealt with and can ask no more. It would not be just.' And so the creditor agreed.

"The mediator turned then to the debtor. 'If I pay your debt, will you accept me as your creditor?' 'Oh yes, yes,' cried the debtor. 'You saved me from prison and showed mercy to me.' 'Then,' said the benefactor, 'you will pay the debt to me and I will set the terms. It will not be easy, but it will be possible. I will provide a way. You need not go to prison.' And so it was that the creditor was paid in full. He had been justly dealt with. No contract had been broken. The debtor, in turn, had been extended mercy. Both laws stood fulfilled. Because there was a mediator, justice had claimed its full share, and mercy was fully satisfied.

"Each of us lives on a kind of spiritual credit. One day the account will be closed, a settlement demanded. However casually we may view it now, when that day comes and the foreclosure is imminent, we will look around in restless agony for someone, anyone, to help us. And, by eternal law, mercy cannot be extended save there be one who is both willing and able to assume our debt and pay the price and arrange the terms for our redemption. Unless there is a mediator . . . the full weight of justice untampered, unsympathetic, must . . . fall on us. The full recompense for every transgression, however minor or however deep, will be extracted from us. . . .

"But know this: Truth, glorious truth, proclaims there is such a Mediator. 'For there is one God, and one mediator between God and men, the man Christ Jesus.' (1 Tim. 2:5). Through Him mercy can be fully extended to each of us without offending the eternal law of justice. . . . All mankind can be protected by the law of justice, and at once each of us individually may be extended the redeeming and healing blessing of mercy. . . . If justice decrees that we are not eligible because of our transgression, mercy provides a probation, a penitence, a preparation to enter in." (Packer, Conf. Report, Apr. 1977).

Through Christ's Atonement, mercy can satisfy justice, and we can become clean and worthy to return to our Heavenly Father's presence. President Harold B. Lee taught, "When you have done all within your power to overcome your mistakes, and have determined in your heart that you will never repeat them again, then . . . peace of conscience [can come to you] by which you will know that your sins have been forgiven." (*quoted in* Uchtdorf, Conf. Report, Apr. 2007).

"Once we have truly repented, Christ will take away the burden of guilt for our sins. We can know for ourselves that we have been forgiven and made clean. The Holy Ghost will verify this to us; He is the Sanctifier. No other testimony of forgiveness can be greater. The Lord said, 'He that repents and does the commandments of the Lord shall be forgiven.' (D&C 1:32)." (Uchtdorf, Conf. Report, Apr. 2007). This is the message of justice and mercy Alma taught his son, Corianton.

Discourse 21: Helaman, "The Rock of Christ" (Helaman 5)

Prophet	Key Doctrines	Scriptures	Audience	Date
Helaman, the son of Helaman, who was the son of Alma the Younger	• Remember prophetic teachings • Build your foundation on the Rock of Christ	Helaman 5	To his sons, Nephi and Lehi	Between 50 B.C. and 39 B.C. Quoted by Nephi in 30 B.C.

INTRODUCTION

The Helaman referred to in the Book of Helaman, chapter 5, was the son of Helaman, who was the son of Alma the Younger. This Helaman became the chief judge of the people known as Nephites in approximately 50 B.C. (Helaman 2:1-2). We are told that Helaman "did fill the judgment seat with justice and equity; yea he did observe to keep the statutes, and the judgments and the commandments of God; and he did do that which was right in the sight of God continually; and he did walk after the ways of his father" (Helaman 3:21). This Helaman had two sons, Nephi and Lehi. (Helaman 3:21). In 39 B.C., Helaman died, and his son, Nephi, began to reign as chief judge.

In 30 B.C., like his great-grandfather, Alma (See Alma 4:20), Nephi gave up the judgment seat in order to "preach the word of God all the remainder of his days" (Helaman 5:1, 4). He had evidently been inspired by the words of his father, Helaman; and, at the outset of his mission, Nephi quoted some of his father's teachings ("these are the words which he [Helaman] spake") in a short discourse recorded in Helaman 5:6-12.[61]

DISCOURSE: Helaman 5

KEY DOCTRINES

- **Remember.** Importance of remembering prophetic teachings

- **Christ (the Rock) as the Foundation.** Christ is the foundation upon which we should build our lives. If we build our foundation on Christ, Satan will have no power over us.

---

[61] 30 B.C. was the date Helaman's words were included in the record by Nephi; they had certainly been delivered by Helaman prior to his death in 39 B.C.

COMMENTARY

Remember

In the seven short verses comprising Helaman's recorded words to his sons, Nephi and Lehi, the word "remember" is repeated thirteen times. Helaman's sons are admonished:

- To remember to keep the commandments. (Helaman 5:6).
- To remember that their names were given to remind them of their faithful ancestors.
- To remember the good works of Lehi and Nephi, and follow their example. (Hel. 5:6-7).
- To remember the words of King Benjamin, who taught "there is no other way nor means whereby man can be saved, only through . . . Jesus Christ" (Helaman 5:9).
- To remember that Christ shall come to redeem the world. (Helaman 5:9).
- To remember the words of Amulek, who taught that Christ will come to redeem the people "<u>from</u> their sins," not "<u>in</u> their sins" (Helaman 5:10).
- To remember to build the foundation of their lives on the "rock of our Redeemer, who is Christ." (Helaman 5:12).

President Spencer W. Kimball taught about the importance of remembering. "When you look in the dictionary for the most important word, do you know what it is? It could be *remember*. Because all of you have made covenants – you know what to do and you know how to do it – our greatest need is to remember. That is why everyone goes to sacrament meeting every Sabbath day – to take the sacrament and listen to the priests pray that they 'may always remember him and keep his commandments which he has given them.' . . . *Remember* is the word. *Remember* is the program." ("Circles of Exaltation," CES meeting, June 28, 1968).

President Henry B. Eyring said that "forgetting God has been . . . a persistent problem among His children since the world began. . . . And the challenge to remember has always been the hardest for those who are blessed abundantly. . . . '[H]ow slow are [those who prosper] to remember the Lord their God, and to give ear unto his counsels.' (Helaman 12:5). . . . Sadly, prosperity is not the only reason people forget God. It can also be hard to remember Him when our lives go badly. . . . The key to remembering that brings and maintains testimony is receiving the Holy Ghost as a companion. . . . Heavenly Father has given a simple pattern for us to receive the Holy Ghost not once but continually in the tumult of our daily lives. The pattern is repeated in the sacramental prayer: We promise that we will always remember the Savior. We promise to take His name upon us. We promise to keep His commandments. And we are promised that if we do that, we will have His Spirit to be with us." (Conf. Report, Oct. 2007).

In addition to the counsel of Helaman and the sacramental prayers, the scriptures also instruct us to:

- Remember to keep His commandments in all things (1 Nephi 15:25);
- Remember to search the scriptures diligently (Mosiah 1:7);
- Remember the words our parents have taught us (Alma 57:21);
- Remember the words spoken by the prophets and apostles (Jude 1:17);
- Remember the awfulness of transgression (2 Nephi 9:39); and
- Remember that the Lord is merciful unto all who believe on his name (Alma 32:22).

(Warner, Conf. Report, Apr. 1996).

Importance of a Name: Remember Our Heritage

The first thing Helaman told his sons is that he named them after their righteous ancestors, Nephi and Lehi. His intent was to help them remember the good works of these righteous prophets and follow their worthy examples each time Nephi and Lehi heard their own names. (Helaman 5:6). Proverbs teaches, "A good name is rather to be chosen than great riches" (Proverbs 22:1).

Elder Carlos E. Asay observed: "Though all of Adam's children may not have received names of significance, many have, and it has made a difference. It made a difference in the lives of Helaman's sons, Nephi and Lehi . . . . The record attests that Nephi and Lehi did pattern their lives after their forebears or namesakes and did bring honor to the names given them." (Asay, Family Pecan Trees, 66-67).

Elder Mervyn B. Arnold reviewed a more recent example of the importance of remembering good works through a good name: "When President George Albert Smith was young, his deceased grandfather George A. Smith appeared to him in a dream and asked, 'I would like to know what you have done with my name.' President Smith responded, 'I have never done anything with your name of which you need be ashamed.'" (Conf. Report, Oct. 2010).

Of this experience, President Smith said: "I have thought of this many times, and I want to tell you that I have been trying, more than ever since that time to take care of that name. So I want to say to the boys and girls, to the young men and women, to the youth of the Church and of all the world: Honor your fathers and mothers. Honor the names that you bear, because some day you will have the privilege and the obligation of reporting to them (and to your Father in heaven) what you have done with their name." ("Your Good Name," *Improvement Era*, Mar. 1947).

Helaman taught his sons to search the scriptures diligently. He specifically referenced prophetic teachings from King Benjamin: "there is no other way nor means whereby man can be saved, only through the atoning blood of Jesus Christ" (Helaman 5:9). He also instructed Nephi and Lehi to remember the words which Amulek spoke to Zeezrom: that the Lord shall "redeem his people" not "*in* their sins," but "*from* their sins" (Helaman 5:10, *emphasis added*). Helaman testified: "And [Christ] hath power given him from the Father to redeem them *from* their sins *because of repentance*" (Helaman 5:11, *emphasis added*). Sincere repentance and constant obedience represent our contributions to the salvation formula.

Brigham Young declared: "We, the Latter-day Saints, certainly believe that Christ will accomplish all that he undertook to do, but he never said he would save a sinner in his sins, but that he would save him *from* his sins. He has instituted laws and ordinances whereby this can be effected." (Journal of Discourses, 13:233). "We are not saved *in* our sins, as by being unconditionally saved through confessing Christ and then, inevitably, committing sins in our remaining lives. We are saved *from* our sins by a weekly renewal of our repentance and cleansing through the grace of God and his blessed plan of salvation." (Oaks, Conf. Report, Apr. 1998, *emphasis in original*).

It was King Benjamin who gathered his people together to give them "a name that never [would] be blotted out, except it be through transgression" (Mosiah 1:12). And, who taught that "there shall be no other name given . . . whereby salvation can come" (Mosiah 3:17). Just as Nephi and Lehi received the names of their righteous ancestors, the people of Benjamin received the name of Christ. We can be similarly blessed. (See "Jesus Christ - Name of Christ" in Topical Index, Mosiah 3-4).

With respect to salvation, Elder Richard G. Scott taught that it is only through the Atonement of Christ that we are saved: "[Heavenly Father] so loves each of us that He was willing to have His perfect, sinless, absolutely obedient, totally righteous Son experience indescribable agony and pain and give Himself in sacrifice for all. Through that atonement we can live in a world where absolute justice reigns in its sphere so the world will have order. But that justice is tempered through mercy attainable by obedience to the teachings of Jesus Christ. Which of us is not in need of the miracle of repentance? . . . Our goal surely must be forgiveness. The only possible path to that goal is repentance, for it is written: 'There is no other way nor means whereby man can be saved, only through the atoning blood of Jesus Christ.'" (Conf. Report, Apr. 1995). We believe that through the Atonement of Christ all mankind may be saved, by obedience to the laws and ordinances of the gospel. (Articles of Faith 3).

When we first enter the waters of baptism, and then regularly partake of the sacramental ordinance, we witness that we are willing to take on ourselves the name of Christ and always remember Him. Similarly, Helaman's remembrances focused his sons on Christ. What were they told to remember? They were instructed to remember that Christ will save us from our sins. They were taught to remember that salvation only comes through Christ. Finally, they were taught to make Christ the very foundation of their lives.

Build Your Foundation on the Rock of Our Redeemer, Jesus Christ

Helaman summarized his teachings with the guiding principle: "it is upon the rock of our Redeemer, who is Christ, the Son of God, that ye must build your foundation; that when the devil shall send forth his mighty winds, yea, his shafts in the whirlwind, yea, when all his hail and his mighty storm shall beat upon you, it shall have no power over you to drag you down to the gulf of misery and endless wo, because of the rock upon which ye are built, which is a sure foundation, a foundation whereon if men build they cannot fall" (Helaman 5:12).

This is an incredible promise: if we build the foundation of our life on the "rock" of Christ, we cannot fall. "Indeed . . . the sure foundation is Jesus Christ. He is the 'Rock of Heaven.' (Moses 7:53). When we build our house upon him, the rains of the latter days may descend, the floods may come, and the winds may blow, but we will not fall. We will not fail, for our home and our family will be founded on Christ." (Hales, Conf. Report, Oct. 2014). Temptations will come from all sides. Nonetheless, if we have built a foundation on Christ, we can withstand not only the wisps of enticement, but also the "mighty winds" of severe temptations that may buffet us.

President Spencer W. Kimball taught: "We . . . are faced with powerful destructive forces unleashed by the adversary. Waves of sin, wickedness, immorality, degradation, tyranny, deceitfulness, conspiracy, and dishonesty threaten all of us. They come with great power and speed and will destroy us if we are not watchful. . . . Without help we cannot stand against it. We must flee to high ground or cling fast to that which can keep us from being swept away. That to which we must cling for safety is the gospel of Jesus Christ. It is our protection from whatever force the evil one can muster. An inspired Book of Mormon prophet counseled his people: 'Remember that it is the rock of our Redeemer, who is Christ, the Son of God, that ye must build your foundation.'" (Conf. Report, Oct. 1978). Jacob identified Christ as both a "sure foundation" and "safe foundation." This "stone," he said, would become "the great, and the last, and the only sure foundation" upon which to build. (Jacob 4:16).

The Lord Jesus Christ is the rock of our salvation, the "corner stone," and the "stone of Israel." The Lord said, "I am the stone of Israel. He that buildeth upon this rock shall never fall" (D&C 50:44). The Lord taught that "whosoever heareth these sayings of mine and doeth them, I will liken him unto a wise man; which built his house upon a rock. And the rain came, and the winds blew, and beat upon that house; and it fell not; for it was founded upon a rock. And every one that heareth these sayings of mine, and doeth them not, shall be likened unto a foolish man, which built his house upon the sand: And the rain descended, and the floods came, and the winds blew, and beat upon that house; and it fell: and great was the fall of it" (Matt. 7:24-27).

President Howard W. Hunter explained: "The words of the Master regarding the house without a foundation say to me that a man cannot have a shallow and reckless notion that he is sufficient to himself and can build his own life on any basis that happens to be easy and agreeable. As long as the weather is fair, his foolishness may not be evident; but one day there will come the floods, the muddy waters of some sudden passion, the rushing current of unforeseen temptation. If his character has no sure foundation in more than just lip service, his whole moral structure may collapse." (Conf. Report, Oct. 1967).

President Russell M. Nelson counseled: "Even firm foundations cannot prevent life's problems. Wayward children cause parents to grieve. Some broken families don't get fixed. Gender disorientation is poorly understood. Married couples, for whatever reason, may not be blessed with children. Even in our day, 'the guilty and the wicked go unpunished because of their money.' (Helaman 7:5). Some things just don't seem fair. With strong underpinnings, however, we are better able to reach upward for help, even when faced with questions without easy answers. . . . Though we don't know all things, we know that God lives and that He loves us. Standing on that firm foundation, we can reach up and find strength to endure the heavy burdens of life. . . . That faith will give hope . . . . It will give us joy here and eternal life hereafter." (Conf. Report, Apr. 2002).

Paul taught the importance of Christ as the foundation of rock: "As a wise masterbuilder, I have laid the foundation. . . . For other foundation can no man lay than that is laid, which is Jesus Christ" (1 Corinthians 3:10-11). "On what are [we] built? How strong is our house?" (Perry, Conf. Report, Apr. 1985). With Christ as the footings, forms and underpinnings of the foundation, we can withstand any storm, and endure the burdens of life.

In the construction of any building, getting the foundation right is incredibly important. Unrepaired foundational deficiencies deteriorate over time. If you skimp on the foundation, and something fails, it is not an easy fix. Often anything built on a faulty foundation must be destroyed or rebuilt. Sufficient time and attention needs to be spent building a strong foundation. Therefore, it generally takes 30% to 40% of the total time building an entire house to make sure the foundation is correct. Corners must be square and level. Adequate bracing is essential. Bolts need to be secure and firm.

These foundational features can be compared to building a strong foundation on the rock of Christ. We cannot skimp in studying His words, and need to spend sufficient time reading and pondering the scriptures, serving others with love, and communicating with our Father in prayer. There can be no shortcuts in obedience – our actions should square with His commandments. Our commitments to covenants, like bolts supporting a structure, need to be secure and firm. And, we need to check our foundation regularly for any wear or cracks, and quickly shore things up – even if we need to alter or rebuild (repent) desires, habits, and attitudes.

Importantly, the Lord's approved ordinances must brace and buttress the foundation of our lives Elder David A. Bednar instructed: "Ordinances and covenants are the building blocks we use to construct our lives upon the foundation of Christ and His Atonement. We are connected securely to and with the Savior as we worthily receive ordinances and enter into covenants, faithfully remember and honor those sacred commitments, and do our best to live in accordance with the obligations we have accepted. We can be blessed . . . as we firmly establish our desires and deeds on the sure foundation of the Savior through our ordinances and covenants." (Conf. Report, Apr. 2015).

Bishop Dean M. Davies encouraged us to build a strong foundation analogous to the foundation of a temple, which is specifically designed to withstand the storms and calamities to which it will be subjected. (Conf. Report, Apr. 2013). He counseled: "But the foundation is just the beginning. A temple is composed of many building blocks, fitted together according to predesigned patterns. If our lives are to become the temples each of us is striving to construct as taught by the Lord (1 Cor. 3:16-17), we could reasonably ask ourselves, 'What building blocks should we put in place in order to make our lives beautiful, majestic, and resistant to the storms of the world?'" ("Come, Listen to a Prophet's Voice," Conf. Report, Oct. 2018).

The **bedrock** elements in the foundation are the **first principles** of faith, repentance, baptism and the Holy Ghost; and the **building blocks** are the **ordinances and covenants** we receive in the temple, as well as the Christlike attributes we strive to develop in our lives. (See "Divine Attributes" in Topical Guide, Alma 7).

Elder L. Tom Perry observed: "We have been taught by the prophets concerning foundations. President Joseph F. Smith has said: 'But the men and the women who are honest before God, who humbly plod along, doing their duty, paying their tithing . . . and who honor the holy Priesthood, who do not run into excesses, who are prayerful in their families, and who acknowledge the Lord in their hearts, *they will build up a foundation that the gates of hell cannot prevail against*; and if the floods come and the storms beat upon their house, it shall not fall, for it will be built upon the rock of eternal truth.'" (Conf. Report, Apr. 1985, *emphasis added*). Elder Perry added: "To build a foundation strong enough . . . requires the best effort of each of us . . . . Each must contribute energy and effort in driving piles right down to the bedrock of the gospel until the foundation is strong enough to endure through the eternities." (Conf. Report, Apr. 1985).

Discourse 22: Samuel the Lamanite, "Signs of Christ" (Helaman 13-15)

Prophet	Key Doctrines	Scriptures	Audience	Date
Samuel the Lamanite	<ul><li>Listen to the Prophets</li><li>Signs of the Coming of Christ</li><li>Conditions of Repentance</li></ul>	Helaman 13-15	To people in the city of Zarahemla	6 B.C.

INTRODUCTION

The Nephites had become prideful and wicked, and ignored their own prophets. Consequently, a few years before the Savior's birth, the Lord sent Samuel, a Lamanite prophet, to the city of Zarahemla to prepare the people for the coming of the Lord, and to warn them to repent. The people would not allow Samuel to enter the city, so he stood on top of the city wall and "prophesied unto the people whatsoever things the Lord put into his heart" (Helaman 13:4). Samuel told the people that "for this intent [he came] up upon the walls of this city," that the people might:

1. Know of the judgments of God.
2. Know of the coming of Jesus Christ, and the signs of his coming and his death.
3. Know the conditions of repentance. (Helaman 14:11-14).

As he preached and prophesied of Christ's coming, the people attacked him with rocks and arrows; however, he stood fast, and delivered his message from the Lord.

President Spencer W. Kimball observed: "Has the world ever seen a more classic example of indomitable will, of faith and courage than that displayed by Samuel the Prophet: 'One of the Lamanites who did observe strictly to keep the commandments of God.' (Helaman 13:1). Visualize, if you can, this despised Lamanite standing on the walls of Zarahemla and while arrows and stones were shot at him, crying out to his accusers that the sword of justice hung over them. So righteous was he that God sent an angel to visit him. . . . So great faith had he that the multitudes could not harm him until his message was delivered and so important was his message that subsequently the Savior required a revision of the records to include his prophecies concerning the resurrection of the Saints." (Conf. Report, Apr. 1949).[62]

---

[62] Samuel's words were later endorsed by the Savior, who stated that they had been fulfilled. (3 Nephi 23:9-13).

DISCOURSE: Helaman 13-15

KEY DOCTRINES

- **Listen to the Prophets.** Know the judgments of God.

- **Prophesies of the Coming of Christ.** Signs and wonders and the life of Christ.

- **Conditions of Repentance.** Repent or be destroyed (Helaman 13:11).

COMMENTARY

Listen to the Prophets

Prophets deliver messages they receive from God. Samuel the Lamanite taught the people "whatsoever things the Lord put into his heart" (Helaman 13:4). He chastened the people of Zarahemla for not following the words of other prophets: "ye do cast out the prophets, and do mock them and cast stones at them" (Helaman 13:24). He reprimanded them for only accepting the words of prophets that validated their actions. "But behold, if a man shall come among you and shall say: Do this, and there is no iniquity; do that and ye shall not suffer . . . do whatsoever your heart desireth . . . ye will receive him, and say that he is a prophet" (Helaman 13:27). On the other hand, Samuel warned: "if a prophet come among you and declareth unto you the word of the Lord, which testifieth of your sins and iniquities, ye are angry with him and cast him out and . . . say that he is a false prophet" (Helaman 13:26).

Joseph Smith said: "The world always mistook false prophets for true ones, and those that were sent of God, they considered to be false prophets, and hence they killed, stoned, punished and imprisoned the true prophets . . . . whilst they cherished, honored and supported knaves, vagabonds, hypocrites, imposters, and the basest of men." (Teachings of the Prophet Joseph Smith, 206). "We wonder how often hearers first rejected the prophets because they despised them, and finally despised the prophets even more because they rejected them . . . . The holy prophets have not only refused to follow erroneous human trends, but have pointed out these errors. No wonder the response to the prophets has not always been one of indifference. So often the prophets have been rejected because they first rejected the wrong ways of their own society. . . . Of course, rejection of the holy prophets comes because the hearts of people are hardened, as people are shaped by their society. . . .Prophets have a way of jarring the carnal mind. . . . [but they] are the most loving of men. It is because of their love and integrity that they cannot modify the Lord's message merely to make people feel comfortable." (Kimball, Conf. Report, Apr. 1978).

Samuel warned that if we reject the words of the true prophets, we will experience regret and sorrow. (Helaman 13:24-30). Prophets provide warnings, and preach repentance. They counsel, challenge, and correct. They testify of Christ. Elder Dallin H. Oaks taught: "A message given by a General Authority at a general conference – a message prepared under the influence of the Spirit to further the work of the Lord – is not given to be enjoyed. It is given to inspire, to edify, to challenge, or to correct. It is given to be heard under the influence of the Spirit of the Lord, with the intended result that the listener learns from the talk and from the Spirit what he or she should *do* about it." (CES Fireside for Young Adults, May 1, 2005).

(See "Prophets" in Topical Index, 2 Nephi 1).

Prophesy of Christ

Samuel was specifically instructed to prophesy about the imminent coming of the Savior, and the many signs and wonders that would occur in connection with his birth and death.

Samuel's Prophesy	Fulfillment
His birth will be in five years (Helaman 14:2)	3 Nephi 1:13
No darkness the night before His birth (Helaman 14:3-4)	3 Nephi 1:15
A new star would arise (Helaman 14:5)	3 Nephi 1:21
There will be signs and wonders in heaven (Helaman 14:6)	3 Nephi 2:1
People will be amazed and fall to the earth (Helaman 14:7)	3 Nephi 1:16-17
At His death, the sun will be darkened for 3 days (Hel. 14:20, 27)	3 Nephi 8:19-23
Thunder, lightning, and earthquakes will occur (Helaman 14:21)	3 Nephi 8:6-7
The earth will be broken up (Helaman 14:22)	3 Nephi 8:12, 17-18
Mountains will be laid low, valleys rise (Helaman 14:23)	3 Nephi 8:9-10
Highways and cities will be destroyed (Helaman 14:24)	3 Nephi 8:8-11, 13-14
Graves will open and resurrected saints appear (Helaman 14:25)	3 Nephi 23:9-13

Book of Mormon Student Manual, 283.

Samuel taught that these signs and wonders would be given so that there should be "no cause for unbelief" (Helaman 14:28). However, the impact of these signs and wonders did not last. Elder Gerald Causse warned: "Our ability to marvel is fragile. Over the long term, such things as casual commandment keeping, apathy, or even weariness may set in and make us insensitive to even the most remarkable signs and miracles of the gospel. The Book of Mormon describes a period, very similar to our own, that preceded the coming of the Messiah to the Americas. Suddenly the signs of His birth appeared in the heavens. The people were so stricken with astonishment that they humbled themselves, and nearly all were converted. However, only a short four years later, 'the people began to forget those signs and wonders which they had heard. . . and began to disbelieve all which they had heard and seen.' (3 Nephi 2:1)." (Conf. Report, Apr. 2015).

President Uchtdorf observed: "It seems to be human nature: as we become more familiar with something, even something miraculous and awe-inspiring, we lose our sense of awe and treat it as commonplace." (Conf. Report, Oct. 2016.)

Repent and Re-Turn to God

In addition to prophesies about the signs and wonders accompanying the Savior, Samuel was instructed to call the Nephites to repentance. Over and over, Samuel urged the people to repent: "if ye will repent and return unto the Lord your God I will turn away mine anger, saith the Lord . . . blessed are they who will repent and turn unto me, but wo unto him that repenteth not" (Helaman 13:11). He also warned:

- "Nothing can save this people save it be repentance . . . ." (Helaman 13:6).
- "Repent ye, repent ye, lest by knowing these things and not doing them ye shall suffer yourselves to come under condemnation" (Helaman 14:19).
- "Except ye shall repent your houses shall be left unto you desolate" (Helaman 15:1).
- "And now behold, saith the Lord, concerning the people of the Nephites: If they will not repent, and observe to do my will, I will utterly destroy them. . . ." (Helaman 15:17).

Samuel explained that faith and belief in Christ leads to repentance. "And if ye believe on his name, ye will repent of all your sins, that thereby ye may have a remission of them through his *merits*" (Helaman 14:13, *emphasis added*).

Samuel summarized the process to receive a remission of sins as follows: (1) believe the holy scriptures; (2) have faith in Christ; (3) repent, which brings a change of heart; and (4) return to the Lord, and remain firm and steadfast in the faith. (Helaman 15:7-8). It is belief in the holy scriptures, Samuel taught, which leads to faith, repentance and a change of heart. (Helaman 15:7). This is similar to Alma's message to the Zoramites that faith begins with belief in the "word." (See Alma 32).

"Biblical teachings from the books of Genesis to Revelation teach repentance . . . . References to repentance are even more frequent in the Book of Mormon. The word repent in any of its forms appears 72 times in the King James Version of the Bible. . . . In the Book of Mormon, the word repent in any of its forms appears 360 times. . . . The word repent in any of its forms appears in 47 of the 138 sections of the Doctrine and Covenants." (Nelson, Conf. Report, Apr. 2007).

Samuel's discourse weaves together the principles of repentance and agency with his prophesy about the coming of the Son of God, a Savior, who would atone for the sins of the people, and enable those who would choose to turn away from sin, and turn toward God, and "repent of all [their] sins, that thereby [they] might have a remission of them through his merits" (Helaman 14:13). He admonishes the Nephites to use their agency and choose repentance: "[Y]e are free; ye are permitted to act for yourselves. . . . He hath given unto you that ye might know good from evil, and he hath given unto you that ye might choose life or death" (Helaman 14:30-31). To repent and turn toward God is to choose life, but the choice is ours.

(See "Repentance" in Topical Index, Alma 36).

Discourse 23: Mormon, "Faith, Hope & Charity" (Moroni 7)

Prophet	Doctrines	Scriptures	Audience	Date
Mormon	• Real Intent • Light of Christ • Faith, Hope & Charity	Moroni 7	To the people in an un-named synagogue (recorded by Moroni)	Before A.D. 401

INTRODUCTION

Elder Sterling W. Sill provided the following brief summary of the life of Mormon: "When he was only ten years of age, Mormon received the divine call to his life's work of compiling this book for our benefit. Then, like young Samuel at Shiloh, he received a personal visitation from the Lord at age 15. At age 16 he was appointed to lead the armies of the Nephite republic against its adversaries, the Lamanites, and his commission extended over 58 years, until his death at age 74. No weakling or coward survives a test like that. Mormon was a prophet, an author, a historian, and he had the most extended military career on record." (Conf. Report, Oct. 1970).

There are four recorded sermons by the prophet Mormon. These include two epistles to his son, Moroni; an invitation from the prophet/warrior to his enemies to repent and be saved, spiritually; and a comprehensive discourse, recorded in the Book of Moroni, Chapter 7, which had been delivered by Mormon in a Nephite synagogue to those "that are of the church, that are the peaceable followers of Christ" (Moroni 7:1-3).

Moroni chapter 7 is Moroni's "recording of his father's masterful teaching on . . . faith, hope, and charity. Mormon's sermon was directed unto those 'that are of the church, that are the peaceable followers of Christ.' . . . Teaching that 'all things which are good cometh of God; and that which is evil cometh of the devil,' Mormon taught that everyone can make this assessment – a variation on Lehi's teaching about opposition in all things – because 'the Spirit of Christ is given to every man, that he may know good from evil.' . . . The ability to see these choices clearly and accurately is provided by the 'light of Christ,' a free gift to all even if it is not always received or cultivated." (Holland, Christ and the New Covenant, 332-333).

"One of the most tightly woven and forceful sermons in the Book of Mormon is that recorded by Moroni as given by his father, Mormon, on faith, hope and charity. . . . We can also imagine that Moroni is rereading this sermon to strengthen his own faith, hope and charity – a topic Moroni addresses in his concluding words in the Book of Mormon." (Rust, Feasting on the Word, 140-141).

"And now, I Moroni, write a few of the words of my father Mormon, which he spake concerning faith, hope, and charity; for after this manner did he speak unto the people, as he taught them in the synagogue which they had built for the place of worship" (Moroni 7:1).

DISCOURSE: Moroni 7

KEY DOCTRINES

- **Righteous Acts Require Real Intent.** (Moroni 7:5-14).

- **The Light of Christ** is given to every person to know good from evil (Moroni 7:16).

- **Faith, Hope & Charity**.
    - We must have faith in Christ to be saved (Moroni 7:26-39).
    - We hope for eternal life through Christ's atonement (Moroni 7:40-43).
    - Charity, or the pure love of Christ, suffers long, is kind, envies not, and seeks not her own (Moroni 7:44-48).

COMMENTARY

Real Intent: Motives, Actions and the "As If" Principle

Mormon taught that "good works" require good motives. It is not just our outward actions that demonstrate righteousness, but the intent of our hearts. The key to good works that are "counted . . . for righteousness" (Moroni 7:7) is **real intent**. A person may "offereth a gift, or "prayeth unto God"; however, "except he shall do it with *real intent* it profiteth him nothing" (Moroni 7:6, *emphasis added*; 1 Cor. 13:3). "If our works are to be credited for good, they must be done for the right reasons." (Oaks, Conf. Report, Oct. 1984).

Elder Dallin H. Oaks explained: "We must not only *do* what is right. We must act for the right reasons. The modern term is *good motive*. The scriptures often signify this appropriate mental attitude with the words *full purpose of heart* or *real intent*. The scriptures make clear that God understands our motives and will judge our actions accordingly." (Oaks, Pure in Heart, 15). "For I, the Lord, will judge all men according to their works, according to the desire of their hearts" (D&C 137:9; see also, Alma 29:4-5).

"Real intent" can be a challenge even for the righteous. Mormon was addressing the saints, the "peaceable followers of Christ" (Moroni 7:3), in his sermon. President Marion G. Romney shared the following personal experience about the difficulty and importance of righteous motivations: "About a quarter of a century ago Sister Romney and I moved into a ward in which they were just beginning to build a meetinghouse. The size of the contribution the bishop thought I ought to contribute rather staggered me. I thought it was at least twice as much as he should have asked. However, I had just been called to a rather high Church position, so I couldn't very well [say no]. Therefore, I said, 'Well, I will pay it, Bishop, but I will have to pay it in installments because I don't have the money.' And so I began to pay. And I paid and paid until I was down to about the last three payments, when, as is my habit, I was reading the Book of Mormon, and came upon the scripture which said: 'If a man . . . giveth a gift . . . grudgingly; wherefore it is counted unto him the same as if he had retained the gift; wherefore he is counted evil before God.' (Moroni 7:8). This shocked me because I was out about a thousand dollars. Well, I went on and paid the three installments I had promised to pay, and then I paid several more installments to convince the Lord that I had done it with the right attitude." (*Relief Society Magazine*, Feb. 1968).

If our intent is not righteous, our outward actions may not be acceptable to the Lord. Mormon uses the metaphor of a fountain of water: a "bitter fountain cannot bring forth good water" (Moroni 7:11). "There are some, for vanity or other superficial reasons, who may seemingly offer a good gift, but only to deceive . . . . God recognizes no sense of good which is but a cloak of how the inner person really feels in opposition thereto." (Dyer, Conf. Report, Apr. 1965).

During His earthly ministry, the Savior warned that outwardly "good" actions must be accompanied by the right motives. For example, to pray or to fast only to be "seen of men" brings no heavenly approbation (Matthew 6:5-16). He condemned the hypocrites who "outwardly appear righteous unto men, but within . . . are full of hypocrisy and iniquity" (Matt. 23:28). Speaking of hypocrisy, the Lord observed: "Well hath Isaiah prophesied of you hypocrites, as it is written, this people honoureth me with their lips, but their heart is far from me" (Mark 7:6; see Isaiah 29:13). As Mormon taught, outwardly righteous acts must be accompanied by inwardly righteous motives to be fully accepted by God.

Developing Real Intent: The "As If" Principle

What about the situation where the intent may not be "bitter" or "deceitful," but "grudging" or "reluctant"? We may not be hypocritical, but we may not be enthusiastic, either. How then to develop righteous intent? President Marion G. Romney taught: "Some may ask . . . 'How do I overcome giving grudgingly?'. . . To those I would say: Faithfully live the commandments, give of yourselves, care for your families, serve in church callings, perform missionary work, pay tithes and offerings, study the scriptures – and the list could go on." (Conf. Report, Oct. 1981).

Mormon said that if a person prays without real intent, "it profiteth him nothing, for God receiveth none such" (Moroni 7:9). In Shakespeare's Hamlet, King Claudius says: "My words fly up; my thoughts remain below. Words without thoughts never to heaven go." (Hamlet Act 3, Scene 3). In this scene, the King kneels in prayer, but does not truly seek forgiveness for his heinous act of killing his brother. When he rises up, he recognizes that his prayers were in vain, consisting of words, but no true feelings of remorse. Does this mean that if we don't pray with real intent, we should just cease praying? Of course not. President Brigham Young counseled: "It matters not whether you or I feel like praying, when the time comes to pray, pray. If we do not feel like it, we should pray till we do." (Journal of Discourses, 13:150).

In the act of performing good works, our desire to do those works for the right reasons may actually increase. This is often the case when we serve others. (See "Service" in Topical Index, Mosiah 2). While we may not be serving with wicked motivations, we may be serving more out of duty, or rote obedience, than love. In this circumstance, it is important to keep serving. And, as we serve, God will help us grow, "so that we may serve one another for the highest and best reason, the pure love of Christ." (Oaks, Conf. Report, Oct. 1984).

This is similar to what the philosopher William James called the "as if" principle. He said, "If you want a quality act as if you already had it." (*Quoted* in Peale, Norman Vincent, Enthusiasm Makes the Difference. 13, 1958). "It is a proven law of human nature that as you imagine yourself to be and as you act on the assumption that you are what you see yourself as being, you will in time strongly tend to become, provided you persevere in the process." (Ibid.)

When we act "as if" we already possess a righteous quality or attribute, we may be able to attain that quality or attribute over time. In this way, righteous acts may help develop righteous motivations. "If you want to be faithful, act 'as if' you are already faithful. Do the things that faithful people do. Go to church, say your prayers, love God, refrain from evil, study the scriptures, be honest with yourself and everyone else. And if you would like to be perfect, act 'as if' you were already perfect. Don't go around glorying in your sins and weaknesses. We can come very close to perfection if we really get the spirit of it in our hearts. If we really want to obey God, we should act 'as if' we were already obedient. We should think obedience, love obedience, practice obedience, and we should allow no exceptions to obedience. The fewer the exceptions to perfection, the nearer we get to perfection." (Sill, Conf. Report, Oct. 1962). "If we want to increase our faith, then let's do things that require faith." (Villar, Conf. Report, Apr. 2019). Act "as if."

As we honestly try to do good, the Lord can help purify our motives until we "serve one another for the highest and best reason." "We train our spiritual senses by doing good things." (Grassli, Conf. Report, Oct. 1989). Doing what is right can lead to doing what is right with real intent. Through righteous living, the Lord can help us transform rote to real. As the disciple said, "Lord, I believe; help thou mine unbelief" (Mark 9:24). The Lord will be merciful in our weaknesses; it is our hypocrisy that earns his condemnation. (Scott, Conf. Report, Oct. 2013).

Good Comes from God

Mormon taught: "everything which inviteth and enticeth to do good, and to love God, and to serve him, is inspired of God" (Moroni 7:13). President Brigham Young counseled: "When we see anything that has solidity and permanency, that produces good, that builds up, creates, organizes, sustains, and betters the condition of the people, we pronounce that good and from God." (Journal of Discourses, 13:261).

It is the nature of God to always seek what is best for us, and inspire, invite, and entice us to do good. Elder B.H. Roberts taught: "He is the All-Wise One! The All-Powerful One! What he tells other Intelligences to do must be precisely the wisest, fittest thing that they could anywhere or anyhow learn – the thing which it will always behoove them, with right loyal thankfulness, and nothing doubting, to do. There goes with this, too, the thought that this All-Wise One will be the Unselfish One, the All-Loving One, the One who desires that which is highest, and best; not for himself alone, but for all.'" (Teachings of the Prophet Joseph Smith, 353, f.n. 8).

Elder Jose A. Teixeria counseled: "One gift that will help us navigate our lives is the gift He has given to all, the ability and power to choose. . . . This gift is an extraordinary sign of trust in us and simultaneously a cherished personal responsibility to use wisely. Our Father in Heaven respects our freedom to choose and will never force us to do what is right, nor will he impede us from making mediocre choices. His invitation, however, concerning this important and vital gift is clearly expressed in the scriptures: 'that which is of God inviteth and enticeth to do good continually.' (Moroni 7:13). The words 'to do good continually' depict well the standard we need to apply as we use our agency." (Conf. Report, Apr. 2009).

On the other hand, that which "inviteth and enticeth to sin" comes from the devil. (Moroni 7:12). Because the devil is "miserable forever," he seeks the "misery of all mankind" (2 Nephi 2:18). The devil is the source of anything which persuades us to deny Christ, "and serve him not" (Moroni 7:16, 17).

President Brigham Young observed: "when we see that that injures, hurts, destroys, produces confusion in a community, disturbance and discord, strife and animosity, hatefulness and bitter feelings one towards another, we at once pronounce it evil, and declare that it springs from beneath. All evil is from beneath, while all that is good is from God." (Journal of Discourses, 13:261).

Elder Neil L. Andersen stated: "Let's begin with what we know. Good comes from God; evil comes from the devil. (Moroni 7:12). They are not, however, equal forces that are fighting each other in the universe. At the head of all that is good is the Christ. . . . The devil, on the other hand, 'persuadeth men to do evil.' (Moroni 7:17). 'He [has] fallen from heaven . . . [and has] become miserable forever,' (2 Nephi 2:18) and now works 'that all men might be miserable like unto himself.' (2 Nephi 2:27). He is a liar and a loser. The power of the Savior and the power of the devil are not truly comparable. . . . On this planet, however, evil has been allowed a position of influence to give us the chance to choose between good and evil." (Conf. Report, Apr. 2005).

The Light of Christ

All men have the fundamental power to choose good over evil through the Spirit of Christ, also known as the "light of Christ" (Moroni 7:16, 19). Elder Richard G. Scott taught: "The Light of Christ is that divine power or influence that emanates from God through Jesus Christ. It gives light and life to all things. It prompts all rational individuals throughout the earth to distinguish truth from error, right from wrong. It activates your conscience." (Conf. Report, Oct. 2004). Every person is given the gift of the light of Christ.

<u>The Light of Christ is Given to All People</u>
President Boyd K. Packer taught: "Regardless of whether this inner light, this knowledge of right and wrong, is called the Light of Christ, moral sense, or conscience, it can direct us to moderate our actions. . . . Every man, woman, and child of every nation, creed, or color – everyone, no matter where they live or what they believe or what they do – has within them the imperishable Light of Christ." ("The Light of Christ," *Ensign*, Apr. 2005). President Packer later affirmed: "All are born with the Light of Christ, a guiding influence which permits each person to recognize right from wrong. What we do with that light and how we respond to those promptings to live righteously is part of the test of mortality." (Conf. Report, Apr. 2013).

We are taught that the light of Christ powers the Universe. "Jesus Christ is the light of the world because he is the source of the light which 'proceedeth forth from the presence of God to fill the immensity of space.'" (D&C 88:12). (Oaks, Conf. Report, October 1987). Jesus Christ is "the true Light, which lighteth every man that cometh into the world" (John 1:9; D&C 93:2). Jesus, Himself, testified: "Behold, I am the light of the world" (3 Nephi 11:11; D&C 12:9). Christ is the light of creation, the creator of this and other worlds. The third verse of the creation story at the very beginning of the Old Testament reads "Let there be Light" (Genesis 1:3). If Christ is the Light, perhaps the Old Testament should begin with the phrase "Let there be Christ." And, the next verse should read, "And God saw Christ, that He was good" (Genesis 1:4).

What comes to mind when we think of light? Illumination, power, cleanliness, warmth, a universal constant . . . the absence of darkness. These terms also describe Jesus Christ.

First, Light is Illumination. Just as light provides illumination and helps us perceive and understand our physical surroundings, Christ's teachings provide illumination and greater understanding of spiritual and moral truths. Elder Dallin Oaks testified that Jesus Christ is the light of the world because his example and his teachings illuminate the path we should walk to return to the presence of our Father in Heaven. (Conf. Report, Oct. 1987). During His ministry, the Savor taught, "Behold I am the light; I have set an example for you" (3 Nephi 18:16). He told His Apostles, "Behold I am the light which ye shall hold up – that which ye have seen me do" (3 Nephi 18:24).

President James E. Faust taught that the light of Christ has influenced and illuminated many world leaders and teachers: "The First Presidency has stated: 'The great religious leaders of the world such as Mohammed, Confucius, and the Reformers, as well as philosophers including Socrates, Plato, and others, received a portion of God's light. Moral truths were given to them by God to enlighten whole nations and to bring a higher level of understanding to individuals.'" (Conf. Report, Apr. 1980). Elder Dallin H. Oaks taught: "We believe that most religious leaders and followers are sincere believers who love God and understand and serve Him to the best of their abilities. We are indebted to the men and women who kept the light of faith and learning alive through the centuries to the present day. We want all who investigate our church from other churches or systems of belief to retain everything they have that is good and to come and see how we can add to their understanding of truth and to their happiness as they follow it." (Oaks, "The Only True and Living Church," June 25, 2010, Seminar for New Mission Presidents).

Second, Light is Power. In the physical world, light overcomes darkness. In the spiritual world, darkness cannot abide the light. "Jesus said, 'I am the light [that] shineth in darkness, and the darkness comprehendeth it not.' (D&C 6:21). That means no matter how hard it tries, the darkness cannot put out the light. Ever. You can trust His light will be there for you." (Eubank, Conf. Report, Apr. 2019).

However, at times, we, or people we love, may temporarily go dark, through sin. And, those who sin will often wish to avoid the light, and places where there is light. Consider the example of Adam and Eve in the garden, who hid from the presence of the Lord after their transgression.

When I lived in an apartment in New York City, we had other tenants in the form of an extended family of cockroaches. They were not welcome visitors. We soon learned that the cockroaches hated the light. Turning on the light in the kitchen would make the cockroaches scurry and disappear. Similarly, the light of Christ can chase away the cockroaches of darkness. Doubt and despair disappear when we turn on His light in our lives, and obey His commandments. The Savior emphasized the close relationship between His light and His commandments when he taught the Nephites, "Behold, I am the law, and the light" (3 Nephi 15:9, *emphasis added*).

Often, when we sin, we avoid areas of light (churches and temples) and seek zones of darkness, just like those cockroaches in my New York City apartment. But, when we repent and welcome the light of Christ back into our lives through repentance and obedience to the commandments, we are able to bask in the power of the light of Christ. When we are clean and pure, we embrace the light. Just as light overcomes dark, the power of the light of Christ helps us overcome temptation, darkness, and sin.

Third, Light is Cleanliness. Justice Louis D. Brandeis said, "sunlight is said to be the best of disinfectants, and electric light the most efficient policeman" ("What Publicity Can Do," Harper's Weekly, 1913). Just as light can serve as a disinfectant, or cleansing agent, Christ's Light, through the Atonement allows us to be clean, and stay clean. President Boyd K. Packer described the Atonement's cleansing power as follows: "The Atonement leaves no tracks, no traces. What it [cleanses] is [clean] . . . The Atonement . . . can wash clean every stain no matter how difficult or how long or how many times repeated." (Conf. Report, Apr. 2015). "Christ's light brings hope, happiness, and healing of any spiritual wound or ailment." (Uchtdorf, Conf. Report, Oct. 2017). The light Christ provides through the Atonement is the best of disinfectants.

Fourth, Light is Warmth. There is great warmth in the love of Christ. The scriptures say that Christ "encircles [us] in the arms of safety" (Alma 34:16), in a warm embrace. This is a vivid image. Any child knows that the feeling to be held in the arms of a parent, is one of warmth and love. We are warm and safe in the light. Elder David A. Bednar explained, "Because of His [Atonement], Christ has perfect empathy and can reach out and extend to us His arm of mercy." (Conf. Report, Apr. 2014). He can comfort us and warm our souls.

Fifth, Light is Constant. Light travels 186,000 miles per second (its exact value is 299,792,458 meters per second). Light's speed in a vacuum is the universal physical constant used to measure other phenomenon. It never varies; it never changes speed. Christ's teachings are the universal spiritual constants. Christ does not change; He does not waver from what He says, or who He is. He is "the same yesterday, today, and forever" (2 Nephi 27:23; see Moroni 10:19; Hebrews 13:8). We can rely on Him completely to provide universal and unchanging standards, against which we will be measured, and to serve as the example of righteousness toward which we can align our thoughts, words and actions.

"Jesus Christ is the light of the world because his example and his teachings illuminate the path we should walk to return to the presence of our Father in Heaven. . . . Jesus Christ is also the light of the world because his power persuades us to do good. . . . 'Whatsoever thing persuadeth men to do good is of me' (Ether 4:11). . . . And so we see that Jesus Christ is the light of the world because he is the source of the light that quickens our understanding, because his teachings and his example illuminate our path, and because his power persuades us to do good." (Oaks, Conf. Report, Oct. 1987).

The Light of Christ Differs from the Holy Ghost
"The Holy Ghost and the Light of Christ are different . . . While they are sometimes described in the scriptures with the same words, they are two different and distinct entities." (Packer, *Ensign*, Apr. 2005). "The Holy Ghost is . . . a third member of the Godhead, a distinct personage of spirit with sacred responsibilities." (Hales, Conf. Report, Apr. 2016). "The Light of Christ is not a person. It is a power and influence that comes from God and when followed can lead a person to qualify for the guidance and inspiration of the Holy Ghost." (Scott, Conf. Report, Oct. 2004). "The light of Christ should not be confused with the personage of the Holy Ghost, for the light of Christ is not a personage at all." (Bible Dictionary, "Light of Christ," 725). "The Light of Christ is given to all men and women that they may know good from evil; manifestations of the Holy Ghost are given to lead sincere seekers to gospel truths that will persuade them to repentance and baptism." (Oaks, Conf. Report, Oct. 1996).

Faith

In the remainder of his discourse, Mormon teaches the people how to use the light of Christ to "lay hold on every good thing" (Moroni 7:19). This is possible through developing *faith, hope, and charity*. These are the attributes that allow the light of Christ within us to discern good (from God) and avoid evil (from the devil). (See Moroni 7:15-20, 33, 40, 44-45). These are the attributes that enable us to follow the light, become a "child of Christ" (Moroni 7:19), and ultimately "be like him" (Moroni 7:48). (See "Faith" in Topical Index, Alma 32).

First, faith. Joseph Smith taught that faith is the first principle in religion, a foundation of righteousness, and a principle of power. (See Lectures on Faith). He said that faith in Christ [God] includes a correct idea of His character and attributes. "First, that he was God before the world was created and the same God that he was after it was created. Second, that he is merciful and gracious, slow to anger, abundant in goodness, and that he was so from everlasting and will be so to everlasting. Third, that he changes not, neither is there variableness with him, and that his course is one eternal round. Fourth, that he is a God of truth and cannot lie. Fifth, that he is no respecter of persons. And sixth, that he is love." (*quoted in* McConkie, Conf. Report, Oct. 1953).

"Faith comes by righteousness, and without righteousness and obedience we cannot have the measure of faith that will save us." (McConkie, Conf. Report, Oct. 1953). This is part of what Mormon was teaching when he said: "By every word which proceeded out of the mouth of God, men began to exercise faith in Christ, and thus by faith, they did lay hold upon every good thing" (Moroni 7:25).

President Henry B. Eyring taught: "It is by faith you can lay hold upon every good thing. . . . . The way through difficulties has always been prepared for you, and you will find it if you exercise faith. You must have faith to pray. You must have faith to ponder the word of God. You must have faith to do those things and go to those places which invite the Spirit of Christ and the Holy Ghost." (Conf. Report, Apr. 2008). "As we desire to 'lay hold upon every good thing,' we of necessity choose actions that increase our faith: We set aside meaningful time for prayer. We remember and renew our covenants regularly through partaking of the sacrament and visiting the temple. We use the scriptures as a personal road map to guide us in our actions. We cultivate friendships with people who help us build our testimonies. We make service part of our daily routine" (Relief Society Visiting Teaching Message, "Lay Hold upon Every Good Thing," *Ensign*, March 1991).

Mormon quoted the words of Christ: "If ye will have faith in me ye shall have power to do whatsoever thing is expedient in me" (Moroni 7:33). Faith in Christ is a principle of power, and can lead to needed blessings, even miracles, in our lives. Mormon teaches, "it is by faith that miracles are wrought" (Moroni 7:37). "Remember, faith precedes and produces miracles for which we have no immediate explanation within our experience. . . . the Lord will, according to our faith, fulfill His promises and work with us to overcome every challenge. . . . Because He is a 'God of Miracles' . . . He will likewise bless each of us with hope, protection, and power according to our faith in Him." (Nash, Conf. Report, Oct. 2012). (See "Miracles" in Topical Index, Mormon 9).

Hope

After faith, comes hope: "if a man have faith he must needs have hope" (Moroni 7:42). "Hope comes of faith, for without faith, there is no hope. In like manner faith comes of hope, for faith is 'the substance of things hoped for' (Hebrews 11:1)." (Uchtdorf, Conf. Report, Oct. 2008). The Apostle Paul taught that the scriptures were written to the end that we "might have hope" (Romans 15:4). Hope has the power to fill our lives with happiness. Its absence can make "the heart sick" (Proverbs 13:12).

In discussing the definition of "hope," Elder Neal A. Maxwell observed: "Our everyday usage of the word hope includes how we 'hope' to arrive at a certain destination by a certain time. We 'hope' the world economy will improve. We 'hope' for the visit of a loved one. Such typify our sincere but proximate hopes. . . . Ultimate hope is a different matter. It is tied to Jesus and the blessings of the great Atonement, blessings resulting in the universal Resurrection. . . . Mormon confirmed: '*What is it that ye shall hope for? Behold I say unto you that ye shall have hope through the atonement of Christ*' (Moroni 7:41). Real hope, therefore, is not associated with things mercurial, but rather with things immortal and eternal." (Conf. Report, Oct. 1998, *italics added*). Hope is a gift of the Spirit that through the Atonement of Jesus Christ and the power of His resurrection, we shall be raised unto life eternal.

"From this triumphal act [the Atonement], resulting in the eventual resurrection of all mankind, so many lesser hopes derive their significance . . . . Thus, real hope is much more than wishful musing. It stiffens, not slackens, the spiritual spine. It is composed, not giddy, eager without being naïve, and pleasantly steady without being smug. . . . Such hope allows us to 'press forward' even when dark clouds oppress. . . . Hope keeps us 'anxiously engaged' in good causes even when these appear to be losing causes. . . . Hope feasts upon the words of Christ, that through the 'comfort of the scriptures [we] might have hope' (Romans 15:4). . . . Hope beckons all of us to come home where a glow reflects the Light of the World, whose 'brightness and glory defy all description' (JS-H 1:17). Jesus waits with open arms to receive those who finally overcome by faith and hope." (Maxwell, Conf. Report, Oct. 1994).

President James E. Faust concluded: "Hope is the anchor of our souls. I know of no one who is not in need of hope – young or old, strong or weak, rich or poor. . . Everybody in this life has challenges and difficulties. That is part of our mortal test. The reason for some of these trials cannot be readily understood except on the basis of faith and hope because there is often a larger purpose which we do not always understand. Peace comes through hope. . . . We can all find hope form our personal prayers and gain comfort from the scriptures. . . . Hope also comes from direct personal revelation, to which we are entitled if we are worthy. . . . The unfailing source of our hope is that we are sons and daughters of God and that His Son, the Lord Jesus Christ, saved us from death. . . . Our greatest hope comes from the knowledge that the Savior broke the bands of death." (Conf. Report, Oct. 1999).

If faith leads to knowledge, hope leads to trust. "Hope is not knowledge, but rather the abiding trust that the Lord will fulfill His promise to us. It is confidence that if we live according to God's laws and the words of His prophets now, we will receive desired blessings in the future. It is believing and expecting that our prayers will be answered. It is manifest in confidence, optimism, enthusiasm, and patient perseverance. . . . With hope comes joy and happiness. With hope, we can 'have patience, and bear . . . [our] afflictions.' (Alma 34:41)" (Uchtdorf, Conf. Report, Oct. 2008).

"Hope is critical to both faith and charity. When disobedience, disappointment, and procrastination erode faith, hope is there to uphold our faith. When frustration and impatience challenge charity, hope braces our resolve and urges us to care for our fellowmen even without expectation of reward." (Uchtdorf, Conf. Report, Oct. 2008).

Elder Jeffrey R. Holland concluded: "It is to have 'hope through the atonement of Christ and the power of his resurrection, to be raised unto life eternal, and this because of your faith in him according to the promise' (Moroni 7:41). That is the theological meaning of hope in the faith-hope-charity sequence. With an eye to that meaning, Moroni 7:42 then clearly reads, 'If a man have faith [in Christ and his atonement] he must needs [as a consequence] have hope [in the promise of the resurrection because the two are inextricably linked]; for without faith [in Christ's atonement], there cannot be any hope [in the resurrection].'" (Holland, Christ and the New Covenant, 334-335).

Charity

Mormon taught that a man "cannot have faith and hope, save he shall be meek and lowly of heart . . . and if a man be meek and lowly of heart . . . he must have charity; for if he have not charity, he is nothing" (Moroni 7:43-44). Thus, faith leads to hope, which leads to meekness and humility, which leads ultimately to charity.

The divine attributes of faith, hope, and charity "should become fixed in our hearts and minds to guide us in all of our actions. . . . When we keep the Lord's commandments, faith, hope and charity abide with us. . . . As I read and ponder the scriptures, I see that developing faith, hope and charity within ourselves is a step-by-step process. Faith begets hope, and together they foster charity. . . . These three virtues may be sequential initially, but once obtained, they become interdependent. Each one is incomplete without the others. They support and reinforce each other." (Wirthlin, Conf. Report, Oct. 1998).

"Three divine principles form a foundation upon which we can build the structure of our lives. They are faith, hope, and charity. Together they give us a base of support like the legs of a three-legged stool. Each principle is significant within itself, but each also plays an important supporting role. Each is incomplete without the others. . . The principles of faith and hope working together must be accompanied by charity, which is the greatest of all. . . . Working together, these three eternal principles will help give us the broad eternal perspective we need to face life's toughest challenges, including the prophesied ordeals of the last days. Real faith fosters hope for the future; it allows us to look beyond ourselves and our present cares. Fortified by hope, we are moved to demonstrate the pure love of Christ through daily acts of obedience and Christian service." (Ballard, Conf. Report, Oct. 1992).

With respect to the "three-legged stool" of faith, hope and charity, President Dieter F. Uchtdorf observed: "Faith, hope, and charity complement each other, and as one increases, the others grow as well. . . . The brighter our hope, the greater our faith. The stronger our hope, the purer our charity. The things we hope for lead us to faith, while the things we hope in lead us to charity. These three qualities – faith, hope, and charity – working together, grounded on the truth and light of the restored gospel of Jesus Christ, lead us to abound in good works." (Conf. Report, Oct. 2008).

Thus the progression from faith to hope, to meekness and humility, ultimately leading to charity, or the "pure love of Christ" (Moroni 7:47). As Elder Neal A. Maxwell taught, faith, hope, and charity, individually, and collectively, all point to Jesus Christ: "Unsurprisingly the triad of faith, hope and charity, which brings us to Christ, has strong and converging linkage: faith is in the Lord Jesus Christ, hope is in His atonement, and charity is the 'pure love of Christ.'" (Conf. Report, Oct. 1994).

What Is Charity?

Mormon declared: "And charity suffereth long, and is kind, and envieth not, and is not puffed up, seeketh not her own, is not easily provoked, thinketh no evil, and rejoiceth not in iniquity but rejoiceth in the truth, beareth all things, believeth all things, hopeth all things, endureth all things" (Moroni 7:45). This language is very similar to Paul's description of charity in 1 Corinthians 13:4-7.[63]

President Thomas S. Monson asked, "What is charity?" and then answered: "Charity is having patience with someone who has let us down. It is resisting the impulse to become offended easily. It is accepting weaknesses and shortcomings. It is accepting people as they truly are. It is looking beyond physical appearances to attributes that will not dim through time. It is resisting the impulse to categorize others. . . . Mother Theresa . . . spoke this profound truth: 'If you judge people, you have no time to love them.' . . . There is a serious need for the charity that gives attention to those who are unnoticed, hope to those who are discouraged, aid to those who are afflicted. True charity is love in action." (Conf. Report, Oct. 2010).

Elder Gene R. Cook asked: "Is there a difference between charity and love? The Lord referred to them separately a number of times (e.g., D&C 4:5). Some have said charity is love plus sacrifice – a seasoned love." (Conf. Report, Apr. 2002). President Brigham Young stated: "There is one virtue, attribute, or principle, which, if cherished and practiced by the Saints, would prove salvation to thousands upon thousands. I allude to charity, or love, from which proceed forgiveness, long suffering, kindness, and patience." (Deseret News, Jan. 11, 1860, quoted in Cook, Conf. Report, Apr. 2002).

"What is charity? How do we obtain charity?" asked Sister Silvia H. Allred. "The prophet Mormon defines charity as 'the pure love of Christ,' while Paul teaches that 'charity . . . is the bond of perfectness,' (Colossians 3:14), and Nephi reminds us that . . . 'charity is love.' (2 Nephi 26:30). In reviewing Paul's description of charity, we learn that charity is not a single act or something we give away but a state of being, a state of the heart, kind feelings that engender loving actions. Mormon also teaches that charity is bestowed upon the Lord's true disciples and that charity purifies those that have it. (Moroni 7:48)." (Conf. Report, Oct. 2011).

In essence, love is a feeling; charity is a condition, or state of being – it is, in President Monson's words, "love in action." (Conf. Report, Oct. 2010).

---

[63] Elder Jeffrey R. Holland observed: "The fact that Paul uses comparable language without having the benefit of Mormon and Moroni's text suggests the possibility of an ancient source available to both Book of Mormon and New Testament writers. It may also simply be another evidence that the Holy Ghost can reveal a truth in essentially the same words to more than one person." (Christ and the New Covenant, 413).

Elder Dallin H. Oaks explained: "Charity, 'the pure love of Christ' is not an act but a condition or state of being. Charity is attained through a succession of acts that result in a conversion. Charity is something one becomes. Thus as Moroni declared, 'except men shall have charity they cannot inherit' the place prepared for them in the mansions of the Father (Ether 12:34)." (Conf. Report, Oct. 2000). Elder C. Max Caldwell taught: "Charity is not just a precept or a principle, nor is it just a word to describe actions or attitudes. Rather, it is an internal condition that must be developed and experienced in order to be understood. We are possessors of charity when it is part of our nature." (Conf. Report, Oct. 1992).

Elder Marvin J. Ashton observed: "Charity is, perhaps in many ways a misunderstood word. We often equate charity with visiting the sick, taking in casseroles to those in need, or sharing our excess with those who are less fortunate. But really, true charity is much, much more. Real charity is not something you give away; it is something you acquire and make a part of yourself. . . . Perhaps the greatest charity comes when we are kind to each other, when we don't judge or categorize someone else, when we simply give each other the benefit of the doubt or remain quiet. Charity is accepting someone's differences, weaknesses, and shortcomings; having patience with someone who has let us down; or resisting the impulse to become offended when someone doesn't handle something the way we might have hoped. Charity is refusing to take advantage of another's weakness and being willing to forgive someone who has hurt us. Charity is expecting the best of each other." (Conf. Report, Apr. 1992).

Elder Robert L. Oaks observed, "Mormon, after pointing out that if a man 'have not charity he is nothing' . . . goes on to name the 13 elements of charity, or the pure love of Christ. I find it interesting that 4 of the 13 elements of this must-have virtue relate to patience. . . . First, 'charity suffereth long.' That is what patience is all about. Charity 'is not easily provoked' is another aspect of this quality, as is charity 'beareth all things.' And finally, charity 'endureth all things' is certainly an expression of patience. From these defining elements it is evident that without patience gracing our soul, we would be seriously lacking with respect to a Christlike character. . . . Patience may well be thought of as a gateway virtue, contributing to the growth and strength of its fellow virtues of forgiveness, tolerance, and faith." (Conf. Report, Oct. 2006). As Joseph Smith stated: "Patience is heavenly." (History of the Church, 6:427).

Sister Aileen H. Clyde taught that "understanding charity or being charitable is not easy. . . . Even 'charity suffereth long' requires our thoughtful interpretation. The 'suffering' that may come from loving is the result of our great caring. It comes because another matters to us so much . . . . As an antidote against the suffering that will surely come as we have loved ones die, or see them struggle or be misled, or have them misunderstand us or even betray us, we can find relief in charity to others." (Conf. Report, Oct. 1991).

How Do We Develop Charity?

Charity is a divine gift which we must seek, cultivate and pray for. Mormon exhorted us to "pray unto the Father with all the energy of heart," that we may be filled with charity. "Note that charity is given only to those who seek it ." (Wirthlin, Conf. Report, Oct. 1998). "If we lack this love for others, we should pray for it." (Oaks, Conf. Report, Oct. 2001).

"There is no salvation without true charity," Elder Mark E. Petersen taught, "and true charity embraces the spirit of brotherly love to the point that it permits no injustice on the part of any one of us toward our fellowmen – no deceptions, no dishonesty, and no predatory designs." (Conf. Report, Oct. 1966).

We can start developing charitable traits in our own homes. President Thomas S. Monson instructed: "To my mind come the words of the scripture: 'Charity is the pure love of Christ' . . . Brothers and sisters, some of the greatest opportunities to demonstrate our love will be within the walls of our own homes. Love should be the very heart of family life . . . I would hope that we would strive always to be considerate and to be sensitive to the thoughts and feelings and circumstances of those around us. . . . Love is expressed in many recognizable ways: a smile, a wave, a kind comment, a compliment. . . . Dale Carnegie, a well-known American author and lecturer, believed that each person has within himself or herself the 'power to increase the sum total of [the] world's happiness . . . by giving a few words of sincere appreciation to someone who is lonely or discouraged.'" (Conf. Report, Apr. 2014).

In speaking of charity, Elder Marvin J. Ashton counseled: "Be one who nurtures and who builds. Be one who has an understanding and a forgiving heart, who looks for the best in people. Leave people better than you found them. Be fair with your competitors, whether in business, athletics, or elsewhere. . . . Lend a hand to those who are frightened, lonely, or burdened." (Conf. Report, Apr. 1992). "It is a time-honored adage that love begets love. Let us pour forth love – show forth our kindness unto all mankind, and the Lord will reward us with everlasting increase; cast our bread upon the waters and we shall receive it after many days, increased to a hundredfold." (Teachings of the Prophet Joseph Smith, 316). The power of charity can increase through use: "love begets love, compassion begets compassion, virtue begets virtue, commitment begets loyalty, and service begets joy." (Christofferson, Conf. Report, Apr. 2009).

Charity: The Pure Love of Christ

Mormon teaches that "charity is the pure love of Christ, and it endureth forever" (Moroni 7:47). Sister Bonnie D. Parkin said: "The pure love of Christ. Let's look at that. What does this phrase mean? We find part of the answer in Joshua: 'Take diligent heed . . . to love the Lord your God . . . and to serve him with all your heart and with all your soul.' (Joshua 22:5). Charity is *our* love for the Lord, shown through our acts of service, patience, compassion, and understanding for one another. . . . Charity is also *the Lord's* love for us, shown through His acts of service, patience, compassion, and understanding. The 'pure love of Christ' refers not only to *our* love for the Savior but to *His* love for each of us." (Conf. Report, Oct. 2003, *emphasis in original*).

Elder Henry D. Taylor observed: "Charity can and should mean not only the pure love *of* Christ, but it should also mean pure love *for* him and his love for us." (Conf. Report, Apr. 1969). Elder C. Max Caldwell observed: "The phrase '[pure] love of Christ' might have meaning in three dimensions:

1. Love *for* Christ
2. Love *from* Christ
3. Love *like* Christ

"***First***, love *for* Christ. This concept proclaims Jesus as the object of our love, and our lives should be an external expression of gratitude for him. . . . Is our love for him evident by our behavior and our attitude? Charity, or love *for* Christ, sustains us in every need and influences in every decision. A ***second*** dimension of the meaning of charity is love *from* Christ. . . . Through his compliance with the severe requirements of the Atonement, the Savior offered the ultimate expression of love. 'Greater love hath no man than this, that a man lay down his life for his friends.' (John 15:13). . . . This gift of charity is to be received. . . . A ***third*** perception of charity is to possess a love that is *like* Christ. In other words, people are the object of Christlike love. . . . Jesus' love was inseparably connected to and resulted from his life of serving, sacrificing, and giving on behalf of others. We cannot develop Christlike love except by practicing the process prescribed by the Master. . . . People who have charity have a love for the Savior, have received of his love, and love others as he does." (Caldwell, Conf. Report, Oct. 1992, *emphasis added*). "Charity encompasses His love for us, our love for Him, and Christlike love for others." (Cook, Conf. Report, Apr. 2002).

President Ezra Taft Benson taught: "If we would truly seek to be more like our Savior and Master, then learning to love as He loves should be our highest goal. Mormon called charity 'the greatest of all.' (Moroni 7:46). The world today speaks a great deal about love, and it is sought for by many. But the pure love of Christ differs greatly from what the world thinks of love. Charity never seeks selfish gratification. The pure love of Christ seeks only the eternal growth and joy of others." (Conf. Report, Oct. 1986).

President David O. McKay taught that charity or "love for fellow men" is "the power of the greatest thing in all the world . . . The poet Browning has Paracelsus say to his friend Festus, 'There was a time when I was happy; the secret to life was in that happiness . . . . The answer to the passionate longings of the human heart for fullness is this: Live in all things outside yourself by love and you will have joy. That is the life of God; it ought to be our life. In him it is accomplished and perfect; but in all created things it is a lesson learned slowly and through difficulty.'" (Conf. Report, Apr. 1951).

President Dieter F. Uchtdorf counseled: "The love of Christ is not a pretend love. It is not a greeting-card love. It is not the kind of love that is praised in popular music and movies. This love brings about real change of character. It can penetrate hatred and dissolve envy. It can heal resentment and quench the fires of bitterness. It can work miracles. . . . When your primary thoughts are focused on how things will benefit you, your motivations may be selfish and shallow. . . . But when your primary thoughts and behaviors are focused on serving God and others – when you truly desire to bless and lift up those around you – then the power of the pure love of Christ can work in your heart and life." (Conf. Report, Apr. 2013).

Mormon taught that "charity never faileth" (Moroni 7:46). "Life has its share of fears and failures. Sometimes things fall short. Sometimes people fail us, or economies or businesses or governments fail us. But one thing in time or eternity does not fail us – the pure love of Christ." (Holland, Christ and the New Covenant, 337). Elder Holland testified: "Only the pure love of Christ will see us through. It is Christ's love which suffereth long, and is kind. It is Christ's love which is not puffed up nor easily provoked. Only his pure love enables him – and us – to bear all things, believe all things, hope all things, and endure all things. . . . His pure love never fails us. Not now. Not ever." (Conf. Report, Oct. 1989).

Discourse 24: Mormon, "Baptism of Little Children" (Moroni 8)

Prophet	Key Doctrines	Scriptures	Audience	Date
Mormon	• Baptism of Little Children • A Path to Perfect Love	Moroni 8	Epistle to Moroni	Before A.D. 401

INTRODUCTION

Chapter 8 of the Book of Moroni includes the first of two recorded epistles from Mormon to his son, Moroni. The first is a letter Mormon sent to Moroni addressing the question whether little children need baptism. We don't know when this epistle was sent, but it was likely before Mormon's epistle in Moroni 9, as it relates to instructional and administrative matters in the church, which would be more applicable before the destruction of the Nephites.

The source of Mormon's instruction on this topic came by the "word of the Lord . . . by the power of the Holy Ghost" (Moroni 8:7). In this first recorded epistle to Moroni, Mormon teaches about the mercy of God, and that Christ's Atonement redeems little children. Because of the Atonement, "little children are whole" (Mormon 8:8) and do not need baptism. Those who have reached the age (or mental state) of accountability, however, are required to exercise faith, repent and be baptized, and then live in accordance with the commandments of God, to be saved.

DISCOURSE: Moroni 8

KEY DOCTRINES

- **Baptism of Little Children Not Necessary.** Repentance and baptism are only required for those who are accountable and capable of committing sin. Little children are "alive in Christ" and saved by the Atonement.

- **A Pathway to Perfect Love.** For the accountable, the path of faith, repentance, baptism, humility, the Holy Ghost and perfect love, or charity, leads to life with our Heavenly Father. (Moroni 8:25-26).

COMMENTARY

Baptism of Little Children

Mormon taught that only those "capable of committing sin" should be baptized. (Moroni 8:10). Baptism for the remission of sins is not necessary for little children because they are not capable of sinning. "Little children are redeemed from the foundation of the world through mine Only Begotten. Wherefore, they cannot sin, for power is not given unto Satan to tempt little children, until they begin to become accountable before me" (D&C 29:46-47).

Elder Merlin R. Lybbert observed: "The Lord extends special protection to children. . . . They cannot sin until they reach the age of accountability, which the Lord has declared to be eight years (see D&C 18:42; D&C 29:47). In fact, the power to even tempt them to commit sin has been taken from Satan. The prophet Mormon taught that 'little children are whole, for they are not capable of committing sin.' (Moroni 8:8). . . . Because they cannot sin, they have no need of repentance, neither baptism. Adam's original transgression has no claim as a result of the atonement of Jesus Christ. . . . Because all children who die before the age of accountability are pure, innocent, and wholly sin-free, they are saved in the celestial kingdom of heaven. Understanding the special status of little children before God, because of their pure and innocent nature, brings understanding of the Lord's commandment to 'repent, and become as a little child, and be baptized in [His] name.' (3 Nephi 11:37)." (Conf. Report, Apr. 1994).

Elder Dallin H. Oaks instructed: "We understand from our doctrine that before the age of accountability a child is 'not capable of committing sin' (Moroni 8:8). During that time, children can commit mistakes, even very serious and damaging ones that must be corrected, but their acts are not accounted as sins." ("Sins and Mistakes," Ensign, Oct. 1996). Joseph Smith taught: "Baptism is for remission of sins. Children have no sins. . . . Children are all made alive in Christ, and those of riper years through faith and repentance." (Teachings of the Prophet Joseph Smith, 314).

Elder Bruce R. McConkie instructed: "Accountability does not burst full-bloom upon a child in any given moment in his life. Children become accountable gradually, over a number of years. Becoming accountable is a process. . . There comes a time, however, when accountability is real and actual and sin is attributed in the lives of those who develop normally. It is eight years of age, the age of baptism." (McConkie, "The Salvation of Little Children," Ensign, Apr. 1977). President Joseph Fielding Smith also taught that others who are not accountable, such as people with mental disabilities or who are not capable of understanding the gospel, have no need for repentance and are redeemed through the Atonement of Christ: "They are redeemed without baptism and will go to the celestial kingdom of God, there, we believe, to have their faculties or other deficiencies restored according to the Father's mercy and justice." (Smith, Answers to Gospel Questions, 3:21).

President Wilford Woodruff taught: "There is no infant or child that has died before arriving at the years of accountability, but what is redeemed, and is therefore entirely beyond the torments of hell, to use a sectarian term. And any doctrine, such as the sprinkling of infants or any religious rite for little children is of no effect. . . . I will say again that [infants] are redeemed by the blood of Jesus Christ, and when they die, whether of Christian, Pagan or Jewish parentage, their spirits are taken home to God who gave them, and never go to suffer torments of any kind." (Journal of Discourses, 23:124).

Mormon criticized infant baptism, characterizing it as "solemn mockery before God" (Moroni 8:9). This is because a belief in the need to baptize infants reflects a lack of faith in the efficacy of the Atonement. Joseph Smith taught: "The doctrine of baptizing children, or sprinkling them, or they must welter in hell, is a doctrine not true, not supported in Holy Writ, and is not consistent with the character of God. All children are redeemed by the blood of Jesus Christ, and the moment that children leave this world, they are taken to the bosom of Abraham." (Teachings of the Prophet Joseph Smith, 197).

President Boyd K. Packer shared a story about the comfort this doctrine can bring to parents of children who die before the age of accountability: "A neighbor once told me that as a missionary in earlier days he and his companion were walking along a ridge in the mountains of the South. They saw people gathering in a clearing near a cabin some distance down the hillside. They had come for a funeral. A little boy had drowned, and his parents had sent for the preacher to 'say words.' . . . .The elders stayed in the background as the minister stood before the grieving family and began his sermon. If the parents had hoped for consolation from this man of the cloth, they were disappointed. He scolded them severely because the little boy had not been baptized. He told them bluntly that their little son was lost in endless torment, and it was their fault. After the grave was covered and the neighbors had gone, the elders approached the grieving parents. 'We are servants of the Lord,' they told the sobbing mother, 'and we've come with a message for you.' As the grief-stricken parents listened, the elders unfolded the plan of redemption. They quoted from the Book of Mormon, 'Little children need no repentance, neither baptism' (Moroni 8:11) and then bore testimony of the restoration of the gospel. . . . What comfort the truth brings at times of sorrow!" (Conf. Report, Oct. 1988).

Another example was provided by Elder Shayne M. Bowen about a woman whose child died as an infant and was comforted when she learned the doctrines in Moroni 8. She said: "Six years ago I had a baby boy. He died before we could have him baptized. Our priest told us that because he had not been baptized, he would be in limbo for all eternity. For six years I have carried that pain and guilt. After reading this scripture [Moroni 8:10-12], I know by the power of the Holy Ghost that it is true. I have felt a great weight taken off of me." (Conf. Report, Oct. 2012). Joseph Smith taught: "The Lord takes many away, even in infancy, that they may escape the envy of man, and the sorrows and evils of this present world; they were too pure, too lovely, to live on earth; therefore, if rightly considered, instead of mourning we have reason to rejoice as they are delivered from evil, and we shall soon have them again." (*quoted in* Bowen, Conf. Report, Oct. 2012).

Baptism and the Path to Perfect Love

After Mormon instructed Moroni that baptism is not necessary for little children, he taught his son that baptism and other fundamental gospel ordinances are necessary for the accountable. In two succinct verses, Mormon outlines the path from repentance to baptism, and ultimately, to life with our Father in Heaven. "And the first fruits of repentance is baptism; and baptism cometh by faith unto the fulfilling [of] the commandments; and the fulfilling [of] the commandments bringeth remission of sins; And the remission of sins bringeth meekness, and lowliness of heart; and because of meekness and lowliness of heart cometh the visitation of the Holy Ghost, which Comforter filleth with hope and perfect love, which love endureth by diligence unto prayer, until the end shall come, when all the saints shall dwell with God" (Moroni 8:25-26).

Elder Jack H. Goaslind taught: "By obeying the commandments and fulfilling these covenants, we are sanctified, purified, and . . . become vessels worthy of receiving the Holy Spirit. . . . The fulfilling of the commandments, as [Mormon] explained, 'bringeth remission of sins, and the remission of sins bringeth meekness, and lowliness of heart, and . . . the visitation of the Holy Ghost . . . and perfect love.' (Moroni 8:25-26). . . . As noted by Mormon, this perfect love comes as direct result of having our sins remitted." (Conf. Report, Oct. 1983).

Elder Francisco J. Vinas observed: "Once God has accepted repentance, the process that we are describing leads us to participate in ordinances and the covenants associated with them, such as baptism . . . . After receiving a remission of sins and striving to retain it through obedience to the commandments, we will receive, as described in the book of Moroni, meekness and lowliness of heart, which will allow the visitation of the Holy Ghost, which Comforter will fill us with hope and perfect love, love that will be maintained by the diligence we give to the principle of prayer. (Moroni 8:26). The person who obtains meekness and lowliness of heart and who enjoys the company of the Holy Ghost will have no desire to offend or hurt others, nor will he feel affected by any offenses received from others. . . . Principles like faith, repentance, love, forgiveness, and prayer, lived in the process I just described, become the best vaccine to combat the disease of sin. . . . The decision to incorporate them into our lives and the opportunity to begin the process whenever it may be necessary depends solely upon our agency. It is a simple process that is within the reach of all." (Conf. Report, Apr. 2004).

This progression of choices and consequences is similar to the progression of divine attributes outlined by Peter and others, where we progress from the initial step of faith, ultimately to charity. (See 2 Peter 1:4-8; Alma 7:23-34). Mormon teaches Moroni that faith leads to repentance, which leads to baptism, which leads to fulfilling the commandments, which leads to a remission of sins, which leads to meekness and humility, which leads to the Holy Ghost, which leads to charity ("perfect love"), which leads to life with our Heavenly Father. After faith, repentance, and baptism, we can receive the Holy Ghost. By receiving this Comforter in all humility, faithfully obeying the commandments, and being filled with charity, we can prepare to live with God. The description of this path aligns with Mormon's teachings about faith, hope, and charity recorded in Moroni 7.

The process changes our lives, purifies our souls, and creates what President Henry B. Eyring calls a "spirit of righteousness." He taught: "How then can we keep reaching out in a spirit of righteousness, with love and tenderness? The best answer I know comes from . . . Mormon. He wrote a letter to his son Moroni in a time when they met not only rejection but unbridled hatred, and faced not only frustration but almost certain failure. Mormon wanted Moroni to meet even such a test with love and tenderness and the spirit of righteousness. He gave a formula, the same one given by true prophets in all ages. It has always worked. The promise is sure. Here it is, from Mormon's letter: 'And the first fruits of repentance is baptism; and baptism cometh by faith unto the fulfilling the commandments; and the fulfilling the commandments bringeth remission of sins; And the remission of sins bringeth meekness, and lowliness of heart; and because of meekness and lowliness of hart cometh the visitation of the Holy Ghost, which Comforter filleth with hope and perfect love' (Moroni 8:25-26). That tenderness and love, Mormon testified to his son, is the natural result of the atonement of Jesus Christ operating in our lives. Our faith leads to repentance, to the gifts of the Spirit, and from that to the perfect love which the Master Shepherd has, and knows we must have to serve him." (Conf. Report, Oct. 1986).

Discourse 25: Mormon, "Persevere Despite Wickedness" (Moroni 9)

Prophet	Key Doctrines	Scriptures	Audience	Date
Mormon	• Anger • Persevere Despite Wickedness • Let Christ Lift You Up	Moroni 9	2nd Epistle from Mormon to Moroni[64]	Before A.D. 401

INTRODUCTION

Moroni chapter 9 is the second recorded epistle from Mormon to his son, Moroni. This letter reveals the consequences of universal sin and disobedience, as the Nephites had deteriorated as a society to the point that they were "without civilization" (Moroni 9:11), "without order and without mercy" (Moroni 9:18), and "without principle, and past feeling" (Moroni 9:20). The entire Nephite nation, or what was left of it, reveled in wickedness, and faced imminent destruction.

One commentator observed: "It is appropriate that these letters [Moroni 8, 9] follow Mormon's sermon on faith, hope, and charity [Moroni 7] because they put the essence of that sermon to the test. . . . The second letter [Moroni 9] reveals the full strength of Mormon's position. His people, he says, 'have lost their love, one towards another; and they thirst after blood and revenge continually.' (Moroni 9:5). Yet Mormon preserves his 'perfect love' and remains uncontaminated by the evil around him." (Rust, <u>Feasting on the Word</u>, 163-164). In his epistle recorded as Moroni Chapter 9, Mormon encourages his son to persevere in righteousness, despite the wickedness of the world around him.

DISCOURSE: Moroni 9

KEY DOCTRINES

- **Persevere Despite Wickedness**. Despite wickedness and the hardness of the hearts of those around us, we must continue to labor diligently (Moroni 9:6)

---

[64] The superscription to Moroni 9, "The second epistle of Mormon to his son Moroni," was part of the record translated by Joseph Smith, and dictated by him to his scribe.

COMMENTARY

Anger and Wickedness

In his epistle, Mormon describes the Nephite people as unrepentant and angry; "Satan stirreth them up continually to *anger* one with another" (Moroni 9:3). They would "tremble and *anger*" against Mormon when he taught the word of God. (Moroni 9:4). "For so exceedingly do they *anger* that . . . they have lost their love, one towards another; and they thirst after blood and revenge continually" (Moroni 9:5). *Emphasis added.*

Anger is a tool of Satan and a hallmark of the natural man. The Lord taught: "whosoever is angry with his brother without a cause shall be in danger of the judgment" (Matt. 5:22). Elder George A. Smith observed: "It is an old proverb, and one of long standing, that 'whom the gods would destroy, they first make mad.' Peace is taken from the earth, and wrath and indignation among the people is the result: they care not for anything but to quarrel and destroy each other. The same spirit that dwelt in the breasts of the Nephites during the last battles . . . when they continued to fight until they were exterminated. . . . This spirit will in the end lead a man to destruction." (Journal of Discourses, 3:28).

Elder Lynn G. Robbins explained: "A cunning part of [Satan's] strategy is to disassociate anger from agency, making us believe that we are victims of an emotion that we cannot control. . . . This is a myth that must be debunked. No one makes us mad. Others don't make us angry. There is no force involved. Becoming angry is a conscious choice, a decision; therefore, we can make the choice not to become angry." (Conf. Report, Apr. 1998). "You shouldn't give circumstances the power to rouse anger, for they don't care at all." (Marcus Aurelius, Meditations).

As the people hardened their hearts, and chose anger, again and again, Mormon feared that "the Spirit of the Lord hath ceased striving with them" (Moroni 9:4). He describes the wickedness of his people: "O the depravity of my people. They are without order and without mercy . . . And they have become strong in their perversion; and they are alike brutal, sparing none . . . and they delight in everything save that which is good . . . they are without principle, and past feeling" (Moroni 9:18-20).

Elder Neal A. Maxwell observed: "People who wrongly celebrate their capacity to feel finally reach a point where they lose much of their capacity to feel. In the words of three different prophets, such individuals become 'past feeling' (1 Nephi 17:45; Eph. 4:19; Moroni 9:20). When people proceed 'without principle,' erelong they will be 'without civilization,' 'without mercy,' and 'past feeling.'" (Conf. Report, Apr. 1995). Elder Orson Pratt said: "We see the Nephites . . . descending lower and lower in their wickedness, going into idolatry, offering up human sacrifices unto their idol gods, and committing every species of abomination that they had ever known or heard of, all because they had been once enlightened and had apostatized from the truth, and withdrawn from the order of God." (Journal of Discourses, 17:24). It all began with anger.

Persevere Despite Wickedness

At the time Mormon wrote his epistle, the Nephite people are living in a steady state of wickedness and depravity, and have rejected the Lord, and His prophet, Mormon. Notwithstanding these circumstances, Mormon realizes that he cannot give up, but must persevere and continue to labor for their benefit. "Behold, I am laboring with them continually . . ." (Moroni 9:4). In his epistle, Mormon encourages his son, Moroni, to do likewise: "And now, my beloved son, notwithstanding their hardness, let us labor diligently; for if we should cease to labor, we should be brought under condemnation" (Moroni 9:6).

President Joseph F. Smith taught: "After we have done all we could do for the cause of truth and withstood the evil that men have brought upon us, and we have been overwhelmed by their wrongs, it is still our duty to stand. We cannot give up; we must not lie down. . . . To stand firm in the face of overwhelming opposition, when you have done all you can, is the courage of faith." (Smith, Gospel Doctrine, 119).

Elder Joseph B. Wirthlin observed: "The life of Moroni is especially instructive in teaching perseverance. The obstacles he faced may seem beyond belief to us. He saw the entire Nephite nation destroyed by the sword in a terrible war because of the wickedness of the people. His father and all of his kinsfolk and friends were slain. He was alone for about twenty years, perhaps hiding and fleeing from savage Lamanites who sought to take his life. Yet he continued to keep the record as his father had commanded him." (Conf. Report, Oct. 1987). Elder Neal A. Maxwell said: "Our discipleship should not be dried out by discouragement . . . nor should dismaying, societal symptoms 'weigh us down.'" (Conf. Report, Oct. 2002).

Elder Delbert L. Stapley said: "Our position and responsibility are the same now as Mormon expressed to his son Moroni centuries ago . . . 'notwithstanding their hardness, let us labor diligently' (Moroni 9:6). Striving to exert the power of good example by living gospel principles, maintaining proper standards, and holding firm to righteous ideals, while not always easy, will reward us in this life and in the eternal worlds to come." (Conf. Report, Apr. 1969).

There are several examples of other Book of Mormon prophets who continued to perform their assignments despite the people's wickedness and rejection. These include: (i) Abinadi in Zeniff's colony (Mosiah 11:20-29; Mosiah 12-15); (ii) Alma in Ammonihah (Alma 8:11-32); and, (iii) Samuel the Lamanite in Zarahemla (Helaman 13-15).

1. **Abinadi** was called to preach repentance to the people of King Noah in the land of Lehi-Nephi (Mosiah 11:20). The people rejected Abinadi's teachings, and were "wroth with" Abinadi; they "sought to take away his life" (Mosiah 11:26). King Noah commanded that Abinadi be brought to him to be killed. The Lord, however, delivered Abinadi from King Noah and the people, and he initially escaped the death sentence. Nonetheless, and notwithstanding the wickedness of the people, Abinadi returned to prophesy and preach repentance "in disguise" (Mosiah 12:1). Abinadi paid the ultimate price for his testimony and preaching, but fulfilled his mission, and died as a martyr with honor. His perseverance in teaching led to the conversion of one of King Noah's priests, Alma, and ultimately brought salvation to thousands. See Mosiah 12-15.

2. **Alma the Younger**, the son of the Alma who was converted by Abinadi, had been serving as chief judge. As the people increased in wickedness, Alma resigned from his government position to preach full time among the cities of the Nephites. One of the most wicked cities was Ammonihah, where "Satan had gotten great hold upon the hearts of the people" (Alma 8:9). The people would not listen to Alma, and "reviled him, and spit upon him, and caused that he should be cast out of their city" (Alma 8:13). After Alma left Ammonihah, he was visited by an angel, who instructed him to return and "preach again" (Alma 8:16) repentance to the people. After receiving this message from the angel, Alma "returned *speedily*" (Alma 8:18) to Ammonihah. Upon his return, Alma met Amulek and Zeezrom, who both assisted in teaching and converting many to follow the Lord. See Alma 8-13.

3. **Samuel** the Lamanite was sent to the city of Zarahemla to preach to a Nephite people who did "remain in wickedness" (Helaman 13:1). Samuel preached repentance "many days," but the people "cast him out" (Helaman 13:2). Samuel was about to return to his own land, but was instructed to return. The wicked Nephites would not let him enter the city, but Samuel persevered. He climbed the walls of the city and cried with a loud voice, preaching repentance and prophesying about the coming of Christ. The people were angry with Samuel and "cast stones at him upon the wall," and "shot arrows" at him. (Helaman 16:2). However, the Spirit of the Lord was with Samuel and the Nephites could not hit him. Samuel finished his message, and then departed from Zarahemla and returned to "his own country, and began to preach and to prophesy among his own people" (Helaman 16:7). See Helaman 13-16.

Each of these prophets fulfilled his mission to preach despite the anger and wickedness of the people, despite rejection, and despite threats of death. They are excellent examples of Mormon's admonition to "labor diligently" notwithstanding the "hardness" of the people (Moroni 9:6).

May Christ Lift You Up

Elder Marion D. Hanks taught: "In the last recorded letter of the great prophet Mormon to his son Moroni are written the lamentings of the prophet over wickedness of the people, described in the record to be 'without principle, and past feeling.' Mormon's final testimony to his beloved son included the marvelous admonition and explanation of the effect Christ's gifts should have in all of our lives: 'My son, be faithful in Christ; and may not the things which I have written grieve thee to weigh thee down unto death; but may Christ lift thee up, and may his sufferings and death, and the showing his body unto our fathers, and his mercy and long-suffering, and the hope of his glory and of eternal life, rest in your mind forever' (Moroni 9:25)." (Conf. Report, Apr. 1973).

President Henry B. Eyring observed: "Both Mormon and Moroni were facing days of difficulty that make [our] challenges pale. Mormon knew his son might be overcome with gloom and foreboding, so he told him the perfect antidote. He told him that he could choose, by what he put in his mind, to become an example of hope." (Conf. Report, Oct. 1986).

There was unspeakable wickedness in Mormon's time. There is unspeakable wickedness in modern times. The last 100 years have witnessed atrocities ranging from the Nazi holocaust to genocides in Russia, Rwanda, Cambodia, Armenia and throughout the Middle East. Elder Dallin H. Oaks observed: "The mass-murders of the twentieth century are among the bloodiest crimes ever committed against humanity. We can hardly comprehend the magnitude of the Nazi holocaust murders of over five million Jews in Europe, Stalin's purges and labor camps that killed five to ten million in the Soviet Union, and the two to three million noncombatants who were killed or who died of hunger in the Biafra War." (Conf. Report, Apr. 1990).

Today, terrorists torture and execute their victims on live video feeds, and instill fear with random acts of violence. Throughout the world, evil men (and women) commit violent and abominable acts. It is difficult to not let these things "grieve" us; however, Mormon's message is that no matter how bad the world gets, no matter whether wickedness and abominations surround us, we can still look to Christ with hope. In both Mormon's time and today, faith and hope in Christ is the antidote from the oppressive and discouraging impact of the wickedness of men.

Elder Dallin H. Oaks counseled: "As we struggle with the challenges of mortality, I pray for each of us, as the prophet Mormon prayed for his son, Moroni: "May Christ lift thee up, and may his sufferings and death . . . and his mercy and long-suffering, and the hope of his glory and of eternal life, rest in your mind forever." (Conf. Report, Oct. 2006).

Discourse 26: Mormon, "Invitation to Believe" (Mormon 7)

Prophet	Doctrines	Scriptures	Audience	Date
Mormon	• Invitation to Believe	Mormon 7	To the Lamanites ("the remnant of this people who are spared")	About A.D. 385

INTRODUCTION

In his final recorded words, chronologically,[65] Mormon speaks to "the remnant of this people who are spared . . . ye remnant of the house of Israel" (Morm. 7:1). Although Mormon had fought the Lamanites his entire life, he encourages his mortal enemies to repent and be baptized, and to come unto Christ to be saved. He teaches them things they need to "know," and things they need to "do" so that "it shall be well with [them] in the day of judgment" (Mormon 7:10).

The ten verses in Mormon chapter 7 include Mormon's last message in the Book of Mormon. Although Moroni later included some of his father's earlier epistles (see Moroni 7-9), Mormon chapter 7 is likely Mormon's final recorded discourse – succinct and direct. This brief discourse illustrates the compassionate character of the battle-weary prophet, Mormon.

After a lifetime of war with the Lamanites, and a final battle where the Nephites are basically exterminated (see Mormon 6), Mormon magnanimously pleads for the Lamanites' repentance, that the descendants of his enemies might be saved through the redemption of Christ and that it "shall be well" with them "in the day of judgment" (Mormon 7:10).

DISCOURSE: Mormon 7

KEY DOCTRINES

- **Invitation to Lamanites to Believe**. What the Lamanites need to know and to do in order to be saved. The Lord will offer salvation to all those who will repent, be baptized, and follow His teachings. "Lay hold" upon the gospel in the Book of Mormon and the Bible.

---

[65] Although this is Mormon's first recorded discourse in the Book of Mormon, it apparently occurred chronologically after his letters were written to Moroni about the baptism of little children and the dissolution of Nephite society, and his sermon on faith, hope, and charity was delivered. The latter three discourses, however, are presented in subsequent chapters of the Book of Mormon - in the Book of Moroni.

COMMENTARY

Invitation to the Lamanites: Know and Do

Mormon teaches the Lamanites that they must "know" several things:

- That they are of the house of Israel. (Mormon 7:2).
- That they need to repent or they can't be saved. (Mormon 7:3).
- That they must give up their culture of war. (Mormon 7:4).
- That they must believe in Christ, that He is the Son of God, and was slain and resurrected, and that all men will be judged by Him. (Mormon 7:5).
- That they are a remnant of the seed of Jacob and numbered among the covenant people. (Mormon 7:10).

Elder Jeffrey R. Holland taught: "In a soliloquy of death, Mormon reached across time and space to all, especially to that 'remnant of the house of Israel' who would one day read his majestic record. Those of another time and place must learn what those lying before him had forgotten – that all must 'believe in Jesus Christ, that he is the Son of God,' that following his crucifixion in Jerusalem he had, 'by the power of the Father . . . risen again, whereby he hath gained the victory over the grave; and also in him is the sting of death swallowed up' (Mormon 7:2, 5). . . . To 'believe in Christ,' especially when measured against such tragic but avoidable consequences, was Mormon's last plea and his only hope. It is the ultimate purpose of the entire book that would come to the latter-day world bearing his name." (Holland, Christ and the New Covenant, 321-322).

Mormon's invitation to the Lamanites is not only "to know," but "to do." He admonishes them to:

- Delight no more in the shedding of blood, and lay down their weapons of war (Mormon 7:4)
- Repent and be baptized in the name of Jesus (Mormon 7:8).
- "Lay hold" upon the gospel of Christ (Mormon 7:8).
- Study and believe in the writings of "this record" (the Book of Mormon), as well as the record that will come to the Gentiles from the Jews (the Bible) (Mormon 7:8).
- Be baptized with fire and with the Holy Ghost (Mormon 7:10).
- Follow the example of Christ (Mormon 7:10).

These instructions follow the basic doctrine of Christ preached by Nephi nearly 1,000 years earlier, and mirror the first principles of the gospel: faith in Christ, repentance, baptism, and the gift of the Holy Ghost. (See 2 Nephi 31). It is fitting that the doctrine of Christ serves as one of the constant themes addressed by prophets from Nephi to Mormon. And, in similar fashion to their Lamanite forefathers who were converted in the time of Ammon and buried their weapons of war, future Lamanites are instructed to "lay down your weapons of war . . . and take them not again," unless "God shall command you" (Mormon 7:4), as part of their repentance and turning to God.

The Bible and The Book of Mormon Support Each Other

Mormon admonishes the Lamanites to "lay hold of the gospel" that is contained "not only in this record but also in the record which shall come unto the Gentiles from the Jews," or the Bible. (Mormon 7:8). The Bible teachings support those in the Book of Mormon; and the Book of Mormon teachings support those in the Bible. Mormon says, "*this* [the Book of Mormon] is written than ye may believe *that* [the Bible]; and if ye believe *that* [the Book of Mormon] ye will believe *this* [the Bible] also" (Morm. 7:9, *emphasis added*). President Brigham Young declared: "No man can say that this book [the Bible] is true . . . and at the same time say, that the Book of Mormon is untrue; if he has had the privilege of reading it, or of hearing it read, and learning its doctrines. There is not that person on the face of the earth who has had the privilege of learning the Gospel of Jesus Christ from these two books who can say that one is true, and the other is false. If one be true, both are; and if one be false, both are false. " (Journal of Discourses, 1:37).

(See "Scriptures – Book of Mormon" in Topical Index, Moroni 10).

Discourse 27: Moroni, "Voice of Warning; The Last Days" (Mormon 8-9)

Prophet	Key Doctrines	Scriptures	Audience	Date
Moroni	• Warning about Disobedience • Coming forth of the Book of Mormon • Conditions in the Last Days • God Performs Miracles: Yesterday, Today, and Tomorrow	Mormon 8-9	To future members of the church; to those who have not accepted the gospel	A.D. 401

INTRODUCTION

After witnessing the final wars between the Lamanites and Nephites, Moroni was commanded by his father, Mormon, to "write the sad tale of the destruction of my people," to preserve the records, and to "hide them up in the earth" (Mormon 8:3-4). Before he hid the records, Moroni wrote the last part of his father's book (Mormon 8-9), abridged the records of the Jaredites (the Book of Ether), and wrote his own book (the Book of Moroni). Moroni's discourse contained in Mormon chapters 8 and 9 is a warning directed to those who will receive the record of the Book of Mormon in the future, both to members of the church, and to "those who do not believe in Christ" (Mormon 9:1).

Moroni declares: "I speak unto you as if ye were present, and yet ye are not. But behold, Jesus Christ hath shown you unto me, and I know your doing" (Mormon 8:35). Elder L. Tom Perry said: "imagine we are standing in the place where Moroni, the last of the great Nephite prophets, stood. The assignment his father gave to him to complete the record, which was entrusted to his care, was very difficult. He must have been in a state of shock as he described the total destruction of his people. . . . All he has is the faith that the Lord will preserve him long enough to complete the record and that someday it will be found by one chosen of the Lord. He realizes that the record will be a voice of warning to future generations of what occurs when nations like his own turn away from the teachings of the Lord. It is from the depths of his heart that Moroni cries out to those who will eventually receive the record. He wants to spare those who read his account the heartache and misery which comes from disobedience. He writes first to the members of the Church and then to those who have not embraced the gospel of Jesus Christ. Moroni's last words to the members of the Church are written as a voice of warning. He writes as one who sees the history of his people repeating itself in the future." (Conf. Report, Oct. 1992).

Elder Mark E. Petersen instructed: "[Moroni] wrote a description of the last battle [between the Nephites and Lamanites] and added: 'I . . . remain alone to write the sad tale of the destruction of my people . . . . Therefore I will write and hide up the records in the earth. . . . My father hath been slain in battle, and all my kinsfolk, and I have not friends nor wither to go; and how long the Lord will suffer that I may live I know not.' (Mormon 8:3-5). As he wrote his fateful words, he said again that his people were annihilated because they loved wickedness, rejected the counsel of God, and gave themselves over to seeking wealth and corruption. This made up the deadly concoction which brought about their extinction." (Conf. Report, Oct. 1978).

President Marion G. Romney explained: "The tragic fate of the . . . Nephite civilizations is proof positive that the Lord meant it when he said that this 'is a land of promise; and whatsoever nation shall possess it shall serve God, or they shall be swept off when the fullness of his wrath shall come upon them. And the fullness of his wrath cometh upon them when they are ripened in iniquity.' (Ether 2:9). This information, wrote Moroni, addressing himself to us who today occupy this land . . . 'cometh unto you . . . that ye may repent, and not continue in your iniquities until the fullness come.' (Ether 2:11)." (Conf. Report, Oct. 1975).

"Following this dismaying decline of Nephite civilization documented by his father, Moroni picked up the recorder's task, but he did not write to any living audience. Rather, he directed his final testimony . . . to those who would receive the record in the last days . . . . Calling out to those in the latter days who would receive the Book of Mormon . . . Moroni focused inexorably upon the future reader. 'Behold, I speak unto you as if ye were present,' he wrote, 'and yet ye are not. But behold, Jesus Christ hath shown you unto me, and I know your doing.' (Mormon 8:35). His despair, which was tinged with both disappointment and anger, is evident in his words." (Holland, Christ and the Covenant, 323).

DISCOURSE: Mormon 8-9

KEY DOCTRINES

- **A Voice of Warning.** Repent and heed the teachings of the gospel.

- **Coming Forth of the Book of Mormon.** The Book of Mormon shall be brought out of darkness to the people in the latter days. Any imperfections are of man, not God.

- **Conditions of the Last Days.** The Book of Mormon shall come forth in a day with wars, rumors of wars, earthquakes, fires and great pollutions. The people generally will deny miracles and the power of God. There shall be murders, robbing, lying and deceiving and all manner of abominations.

- **God Performs Miracles – Yesterday, Today, and Tomorrow.** God is unchangeable, and will bless us with miracles according to our faith.

COMMENTARY

A Voice of Warning

President Marion G. Romney taught: "In Mormon chapter eight, [Moroni provides] a clear and accurate description of the world in which we now live – a word picture written by a prophet who by the power of God saw in open vision and made record of us, our times and doings, and of the chastening which awaits us, the inhabitants of this land, if we do not repent and heed the teachings of the restored gospel." (Conf. Report, Apr. 1963).

Elder Mark E. Petersen taught: "In prophesy . . . [Moroni] asked why we are so foolish as to revel in sin, why we would reject the Christ, and thereby invite disaster. 'Why are ye ashamed to take upon you the name of Christ?' (Mormon 8:38), he asked, speaking to modern America, knowing full well that many might profess to believe in him and yet refuse to do his works. . . . He made it clear that advance warning is given to us who live today through the very book which he and his father had written and which he was now about to bury in Cumorah. It would be published in our day to give us that warning. . . . His words constituted a people-to-people message, ancient Americans speaking to modern Americans. Theirs was the voice of bitter experience seeking to persuade us to avoid the dreadful conditions which engulfed them." (Conf. Report, Oct. 1978).

This is one of the warnings Moroni issues to those in the last days who are, in name but not in deed, members of the Church of Christ: "O ye wicked and perverse and stiffnecked people . . . Why have ye transfigured the holy word of God, that ye might bring damnation upon your souls. . . . O ye pollutions, ye hypocrites, ye teachers, who sell yourselves for that which will canker, why have ye polluted the holy church of God? . . . Why do ye adorn yourselves with that which hath no life and yet suffer the hungry, and the needy, and the naked, and the sick and the afflicted to pass by you, and notice them not? Yea, why do ye build up your secret abominations to get gain, and cause that widows should mourn before the Lord. . . . Behold, the sword of vengeance hangeth over you; and the time soon cometh that he avengeth the blood of the saints upon you, for he will not suffer their cries any longer" (Mormon 8:33, 38-41).

Based on his vision of our times, Moroni chastises the members of the church for their pride, for abandoning the poor, and for participating in the sinful behavior that would permeate society. Elder L. Tom Perry elaborated: "[W]e see so many members seeking worldly pursuits contrary to the words of the Lord's prophets through the ages. Many of us are more concerned about our fine apparel, the size of our homes, and our cars and their gadgets than we are about the needs of the poor and the needy. We have also seen the threat of legalized abortion, gambling, pornography, and challenges to public prayer undermining the values that bring us together as a community of Saints." (Conf. Report, Oct. 1992).

President Ezra Taft Benson declared: "Moroni, the last of the inspired writers [of the Book of Mormon], actually saw our day and time. . . . If [he] saw our day and chose those things which would be of greatest worth to us, is not that how we should study the Book of Mormon? We should constantly ask ourselves, 'Why did the Lord inspire Mormon (or Moroni or Alma) to include that in his record? What lesson can I learn from that to help me in that to help me live in this day and age?" (Conf. Report, Oct. 1986).

Coming Forth of the Book of Mormon: Conditions of the Last Days

Conditions of the Last Days

Moroni identifies several conditions of the world in the last days, when the Book of Mormon shall come forth:

1. *It shall come in a day when it shall be said that miracles are done away.* (Mormon 8:26). In our day, a large percentage of the population does not believe in miracles that come from God. This trend has accelerated during the period just prior to, and since, the coming forth of the Book of Mormon. "The intellectual winds of the last three centuries have blown in a direction contrary to belief in miracles." Noted philosophers, Voltaire (1694-1778), said that a "miracle is the violation of mathematical, divine, immutable, eternal laws." David Hume (1711-1776) called belief in miracles "a superstitious delusion." [66] Both men died about 50 years before the publication of the Book of Mormon. Disbelief in miracles has generally accelerated since that time.

2. *It shall come in a day when the blood of the saints shall cry unto the Lord because of secret combinations and the works of darkness.* (Mormon 8:27). Elder Orson Pratt taught that this prophesy "has been literally fulfilled" in the "scores of saints that were shot down in cold blood." (Journal of Discourses, 17:264). Could this prophesy also apply to modern times when secretive terrorist organizations commit acts of violence throughout the world?

3. *It shall come in a day when the power of God shall be denied.* (Mormon 8:28). "Pew Research Center studies have shown the share of Americans who believe in God has declined in recent years, while the share saying they . . . do not believe in God at all – has grown." Nearly a majority of Americans (46%) do not believe in God as described in the Bible. (Pew Research Survey, 2018)[67]

4. *It shall come in a day when churches are defiled and lifted in the pride of their hearts.* (Mormon 8:28). In spite of many churches that help people lead good, moral lives, there are several instances of religious corruption, where ministers become "lifted in the pride of their hearts" and fill their own coffers. The Swiss psychiatrist Carl Jung observed: "In most cases, a religion arises from a good set of beliefs and teachings. . . . As the number of people grows, there is a need for organization. As soon as there is organization, money and power become involved. At this point, unscrupulous and power hungry individuals take control through manipulation and greed. They regulate the teachings to fit their perspective and greed, and consequently, the religion becomes corrupted."[68] One only needs to review the "List of Religious Leaders Convicted of Crimes" in Wikipedia to understand Moroni's words, "when churches are defiled" (Mormon 8:28).[69]

---

[66] Mark L. Larson, "Three Centuries of Objections to Biblical Miracles," *Bibliotheca Sacra*
[67] "When Americans Say They Believe in God, What Do They Mean?" April 25, 2018, pewforum.org.
[68] Collected Works of Carl Jung
[69] Wikipedia, "List of Religious Leaders Convicted of Crimes."

5. *It shall come in a day when there shall be fires, and tempests, and vapors of smoke in foreign lands.* (Mormon 8:29). Large wildfires have become the new normal in many areas of the world. Recent examples include the largest fire on record in the State of California in December 2017, and large scale burning of forests in Southeast Asia which has led to extensive "vapors of smoke" throughout the region.[70]

6. *It shall come in a day when there shall be wars, rumors of wars, and earthquakes in diverse places.* (Mormon 8:30). Between 1870 and 1950, the frequency of wars increased steadily by 2% per year. In the 1990s, the frequency of wars between states rose by 36% per year.[71] (See D&C 45:26). "If it seems like earthquakes and erupting volcanos are happening more frequently, it is because they are. We have recently experienced a period that has had one of the highest rates of great earthquakes ever recorded" (Worldpress.com).[72] Elder Ballard said, "Recently I read . . . statistics from the U.S. Geological Survey indicating that earthquakes around the world are increasing in frequency and intensity. According to the article, only two major earthquakes . . . occurred during the 1920s. In the 1930s, the number increased to five, and then it decreased to four during the 1940s. But in the 1950s, nine major earthquakes occurred, followed by fifteen during the 1960s, forty-six during the 1970s, and fifty-two during the 1980s. Already almost as many major earthquakes have occurred [by 1992] as during the entire decade of the 1980s." (Conf. Report, Oct. 1992).

7. *It shall come in a day when there shall be great pollutions upon the face of the earth.* (Mormon 8:31). Elder Mark E. Peterson observed: "[Moroni] said it would be a time of great pollution. Isn't it interesting that he would speak of great pollution in the earth? Does it remind you of the claims of our modern ecologists? . . . What frightful pollutions these things are!" (Conf. Report, Oct. 1978). "We all hear and read a great deal these days about our polluted physical environment – acid rain, smog, toxic wastes. But . . . there is another kind of pollution that is much more dangerous – the moral and spiritual." (Christensen, Conf. Report, Oct. 1993).

8. *It shall come in a day when there shall be murders, and robbing, and lying.* (Mormon 8:31). Crime and violence cause more than 1.6 million deaths worldwide every year; violence is one of the leading causes of death in all parts of the world for persons ages 15 to 44.[73] "[Moroni] also said that it would be a time of extensive crime, of murders, robberies, lies, deceptions, and immorality. Think of those words in terms of today's cover-ups, bribes, theft, embezzlements, and other fraudulent practices among individuals, in business, and also in government." (Peterson, Conf. Report, Oct. 1978).

At the conclusion of Mormon chapter 8, Moroni rebukes the people of our day for their greed: "For behold, ye do love money, and your substance, and your fine apparel . . . ye hypocrites . . . who sell yourselves for that which will canker . . . why do ye build up your secret abominations to get gain? . . . Behold, the sword of vengeance hangeth over you" (Mormon 8:37-41).

---

[70] "Southeast Asia faces continued choking smoke." (Oct. 19, 2015, http://phys.org/news).
[71] See www.historytoday.com/blog/2011/07/alarming-increase-wars.
[72] See April 2015, https://theextinctionprotocol/worldpress.com.
[73] Krug, World report on violence and health. Geneva, World Health Organization.

God Performs Miracles Yesterday, Today, and Tomorrow

Moroni continues his discourse in Mormon chapter 9 with a warning to "those who do not believe in Christ" (Mormon 9:1). "Promising that one day the Lord would return to assume leadership of his kingdom, with the earth rolling together as a scroll and the elements melting with fervent heat, Moroni asked how the unbelievers would feel standing before the Lamb of God in that fateful day. Stressing the guilt they would surely feel, the inevitable nakedness, and their wish to dwell in hell rather than stand before the 'holiness of Jesus Christ,' Moroni exhorted, 'O then ye unbelieving, turn ye unto the Lord' (Mormon 9:6)." (Holland, Christ and the New Covenant, 325).

Moroni specifically addresses non-believers in the last days who deny miracles: "I speak unto you who deny the revelations of God, and say that they are done away, that there are no revelations, nor prophecies, nor gifts, nor healing, nor speaking with tongues, and the interpretation of tongues" (Mormon 9:7). Moroni teaches with great conviction that there is a God who continues to work miracles among the faithful in the latter days, and makes several arguments to support this assertion.

His reasoning tracks the following logic. God is an unchangeable being, "the same yesterday, today, and forever" (Mormon 9:9). He has performed great miracles in the past, including the creation, the resurrection, and our individual redemption through the Atonement. In addition, according to the scriptures, Christ and the apostles performed "many mighty miracles" (Mormon 9:18); these miracles only ceased when man "dwindled in unbelief" (Mormon 9:20). However, Christ taught that signs and miracles would continue to follow those that believe, and thus would occur whenever his people exercised the requisite faith. (Mormon 9:24). Therefore, if God performed miracles in the past, the same God should be able perform miracles in the future, subject to the condition that men and women exercise sufficient faith in Christ.

Elder Charles W. Penrose taught: "We read that the works of God are one eternal round. He is the same yesterday, today, and forever; without variableness or any change whatever. As He acted in ancient times, then, so may we expect Him to act in latter times." (Journal of Discourses, 24:203). "In other words, if God, who is unchangeable, spoke in ancient times, He will likewise speak in modern times." (Callister, Conf. Report, Oct. 2011). "And we may reasonably infer that if God was a God of revelation hundreds of years ago, he is the same God of revelation today." (Penrose, Journal of Discourses, 23:18). God "changes not, neither is there variableness with him; but that he is the same from everlasting to everlasting, being the same yesterday, to-day, and for ever; and that his course is one eternal round, without variation." (Lectures on Faith, 41-42).

President Spencer W. Kimball stated: "Certainly, if there is no variableness in the Lord, if there is not shadow of changing, and if, as he said, he is the same yesterday, today, and forever, then we may fully expect that the same revelations, visions, healings, and tongues are all available today as in any other day, providing there is necessary faith." (Conf. Report, Oct. 1966). In all times, and in all eras, "necessary faith" must precede the miracle.

Elder Bruce R. McConkie taught: "Where there is faith, there will be gifts of the spirit; there will be the ministering of angels and the working of miracles. . . . By faith the worlds were made; by faith the elements can be controlled, rivers turned out of their courses, mountains removed. By faith we can have angels minister to us, see our sick healed, and the dead raised; and what is more important than all this, by faith we can live so as to become the sons of God and be joint heirs with Jesus Christ." (Conf. Report, Oct. 1953). The Lord told Nephi: "I am a God of miracles; and I will show unto the world that I am the same yesterday, today, and forever; and I work not among the children of men save it be according to their faith" (2 Nephi 27:23).[74]

With respect to miracles of the past, Moroni points to the creation of heaven and earth, and the creation of man. (Mormon 9:11, 17). President Howard W. Hunter taught: "The original creations of the Father constitute a truly wonder-filled world. Are not the greatest miracles the fact we have life and limb and sight and speech in the first place? . . . We are miracles in our own right, every one of us."(Conf. Report, Apr. 1989).

Moroni then cites the miracles of Jesus and the apostles. "And who shall say that Jesus did not do many mighty miracles? And there were mighty miracles wrought by the hands of the apostles" (Mormon 9:18).

Miracles in Modern Times

President Gordon B. Hinckley observed: "The great scientific age of which we are a part does not demand a denial of the miracle that is Jesus. Rather, there was never a time in all the history of man that made more believable that which in the past might have been regarded as supernatural and impossible. . . . Further, it is not difficult to believe that he, possessed of knowledge commensurate with the task of creating the earth, could heal the sick, restore the infirm, return the dead to life. It may have been difficult to believe these things in medieval times, but can one reasonably doubt the possibility of such while witnessing the miracles of healing and restoration that occur daily? . . . Miracles? I should think so. This is the age of miracles. During my brief lifetime, I have witnessed more of scientific advance than did all my forebears together during the previous 5,000 years. With so much of what appears miraculous about me every day, it is easy to believe in the miracle of Jesus." (Conf. Report, Apr. 1966).

Moroni declares with respect to the mighty miracles performed by Christ and the apostles: "And if there were miracles wrought then, why has God ceased to be a God of miracles?" (Mormon 9:19). If God is a "God of Miracles," and performed miracles in ancient times, and during the time of Christ, there is no reason that miracles should cease in the last days. Elder Bruce R. McConkie wrote: "Why do signs and miracles cease in certain ages? . . . Moroni answers 'The reason . . . is because that they dwindle in unbelief, and depart from the right way, and know not the God in whom they should trust.' . . . It is men who have changed, not God; he is the same everlastingly." (A New Witness for the Articles of Faith, 367).

Elder Dallin H. Oaks observed: "Many miracles happen every day in the work of our Church and the lives of our members. Many of you have witnessed miracles, perhaps more than you realize. A miracle has been defined as 'a beneficial event brought about through divine power that mortals do not understand and of themselves cannot duplicate.' (Ludlow, Encyclopedia of Mormonism, 2:908). The idea that events are brought about through divine power is rejected by most irreligious people and even by some who are religious. . . . [However,] miracles worked by the power of the priesthood are always present in the true Church of Jesus Christ." (Oaks, "Miracles," Ensign, June 2001).

---

[74] See also D&C 20:11-12; 1 Nephi 10:18-19; Moroni 10:19. Cf. Hebrews 13:8 ("Jesus Christ the same yesterday, today, and forever"); James 1:17 ("Every good gift . . . is from above, and cometh down from the Father of lights, with whom is no variableness, neither shadow of turning").

President Howard W. Hunter testified: "Among the signs of the true church, and included in the evidences of God's work in the world, are the manifestations of his power which we are helpless to explain or to fully understand. In the scriptures these divine acts and special blessings are variously referred to as miracles or signs or wonders or marvels." (Conf. Report, Apr. 1989). He continued: "In the contemplation of miracles 'we must of necessity recognize the operation of a power transcending our present human understanding' (Talmage, Jesus the Christ, 149). Science and the unaided human mind, he [Talmage] said have not advanced far enough to analyze and explain these wonders. But, he cautioned, to deny the reality of miracles on the ground that the results and manifestations must be fictitious simply because we cannot comprehend the means by which they have happened is arrogant on the face of it." (Conf. Report, Apr. 1989).

Elder Robert D. Hales stated: "Generally, those miracles will not be physical demonstrations of God's power – parting of the Red Sea, raising of the dead, breaking down prison walls, or the appearance of heavenly messengers. By design, most miracles are spiritual demonstrations of God's power – tender mercies gently bestowed through impressions, ideas, feelings of assurance, solutions to problems, strength to meet challenges, and comfort to bear disappointments and sorrow. These miracles come to us as we endure what the scriptures call a 'trial of [our] faith.' (Ether 12:6). Sometimes that trial is the time it takes before an answer is received. . . . The answer may be 'Not now – be patient and wait.'" (Conf. Report, Oct. 2007).

Sister Sydney S. Reynolds observed: "Just as important as these 'mighty miracles' are the smaller 'private miracles' that teach each of us to have faith in the Lord. These come as we recognize and heed the promptings of the Spirit in our lives. . . . I believe that all of us can bear witness to these small miracles. We know children who pray for help to find a lost item and find it. We know of young people who gather the courage to stand as a witness of God and feel His sustaining hand. We know friends who pay their tithing with the last of their money and then, through a miracle, find themselves able to pay their tuition or their rent or somehow obtain food for their family. We can share experiences of prayers answered and priesthood blessings that gave courage, brought comfort, or restored health. These daily miracles acquaint us with the hand of the Lord in our lives." (Conf. Report, Apr. 2001).

Miracles happen. They occur, however, based on faith, and in the Lord's time. As Sister Susan W. Tanner testified: "I delight in the Lord's mercies and miracles. I know that His tender mercies and His miracles, large and small, are real. They come, [however,] in His way and on His timetable. Sometimes it is not until we have reached our extremity. Jesus' disciples on the Sea of Galilee had to toil in rowing against a contrary wind all through the night before Jesus finally came to their aid. He did not come until the 'fourth watch,' meaning near dawn. Yet He did come. (Mark 6:45-51). My testimony is that miracles do come, though sometimes not until the fourth watch." (Conf. Report, Apr. 2008).

Moroni's Summary

In Mormon chapter 9, Moroni teaches that the gospel is available to all, and challenges the non-believers to "come unto the Lord with all your heart, and work out your own salvation, with fear and trembling" (Mormon 9:27). He teaches about the reality of miracles, and the unchanging nature of God. In succinct language, he preaches the first principles of the gospel and the plan of redemption. "Moroni reminded his future readers that the gospel is a gospel of life and redemption. In a remarkable three-verse summary of the great plan of happiness, he wrote: 'Behold, [God] created Adam, and by Adam came the fall of man. And because of the fall of man came Jesus Christ, even the Father and the Son; and because of Jesus Christ came the redemption of man.' (Moroni 9:12)." (Holland, Christ and the New Covenant, 326).

"Moroni at first evidently intended this chapter [Mormon 9] to be the last one in the entire Book of Mormon. . . . [I]n a powerful, logical, and forceful manner he outlines the major teachings of the gospel of Jesus Christ and indicates why all men must understand and apply these principles if they are to find the peace and happiness they desire. He says the gospel is not restricted to a chosen few, but is available 'unto all, even unto the ends of the earth' (Mormon 9:21)." (Ludlow, Companion to Your Study of the Book of Mormon, 307). However, Moroni continued to survive, and his final words and testimony were later recorded in what we now know as Moroni, chapter 10, the final discourse – and chapter – in the Book of Mormon.

Discourse 28: Moroni, "Promise of the Book of Mormon" (Moroni 10)

Prophet	Doctrines	Scriptures	Audience	Date
Moroni	• A Promise to Know the Truth of All Things • Gifts of the Spirit • Come Unto Christ and Be Perfected	Moroni 10	To his "brethren the Lamanites," and those who receive the record in the future	A.D. 421

INTRODUCTION

Moroni chapter 10 contains Moroni's exhortation to the Lamanites, and all who "read these things," at the close of his record: "Now I, Moroni, write somewhat as seemeth me good; and I write unto my brethren, the Lamanites.... And I seal up these records, after I have spoken a few words of exhortation unto you" (Moroni 10:1-2).[75] His words of exhortation include three key doctrines. First, Moroni provides guiding principles for all who receive the records to obtain a witness of their truth. (Moroni 10:4-5). Second, he gives a charge to acknowledge and acquire spiritual gifts ("lay hold upon every good gift") (Moroni 10:8-19, 30). Finally, he exhorts the reader to "come unto Christ and be perfected in him" (Moroni 10:32-33).

DISCOURSE: Moroni 10

KEY DOCTRINES

- **Book of Mormon Promise.** When we ask God in faith, in the name of Christ, if the Book of Mormon is true, He will manifest the truth of the record by the power of the Holy Ghost (Moroni 10:3-5). By the power of the Holy Ghost we may know the truth of all things.

- **Gifts of the Spirit.** The gifts of God are given for our benefit (Moroni 10:8-19).

- **Come unto Christ and Be Perfected.** Come unto Christ, and be perfected in Him through His grace (Moroni 10:32).

---

[75] Moroni uses the word, "exhort," eight times in his discourse. "Exhort" means to strongly encourage, or urge, someone to do something.

COMMENTARY

Promise of the Book of Mormon

The first part of Moroni's sermon focuses on gaining a testimony of the Book of Mormon. He says: "Behold, I would exhort you, that when ye shall read these things . . . that ye would remember how merciful the Lord hath been unto the children of men . . . and ponder it in your hearts. And when ye shall receive these things, I would exhort you that ye would ask God, the Eternal Father, in the name of Christ, if these things are not true; and if ye shall ask with a sincere heart, with real intent, having faith in Christ, he will manifest the truth of it unto you, by the power of the Holy Ghost" (Moroni 10:3-4). In this exhortation, Moroni identifies things we should do to receive a witness that the Book of Mormon is true:

1. *"Read these things."* (Moroni 10:3).

The first step in learning whether the Book of Mormon is true is to read the book. President Ezra Taft Benson said, "how are we to use the book? We must first read it." (Conf. Report, Oct. 1984). Elder Mark E. Petersen admonished us: "Moroni came back from the dead to deliver [the Book of Mormon] – in these modern times. . . . We now have it in our hands. It is published to the world. It carries God's message to all. . . . Read it! . . . It can lead us unerringly to Christ!" (Conf. Report, Oct. 1978). "Read the Book of Mormon! It will bring you closer to the Lord and His loving power." (Nelson, Conf. Report, Oct. 1999).

"This morning I speak about the power of the Book of Mormon and the critical need we have as members of this Church to study, ponder, and apply its teachings in our lives. The importance of having a firm and sure testimony of the Book of Mormon cannot be overstated. . . . If you are not reading the Book of Mormon each day, please do so. If you will read it prayerfully and with a sincere desire to know the truth, the Holy Ghost will manifest its truth to you." (Monson, Conf. Report, April 2017).

B-17 Flight Checklists

The first time I read the Book of Mormon as a teenager, I was having difficulty getting through some of the early chapters. To help me read the entire book, I made a chart with a daily schedule and checklist. The simple act of checking a box each day when I finished a chapter helped me read the Book of Mormon for the first time cover-to-cover. It was not a sophisticated method, but it worked for me, and ultimately led to multiple readings and a testimony of the truth of the book and its witness of Christ.

A simple checklist may sound routine, but several examples demonstrate the power of this basic tool. (See, generally, Gawande, Atul, The Checklist Manifesto). One of these examples involves the adoption of the B-17 "Flying Fortress" bomber by the U.S. Army Air Corps.

In the 1930s, a competition was held for airplane manufacturers to build a long-range bomber for the military. Boeing produced the B-17, which could fly faster and carry five times as many bombs as the army requested. On the day Boeing demonstrated the plane, however, it lifted off, then stalled at 300 feet, and crashed in a fiery explosion. Investigators found that the crash was not caused by mechanical malfunction, but pilot error. The new bomber was a more complex plane to operate than other aircraft of the time. Unlike other planes, the B-17 required the pilot to pay attention to four different engines, wing flaps, trim tabs and much more – tasks that aircraft pilots were not accustomed to doing at the time.

In the case of the demonstration crash, the pilot was so preoccupied with the different systems, he forgot to release a new locking mechanism on the rudder controls. Overlooking this simple task killed the crew. The U.S. Army Air Corps concluded the plane was too complicated, and awarded the contract to another company.

However, several test pilots believed the B-17 was a superior plane, and devised a simple way to enable pilots to fly it. They created a pre-flight checklist that spelled out all the basic tasks required to fly the plane successfully, like checking if battery switches and radio were on before taking off. Subsequent tests demonstrated the safety of the aircraft. Ultimately, just by using the pre-flight checklist, pilots were able to fly the B-17 bomber more than 1.8 million miles without incident.

And, due in part to the use of a simple checklist, the Air Corps ordered 13,000 Boeing bombers and the B-17 became one of the most successful aircraft in wartime history. Today, flight checklists are standard practice in aviation.

A simple checklist can be a helpful tool to read the Book of Mormon, and may be designed as a "check the box" chart that lists chapters, verses, and/or pages of the Book of Mormon; a daily checklist of items to accomplish that includes "read such-and-such chapter (or pages) in the Book of Mormon"; or some other system that can help motivate us to complete a regular reading regimen.

We must be careful, however, to not use the tool of checklists inappropriately whereby the process obscures the principle. "Sometimes as members of the Church we segment, separate, and apply the gospel in our lives by creating lengthy checklists of individual topics to study and tasks to accomplish. But such an approach potentially can constrain our understanding and vision. We must be careful because pharisaical focus upon checklists can divert us from drawing closer to the Lord. . . . [Spirituality] cannot be obtained merely by performing and checking off all the spiritual things we are supposed to do." (Bednar, Conf. Report, Oct. 2018).

The point is that a checklist can be a useful tool to regularly record our progress in studying the Book of Mormon, but it is merely a means to an ends: we must prayerfully ponder the message of the book and strive to understand the doctrines contained therein, rather than to merely check off boxes in a perfunctory spiritual "to do" list.

2. *"Remember how merciful the Lord hath been."* (Moroni 10:3).

At the outset of the Book of Mormon, Nephi declares that he will demonstrate the "tender mercies of the Lord" (1 Nephi 1:20). Later, Lehi and Ether both speak of the "multitude of [the Lord's] tender mercies" (1 Nephi 8:8; Ether 6:12). Moroni exhorts us to remember the tender mercies of the Lord to mankind generally "since the creation of Adam even down to the time that ye should receive these things" (Moroni 10:3).

These tender mercies exist throughout the Book of Mormon, and in our own lives. Elder Neal A. Maxwell observed: "There are clusters of memories embedded in each of your lives. And these can help us to 'remember how merciful the Lord hath been'" (Maxwell, Conf. Report, Apr. 2004).

Elder David A. Bednar taught: "Through personal study, observation, pondering, and prayer, I believe . . . that the Lord's tender mercies are the very personal and individualized blessings, strength, protection, assurances, guidance, loving kindnesses, consolation, support, and spiritual gifts which we receive from and because of and through the Lord Jesus Christ." (Conf. Report, Apr. 2005). Moroni exhorts us to remember these tender mercies as we read the record.

3. *"Ponder it in your hearts."* (Moroni 10:3).

"Dictionaries say that *ponder* means to weigh mentally, think deeply about, deliberate, meditate," taught Elder Marvin J. Ashton. "By pondering, we give the Spirit an opportunity to impress and direct. Pondering is a powerful link between the heart and the mind. As we read the scriptures, our hearts and minds are touched." (Ashton, Conf. Report, Oct. 1987). "The act of pondering on the scriptures and the things we have seen and heard invites personal revelation to come into our lives." (Oswald, Conf. Report, Oct. 2008). The scriptures contain several examples where pondering led directly to revelation, including Nephi's panoramic vision of the world. (See "Ponder" in Topical Index, 1 Nephi 11).

Elder Gene R. Cook explained the meaning of Moroni's exhortation to "ponder it" as follows: "What is the antecedent of '*it'* – the thing that we are to ponder? It is 'how merciful the Lord hath been unto the children of men, from the creation of Adam even down until the time that ye shall receive these things.' We are to remember how loving, how provident, how good, how forgiving our Heavenly Father has been toward us. What happens to us when we begin to ponder how merciful the Lord has been to mankind? To us personally? . . . Is it not true that our hearts turn to the Lord in love and gratitude? Yes, and that, in my judgment, is the impact of verse 3 – following the counsel therein helps us to become more humble, more willing and ready to receive new information and knowledge with an open mind." ("Moroni's Promise," *Ensign*, Apr. 1994).

President Marion G. Romney observed: "Pondering is, in my feeling, a form of prayer. It has, at least, been an approach to the Spirit of the Lord on many occasions. . . . Desiring, searching, and pondering . . . as important as they are, would be inadequate without prayer." (Conf. Report, Apr. 1973). And, Moroni's suggested subsequent step is sincere prayer: to "ask God."

4. *"Ask God with a sincere heart, with real intent, having faith in Christ."* (Moroni 10:4)

When we "pray sincerely and have real intent," it means we "intend to act on the answer [we] receive from God." (Preach My Gospel, 111). "'Real intent' means that one really intends to follow the divine direction given." (Nelson, Conf. Report, Oct. 2009). (See Discussion of "Real Intent" in Moroni 7).

Elder Dallin H. Oaks taught: "Moroni did not promise a manifestation of the Holy Ghost to those who seek to know the truth of the Book of Mormon for hypothetical or academic reasons, even if they 'ask with a sincere heart.' The promise of Moroni is for those who are committed in their hearts to act upon the manifestation if it is received. Prayers based on any other reason have no promise because they are not made 'with real intent.'" (Pure in Heart, 19-20). God answers our prayers when we have a sincere heart and "real intent." "He does not answer just to respond to our curiosity." (Martino, Conf. Report, Oct. 2015).

Obtaining a Testimony of the Book of Mormon

If we follow these steps, Moroni promises that God "will manifest the truth of [the Book of Mormon] unto you, by the power of the Holy Ghost" (Moroni 10:4). President Dieter F. Uchtdorf testified, "If you do these things, you have a promise from God – who is bound by His word (D&C 82:10) – that He will manifest the truth to you by the power of the Holy Ghost." (Conf. Report, Oct. 2014). President Gordon B. Hinckley observed, "The Book of Mormon is the only book ever published, of which I know, that carries in it a promise that one who reads it prayerfully and asks concerning it in prayer will have revealed to him by the power of the Holy Ghost a knowledge that it is true." (Conf. Report, Oct. 2007).

President Boyd K. Packer related his own experience in gaining a testimony of the Book of Mormon: "When I first read the Book of Mormon from cover to cover, I read the promise [in Moroni 10:3-4] . . . . I tried to follow those instructions as I understood them. If I expected a glorious manifestation to come at once as an overpowering experience, it did not happen. Nevertheless, it felt good, and I began to believe. . . . My experience has been that a testimony does not burst upon us suddenly. Rather, it grows. . . . Do not be disappointed if you have read and reread and yet have not received a powerful witness. You may be somewhat like the disciples spoken of in the Book of Mormon who were filled with the power of God in great glory 'and they know it not' [3 Nephi 9:20]. Do the best you can." (Conf. Report, Apr. 2005).

Elder Bruce R. McConkie declared: "There is another simpler test that all who seek to know the truth might well take. It calls for us simply to read, ponder, and pray – all in the spirit of faith and with an open mind. To keep ourselves alert to the issues at hand – as we do read, ponder, and pray – we should ask ourselves a thousand times, 'Could any man have written this book?' And it is absolutely guaranteed that sometime between the first and thousandth time this question is asked, every sincere and genuine truth seeker will come to know by the power of the Spirit that the Book of Mormon is true." (Conf. Report, Oct. 1983).

Elder Richard G. Scott testified, "Try reading the Book of Mormon because you want to, not because you have to. Discover for yourself that it is true. As you read each page ask, 'Could any man have written this book or did it come as Joseph Smith testified?' Apply the teachings you learn. . . . Follow Moroni's counsel. Sincerely ask God the Father, in the name of Jesus Christ, with real intent, if the teachings of the Book of Mormon are true. Ask with a desire to receive a confirmation personally, nothing doubting. . . . I know that you can receive a spiritual confirmation that it is true." (Conf. Report, Oct. 2003).

Elder Joseph B. Wirthlin observed: "A testimony of the truth . . . does not come the same way to all people. Some receive it in a unique, life-changing experience. Others gain a testimony slowly, almost imperceptibly until, one day, they simply know." (Conf. Report, Oct. 2000). President Henry B. Eyring said: "The answer may not come in a single and powerful spiritual experience. For me it came quietly at first. But it comes more forcefully each time I have read and prayed over the Book of Mormon" (Conf. Report, Apr. 2011).

Elder Perry taught: "Each time we read the book we should probably ask ourselves: 'Why did these writers choose these particular stories or events to include in the record? What value are they for us today?' Among the lessons we learn from the Book of Mormon are the cause and effect of war and under what conditions it is justified. It tells of evils and dangers of secret combinations, which are built up to get power and gain over the people. It tells of the reality of Satan and gives an indication of some of the methods he uses. It advises us on the proper use of wealth. It tells us of the plain and precious truths of the gospel and the reality and divinity of Jesus Christ and His atoning sacrifice for all mankind. It informs us of the gathering of the house of Israel in the last days. It tells us of the purpose and principles of missionary work. It warns us against pride, indifference, procrastination, the dangers of false traditions, hypocrisy, and unchastity. Now it is up to us to study the Book of Mormon and learn of its principles and apply them in our lives." (Conf. Report, Oct. 2005).

The main purpose of the Book of Mormon, and of all scripture, is to testify of Christ, and declare true doctrines, principles and ordinances. President Russell M. Nelson testified: "The purpose of the Book of Mormon is to 'make known to all kindreds, tongues, and people, that the Lamb of God is the Son of the Eternal Father, and the Savior of the world; and that all men must come unto him, or they cannot be saved.' (1 Nephi 13:40)." (Conf. Report, Oct. 2007). "The Book of Mormon provides the fullest and most authoritative understanding of the Atonement of Jesus Christ to be found anywhere. It teaches what it really means to be born again. From the Book of Mormon we learn about the gathering of scattered Israel. We know why we are here on earth. These and other truths are more powerfully and persuasively taught in the Book of Mormon than in any other book. The full power of the gospel of Jesus Christ is contained in the Book of Mormon. Period. The Book of Mormon both illuminates the teachings of the Master and exposes the tactics of the adversary. (2 Nephi 26-33). The Book of Mormon teaches true doctrine to dispel false religious traditions -- such as the erroneous practice of performing infant baptisms. (Moroni 8:11-15). The Book of Mormon gives purpose to life by urging us to ponder the potential of eternal life and 'never-ending happiness' (Mosiah 2:41; Alma 28:12). The Book of Mormon shatters the false belief that happiness can be found in wickedness (Alma 41:10-11), and that individual goodness is all that is required to return to the presence of God. It abolishes forever the false concepts that revelation ended with the Bible and that the heavens are sealed today. . . . The truths of the Book of Mormon have the power to heal, comfort, restore, succor, strengthen, console, and cheer our souls." (Nelson, Conf. Report, Oct. 2017).

Although "the Book of Mormon is the most correct of any book on earth" (History of the Church, 4:461), this does not mean that the book was or is grammatically perfect. It is the revelations and doctrines that are perfect, not the punctuation or wording. Moroni saw this. After compiling some of the revelations, Moroni said, "if there be faults they be the faults of a man . . . he that condemneth, let him be aware lest he shall be in danger of hell fire" (Mormon 8:17). He also said: "And whoso receiveth this record, and shall not condemn it because of the imperfections which are in it, the same shall know of greater things than these" (Mormon 8:12).

Since the first publication of the Book of Mormon in 1830, several minor changes have been made. Punctuation, grammar and transcription errors have been corrected. Elder Orson Pratt taught: "'But,' says one, 'what imperfections could there be in the writings of an inspired man?' I will tell you. Imperfections may creep in through the printing press . . . . There might be imperfections creep in through the persons that recorded these things – Moroni and the various prophets that preceded him who wrote upon the plates. Imperfections might occur through omission of some words. . . . Probably the individual in reading the first edition of the Book of Mormon from the hands of the printer knew of no error so far as the printing was concerned. But when we came to examine the first edition, and even all the editions, we found some few little imperfections that were introduced chiefly of a typographical nature. Well, those who will not condemn the work of God because of such little things, have the promise that they shall know of greater things than these." (Journal of Discourses, 20:62).

President Boyd K. Packer stated: "Some have alleged that these books of revelation are false, and they place in evidence changes that have occurred in the texts of these scriptures since their original publication. . . . Of course there have been changes and corrections. Anyone who has done even limited research knows that. When properly reviewed, such corrections become a testimony for, not against, the truth of the books. The Prophet Joseph Smith was an unschooled farm boy. To read some of his early letters in the original shows him to be somewhat unpolished in spelling and grammar and in expression. That the revelations came through him in any form of literary refinement is nothing short of a miracle. That some perfecting should continue strengthens my respect for them. Now, I add with emphasis that such changes have been basically minor refinements in grammar, expression, punctuation, clarification. Nothing fundamental has been altered . . . they have absolutely nothing to do with whether the books are true." (Conf. Report, Apr. 1974).

As Joseph Smith testified, "I never told you I was perfect – but there is no error in the revelations which I have taught." (Maxwell, Conf. Report, Oct. 2003, *quoting* The Words of Joseph Smith, 369). The truth of the revealed doctrines contained in the Book of Mormon is not diminished through corrections of grammar or punctuation over time. The fundamental doctrines and testimony of Jesus Christ remain clear, comprehensive, and unadulterated. The Lord, Himself, testifies that the Book of Mormon "contains the fullness of the gospel of Jesus Christ" (D&C 20:9). Nephi testified that the book contains "the words of Christ" (2 Nephi 33:10), and Moroni later testified that "these things are true" (Moroni 7:35).

President Nelson testified: "I promise that as you prayerfully study the Book of Mormon every day, you will make better decisions – every day. I promise that as you ponder what you study, the windows of heaven will open and you will receive answers to your own questions and direction for your own life. I promise that as you daily immerse yourself in the Book of Mormon, you can be immunized against the evils of the day." (Conf. Report, Oct. 2017).

President Nelson's Book of Mormon Lists

President Russell M. Nelson said: "I've made lists of what the Book of Mormon *is*, what it *affirms*, what it *refutes*, what it *fulfills*, what it *clarifies* and what it *reveals*. Looking at the Book of Mormon through these lenses has been an insightful and inspiring exercise. I recommend it to each of you." (Conf. Report, Oct. 2017).

A summary of President Nelson's lists is set forth below, with additional scriptural references.

The Book of Mormon *is*:

- Another testament of Jesus Christ. Its major writers were all eyewitnesses of the Lord. (2 Nephi 11:2-3; 2 Nephi 2:4; Alma 19:13; Ether 3:6-17; Ether 12:39; Mormon 8:35)
- A record of His ministry to people who lived in ancient America. (3 Nephi 11-28)
- True, as attested by the Lord Himself. (D&C 17:6)

The Book of Mormon *affirms*:

- The individual identity of Heavenly Father and His Beloved Son, Jesus Christ. (3 Nephi 11:3-11; 2 Nephi 31:15)
- The necessity of the Fall of Adam and the wisdom of Eve, that men might have joy. (2 Nephi 2:25)

The Book of Mormon *refutes* notions that:

- Revelation ended with the Bible. (2 Nephi 27:6-11; Mormon 9:7-9)
- Infants need to be baptized. (Moroni 8:11-15)
- Happiness can be found in wickedness. (Alma 41:10-11; Helaman 13:38)
- Individual goodness is inadequate for exaltation (ordinances and covenants are needed). (2 Nephi 31:3-13, 17-18, 21; Mosiah 3:17)
- The Fall of Adam tainted mankind with 'original sin.' (2 Nephi 2:22-27)

The Book of Mormon *fulfills biblical prophesies* that:

- 'Other sheep' shall hear His voice. (3 Nephi 16:1-3)
- God will do a 'marvelous work and a wonder,' speaking 'out of the dust.' (2 Nephi 27:9, 26; 2 Nephi 26:16)
- The 'stick of Judah' and the 'stick of Joseph' will become one (2 Nephi 3:12)
- Scattered Israel will be gathered in the latter days, and how that will be done (1 Nephi 19-22)
- The land of inheritance for the lineage of Joseph is the Western Hemisphere. (2 Nephi 3:3-5; 2 Nephi 1:5, 9)

The Book of Mormon *clarifies* understanding about:

- Our premortal existence. (Alma 13:3-5)
- Death. It is a necessary component of God's great plan of happiness. (Alma 42:4-15)
- Post-mortal existence, which begins in paradise. (Alma 40:11-12)
- How the resurrection of the body, reunited with its spirit, becomes a mortal soul. (Alma 11:43-44; Alma 40:23; Alma 41:2)
- How judgment by the Lord will be according to our deeds and the desires of our hearts. (Alma 41:3-6; Mosiah 4:30; Alma 12:14)
- How ordinances are properly performed. (Moroni 3-5)
- The Atonement of Jesus Christ. (2 Nephi 9:1-27; Mosiah 13:28; Alma 7:10-13; 34:8-16)
- The Resurrection. (Alma 11:40-45; 2 Nephi 9:3-6; Mosiah 15:18-26; Alma 40:2-10,15-26)
- The important role of angels. (Visitations: Nephi – 1 Nephi 11:14; Lehi – 1 Nephi 1:8; Jacob – 2 Nephi 10:3; King Benjamin – Mos. 3:2-4; Alma – Mos. 27:11-18; Alma 8:15) (Ministering: Alma 12:29; Moroni 7:25, 29-31, 36)
- The eternal nature of priesthood. (Alma 13:6-20).
- How human nature is influenced more by the power of the word than the power of the sword. (Alma 31:5-6)

The Book of Mormon *reveals information previously unknown*:

- Baptisms were performed before Jesus Christ was born. (Mosiah 18:8-16)
- Temples were built and used by people in ancient America. (2 Nephi 5:16; Mosiah 2:1-6)
- Joseph, the 11th son of Israel, foresaw the prophetic role of Joseph Smith. (2 Nephi 3)
- Nephi (in 600-592 BC) foresaw the discovery and colonizing of America. (1 Nephi 13)
- Plain and precious parts of the Bible have been lost. (1 Nephi 13:28-34)
- The Light of Christ is given to each person. (Moroni 7:16-20)
- The importance of individual agency and the need for opposition in all things. (2 Nephi 2:11-16, 27-30; 2 Nephi 10:23; Helaman 14:30)
- Warnings about 'secret combinations.' (Ether 8:18-25)

See Nelson, Russell M., "The Book of Mormon: What Would Your Life Be Like Without It?" Conference Report, Oct. 2017.

The Holy Ghost; Revelation

Moroni testifies that not only will the power of the Holy Ghost manifest the truth of the Book of Mormon, but also "by the power of the Holy Ghost ye may know the truth of *all things*" (Moroni 10:5, *emphasis added*). Through the Holy Ghost, we gain a testimony of true principles and doctrines.

Elder Eldred G. Smith declared: "The power and function of the Holy Ghost is to testify of the truth, and especially to testify of the Son. The Holy Ghost, being a personage of Spirit, speaks through our spirits. . . . When we receive promptings from the Holy Ghost, it is like opening an imaginary door between the spirit mind and the mortal mind. When this happens, we receive knowledge which we cannot deny. . . . By the Holy Ghost you may know the truths of the gospel. I'd like to mention just a few of these . . . . You may know of a surety of the visitation of God the Father and his Son Jesus Christ to the Prophet Joseph Smith in the Sacred Grove . . . the true concept of Deity . . . the restoration of the gospel with the priesthood of God . . . the divine purpose of temple work . . . the principle of continued revelation . . . that the resurrection is real and will be universal. . . ." (Conf. Report, Apr. 1963).

As we learn the truths of the gospel, the Holy Ghost will confirm these truths, and we can gain a testimony. President Dieter F. Uchtdorf taught: "A testimony is very personal and may be a little different for each of us, because everyone is a unique person. However, a testimony of the restored gospel of Jesus Christ will always include these clear and simple truths: (i) God lives. He is our loving Father in Heaven, and we are His children; (ii) Jesus Christ is the Son of the living God and the Savior of the world; (iii) Joseph Smith is the prophet of God through whom the gospel of Jesus Christ was restored in the latter days; (iv) the Book of Mormon is the word of God; (v) [the prophet], his counselors, and the members of the Quorum of the Twelve Apostles are the prophets, seers, and revelators in our day. As we acquire a deeper knowledge of these truths and of the plan of salvation by the power and the gift of the Holy Ghost, we can come to 'know the truth of all things' (Moroni 10:5)." (Conf. Report, Oct. 2006).

Elder Dallin H. Oaks taught that the Holy Ghost "teaches us all things and brings all things to our remembrance. (John 14:26). He guides us into truth and shows us things to come. (John 16:13). He testifies of the Son. (John 15:26). . . . The Holy Ghost is the means by which God inspires and reveals his will to his children. (D&C 8:2-3). The Holy Ghost bears record of the Father and of the Son. (3 Nephi 28:11). He enlightens our minds and fills us with joy. (D&C 11:13). By the power of the Holy Ghost we may know the truth of all things. (Moroni 10:5). By his power we may have the mysteries of God unfolded to us, all things which are expedient. (D&C 18:18). The Holy Ghost shows us what we should do." (Conf. Report, Oct. 1996).

"It is important to remember that the illumination and revelation that come to an individual as a result of the gift of the Holy Ghost do not come suddenly or without seeking. President Spencer W. Kimball taught that the Holy Ghost 'comes a little at a time as you merit it. And as your life is in harmony, you gradually receive the Holy Ghost in great measure.' The blessings available through the gift of the Holy Ghost are conditioned upon worthiness. . . . Even though we have a right to his constant companionship, the Spirit of the Lord will dwell only with us when we keep the commandments. He will withdraw when we offend him by profanity, uncleanliness, disobedience, rebellion, or other serious sins." (Oaks, Conf. Report, Oct. 1996).

"The gift of the Holy Ghost is so important to our faith that [Joseph Smith] gave it unique emphasis in a conversation with the president of the United States [President Martin Van Buren]. . . . Joseph Smith was asked how this church differed from the other religions of the day. The Prophet replied that 'we differ in mode of baptism, and the gift of the Holy Ghost by the laying on of hands.' (History of the Church, 4:42). He later explained that this answer was given because 'all other considerations were contained in the gift of the Holy Ghost' (History of the Church, 4:42)." (Oaks, Conf. Report, Oct. 1996).

"The Holy Ghost testifies of Christ and helps us recognize the truth. He provides spiritual strength and helps us do what is right. He comforts us during times of trial or sorrow. He warns us of spiritual or physical danger. The Holy Ghost provides the power by which we teach and learn. The gift of the Holy Ghost is one of our Heavenly Father's most precious gifts." (Preach My Gospel, p. 65). We are instructed to "receive" the gift of the Holy Ghost. We receive the Holy Ghost by striving to follow the Savior and keep His commandments.

The gift of the Holy Ghost "is the right and opportunity to have the Holy Ghost as a constant companion. If we listen to and obey His still small voice, He will keep us on the covenant path we entered through baptism, warn us when we are tempted to depart from it, and encourage us to repent and adjust as necessary. . . . The Holy Ghost can be with us only to the degree we keep our lives clean and free from sin. For this reason, the Lord has provided a way for us to continually refresh the purifying effect of our baptism through another ordinance – the sacrament." (Pieper, Conf. Report, Oct. 2018). If we repent and partake of the sacrament, "the Savior performs His cleansing miracle yet again and qualifies us to have the continuing influence of the Holy Ghost." (Pieper, Conf. Report, Oct. 2018).

The Prophet Joseph Smith described the process of revelation through the Holy Ghost: "A person may profit by noticing the first intimation of the spirit of revelation; for instance, when you feel pure intelligence flowing into you, it may give you sudden strokes of ideas, so that by noticing it, you may find it fulfilled the same day or soon; those things that were presented unto your minds by the Spirit of God will come to pass; and thus by learning the Spirit of God and understanding it, you may grow unto the principle of revelation, until you become perfect in Christ Jesus." (Teachings of the Prophet Joseph Smith, 151, *quoted in* Lee, Conf. Report, Apr. 1968).

With respect to the process of revelation, President Boyd K. Packer taught: "Revelation comes as words we feel more than hear. Nephi told his wayward brothers, who were visited by an angel, 'Ye were past feeling, that ye could not feel his words.' The scriptures are full of such expressions as 'The veil was taken from our minds, and the eyes of our understanding were opened' (D&C 110:1), or 'I will tell you in your mind and in your heart' (D&C 8:2), or 'I did enlighten thy mind' (D&C 6:15), or 'Speak the thoughts that I shall put into your hearts' (D&C 100:5). There are hundreds of verses which teach of revelation." (Conf. Report, Oct. 1994).

President Kimball taught that revelations come in different forms. "Joseph Smith's revelations were spectacular. . . . [However], revelation does not always mean 'walking with God,' nor 'face-to-face,' nor 'lips-to-ear.' There are many kinds of revelation – some more and some less spectacular. . . . Many recorded revelations in the Doctrine and Covenants and in the Bible were from deep feelings and an impressive consciousness of direction from above." (Conf. Report, Oct. 1966).

"The Spirit speaks to different people in different ways, and He may speak to the same person in different ways at different times. As a result, learning the many ways He speaks to us is a lifelong quest. Sometimes, He speaks to our 'mind and in [our] heart' (D&C 8:2) in a voice that is small yet powerful, piercing . . . . Other times His impressions 'occupy [our] mind[s]' or 'press . . . upon [our] feelings' (D&C 128:1). Other times our bosom will 'burn within [us]' (D&C 9:8). Still other times He fills our souls with joy, enlightens our minds (D&C 11:13; D&C 6:15), or speaks peace to our troubled hearts (D&C 6:22-23). We will find our Father's voice in many places. We will find it when we pray, study the scriptures, attend church, engage in faithful discussions, or go to the temple." (Homer, Conf. Report, Apr. 2019).

Elder Parley P. Pratt described the extensive, animating influence the Holy Ghost can have on us: "The gift of the Holy Spirit adapts itself to all these organs or attributes. It quickens all the intellectual faculties, increases enlarges, expands, and purifies all the natural passions and affections and adapts them, by the gift of wisdom, to their lawful use. It inspires, develops, cultivates, and matures all the fine-toned sympathies, joys, tastes, kindred feelings, and affections of our nature. It inspires virtue, kindness, goodness, tenderness, gentleness, and charity. It develops beauty of person, form, and features. It tends to health, vigor, animation, and social feeling. It invigorates all the faculties of the physical and intellectual man. It strengthens and gives tone to the nerves. In short, it is, as it were, marrow to the bone, joy to the heart, light to the eyes, music to the ears, and life to the whole being." (Pratt, Key to the Science of Theology, 101, *quoted in* Perry, Conf. Report, Apr. 1997).

Gifts of the Spirit

In addition to, and in combination and conjunction with, the gift of the Holy Ghost, Moroni taught that there are several other "gifts of God" that are "given by the manifestations of the Spirit of God unto men" (Moroni 10:8). Elder LeGrand Richards observed that after Moroni writes about "the marvelous gifts of the Holy Ghost . . . he warns us that we deny not the gifts of God, and enumerates them and then adds that these gifts shall never be taken away as long as the world shall stand, except according to the unbelief of the children of men. (Moroni 10:7-25)." (Conf. Report, Oct. 1943).

Moroni identifies the following gifts of the Spirit (See Moroni 10:9-18):

- To teach the word of wisdom;
- To teach the word of knowledge;
- To have exceedingly great faith;
- To perform healing;
- To work mighty miracles;
- To prophesy;
- To behold angels and ministering spirits;
- To exhibit all kinds of tongues;
- To interpret languages and divers kind of tongues

"And all these gifts come by the Spirit of Christ; and they come unto every man severally, according as he will" (Moroni 10:17).

Elder Stephen L. Richards testified, "I believe that these listed gifts and others of comparable seemingly supernatural nature have come to men and women of faith, and I believe that they will continue to come from time to time as conditions and circumstances warrant." (Conf. Report, Apr. 1950).

Such gifts are core features in the Lord's church, part of the bedrock. Elder Bruce R. McConkie concluded. "Their presence is proof of the divinity of the Lord's work; where they are not found, there the Church and kingdom of God is not." (McConkie, Mormon Doctrine, 314).

Paul referred to similar gifts as present in Christ's church in the meridian of time: "For to one is given by the Spirit the word of wisdom; to another the word of knowledge by the same Spirit; to another faith by the same Spirit; to another the gifts of healing by the same Spirit; to another the working of miracles; to another prophecy; to another discerning of spirits; to another diverse kinds of tongues; to another the interpretation of tongues" (1 Corinthians 12:8-10). "These were the fruits of the spirit in the days of the Apostles. Now, if this same spirit [the Holy Ghost] is given to the people today, through obedience to the gospel, it will bring forth the same fruits." (Penrose, Journal of Discourses, 22:155). The Prophet Joseph Smith states this foundational doctrine as follows: "We believe in the gift of the Holy Ghost being enjoyed now, as much as it was in the Apostles' day . . . we also believe in prophecy, in tongues, in visions, and in revelations, in gifts, in and healings; and that these things cannot be enjoyed without the gift of the Holy Ghost." (History of the Church, 5:27; See also, Moroni 10:9-16; D&C 46:13-25; and 1 Cor. 12:8).

"Within a year from the organization of the Church," President Marion G. Romney taught, "the Lord set forth in a revelation the gifts which were to be enjoyed in the restored Church. He named all those listed by Paul, to which were added the following: 'To some it is given by the Holy Ghost to know that Jesus Christ is the Son of God, and that he was crucified for the sins of the world. To others it is given to believe on their words, that they also might have eternal life if they continue faithful. And again, to some it is given by the Holy Ghost to know the differences of administration . . . And . . . to some to know the diversities of operations, whether they be of God.' (D&C 46:13-16)." (Conf. Report, Apr. 1956).

Purpose of Spiritual Gifts
Moroni teaches that spiritual gifts come according to a person's desires. (Moroni 10:17). "Faithful persons are expected to seek the gifts of the Spirit with all their hearts. They are to 'covet earnestly the best gifts' (1 Cor. 12:31), to 'desire spiritual gifts' (1 Cor. 14:1)." (McConkie, Mormon Doctrine, 314). The Lord admonished us to "seek earnestly" the best gifts. (D&C 46:8). "Because of Christ's Atonement, we are eligible to receive the gift of the Holy Ghost and its accompanying spiritual gifts. These gifts are the attributes of godliness; therefore, each time we acquire a gift of the Spirit, we become more like God." (Callister, Conf. Report, Apr. 2019).

President Boyd K. Packer counseled: "I must emphasize that the word 'gift' is of great significance, for a gift may not be demanded or it ceases to be a gift. It may only be accepted when proffered. Inasmuch as spiritual gifts are gifts, the conditions under which we may receive them are established by him who offers them to us. Spiritual gifts cannot be forced, for a gift is a gift. They cannot, I repeat, be forced, nor bought, nor 'earned' in the sense that we make some gesture in payment and expect them to automatically be delivered on our own terms. ("Gifts of the Spirit," BYU Fireside, Jan. 4, 1987, *quoted in* L.D.S. Institute, Book of Mormon Student Manual, Ch. 56: Moroni 10).

We must seek these gifts for the right purpose: "remembering for what they are given" (D&C 46:8). The Lord gives us these gifts for our own benefit, and to benefit others, "that all may be profited thereby" (See D&C 46:9-12). Elder Bruce R. McConkie described some of the purposes of spiritual gifts: "to enlighten, encourage, and edify the faithful so that they will inherit peace in this life and be guided toward eternal life in the world to come" (McConkie, <u>Mormon Doctrine</u>, 314). "Spiritual gifts are numerous and varied and come to us as we seek them and use them appropriately. We enjoy them because of the power of the Holy Ghost, which is in and around and woven through our lives." (Beck, Conf. Report, April 2006).

<u>Other Gifts</u>

In addition to the gifts enumerated by Moroni and Paul, and those set forth in D&C 46, there are other gifts: "there are many gifts, and to every man is given a gift by the Spirit of God" (D&C 46:11). Elder Marvin J. Ashton identified some of these other gifts as the "less-conspicuous gifts. . . . Taken at random, let me mention a few gifts that are not always evident or noteworthy but that are very important. Among these may be your gifts – gifts not so evident but nevertheless real and valuable. Let us review some of these less-conspicuous gifts: the gift of asking; the gift of listening; the gift of hearing and using a still, small voice; the gift of being able to weep; the gift of avoiding contention; the gift of being agreeable; the gift of avoiding vain repetition; the gift of seeking that which is righteous; the gift of not passing judgment; the gift of looking to God for guidance; the gift of being a disciple; the gift of caring for others; the gift of being able to ponder; the gift of offering prayer; the gift of bearing a mighty testimony; and the gift of receiving the Holy Ghost." (Conf. Report, Oct. 1987).

Similarly, President Stephen L. Richards taught that while the diversity of gifts set forth in Moroni 10:9-16 "may bring to our Father's children greatly varying talents and capacities, I feel sure that there are some highly important gifts of the gospel, which it is intended that *all* men of faith shall enjoy at least to some extent." (Conf. Report, Apr. 1950, *emphasis added*). He specifically identified three gifts that fit this category: (1) The Gift of Discernment; (2) The Gift of Wisdom; and (3) The Gift of Comfort.

1. The **Gift of Discernment** is the power to discriminate between right and wrong. When highly developed, it can ascertain hidden motives, and "find the good that may be concealed."
2. The **Gift of Wisdom** is similar to discernment, but involves other factors. He defines wisdom as "the beneficent application of knowledge in a decision." Wisdom is the functional basis for choices and determinations. "Your testimony, your spirit and your service will direct the application of your knowledge; that is wisdom."
3. The **Gift of Comfort** brings "consolation, peace of mind and soul, resignation, tranquility, and serenity in times of bereavement, suffering, fear, doubt, and uncertainty." We all need comfort. (Conf. Report, Apr. 1950).

President Richards concluded that "these [three] precious gifts [are] available to all the Church, and too many good men and women outside the Church. . . . I am aware that in the Christian world and perhaps out of it as well, there are countless thousands of our Father's children who are the beneficiaries of the gifts of the gospel. There are many of all faiths and conditions of life who love the Lord; and in return for this love and obedience to his commandments, he blesses them with his spirit. I am grateful indeed that it is so; but . . . with the gift of the Holy Ghost, how much more should we so favored enjoy its precious gifts!" (Conf. Report, Apr. 1950).

Come Unto Christ and Be Perfected

In the last few verses of his discourse, Moroni exhorts us to "come unto Christ" and "be perfected in him" (Moroni 10:32). This doctrine echoes the admonition of Christ, Himself: "I would that ye should be perfect, even as I, or your Father who is in heaven is perfect" (3 Nephi 12:48). Elder Joseph B. Wirthlin observed: "In both his Old and New World ministries, the Savior commanded, 'Be ye therefore perfect.' (Matthew 5:48; 3 Nephi 12:48). A footnote to this scripture explains that the Greek word translated as perfect means "complete, finished, fully developed." (Conf. Report, Apr. 1998).

Although we seek perfection, this lofty goal may be difficult, if not impossible, to fully achieve in this life. President Russell M. Nelson observed: "We need not be dismayed if our earnest efforts toward perfection now seem so arduous and endless. Perfection is pending." (Conf. Report, Oct. 1995). "Only one man was able to live perfectly while dwelling on this telestial planet. That was Jesus Christ. Although we may not be perfect . . . , we can be worthy: worthy to partake of the sacrament, worthy of temple blessings, and worthy to receive personal revelation." (Craven, Conf. Report, Apr. 2019).

And, we can always *strive* to attain the *attributes* of perfection. "Our heavenly Father wants us to use this mortal probation to 'fully develop' ourselves, to make the most of our talents and abilities." (Wirthlin, Conf. Report, Apr. 1998). "Christlike attributes are gifts from God. [These attributes] come as [we] use [our] agency righteously . . . With a desire to please God, [we have to] recognize [our] weaknesses and be willing and anxious to improve." (Preach My Gospel, 115). President Lorenzo Snow taught, "It is our duty to try to be perfect . . . to improve each day, and look upon our course last week and do things better this week; do things better today than we did them yesterday." (Conf. Report, Apr. 1898). (See "Divine Attributes" in Topical Index, Alma 7).

We should not be discouraged or depressed if we do not attain perfection quickly. "Perfection is a glorious objective," President Russell M. Nelson counseled, and encouraged us to "do the best we can and try to improve each day. When our imperfections appear, we can keep trying to correct them. We can be more forgiving of flaws in ourselves and among those we love. We can be comforted and forbearing. The Lord taught . . . 'continue in patience until ye are perfected.' (D&C 67:13)." (Conf. Report, Oct. 1995).

In order to be perfected in Christ, we need to be cleansed from past sins and mistakes. This can be achieved through both our efforts to sincerely repent, and the Lord's grace - the power of the Atonement. "His grace will make you clean, even holy. Eventually, you will become like Him, 'perfect in Christ.'" (Christofferson, Conf. Report, Apr. 2011). "Moroni would close the Book of Mormon with his final reassurance of the grace of God, but noting it is a grace that requires our honest effort to claim and enjoy." (Holland, Christ and the New Covenant, 237).

The Grace of Christ

If we "come unto Christ . . . deny ourselves of all ungodliness . . . and love God" (Moroni 10:32), then *through Christ's grace*, the day will come when we may be perfect in him. Nephi taught that "it is by grace that we are saved, after all we can do" (2 Nephi 25:23). And, Jacob instructed: "remember, after ye are reconciled unto God, that it is only in and through the grace of God that ye are saved" (2 Nephi 10:24).

President Dieter F. Uchtdorf taught, "it is by God's amazing grace that His children can overcome the undercurrents and quicksands of the deceiver, rise above sin, and 'be perfect[ed] in Christ.' Though we all have weaknesses, we can overcome them. Indeed, it is by the grace of God that, if we humble ourselves and have faith, weak things can become strong." (Conf. Report, Apr. 2015).

"Indeed, the essence of the gospel of Jesus Christ entails a fundamental and permanent change in our very nature made possible through our reliance upon 'the merits, and mercy, and *grace* of the Holy Messiah.' (2 Nephi 2:8)." (Bednar, Conf. Report, Apr. 2007, *emphasis in original*). "The requirement to put off the natural man and become a saint, to avoid and overcome bad and to do and become good . . . is a recurring theme throughout the Book of Mormon. In fact, Moroni's concluding invitation at the end of the book is a summary of this theme. . . . 'And again, if ye by the grace of God are perfect in Christ, and deny not his power, then are ye sanctified in Christ by the grace of God, through the shedding of the blood of Christ, which is in the covenant of the Father unto the remission of your sins, that ye become holy, without spot.' (Moroni 10:33)." (Bednar, Conf. Report, Oct. 2007).

It is only through the grace of Christ, and the power of the Atonement, whereby we can achieve perfection. While grace is a prerequisite for perfection; perfection is not a prerequisite for grace. "To obtain grace, one does not have to be perfect but he does have to be trying to keep the commandments the best that he can." (Cook, Conf. Report, Apr. 1993). "The Atonement advances our mortal course of learning by making it possible for our natures to become perfect. All of us have sinned and need to repent to fully pay our part of the debt. When we sincerely repent, the Savior's magnificent Atonement pays the rest of that debt. . . . After all we can do to . . . make right our wrongs, the Savior's grace is activated through the Atonement, which purifies us and can perfect us." (Faust, Conf. Report, Oct. 2001).

We thus become perfected through (i) coming to Christ; (ii) striving to adopt His attributes; (iii) denying ourselves of all ungodliness; and (iv) activating his grace through repentance and the power of the Atonement. Moroni calls the latter being "sanctified in Christ by the grace of God, through the shedding of the blood of Christ" (Moroni 10:33). "Through obedience motivated by a wholehearted love of God, we come fully unto Christ and allow His grace, through the Atonement, to lead us unto perfection." (Elder Joseph B. Wirthlin, Conf. Report, Oct. 1996).

Moroni closes his testimony, and the entire abridged record, with an invitation to "come unto Christ and be perfected in him" (Moroni 10:32). He testifies that if, through the grace of Christ, we do become perfect in him, we are sanctified through His Atonement, whereby we may become "holy, without spot" (Moroni 10:33).

In conclusion, Moroni declares: "And now I bid unto all farewell." The weary fugitive says, "I soon go to rest in the paradise of God until my spirit and body shall again reunite, and I am brought forth triumphant through the air to meet you before the pleasing bar of the great Jehovah, the Eternal Judge of both quick and dead. Amen" (Moroni 10:34).

Moroni's final message, as well as the entire Book of Mormon, concludes with a witness of the grace, divinity, and power of the Lord Jesus Christ. The Book of Mormon is, in every sense, "Another Testament of Jesus Christ."

Appendix A: Another Testament of Jesus Christ

A recurring theme that ties together every Book of Mormon discourse is a witness of Jesus Christ.

Discourse	Summary Reference(s) to Christ
Lehi (1 Nephi 8) "The Tree of Life"	The tree of life represents the love of God manifest through the gift of His Son. The fruit of the tree represents the Atonement of Christ.
Lehi (2 Nephi 1) "Awake and Repent"	Those who come to the land of promise are led by the Lord. Lehi has beheld the glory of Christ and is encircled about in the arms of his love.
Lehi (2 Nephi 2) "The Gift of Agency"	In the plan of salvation, we are redeemed through the Atonement. Christ satisfies the demands of justice, and intercedes for those who repent. The Messiah will come in the fullness of time to redeem the children of men. The Savior offers himself a sacrifice for sin. It is by his grace we are saved, after all we can do. Look to Christ as the great Mediator, hearken to his commandments, and be faithful unto his words to obtain eternal life.
Lehi (2 Nephi 3) "A Choice Seer"	In the latter days, the Messiah will be made manifest to a branch of the house of Israel that are descendants of Joseph. The Lord will raise up a choice seer, who shall have power to bring forth the words of Christ. The Lord will bless the seer, and the Lord will restore the House of Israel, and bring the descendants of Joseph unto salvation.
Nephi (1 Nephi 11-14) "Panoramic Vision of the Future"	Nephi has a vision of the birth, baptism, ministry and death of Christ. He receives a revelation about the condescension of God. He sees a vision of the resurrected Savior visiting the New World. The Lamb of God is the Son of the Eternal Father and the Savior of the world. All men must come unto him, or they cannot be saved.
Nephi (1 Nephi 19-22) "Hope in the Lord"	Purpose of scripture is to persuade men to believe in the Lord their redeemer, and testify of Christ. Christ will not forget or forsake the House of Israel. "I have graven thee upon the palms of my hands." The Messiah will be a light to the Gentiles. All mankind will know that the Lord is the Savior and Redeemer, the Mighty One of Jacob.
Nephi (2 Nephi 25-33) "Press Forward in Christ"	Isaiah predicts the coming of Christ, and teaches that unless Christ should come all men must perish. Nephi teaches: "We talk of Christ, rejoice in Christ, preach of Christ, and prophesy of Christ that our children may know to what source to look for remission of sins." The doctrine of Christ includes faith, repentance, baptism, the gift of the Holy Ghost and endurance to the end. Christ invites all to come unto him. If we press forward, feasting on the word of Christ, and endure to the end, we shall have eternal life.

Jacob (2 Nephi 6-10) "The Infinite Atonement"	The Savior will redeem the House of Israel. Christ will accomplish an infinite and eternal Atonement. Christ's resurrection will overcome physical death for all people; his atonement will overcome spiritual death for those who repent. After the resurrection, all men must appear before the judgment seat of Christ (the Holy One of Israel). Isaiah prophesies of Christ's ministry, crucifixion, resurrection, and millennial reign. Jacob learns the name of Christ from an angel.
Jacob (Jacob 2-3) "A Warning about Sin"	Seek first for the kingdom of God – after you have attained a hope in Christ, you shall obtain riches, if you seek them. The Lord delights in chastity.
King Benjamin (Mosiah 2-4) "Service and Salvation"	Salvation only comes through Jesus Christ. There is no other name given or way that salvation comes other than through Christ. The Atonement of Christ overcomes the Fall. Benjamin has a vision of the coming of Christ: his mission and ministry. "He shall be called Jesus Christ . . . and his mother shall be called Mary." The people take on the name of Christ and receive a remission of their sins because of their exceeding faith in Jesus Christ.
Abinadi (Mos. 13-16) "Redemption through Christ"	The law of Moses is fulfilled through Christ. Christ will come to earth to redeem his people and accomplish the resurrection. Details about the Lord's ministry and life are taught by Isaiah (Isa. 53). Christ shall take upon himself the iniquities and infirmities of all mankind. He has "borne our grief" and "carried our sorrows." He is filled with mercy and compassion. He shall be crucified and slain, but will break the bands of death and be resurrected. He shall have the power of judgment and make intercession for the children of men. Christ is both the Father and the Son.
Alma (Alma 5) "A Mighty Change in Heart"	We experience a mighty change in heart through faith in Christ, repentance, and obedience to his commandments. We can be cleansed through the blood of Christ, who will come to redeem his people. Alma's testimony: "I know that Jesus Christ shall come . . . the Son of God comes in his glory, in his might, majesty, power and dominion."
Alma (Alma 7) "Our Duty to God"	Alma recounts the Spirit's teachings about the coming of Christ. He shall be born of Mary, and go forth suffering pains and afflictions. He will take upon him the pains of his people. He will die that the he may loose the bands of death. He will suffer that he might take on the sins of his people and blot out their transgressions. Through the Atonement, Christ not only suffered for our sins but for our infirmities. It is our duty to walk after the holy order of Christ, and emulate his divine attributes.

Amulek (Alma 11) "Resurrection"	Christ shall come into the world to redeem his people. Christ shall loose the bands of temporal death, and his resurrection shall apply to all people.
Alma (Alma 12-13) "Life is a Probationary State; the High Priesthood"	We must prepare in this life to meet God (Christ). After the resurrection, we will come forth and stand before him to be judged. If we repent, God will have mercy upon us through his Only Begotten Son, and we can be saved. High priests were ordained after the order of the Son of God, who is the Only Begotten of the Father and full of grace, equity and truth. Melchizedek's ministry foreshadowed the ministry of Jesus Christ.
Alma (32-33) "Nourish Faith with the Word of God"	Belief in Jesus Christ is the foundation of faith. "If ye have read the scriptures . . . how can ye disbelieve in the Son of God." The prophets speak of Christ – Moses, for example, raised up a type of Christ in the wilderness that whosoever would look upon it and live. Believe in Christ, that he will come to redeem his people, that he will suffer and die to atone for our sins, that he shall rise from the dead, and that all men shall be judged by him at the last and judgment day. This is the word, the seed of faith that should be planted and nourished to grow into a strong testimony.
Amulek (Alma 34) "The Atonement; Prayer; Procrastination"	The infinite and eternal atonement of Jesus Christ brings salvation to all mankind. Christ shall come among the children of men to take upon him the transgressions of his people. He shall atone for the sins of the world. Christ shall make a great and last sacrifice, an infinite and eternal sacrifice. Through Christ's sacrifice, mercy can satisfy the demands of justice. We must exercise faith unto repentance to be saved. Do not procrastinate, but repent and take on the name of Christ now.
Alma (Alma 36-37) "Repentance; Small and Simple Things"	When we repent, the Atonement removes pain and brings joy. Alma was racked with torment for past sins, but received forgiveness through the mercies of Christ. The words of Christ lead to eternal life. It is as easy to give heed to the word of Christ as it was for Lehi's family to follow the Liahona.
Alma (Alma 38) "Effective Teaching"	Alma cried out to the Lord Jesus Christ, and found peace to his soul. If we trust in Christ, we will be delivered from trials. There is no other way man can be saved, only in and through Christ. He is the life and light of the world. He is the word of truth – we should teach that truth in the manner described by Alma.

Alma (Alma 39-42) "Justice & Mercy"	Christ shall come to take away the sins of the world, and to declare salvation. It is important to share these "glad tidings" with others. Christ will bring to pass the resurrection, and there will be no resurrection until His coming. After Christ's resurrection, there is a time appointed for everyone to be resurrected. In the resurrection, the spirit and the body will be restored to their proper and perfect frame. Good will be restored to good, and evil to evil. For those who repent, Christ's mercy can satisfy the demands of justice. Justice, mercy and repentance work together through the Atonement to erase transgressions. "The plan of mercy could not be brought about except an atonement should be made."
Helaman (Helaman 5) "The Rock of Christ"	Remember there is no other way nor means whereby man can be saved, only through the atoning blood of Jesus Christ. It is upon the rock of our Redeemer, who is Christ, the Son of God, that we must build our foundation.
Samuel the Lamanite (Helaman 13-15) "Prophesy of Christ"	Samuel gives several signs of the coming of Christ, and His death: no darkness at His birth; a new star; darkness and destruction at His death. The death of Christ brings about the resurrection and redeems all men from physical death. If we believe in Christ and repent of our sins, we can obtain a remission of sins. Christ will redeem mankind through his atonement and resurrection.
Mormon (Mormon 7) "Invitation to Believe"	We must repent of our sins and believe in Jesus Christ, that he is the Son of God, that he was slain by the Jews, but by the power of the Father he has risen again, and gained the victory over the grave. We should believe that he has brought to pass the resurrection of the dead whereby man will be raised to be judged, and that he has brought to pass the redemption of the world.
Mormon (Moroni 7) "Faith, Hope and Charity"	The Spirit of Christ is given to every man to know good from evil. God sent his angels to minister unto men to make known the coming of Christ. All things which are good come of Christ. We need to have faith in Christ to be saved. We should have hope in Christ that through the atonement and the power of his resurrection, we may be raised to eternal life. Charity is the pure love of Christ, and endures forever. We should pray that we will be filled with charity, and that when Christ shall appear, we will be like him, and be purified even as he is pure.
Mormon (Moroni 8) "Baptism of Little Children"	Little children are alive in Christ, and are redeemed through his Atonement. The power of Christ's redemption also applies to all those who died without the law. There is no need to baptize little children; to do so would effectively deny the mercy of Christ.

Mormon (Moroni 9) "Persevere Despite Wickedness"	May Christ lift us up despite the wickedness around us, and may his sufferings and death, and his showing his body, and his mercy and long-suffering, and the hope of his glory and of eternal life, rest in our minds forever.
Moroni (Mormon 8-9) "A Voice of Warning; Conditions in the Last Days"	"Jesus Christ has shown you unto me, and I know your doing." Because of the fall of man came Jesus Christ. Because of Jesus Christ came the redemption of man. Because of the redemption of man, we can be brought back into the presence of the Lord. Because of the resurrection of Jesus Christ, all shall be loosed from temporal death. Jesus performed many mighty miracles. Whosoever believes in Christ, doubting nothing, can also perform miracles.
Moroni (Moroni 10) "A Promise & Gifts of the Spirit"	When we ask God, in faith, in the name of Christ, with real intent, whether the Book of Mormon is true, He will manifest the truth unto us by the power of the Holy Ghost. Nothing that is good denies Christ, but acknowledges that He is. Come unto Christ and lay hold upon every good gift. Come unto Christ, and be perfected in Him. Deny all ungodliness, love God with all your might, mind and strength, and be perfected in Christ through His grace. We can be sanctified in Christ though the shedding of his blood, and can receive a remission of sins and become holy, like Him.

Appendix B: Testimonies of the Book of Mormon by Latter-Day Prophets

Joseph Smith, the Prophet

"I told the brethren that the Book of Mormon was the most correct of any book on earth, and the keystone of our religion, and a man would get nearer to God by abiding its precepts, than by any other book." (History of the Church, 4:461). "We say . . . that the Book of Mormon is true." (Teachings of the Prophet Joseph Smith, 148).[76]

President Brigham Young

"When the Book of Mormon was first printed, it came to my hands in two or three weeks afterwards. . . . I considered it to be my right to know for myself, as much as any other man on earth. I examined the matter studiously for two years before I made up my mind to receive that book. I knew it was true, as well as I knew that I could see with my eyes, or feel by the touch of my fingers, or be sensible of the demonstration of any sense." (Journal of Discourses, 3:91). "All creation could ask for no more witnesses than they have . . . that the Book of Mormon is true, and that Joseph Smith was a Prophet and Revelator." (Journal of Discourses, 2:179).

President John Taylor

"[T]here were eleven witnesses in relation to the Book of Mormon, who testify that the Book of Mormon was a divine revelation from God. And some of these witnesses tell us that an angel of God came and laid before them the plates from which the Book of Mormon was translated, and they knew that their testimony was true and faithful. . . . I have conversed with several of those men who say they have seen the plates that Joseph Smith took out of the hill Cumorah; I have also conversed with Joseph Smith, who has told me of these things and many more. . . . Did I know because Joseph Smith knew? Not exactly. . . . After I had been baptized in the name of Jesus for the remission of sins, and received the Holy Ghost . . . there was an inward evidence – an invisible manifestation of the Spirit of the living God, bearing witness that this was the work of God . . . and I knew it for myself and not because anybody said so. At first I believed it on the testimony of others, and then obtained a knowledge for myself." (Journal of Discourses, 10:23).

---

[76] Even several early church leaders who left the church maintained their testimony of the Book of Mormon. After Oliver Cowdery apostatized, he did not deny his witness of the Book of Mormon: "The Book of Mormon is true. It was translated by the gift and power of God. We saw the angel, and we heard his voice as he declared the truthfulness of this sacred record." (*quoted in* Young, Conf. Report, Oct. 1954). See also, Brigham Young, Journal of Discourses, 7:54 ("What did Oliver Cowdery say after he had been away from the Church years and years? . . . 'I know the Book of Mormon to be true.'"). Similarly, although David Whitmer was out of the church, he never denied the truthfulness of the Book of Mormon, "Yes, I held the golden plates in my hands, and they were shown to us by an angel. My testimony of the Book of Mormon is true." (*quoted in* Faust, Conf. Report, Oct. 2000).

President Wilford Woodruff

"All the ingenuity of all the men under heaven could not compose and present to the world a book like the Book of Mormon. Its principles are divine – they are from God." (Journal of Discourses, 16:32). "I believe the Book of Mormon . . . and I believe the predictions [it contains] will in their fulfillment roll upon our heads." (Journal of Discourses, 21:296). "Joseph Smith received . . . a record called the Book of Mormon, which is a record of the ancient inhabitants of this continent. That record is true. . . . I bear my testimony of these things to the world, for I know they are true." (Journal of Discourses, 24:236).

President Heber J. Grant

"I read the Book of Mormon prayerfully and supplicated God for a testimony in my heart and soul of the divinity of it, and I have accepted it and believe it with all my heart." (Conf. Report, Apr. 1929).

President George Albert Smith

"I hold in my hand the American volume of scripture called the Book of Mormon, containing approximately five hundred pages translated from gold plates. We have all that the world has, the scripture that came from the old world, but we have the scripture of the new world which is the Book of Mormon added to that. . . . I desire to call your attention to the fact that these are precious truths, and they contain the revealed word of the Lord printed and published to the world for the purpose of preparing his children for a place in the celestial kingdom." (Conf. Report, Oct. 1948). "Brothers and sisters, we have all the information that our Christian brothers and sisters do with regard to the life of the Savior in the Bible, and in addition to that, we have the story of his coming to his people on this western hemisphere, as recorded in the Book of Mormon. . . . I have known many people, who, having read it, and prayed about it, have received a witness that it is true." (Conf. Report, Oct. 1950).

President David O. McKay

"I bear you my testimony that the head of this Church is our Lord and Savior, Jesus Christ. He is the Redeemer of the world. I know of the reality of his existence, of his willingness to guide and direct all who serve him. I know that in this dispensation he restored with his Father, through the Prophet Joseph Smith, the gospel of Jesus Christ in its fullness [in the Book of Mormon]. I know that one of the glorious messages given by Christ, our Redeemer, is that the spirit of man passes triumphantly through the portals of death into everlasting life." (Conf. Report, Oct. 1969). "I know that [Jesus Christ] lives. . . . I know that he will confer with his servants who seek him in humility and in righteousness. I know because I have heard his voice, and I have received his guidance in matters pertaining to his kingdom here on earth. I know that his Father, our Creator lives. I know that they appeared to the Prophet Joseph Smith and revealed the revelations which we now have recorded in the . . . [Book of Mormon]. This knowledge is as real to me as that which occurs in our daily lives." (Conf. Report, Apr. 1968).

President Joseph Fielding Smith

"I am just as firmly convinced that this Book of Mormon . . . is the word of God and was revealed, as Joseph Smith declared it was revealed, as I am that I stand here looking into your faces. . . . My witness to all the world is that this book is true. I have read it many, many times. I have not read it enough. It still contains truths that I still may seek and find, for I have not mastered it, but I know it is true." (Conf. Report, Oct. 1949).

"I bear witness to you that the Lord has made it very clear to me by revelation which I have received . . . that these things [the Book of Mormon] are true, and that it is the privilege of any sincere person who will endeavor to read with a prayerful spirit and a desire to know whether the book is true or not; and he will receive that testimony according to the promise that was made by Moroni, who sealed the record to come forth in the Dispensation of the Fullness of Times." (Conf. Report, Oct. 1956). "I know the Book of Mormon is true just as well as I know I am standing here in this building facing you." (Conf. Report, Oct. 1961).

President Spencer W. Kimball

"Joseph [Smith] obtained from the angel Moroni the records of a people who anciently inhabited this land; and through the gift and power of God, he translated that record, now known as the Book of Mormon. . . . I testify that the Book of Mormon is a translation of an ancient record of nations who once lived in this western hemisphere, where they prospered and became mighty when they kept the commandments of God, but who were largely destroyed through terrible civil wars when they forgot God. This book bears testimony of the living reality of the Lord Jesus Christ as the Savior and Redeemer of mankind." (Conf. Report, Apr. 1980).

"In the final chapter of the [Book of Mormon] is the never-failing promise that every person who will read the book with a sincere, prayerful desire to know of its divinity shall have the assurance. The book of which I speak is the keystone of true religion, the ladder by which one may get near to God by abiding its precepts. It has been named 'The most correct of any book on earth.' My beloved friends, I give to you the Book of Mormon. May you read it prayerfully, study it carefully, and receive for yourselves the testimony of its divinity." (Conf. Report, Apr. 1963).

President Ezra Taft Benson

"As a special witness of Jesus Christ, and as His humble servant, it is now my obligation and privilege, as the Spirit dictates, to bear pure testimony and witness to that which I know to be true. . . . I testify that through the Book of Mormon God has provided for our day tangible evidence that Jesus is the Christ and that Joseph Smith is His prophet. This other testament of Jesus Christ is a scriptural account of the early inhabitants of America. It was translated by Joseph Smith through the gift and power of God. Those who will read and ponder the Book of Mormon and ask our Eternal Father in the name of Christ if it is true may know for themselves of its truthfulness through the power of the Holy Ghost, provided they will ask with a sincere heart, with real intent, having faith in Christ." (Conf. Report, Oct. 1988). "What, then, are we to say of the Book of Mormon? I bear witness that it is verily true. I know this as I know that I live." (Conf. Report, Apr. 1975).

President Gordon B. Hinckley

"The Book of Mormon is true. It speaks as a voice from the dust in testimony of the divinity of the Lord." (Conf. Report, Oct. 1999). "The Book of Mormon is true. It testifies of the Lord Jesus Christ." (Conf. Report, Apr. 1999). "I give you my testimony that [the Book of Mormon] is true. That I know by the witness of the Holy Ghost, and that knowledge to me is certain. Sidney Rigdon did not write it. Oliver Cowdery did not write it. It is not the product of a myth-maker. . . . Joseph Smith did not write it. He, the Prophet of this dispensation, translated the writings of prophets of old under the power of God, to testify in our day. We invite all men everywhere to read it. Its witness lies within itself. I so testify." (Conf. Report, Oct. 1959).

President Thomas S. Monson

"This morning I speak about the power of the Book of Mormon and the critical need we have as members of this Church to study, ponder, and apply its teachings in our lives. The importance of having a firm and sure testimony of the Book of Mormon cannot be overstated. . . . If you are not reading the Book of Mormon each day, please do so. If you will read it prayerfully and with a sincere desire to know the truth, the Holy Ghost will manifest its truth to you. If it is true – and I solemnly testify that it is – then Joseph Smith was a prophet who saw God the Father and His Son, Jesus Christ. Because the Book of Mormon is true, The Church of Jesus Christ of Latter-day Saints is the Lord's Church on earth." (Conf. Report, April 2017).

"Whether you are 12 or 112 – or anywhere in between – you can know for yourself that the gospel of Jesus Christ is true. We have the promise that 'if ye shall ask with a sincere heart, with real intent, having faith in Christ, he will manifest the truth of it unto you, by the power of the Holy Ghost.' (Moroni 10:4). When we know the Book of Mormon is true, then it follows that Joseph Smith was a prophet and that he saw God the Eternal Father and His Son, Jesus Christ. . . . [I share] my testimony concerning [these things]. I [am] grateful for my testimony and grateful that I [am] prepared to share it." (Conf. Report, Oct. 2011).

President Russell M. Nelson

"I would like to add my testimony of the divinity of this book. I have read it many times. I have also read much that has been written about it. Some authors have focused upon its stories, its people, or its vignettes of history. Others have been intrigued by its language structure or its records of weapons, geography, animal life, techniques of building, or systems of weights and measures. Interesting as these matters may be, study of the Book of Mormon is most rewarding when one focuses on its primary purpose – to testify of Jesus Christ. . . . The Book of Mormon is the most important religious text to be revealed from God to man since the writings of the New Testament were compiled nearly two millennia ago. Joseph Smith declared the Book of Mormon to be 'the most correct of any book on earth, and the keystone of our religion.' It is the only book that the Lord Himself has testified to be true. (See D&C 17:6). . . . Each individual who prayerfully studies the Book of Mormon can also receive a testimony of its divinity. . . . Read the Book of Mormon! It will bring you closer to the Lord and His loving power. . . . The Book of Mormon is true! I so testify in the name of Jesus Christ." (Conf. Report, Oct. 1999).

Testimonies of the Book of Mormon from Latter-Day Apostles

Elder Parley P. Pratt

"The Spirit of the Lord came upon me, while I read [the Book of Mormon], and enlightened my mind, convinced my judgment, and riveted the truth upon my understanding, so that I knew the book was true, just as well as a man knows the daylight from the dark night." (Journal of Discourses, 5:194).

President Marion G. Romney

"It is about the Book of Mormon I want to talk today. I do so with just one objective in mind: To get you to read it. I have read it a little, I believe in it, and I love it. . . I can testify, as did Nephi, that the things written therein persuadeth all men to do good. (2 Nephi 33:4). . . . I remember reading [the Book of Mormon] with one of my lads when he was very young. . . . We were each reading aloud alternate paragraphs of those last three marvelous chapters of Second Nephi. I heard his voice breaking and thought he had a cold, but we went on to the end of the three chapters. As we finished he said to me, 'Daddy, do you ever cry when you read the Book of Mormon?' 'Yes, son,' I answered. 'Sometimes the spirit of the Lord so witnesses to my soul that the Book of Mormon is true that I do cry.' 'Well,' he said, 'that is what happened to me tonight.' . . . I tell you this book was given to us of God to read and to live by, and it will hold us as close to the Spirit of the Lord as anything I know. Won't you please read it?" (Conf. Report, Apr. 1949).

"I bear you my witness that I have obtained for myself a personal knowledge that the Book of Mormon is all the Prophet Joseph said it is; that from it radiates the spirit of prophecy and revelation; that it teaches in plain simplicity the great doctrines of salvation and the principles of righteous conduct calculated to bring men to Christ; that familiarity with its spirit and obedience to its teachings will move every contrite soul to fervently pray with David, 'Create in me a clean heart, O God; and renew a right spirit within me.' (Psalms 51:10)." (Conf. Report, Oct. 1970).

Elder Milton R. Hunter

"When I was a child and first heard the stories of the Book of Mormon, the Holy Ghost touched my heart and bore a sweet witness to it of the divine authenticity of that ancient record. I knew then as I knew that I was alive that the Book of Mormon is true, is divine. . . . As I grew older, I read the book many times, and each time the same sweet testimony came into my heart, sometimes coming so forcefully that I was filled with emotion to the extent that tears ran down my cheeks. As I read the Book of Mormon now, the Holy Ghost still bears testimony to me that it is the word of God." (Conf. Report, Oct. 1954).

Elder Mark E. Petersen

"And [God] has given me a personal testimony that the Book of Mormon is true. I know it as well as the three witnesses or the eight witnesses who held the plates in their hands. I know it. God has made it known to me, and I give you my testimony." (Conf. Report, Oct. 1955). "With all the fervor of my soul I thank the Almighty that he has given to me a testimony of that book. And what is the testimony? That the Book of Mormon is true, that it is the word of God, a new volume of scripture for this modern world" (Conf. Report, Apr. 1957).

Elder LeGrand Richards

"I bear you my witness that I know that book [the Book of Mormon] is true. Sister Richards and I read it [again] last year as the priesthood were asked to do, and we kept saying as we would read, 'Isn't that wonderful? Isn't that wonderful? How could Joseph Smith at his age written anything like that except by the inspiration of the Almighty?'" (Conf. Report, Apr. 1963).

Elder Bruce R. McConkie

"As one voice among thousands of others, I certify that I know by the promptings of the Spirit that the Book of Mormon is true." (Conf. Report, Apr. 1961). "I am one who knows by the power of the Spirit that this book is true." (Conf. Report, Apr. 1968). "But thanks be to God, [the Book of Mormon] is true! . . . May I quote the words that God himself said in bearing record of the divinity of the Book of Mormon, and make them my testimony also? He said of Joseph Smith, 'he has translated the book, even that part which I have commanded him, and as your Lord and your God liveth it is true.' (D&C 17:6)" (Conf. Report, Apr. 1965).[77]

President N. Eldon Tanner

"We have this promise given by Moroni regarding the Book of Mormon: 'And when ye shall receive these things, I would exhort you that ye would ask God, the Eternal Father, in the name of Christ, if these things are not true: and if ye shall ask with a sincere heart, with real intent, having faith in Christ, he will manifest the truth of it unto you, by the power of the Holy Ghost. And by the power of the Holy Ghost ye may know the truth of all things.' (Moroni 10:4-5). I humbly bear testimony that the truthfulness of these things has been revealed to me" (Conf. Report, Oct. 1972).

President James E. Faust

"To me it is inconceivable that Joseph Smith, without divine help, could have written this complex and profound book. There is no way that Joseph Smith, an unlearned young frontiersman, could have fabricated the great truths it contains, generated its great spiritual power, or falsified the testimony of Christ that it contains. The book itself testifies that it is the holy word of God. . . . I testify through the sure conviction that springs from the witness of the Spirit that it is possible to know things that have been revealed with greater certainty than by actually seeing them. . . . God himself has put his approval on the Book of Mormon, having said, 'As your Lord and your God liveth it is true.' (D&C17:6)." (Conf. Report, Oct. 1983).

---

[77] As President Ezra Taft Benson observed, "Excluding the witnesses to the Book of Mormon, the Doctrine and Covenants is by far the greatest external witness and evidence we have from the Lord that the Book of Mormon is true. At least thirteen sections in the Doctrine and Covenants give us confirming knowledge and divine witness that the Book of Mormon is the word of God. (See D&C 1; D&C 3: D&C 5; D&C 8; D&C 10; D&C 11; D&C 17; D&C 18; D&C 20; D&C 27; D&C 42; D&C 84; D&C 135:3)." (Conf. Report, Apr. 1987).

President Boyd K. Packer

"When I was about 10, I made my first attempt to read the Book of Mormon. The first part was easy-flowing New Testament language. Then I came to the writings of the Old Testament prophet Isaiah. I could not understand them; I found them difficult to read. I laid the book aside. I made other attempts to read the Book of Mormon. I did not read it all until I was on a troop ship with other bomber crew members, headed for the war in the Pacific. I determined that I would read the Book of Mormon and find out for myself whether it is true or not. I read and reread the book. I tested the promise that it contained. That was a life-changing event. After that, I never set the book aside. . . . I love this Book of Mormon. . . . I know it is true." (Conf. Report, Oct. 2001). President Packer testified: "I bear witness that the Book of Mormon is true – that it is another testament of Jesus Christ. I have read the Book of Mormon with a sincere heart, with intent, as a humble serviceman, and thereafter pled with the Lord. I received that revelation. Accompanying that revelation is the revelation that Jesus is the Christ . . . and of Him I bear witness." (Conf. Report, Apr. 1986).

Elder Richard G. Scott

"I've just concluded an audio recording of the Book of Mormon for my family. This has been an experience that has increased my testimony of this divine work and strengthened in me a desire to be more familiar with its pages to distill from these scriptures truths to be used in my service to the Lord. I love this book. I testify with my soul that it is true . . . . All who will study its message in humility, in faith believing in Jesus Christ, will know of its truthfulness and will find a treasure to lead them to greater happiness, peace, and attainment in this life. I testify by all that is sacred, this book is true." (Conf. Report, Oct. 2011).

Elder Jeffrey R. Holland

"I ask that my testimony of the Book of Mormon and all that it implies, given today under my own oath and office, be recorded by men on earth and angels in heaven. . . . I want it absolutely clear when I stand before the judgment bar of God that I declared to the world, in the most straightforward language I could summon, that the Book of Mormon is true, that it came forth the way Joseph said it came forth . . . . For 179 years this book has been examined and attacked, denied and deconstructed, targeted and torn apart like perhaps no other book in modern religious history – perhaps like no other book in any religious history. And still it stands. Failed theories have been born and parroted and have died. . . . None of these frankly pathetic answers for this book has ever withstood examination because there is no other answer than the one Joseph gave as its young unlearned translator. In this I stand with my own great-grandfather [George Q. Cannon], who said simply enough, 'No wicked man could write such a book as this; and no good man would write it, unless it were true and he were commanded of God to do so.'. . . Now, I did not sail with the brother of Jared in crossing an ocean . . . I did not hear King Benjamin speak his angelically delivered sermon. I did not proselyte with Alma and Amulek . . . . I was not among the Nephite crowd who touched the wounds of the resurrected Lord, nor did I weep with Mormon and Moroni over the destruction of an entire civilization. *But my testimony of this record and the peace it brings to the human heart is as binding and unequivocal as was theirs*. Like [the witnesses], 'I give my name unto the world, to witness unto the world that which I have seen.' And like them, 'I lie not, God bearing witness of it.' (Testimony of Eight Witnesses). (Conf. Report, Oct. 2009, *emphasis added*).

Appendix C: Book of Mormon Discourses – Major Doctrinal Topics

Prophet, Discourse, Scripture	Major Doctrinal Topics
Lehi, "The Tree of Life" 1 Nephi 8 (to his family)	• Journey to the Tree of Life • Four Categories of People • Dealing with Wayward Children
Lehi, "Awake and Repent" 2 Nephi 1 (to his children, Laman and Lemuel, sons of Ishmael, Zoram)	• Awake and Repent • Keep the Commandments and Prosper
Lehi, "The Gift of Agency" 2 Nephi 2 (to Jacob)	• The Plan of Salvation: Creation, Fall and Atonement • The Gift of Agency • Opposition in All Things
Lehi, "Joseph: A Choice Seer" 2 Nephi 3 (to Joseph)	• A Choice Seer – Joseph Smith • Power of the Bible and Book of Mormon Together
Nephi, "Panoramic Vision of the Future" 1 Nephi 11-14 (to his brethren)	• Vision of Christ: Condescension of God • Vision of the Future of America: Nephites & Lamanites; Gentiles; Restoration of the Gospel and the Last Days
Nephi, "Hope in the Lord" 1 Nephi 19-22; Isaiah 48-49 (to his brethren in the promised land)	• Purpose of Scripture • Scattering and Gathering of Israel • Preservation of the Righteous
Nephi, "Press Forward in Christ" 2 Nephi 25-33; Isaiah 2-14; 29 (to the people of Nephi, and future generations)	• Delight in the Words of Isaiah • Talk of Christ, Rejoice in Christ • Doctrine of Inclusion • Warnings About False Doctrines • The Doctrine of Christ
Jacob, "The Infinite Atonement" 2 Nephi 6-10; Isaiah 49-52 (to the people of Nephi)	• Redemption of the House of Israel • The Infinite Atonement • Warnings to the Disobedient
Jacob, "A Warning About Sin" Jacob 2-3 (to people of Nephi at the temple)	• The Sin of Pride: Prioritizing Riches • The Sin of Immorality

King Benjamin, "Service and Salvation" Mosiah 2-4 (to people of Zarahemla)	• Service to Others and Our Debt to God • Salvation Comes Only through Christ • The Natural Man is an Enemy to God
Abinadi, "Redemption through Christ" Mosiah 13-16 (to King Noah's court in Shilom)	• Law of Moses Is Fulfilled through Christ • Christ Will Come to Redeem His People: His Mortal Ministry and Mission • Christ as the Father and the Son
Alma, "A Mighty Change of Heart" Alma 5 (to people of Zarahemla)	• Conversion: A Mighty Change of Heart • If You Have Experienced a Change of Heart, Can You Feel So Now?
Alma, "Our Duty to God" Alma 7 (to people of Gideon)	• Mission of Christ: He Takes on Death, Sins, and Our Infirmities • Duty to God: Developing Divine Attributes
Amulek, "Resurrection" Alma 11 (to people of Ammonihah)	• Physical Resurrection is Universal • Attributes of a Resurrected Body: Reunited in Perfect Form
Alma, "Life is a Probationary State and the High Priesthood" Alma 12-13 (to people of Ammonihah)	• Life is a Probationary State • The Melchizedek Priesthood • Foreordination
Alma, "Nourish Faith with the Word of God" Alma 32-33 (to Zoramites in Antionum)	• Humility Prepares Us to Be Taught • Faith: Hope for Things Which are Not Seen • Compare the Word to a Seed: Plant and Nourish
Amulek, "Atonement, Prayer and Procrastination" Alma 34 (to Zoramites in Antionum)	• The Atonement Is the Great, Last Sacrifice • Pray at All Times, in All Places, about All Things • Do Not Procrastinate Repentance
Alma, "Principles of Repentance and Small & Simple Things" Alma 36-37 (to his son, Helaman)	• Principles of Repentance (Alma's Conversion) • Small and Simple Things
Alma, "Steadiness and Faithfulness" Alma 38 (to his son, Shiblon)	• Steadiness and Faithfulness • Effective Teaching

Alma, "Chastity, Justice & Mercy" Alma 39-42 (to his son, Corianton)	• Importance of Chastity • State of the Spirit Between Death and Resurrection • Restoration: Good to Good & Evil to Evil • Wickedness Never Was Happiness • Justice & Mercy
Helaman, "The Rock of Christ" Helaman 5 (to his sons, Nephi and Lehi)	• Remember Prophetic Teachings • Build Your Foundation on the Rock of Christ
Samuel the Lamanite, "Prophesy of Christ" Helaman 13-15 (to the people of Zarahemla)	• Listen to the Prophets • Signs of the Coming of Christ • Conditions of Repentance: Re-turn to God
Mormon, "Faith, Hope & Charity" Moroni 7 (to the people in the synagogue)	• Real Intent: Motives Matter and the "As If" Principle • Good Comes from God • The Light of Christ • Faith, Hope & Charity
Mormon, "Baptism of Little Children" Moroni 8 (to his son, Moroni)	• Baptism of Little Children • A Pathway to Perfect Love
Mormon, "Persevere Despite Wickedness" Moroni 9 (to his son, Moroni)	• Nephite Anger and Wickedness • Persevere Despite Wickedness • Let Christ Lift You Up
Mormon, "Invitation to Believe" Mormon 7 (to the Lamanites)	• Invitation to the Lamanites: Know and Do • The Bible and the Book of Mormon Support Each Other
Moroni, "Voice of Warning: the Last Days" Mormon 8-9 (to future members of the church and those who have not accepted the gospel)	• Coming Forth of the Book of Mormon • Conditions of the Last Days • God Performs Miracles: Yesterday, Today, and Tomorrow
Moroni, "Revelation & Gifts of the Spirit" Moroni 10 (to future readers of the Book of Mormon)	• Promise of the Book of Mormon • The Holy Ghost: the Truth of All Things • Gifts of the Spirit • Be Perfected in Christ

Appendix D: Commentary Sources by Discourse

Discourse 1: Lehi, "The Tree of Life" (1 Nephi 8-10)

Journey to the Tree of Life: Hold Fast to the Iron Rod

Andersen, Neil L., "Hold Fast to the Words of the Prophets," CES Fireside, March 4, 2007

Baxter, David S., "Faith, Service, Constancy," Conference Report, Oct. 2006.

Bednar, David A., "Lehi's Dream," *Ensign*, Oct. 2011.

Benson, Ezra Taft, "The Power of the Word," Conference Report, Apr. 1986.

Holland, Jeffrey R., Christ and the New Covenant: The Messianic Message of the Book of Mormon. 1997.

Maxwell, Neal A., "Lessons from Laman and Lemuel," Conference Report, Oct. 1999.

Packer, Boyd K., "Finding Ourselves in Lehi's Dream," *Ensign*, Aug. 2010.

Stapley, Delbert L., "The Vision of Lehi," Conference Report, Apr. 1966.

Four Categories of People

Bednar, David A., "A Reservoir of Living Water," CES fireside, Feb. 4, 2007.

Bednar, David A., "Lehi's Dream," *Ensign*, Oct. 2011.

Maxwell, Neal A., "How Choice a Seer!" Conference Report, Oct. 2003.

Oaks, Dallin H., "The Parable of the Sower," Conference Report, Apr. 2015.

Pace, Glen L., "They're Not Really Happy," Conference Report, Oct. 1987.

Perry, L. Tom, "If Ye Are Prepared Ye Shall Not Fear," Conference Report, Oct. 1995.

Waddell, W. Christopher, "A Pattern for Peace," Conference Report, Apr. 2016.

Wirthlin, Joseph B., "Running Your Marathon," Conference Report, Oct. 1989.

Zwick, W. Craig, "We Will Not Yield, We Cannot Yield," Conference Report, Apr. 2008.

Dealing with Wayward Children

Bednar, David A., "Faithful Parents and Wayward Children," *Ensign*, Mar. 2014.

Hales, Robert D., "With All the Feeling of a Tender Parent," Conference Report, Apr. 2004.

Hales, Robert D., "Come Follow Me," Conference Report, Oct. 2016.

Soares, Ulisses, "How Can I Understand?" Conference Report, Apr. 2019.

Whitney, Orson F., "Untitled," Conference Report, Apr. 1929.

Discourse 2: Lehi, "Awake and Repent" (2 Nephi 1)

Awake and Repent: Keep the Commandments and Prosper

Asay, Carlos E., "Be Men!" Conference Report, Apr. 1992.

Ashton, Marvin J., "Shake Off the Chains with Which Ye Are Bound," Conf. Report Oct. 1986.

Cook, Quentin L., "The Songs They Could Not Sing," Conference Report, Oct. 2011.

Costa, Claudio R.M., "Obedience to the Prophets," Conference Report, Oct. 2010.

Hinckley, Gordon B., "Rise Up O Men of God," Conference Report, Oct. 2006.

Nelson, Russell M., "In the Lord's Own Way," Conference Report, Apr. 1986.

Nelson, Russell M., "We Can Do Better and Be Better," Conference Report, Apr. 2019.

Parkin, Bonnie D., "Eternally Encircled in His Love," Conference Report Oct. 2006.

Uchtdorf, Dieter F., "Are You Sleeping Through the Restoration?" Conf. Report, Apr. 2014.

Discourse 3: Lehi, "The Gift of Agency" (2 Nephi 2)

The Plan of Salvation and the Gift of Agency

Benson, Ezra Taft, "The Great Commandment – Love the Lord," Conference Report, Apr. 1988.

Clark, Kim B., "Look unto Jesus Christ," Conference Report, April 2019.

Clayton, Weatherford, "Our Father's Glorious Plan," Conference Report, April 2017.

Faust, James E., "The Great Imitator," Conference Report, Oct. 1987.

Hales, Robert D., "The Gift and Blessings of Agency," Conference Report, Apr. 2006.

Maxwell, Neal A., "Joseph the Seer," Conference Report, Oct. 1983.

McConkie, Bruce R., "Christ and the Creation," *Ensign*, June 1982.

Nelson, Russell M., "Addiction or Freedom," Conference Report, Oct. 1988.

Nelson, Russell M., "The Atonement," Conference Report, Oct. 1996.

Oaks, Dallin H., "Opposition in All Things," Conference Report, Apr. 2016.

Oaks, Dallin H., "What Think Ye of Christ?" Conference Report, Oct. 1988.

Oaks, Dallin H., "The Plan and the Proclamation," Conference Report, Oct. 2017.

Oaks, Dallin H., "Truth and the Plan," Conf. Report, Oct. 2018.

Packer, Boyd K., "Do Not Fear," Conference Report, Apr. 2004.

Packer, Boyd K., "For Time and All Eternity," Conference Report, Oct. 1993.

Paul, Wolfgang H., "The Gift of Agency," Conference Report, Apr. 2006.

Scott, Richard G., "Jesus Christ, Our Redeemer," Conference Report, Apr. 1997.

Discourse 4: Lehi, "Joseph: A Choice Seer" (2 Nephi 3)

Ballard, M. Russell, "The Family of the Prophet Joseph Smith," Conference Report, Oct. 1991.

Benson, Ezra Taft, "A New Witness for Christ," Conference Report, Oct. 1984.

Hunter, Milton R., "A Prophet 'Great Like Unto Moses,'" Conference Report, Oct. 1968.

Maxwell, Neal A., "How Choice a Seer!" Conference Report, Oct. 2003.

Maxwell, Neal A., "Joseph the Seer," Conference Report, Oct. 1983.

Maxwell, Neal A., "Premortality, a Glorious Reality," Conference Report, Oct. 1985.

Packer, Boyd K., "Scriptures," Conference Report, Oct. 1982.

Reeve, Rex, "Joseph Smith, the Chosen Instrument," Conference Report, Oct. 1985.

Richards, LeGrand, "Call of the Prophets," Conference Report, Apr. 1981.

Sill, Sterling W., "Famine and Joseph Smith," Conference Report, Apr. 1956.

Smith, Eldred G., "Patriarchal Order of the Priesthood," Conference Report, Apr. 1952.

Discourse 5: Nephi, "Panoramic Vision of the Future," (1 Nephi 11-14)

Pondering Leads to a Marvelous Vision

Ashton, Marvin J., "There are Many Gifts," Conference Report, Oct. 1987.

Christensen, Craig C., "I Know These Things of Myself," Conference Report, Oct. 2014.

Christofferson, D. Todd, "The Blessing of Scripture," Apr. 2010.

McKay, David O., "Consciousness of God," Conference Report, Apr. 1967.

Vision of Christ: The Condescension of God

Hinckley, Gordon B., "Be Not Faithless," Conference Report, Apr. 1978.

Lund, Gerald N., Jesus Christ, Key to the Plan of Salvation. 2009.

Stapley, Delbert L., "The Vision of Lehi," Conference Report, Apr. 1966.

Tingey, Earl C., "The Great Plan of Happiness," Conference Report, Apr. 2006.

Vision of the Americas: The Bible and Book of Mormon

Benson, Ezra Taft, "America: Land of the Blessed," Conference Report, Apr. 1948.

Benson, Ezra Taft, "A Marvelous Work and a Wonder," Conference Report, Apr. 1980.

Hinckley, Gordon B., "Building Your Tabernacle," Conference Report, Oct. 1992.

Hinckley, Gordon B., "A Testimony of the Book of Mormon," Conference Report, Oct. 1999.

Holland, Jeffrey R., "The Will of the Father," BYU Speeches, Jan. 17, 1989.

Hunter, Milton R., "A Marvelous Work and a Wonder," Conference Report, Oct. 1958.

Kimball, Spencer W., "Who Is My Neighbor?" Conference Report, April 1949.

Nelson, Russell M., "Scriptural Witnesses," Conference Report, Oct. 2007.

Robinson, Stephen R., "Warring against the Saints of God," *Ensign*, Jan. 1988.

Smith, George Albert, "Untitled," Conference Report, Oct. 1949.

Smith, Joseph Fielding, "The Kingdom of God Is Eternal," Conference Report, Oct. 1968.

Tanner, N. Eldon, "If They Will But Serve the God of the Land," Conference Report, Apr. 1976.

Discourse 6: Nephi, "Scattering and Gathering" (1 Nephi 19-22)

Furnace of Affliction; Scattering and Gathering: Overcoming Satan

Benson, Ezra Taft, "A Witness and a Warning," Conference Report, Oct. 1979.

Benson, Ezra Taft, "Counsel to the Saints," Conference Report, Apr. 1984

Christofferson, D. Todd, "Firm and Steadfast in the Faith of Christ," Conf. Report, Oct. 2018.

Christofferson, D. Todd, "Preparing for the Lord's Return," Conference Report, Apr. 2019.

Faust, James E., "The Great Imitator," Conference Report, Oct. 1987.

Hanks, Marion D., "Pledged to Obedience and Loyalty," Conference Report, Oct. 1960.

Holland, Jeffrey R., "Broken Things to Mend," Conference Report, Apr. 2006.

Holland, Jeffrey R., "The Will of the Father," BYU Speeches, Jan. 17, 1989.

Johnson, Paul V., "Him That Loved Us," Conf. Report, Apr. 2011.

Kimball, Spencer W., "A Report and a Challenge," Conference Report, Oct. 1976.

Kimball, Spencer W., "Search the Scriptures," Conference Report, Oct. 1958.

McConkie, Bruce R., "Stand Independent above All Other Creatures," Conf. Report, Apr. 1979.

McConkie, Bruce R., A New Witness for the Articles of Faith. 1985.

McConkie, Bruce R., Millennial Messiah: The Second Coming of the Son of Man. 1982.

Oaks, Dallin H., "Bible Stories and Personal Protection," Conference Report, Apr. 1992.

Oaks, Dallin H., "The Challenge to Become," Conference Report, Oct. 2000.

Rasband, Ronald A., "Build a Fortress of Spirituality and Protection," Conf. Report, April 2019.

Uchtdorf, Dieter F., "Point of Safe Return," Conference Report, Apr. 2007.

Uchtdorf, Dieter F., "Perfect Love Casteth Out Fear," Conference Report, Apr. 2017.

Discourse 7: Nephi, "Press Forward in Christ" (2 Nephi 25-33)

Delight in the Words of Isaiah

McConkie, Bruce R., "Ten Keys to Understanding Isaiah," *Ensign*, Oct. 1973.

Nyman, Monte S., Great Are the Words of Isaiah. 1980.

Packer, Boyd K., "The Book of Mormon," Conference Report, Oct. 2001.

We Talk of Christ, Rejoice in Christ, Preach of Christ

Cook, Quentin L., "In Tune with the Music of Faith," Conference Report, Apr. 2012

Cook, Quentin L., "Can Ye Feel So Now?" Conference Report, Oct. 2012.

Hales, Robert D., "In Remembrance of Jesus," Conference Report, Oct. 1997.

Hinckley, Gordon B., "We Look to Christ," Conference Report, Apr. 2002.

Holland, Jeffrey R., "That Our Children Might Know," BYU Speeches, Aug. 25, 1981.

McConkie, Bruce R., "Our Belief in Christ," Conference Report, Oct. 1970.

Nelson, Russell M., "Combatting Spiritual Drift," Conference Report, Oct. 1993.

Nelson, Russell M., "A Testimony of the Book of Mormon," Conference Report, Oct. 1999.

Packer, Boyd K., "Another Testament of Jesus Christ," Conference Report, Apr. 2005.

Packer, Boyd K., "For Time and All Eternity," Conference Report, Oct. 1993.

Perry, L. Tom, "Perfect Love Casteth Out Fear," Conference Report, Oct. 2011.

Doctrine of Inclusion

Ballard, M. Russell, "Doctrine of Inclusion," Conference Report, Oct. 2001.

Cook, Quentin L., "Our Father's Plan," Conference Report, Apr. 2009.

Holland, Jeffrey R., "The Other Prodigal," Conference Report, Apr. 2002.

Holland, Jeffrey R., "Songs Sung and Unsung," Conference Report, Apr. 2017.

Hunter, Howard W., "Conference Time," Conference Report, Oct. 1981.

Hunter, Howard W., "A More Excellent Way," Conference Report, Apr. 1992.

Kimball, Spencer W., "The Evil of Intolerance," Conference Report, April 1954.

Oaks, Dallin H., "All Men Everywhere," Conference Report, Apr. 2006.

Okazaki, Chieko N., "Baskets and Bottles," Conference Report, Apr. 1996.

Uchtdorf, Dieter F., "The Love of God," Conference Report, Oct. 2009.

Nephi's Warnings – False Doctrines

Ashton, Marvin J., "The Tongue Can Be a Sharp Sword," Conference Report, Apr. 1992.

Christiansen, ElRay L., "Who Would Justify – A Little Sin?" Conference Report, Oct. 1959.

Dunn, James M., "Words to Live By," Conference Report, Apr. 2003.

Edgley, Richard C., "Satan's Bag of Snipes," Conference Report, Oct. 2000.

Faust, James E., "Communion with the Holy Spirit," Conference Report, Apr. 1980.

Faust, James E., "Gift of the Holy Ghost – A Sure Compass," Conference Report, Apr. 1989.

Faust, James E., "The Enemy Within," Conference Report, Oct. 2000.

Hinckley, Gordon B., "Building Your Tabernacle," Conference Report, Oct. 1992.

Maxwell, Neal A., "Answer Me," Conference Report, Oct. 1988.

Monson, Thomas S., "Constant Truths for Changing Times," Conference Report, Apr. 2005.

Oaks, Dallin H., "Brother's Keeper," Conference Report, Oct. 1986.

Oaks, Dallin H., "Be Not Deceived," Conference Report, Oct. 2004.

Romney, Marion G., "Satan – The Great Deceiver," Conference Report, Apr. 1971.

Smith, Joseph Fielding, "Procrastination Is the Thief of Eternal Life," Conf. Report, Apr. 1969.

The Doctrine of Christ

Ashton, Brian, "The Doctrine of Christ," Conference Report, Oct. 2016.

Bednar, David A., "That We May Always Have His Spirit," Conference Report, Apr. 2006.

Bednar, David A., "Therefore They Hushed Their Fears," Conference Report, Apr. 2015.

Hales, Robert D., "Healing Soul and Body," Conference Report, Oct. 1998.

Hales, Robert D., "The Covenant of Baptism," Conference Report, Oct. 2000.

Holland, Jeffrey R., "The Cost–and Blessings–of Discipleship," Conference Report, Apr. 2014.

Nelson, Russell M., "Living By Scriptural Guidance," Conference Report, Oct. 2000.

Nelson, Russell M., "Repentance and Conversion," Conference Report, Apr. 2007.

Uchtdorf, Dieter F., "Have We Not Reason to Rejoice?" Conference Report, Oct. 2007.

Wirthlin, Joseph B., "Press On," Conference Report, Oct. 2004.

Discourse 8: Jacob, "The Infinite Atonement" (2 Nephi 6-10)

Bednar, David A., "Therefore They Hushed Their Fears," Conference Report, Apr. 2015.

Bowen, Shane M., "The Atonement Can Clean and Sanctify Our Lives," Conf Report, Oct. 2006.

Callister, Tad R., "The Atonement of Jesus Christ," Conference Report, April 2019.

Faust, James E., "Woman, Why Weepest Thou?" Conference Report, Oct. 1996.

Faust, James E., "The Atonement – Our Greatest Hope," Conference Report, Oct. 2001.

Gong, Gerrit W., "Our Campfire of Faith," Conference Report, Oct. 2018.

Hales, Robert D., "Meeting the Challenges of Today's World," Conference Report, Oct. 2015.

Hinckley, Gordon B., "Reverence and Morality," Conference Report, Apr. 1987.

Hinckley, Gordon B., "Converts and Young Men," Conference Report, Apr. 1997.

Holland, Jeffrey R., Christ and the New Covenant. 1997.

Hunter, Howard W., "He Is Risen," Conference Report, Apr. 1988.

Maxwell, Neal A., "Education of the Whole Man," Conference Report, Apr. 1970.

McConkie, Bruce R., "The Atonement of Christ," Conference Report, Apr. 1950.

McConkie, Bruce R., "Come: Let Israel Build Zion," Conference Report, Apr. 1977.

Nelson, Russell M., "Self-Mastery," Conference Report, Oct. 1985.

Nelson, Russell M., "The Atonement," Conference Report, Oct. 1996.

Nelson, Russell M., "A Testimony of the Book of Mormon," Conference Report, Oct. 1999.

Nelson, Russell M., "The Gathering of Scattered Israel," Conference Report, Apr. 2006.

Oaks, Dallin H., "What Think Ye of Christ?" Conference Report, Oct. 1988.

Oaks, Dallin H., "Alternate Voices," Conference Report, Apr. 1989.

Oaks, Dallin H., "Resurrection," Conference Report, Apr. 2000.

Oaks, Dallin H., "All Men Everywhere," Conference Report, Apr. 2006.

Packer, Boyd K., "The Brilliant Morning of Forgiveness," Conference Report, Oct. 1995.

Packer, Boyd K., "The Touch of the Master's Hand," Conference Report, Apr. 2001.

Romney, Marion G., "How Men Are Saved," Conference Report, Oct. 1974.

Discourse 9: Jacob, "A Warning about Sin" (Jacob 2-3)

Pride and Riches: How to Handle Wealth

Larsen, Dean L., "Beware Lest Thou Forget the Lord," Conference Report, Apr. 1991.

Lee, Harold B., "After All We Can Do," Conference Report, Apr. 1956.

Maxwell, Neal A., "Yet Thou Art There," Conference Report, Oct. 1987.

Oaks, Dallin H., "Spirituality," Conference Report, Oct. 1985.

Oaks, Dallin H., "Strengthened by the Atonement," Conference Report, Oct. 2015.

Packer, Boyd K., "The Choice," Conference Report, Oct. 1980.

Perry, L. Tom, "United in Building the Kingdom of God," Conference Report, Apr. 1987.

Tanner, N. Eldon, "Constancy Amid Change," Conference Report, Oct. 1979.

Taylor, Henry D., "He That Is the Greatest Among You," Conference Report, Oct. 1963.

Uchtdorf, Dieter F., "Pride and the Priesthood," Conference Report, Oct. 2010.

Uchtdorf, Dieter F., "In Praise of Those Who Save," Conference Report, Apr. 2016.

Wirthlin, Joseph B., "The Law of the Fast," Conference Report, Apr. 2001.

The Sin of Immorality

Bednar, David A., "We Believe in Being Chaste," Conference Report, Apr. 2013.

Benson, Ezra Taft, "Cleansing the Inner Vessel," Conference Report, Apr. 1986.

Hinckley, Gordon B., "From My Generation to Yours," Conference Report, Oct. 1970.

Hinckley, Gordon B., "What Are People Asking about Us?" Conference Report, Oct. 1998.

Holland, Jeffrey R., "Place No More for the Enemy of My Soul," Conference Report, Apr. 2010.

Nelson, Russell M., "Addiction or Freedom," Conference Report, Oct. 1988.

Scott, Richard G., "Making the Right Choices," Conference Report, Oct. 1994.

Discourse 10: King Benjamin, "Service and Salvation" (Mosiah 2-4)

Service

Alonso, Jose L., "Doing the Right Thing at the Right Time," Conference Report, Oct. 2011.

Hunter, Howard W., "True Religion," Conference Report, Oct. 1978.

Hunter, Howard W., "To the Women of the Church," Ensign, Nov. 1992.

Hunter, Milton R., "The Modern Scriptures," Conference Report, Oct. 1955.

Monson, Thomas S., "The Search for Jesus," Conference Report, Oct. 1965.

Monson, Thomas S., "An Example of the Believers," Conference Report, Oct. 1992.

Monson, Thomas S., "Search and Rescue," Conference Report, Apr. 1993.

Monson, Thomas S., "To the Rescue," Conference Report, Apr. 2001.

Monson, Thomas S., "The Sacred Road of Service," Conference Report, Apr. 2005.

Monson, Thomas S., "Looking Back and Moving Forward," Conference Report, Apr. 2008.

Monson, Thomas S., "What Have I Done for Someone Today?" Conference Report, Oct. 2009.

Oaks, Dallin H., "Why Do We Serve?" Conference Report, Oct. 1984.

Romney, Marion G., "The Celestial Nature of Self-Reliance," Conference Report, Oct. 1982.

Taylor, Henry D., "Some Rain Must Fall," Conference Report, Apr. 1963.

Gratitude

Hales, Robert D., Conference Report, "Gratitude for the Goodness of God," Apr. 1992.

Nelson, Russell M., "In the Lord's Own Way," Conference Report, Apr. 1986.

Nelson, Russell M., "Let Your Faith Show," Conference Report, Apr. 2014.

Smith, Joseph Fielding, "The Sin of Ingratitude," Conference Report, Oct. 1947.

Wirthlin, Joseph B., "Earthly Debts, Heavenly Debts," Conference Report, Apr. 2004.

Wirthlin, Joseph B., "Journey to a Higher Ground," Conference Report, Oct. 2005.

The Name of Jesus Christ

Brown, L. Edward, "Pray Unto the Father in My Name," Conference Report, Apr. 1997.

Oaks, Dallin H., "Taking on the Name of Jesus Christ," Conference Report, Apr. 1985.

Oaks, Dallin H., "Reverent and Clean," Conference Report, Apr. 1986.

Pieper, Paul B., "All Must Take upon Them the Name Given of the Father," Conf. Rep. Oct. 2018.

The Natural Man

Bednar, David A., "We Believe in Being Chaste," Conference Report, Apr. 2013.

Eyring, Henry B., "As a Child," Conference Report, Apr. 2006.

Maxwell, Neal A., "Put off the Natural Man," Conference Report, Oct. 1990.

Kimball, Spencer W., "Ocean Currents and Family Influences," Conference Report, Oct. 1974.

Nelson, Russell M., "Ask, Seek, Knock," Conference Report, Oct. 2009.

Retaining a Remission of Sins

Asay, Carlos E., "Salt of the Earth: Savor of Men and Saviors of Men," Conf. Report, Apr. 1980.

Bednar, David A., "Clean Hands and a Pure Heart," Conference Report, Oct. 2007.

Bednar, David A., "Always Retain a Remission of Your Sins," Conference Report, April 2016.

Crockett, Keith, "Retaining a Remission of Sin," Conference Report, Oct. 2000.

Eyring, Henry B., "As a Child," Conference Report, Apr. 2006.

Faust, James E., "The Great Imitator," Conference Report, Oct. 1987.

Holland, Jeffrey R., "Are We Not All Beggars?" Conference Report, Oct. 2014.

Oaks, Dallin H., "World Peace," Conference Report, Apr. 1990.

Discourse 11: Abinadi, "Redemption through Christ" (Mosiah 13-16)

Keep the Commandments

Ballard, M. Russell, "Pure Testimony," Conference Report, Oct. 2004.

Hales, Robert D., "Keep the Commandments," Conference Report Apr. 1996.

Maxwell, Neal A., "Deny Yourselves of All Ungodliness," Conference Report, Apr. 1995.

Redemption through Jesus Christ

Benson, Ezra Taft, "Jesus Christ, Our Savior, Our God," *Ensign*, Apr. 1991.

Brown, Victor L., "Upon You My Fellow Servants," Conference Report, Oct. 1970.

Christofferson, D. Todd, "Redemption," Apr. 2013.

Christofferson, D. Todd, "The Resurrection of Jesus Christ," Apr. 2014.

Holland, Jeffrey R., "A High Priest of Good Things to Come," Conf. Report, Oct. 1999.

Benson, Ezra Taft, "Jesus Christ, Our Savior, Our God," *Ensign*, Apr. 1991.

Jesus Christ as Father and Son

Ballard, M. Russell, "Building Bridges of Understanding," *Ensign*, June 1998.

Oaks, Dallin H., "Taking Upon Us the Name of Jesus Christ," Conference Report, Apr. 1985.

Smith, Joseph F., First Presidency Statement June 30, 1916, "The Father and the Son," quoted in *Ensign*, Apr. 2002.

Discourse 12: Alma, "A Mighty Change of Heart" (Alma 5)

Conversion

Ashton, Marvin J., "The Measure of Our Hearts," Conference Report, Oct. 1988.

Ballard, M. Russell, "Now Is the Time," Conference Report, Oct. 2000.

Bednar, David A., "Converted unto the Lord," Conference Report, Oct. 2012.

Christofferson, D. Todd, "When Thou Art Converted," Apr. 2004.

Christofferson, D. Todd, "Born Again," Apr. 2008.

Cook, Quentin L., "Can Ye Feel So Now?" Conference Report, Oct. 2012.

Lawrence, W. Mack, "Conversion and Commitment," Conference Report, Apr. 1996.

Martino, James B., "Turn to Him and Answers Will Come," Conference Report Oct. 2015.

Nelson, Russell M., "Jesus Christ – the Master Healer," Conference Report, Oct. 2005.

Oaks, Dallin H., "Strengthened by the Atonement of Jesus Christ," Conference Report, Oct. 2015.

Renlund, Dale G., "Preserving the Heart's Mighty Change," Conference Report, Oct. 2009.

Romney, Marion G., "According to the Covenants," Conference Report, Oct. 1975.

Samuelson, Cecil O., "Testimony," Conference Report, Apr. 2011.

Avoid Pride, Envy, Self-Aggrandizement

Bowen, Albert E., "The Struggle of Life," Conference Report, Apr. 1949.

Bowen, Albert E., "Forgive and Be Forgiven," Conference Report, Oct. 1951

Clyde, Aileen H., "Covenant of Love," Conference Report, Apr. 1995.

Cowley, Matthew, "Spirit of Discernment," Conference Report, Apr. 1950.

Holland, Jeffrey R., "The Other Prodigal," Conference Report, Apr. 2002.

Holland, Jeffrey R., "The Laborers in the Vinyard," Conference Report, Apr. 2012.

Hunter, Howard W., "A More Excellent Way," Conference Report, Apr. 1992.

McKay, David O., "Unity of Purpose," Conference Report, Oct. 1967.

Monson, Thomas S., "Yellow Canaries with Gray on Their Wings," Conf. Report, Apr. 1973.

Monson, Thomas S., "Love – The Essence of the Gospel," Conference Report, Apr. 2014.

Oaks, Dallin H., "All Men Everywhere," Conference Report, Apr. 2006.

Discourse 13: Alma, "Divine Attributes" (Alma 7)

Christ Takes on Our Infirmities

Bateman, Merrill J., "The Power to Heal from Within," Conference Report, Apr. 1995.

Bednar, David A., "Bear Up Their Burdens with Ease," Conference Report, Apr. 2014.

Faust, James E., "The Atonement – Our Greatest Hope," Conference Report, Oct. 2001.

Grow, C. Scott, "The Miracle of the Atonement," Conference Report, Apr. 2011.

Hafen, Bruce, C., "Beauty for Ashes: The Atonement of Jesus Christ," *Ensign*, Apr. 1990.

Holland, Jeffrey R., "Broken Things to Mend," Conference Report, Apr. 2006.

Oaks, Dallin H., "Strengthened by the Atonement of Jesus Christ," Conference Report, Oct. 2015.

Oaks, Dallin H., "He Heals the Heavy Laden," Conference Report, Oct. 2006.

Developing Divine Attributes

Benson, Ezra Taft, "Godly Characteristics of the Master," Conference Report, Oct. 1986.

Benson, Ezra Taft, "Come Unto Christ and Be Perfected in Him," Conference Report, Oct. 1988.

Hales, Robert D., "Becoming a Disciple of Our Lord Jesus Christ," Conf. Report, Apr. 2017.

Maxwell, Neal A., "Willing to Submit," Conference Report, Apr. 1985.

Monson, Thomas S., "A Royal Priesthood," Conference Report, Oct. 2007.

Nelson, Russell M., "These . . . Were Our Examples," Conference Report, Oct. 1991.

Scott, Richard G., "Jesus Christ, Our Redeemer," Conference Report, Apr. 1997.

Uchtdorf, Dieter F., "Christlike Attributes –Wind Beneath Our Wings," Conf. Report, Oct. 2005.

Discourse 14: Amulek, "Resurrection" (Alma 10-11)

Faust, James E., "The Supernal Gift of the Atonement," Conference Report, Oct. 1988.

Hunter, Howard W., "The Reality of the Resurrection," Conference Report, Apr. 1969.

Hunter, Milton R., "Immortality and Eternal Life," Conference Report, Apr. 1949.

Johnson, Paul V., "And There Shall Be No More Death," Conference Report, Apr. 2016.

Nelson, Russell M., "Life After Life," Conference Report, Apr. 1987.

Nelson, Russell M., "Doors of Death," Conference Report, Apr. 1992.

Nelson, Russell M., "Perfection Pending," Conference Report, Oct. 1995.

Oaks, Dallin H., "Resurrection," Conference Report, Apr. 2000.

Sill, Sterling W., "To Die Well," Conference Report, Oct. 1976.

Wirthlin, Joseph B., "Sunday Will Come," Conference Report, Oct. 2006.

Discourse 15: Alma, "Probationary State; High Priesthood" (Alma 12-13)

Life is a Probationary State

Hunter, Milton R., "Untitled," Conference Report, Oct. 1946.

Hunter, Milton R., "Immortality and Eternal Life," Conference Report, Apr. 1949.

Jensen, Jay E., "Keep an Eternal Perspective," Conference Report, Apr. 2000.

Lee, Harold B., "Time to Prepare to Meet God," Conference Report, Oct. 1970.

McMullin, Keith B., "Welcome Home," Conference Report, Apr. 1999.

Nelson, Russell M., "Doors of Death," Conference Report, Apr. 1992.

Oaks, Dallin H., "The Challenge to Become," Conference Report, Oct. 2000.

Packer, Boyd K., "The Touch of the Master's Hand," Conference Report, Apr. 2001.

Perry, L. Tom, "Proclaim My Gospel from Land to Land," Conference Report, Apr. 1989.

Wickman, Lance, "But If Not," Conference Report, Oct. 2002.

Melchizedek Priesthood; Foreordination

Clark, J. Reuben, "Untitled," Conference Report, Oct. 1950.

Kimball, Spencer W., "The Role of Righteous Women," Conference Report, Oct. 1979.

Maxwell, Neal A., "Premortality, a Glorious Reality," Conference Report, Oct. 1985.

McConkie, Bruce R., "God Foreordains His Prophets and His People," Conf. Report, Apr. 1974.

Nelson, Russell M., "Perfection Pending," Conference Report, Oct. 1995.

Discourse 16: Alma, "Nourish Faith with the Word of God" (Alma 32-33)

Humility

Asay, Carlos E., <u>Family Pecan Trees: Planting a Legacy of Faith at Home</u>. 1992.

Benson, Ezra Taft, "Beware of Pride," Conference Report, Apr. 1989.

Kimball, Spencer W., "Humility," BYU Devotional, Jan. 16, 1963.

Maxwell, Neal A., "Willing to Submit," Conference Report, Apr. 1985.

Maxwell, Neal A., "The Tugs and Pulls of the World," Conference Report, Oct. 2000.

Faith

Anderson, Joseph, "Man's Eternal Horizon," Conference Report, Apr. 1972.

Ballard, M. Russell, "Now Is the Time," Conference Report, Oct. 2000.

Christensen, Craig C., "I Know These Things of Myself," Conference Report, Oct. 2014.

Clayton, L. Whitney, "Choose to Believe," Conference Report, Apr. 2015.

Edgley, Richard C., "Faith – The Choice is Yours," Conference Report, Oct. 2010.

Eyring, Henry B., "The Spark of Faith," Conference Report, Oct. 1986.

Eyring, Henry B., "Opportunities to Do Good," Conference Report, Apr. 2011.

Faust, James E., "Of Seeds and Soils," Conference Report, Oct. 1999.

Holland, Jeffrey R., "Broken Things to Mend," Conference Report, Apr. 2006.

Hunter, Howard W., "Faith – The First Step," Conference Report, Apr. 1975.

Maxwell, Neal A., "Lest Ye Be Wearied and Faint in Your Minds," Conf. Report, Apr. 1991.

Packer, Boyd K., <u>The Shield of Faith</u>. 1998.

Packer, Boyd K., "The Book of Mormon: Another Testament of Jesus Christ – Plain and
     Precious Things," Conference Report, Apr. 2005.

Staheli, Donald L., "Securing Our Testimonies," Conference Report, Oct. 2004.

Uchtdorf, Dieter F., "The Fruits of the First Vision," Conference Report, Apr. 2005.

Uchtdorf, Dieter F., "The Way of the Disciple," Conference Report, Apr. 2009.

Uchtdorf, Dieter F., "Come, Join With Us," Conference Report, Oct. 2013.

Uchtdorf, Dieter F., "Be Not Afraid, Only Believe," Conference Report, Oct. 2015.

Wirthlin, Joseph B., "Cultivating Divine Attributes," Conference Report, Oct. 1998.

Discourse 17: Amulek, "Atonement, Prayer & Procrastination" (Alma 34)

Atonement

Amado, Carlos, "Service, A Divine Quality," Conference Report, Apr. 2008.

Andersen, Neil L., "Repent . . . That I May Heal You," Conference Report, Oct. 2009.

Bednar, David A., "Bear Up Their Burdens with Ease," Conference Report, Apr. 2014.

Benson, Ezra Taft, "Jesus Christ: Our Savior and Redeemer," Conference Report, Oct. 1983.

Edgley, Richard C., "For Thy Good," Conference Report, Apr. 2002.

Jensen, Jay E., "Arms of Safety," Conference Report, Oct. 2008.

Maxwell, Neal A., "A Great Answer to 'The Great Question,' BYU Book of Mormon Symposium, Oct. 10, 1986.

Maxwell, Neal A., "Repentance," Conference Report, Oct. 1991.

Nelson, Russell M., "Combatting Spiritual Drift," Conference Report, Oct. 1993.

Nelson, Russell M., "The Atonement," Conference Report, Oct. 1996.

Nelson, Russell M., "The Creation," Conference Report, Apr. 2000.

Oaks, Dallin H., "Sacrifice," Conference Report, Apr. 2012.

Parkin, Bonnie D., "Eternally Encircled in His Love," Conference Report Oct. 2006.

Scott, Richard G., "Strength through the Atonement of Jesus Christ," Conf. Report, Oct. 2013

Smith, Joseph Fielding, "The Sin of Ingratitude," Conference Report, Oct. 1947.

Uchtdorf, Dieter F., "Point of Safe Return," Conference Report, Apr. 2007.

Uchtdorf, Dieter F., "The Gift of Grace," Conference Report, Apr. 2015.

Prayer

Bednar, David A., "Pray Always," Conference Report, Oct. 2008.

Benson, Ezra Taft, "Prayer," Conference Report, Apr. 1977.

Brown, L. Edward, "Pray Unto the Father in My Name," Conference Report, Apr. 1997.

Christofferson, D. Todd, "When Thou Art Converted," Apr. 2004.

Eyring, Henry B., "Prayer," Conference Report, Oct. 2001.

Romney, Marion G., "The Royal Law of Love," Conference Report, Apr. 1978.

Do Not Procrastinate

Ashton, Marvin J., "Straightway," Conference Report, Apr. 1983.

Eyring, Henry B., "Do Not Delay," Conference Report, Oct. 1999.

Lee, Harold B., Address given to Ricks College, Mar. 3, 1962.

Nelson, Russell M., "Doors of Death," Conference Report, Apr. 1992.

Nelson, Russell M., "Now Is the Time to Prepare," Conference Report, Apr. 2005.

Nelson, Russell M., "Repentance and Conversion," Conference Report, Apr. 2007.

Oaks, Dallin H., "The Challenge to Become," Conference Report, Oct. 2000.

Smith, Joseph Fielding, "Procrastination Is the Thief of Eternal Life," Conf. Report, Apr. 1969.

Stapley, Delbert L., "The Blessings of Righteous Obedience," Conference Report, Oct. 1977.

Discourse 18: Alma, "Repentance; Small and Simple Things" (Alma 36-37)

Repentance

Benson, Ezra Taft, "A Mighty Change of Heart," *Ensign*, Oct. 1989.

Burton, Theodore M., "The Meaning of Repentance," *Ensign*, Nov. 1988.

Christofferson, D. Todd, "The Divine Gift of Repentance," Oct. 2011.

Gong, Garrit W. "Our Campfire of Faith," Conf. Report, Apr. 2018.

Hales, Robert D., "Healing Soul and Body," Conference Report, Oct. 1998.

Hanks, Marion D., "Boys Need Men," Conference Report, Apr. 1974.

Kimball, Spencer W., Miracle of Forgiveness. 1969.

Kimball, Spencer W., "President Kimball Speaks Out on Morality," Conf. Report, Oct. 1980.

Maxwell, Neal A., "Repentance," Conference Report, Oct. 1991.

Nelson, Russell M., "Repentance and Conversion," Conference Report, Apr. 2007.

Oaks, Dallin H., "Joy and Mercy," Conference Report, Oct. 1991.

Packer, Boyd K., "The Brilliant Morning of Forgiveness," Conference Report, Oct. 1995.

Packer, Boyd K., "Washed Clean," Conference Report, Apr. 1997.

Packer, Boyd K., "The Touch of the Master's Hand," Conference Report, Apr. 2001.

Packer, Boyd K., "The Plan of Happiness," Conference Report, Apr. 2015.

Peterson, H. Burke, "Touch Not the Evil Gift, nor the Unclean Thing," Conf. Report, Oct. 1993

Romney, Marion G., "Repentance," Conference Report, Oct. 1980.

Scott, Richard G., "Finding Forgiveness," Conference Report, Apr. 1995.

Uchtdorf, Dieter F., "Point of Safe Return," Conference Report, Apr. 2007.

Small and Simple Things

Ballard, M. Russell, "Small and Simple Things," Conference Report, Apr. 1990.

Ballard, M. Russell, "Finding Joy through Loving Service," Conference Report, Apr. 2011.

Christofferson, D. Todd, "The Blessing of Scripture," Apr. 2010.

Hinckley, Gordon B., "Small Acts Lead to Great Consequences," Conference Report, Apr. 1984.

Kerr, W. Rolfe, Conference Report, "The Words of Christ – Our Spiritual Liahona," Apr. 2004.

Maxwell, Neal A., "Repentance," Conference Report, Oct. 1991.

Romney, Marion G., "Look to God and Live," Conference Report, Oct. 1962.

Zaslow, Jeffrey, "What We Can Learn from Sully's Journey," Wall Street Journal, Oct. 14, 2009.

Discourse 19: Alma, "Steadiness and Faithfulness; Effective Teaching" (Alma 38)

Effective Teaching

Ballard, M. Russell, "Teaching – No Greater Call," Conference Report, Apr. 1983.

Bednar, David A., "We Believe in Being Chaste," Conference Report, Apr. 2013.

Benson, Ezra Taft, "Beware of Pride," Conference Report, Apr. 1989.

Burton, Theodore M., "Light and Truth," Conference Report, Apr. 1981.

Clarke, J. Richard, "My Soul Delighteth in the Scriptures," Conference Report, Apr. 1982.

Cook, Gene R., "Are You a Member Missionary?" Conference Report, Apr. 1976.

Cook, Gene R., "Spiritual Guides for Teachers of Righteousness," Conf. Report, Apr. 1982.

Dunn, Paul H., "Teach 'The Why'," Conference Report, Oct. 1981.

Dyer, Alvin R., "The Nobility of Man in Choosing Good Over Evil," Conf. Report, Oct. 1971.

Hafen, Bruce C. and Marie K. Hafen, <u>The Belonging Heart: The Atonement and Relationships with God and Family</u>. 1994.

Hales, Robert D., "Christian Courage: The Price of Discipleship," Conference Report, Oct. 2008.

Hamula, James J., "Winning the War against Evil," Conference Report, Oct. 2008.

Hillam, Harold G., "Teachers, the Timeless Key," Conference Report, Oct. 1997.

Hinckley, Gordon B., "We Have a Work to Do," Conference Report, Apr. 1995.

Holland, Jeffrey R., "A Teacher Come from God," Conference Report, Apr. 1998.

Kimball, Spencer W., "Ministering to the Needs of Members," Conf. Report, Oct. 1980.

Kimball, Spencer W., "Rendering Service to Others," Conference Report, Apr. 1981.

McKay, David O., "Untitled," Conference Report, Oct. 1916.

Monson, Thomas S., "Thou Art a Teacher Come From God," Conference Report, Oct. 1970.

Monson, Thomas S., "Be Thou an Example," Conference Report, Apr. 2005.

Nelson, Russell M., "Choices," Conference Report, Oct. 1990.

Packer, Boyd K., "The Plan of Happiness," Conference Report, Apr. 2015.

Ringwood, Michael T., "Truly Good and Without Guile," Conference Report, Apr. 2015.

Soares, Ulisses, "How Can I Understand?" Conference Report, April 2019.

Taylor, Henry D., "In the Sweat of Thy Face," Conference Report, Apr. 1961.

Taylor, Russell C., "Making Points for Righteousness," Conference Report, Apr. 1989.

Watson, Kent D., "Being Temperate in All Things," Conference Report, Oct. 2009.

Discourse 20: Alma, "Chastity, Restoration, Justice & Mercy" (Alma 39-42)

Chastity

Beck, Julie B., "Mothers Who Know," Conference Report, Apr. 2007.

Bednar, David A., "We Believe in Being Chaste," Conference Report, Apr. 2013.

Benson, Ezra Taft, "Three Threatening Dangers," Conference Report, Oct. 1964.

Benson, Ezra Taft, "Cleansing the Inner Vessel," Conference Report, Apr. 1986.

Holland, Jeffrey R., "Personal Purity," Conference Report, Oct. 1998.

Hunter, Milton R., "The Blessings of Eternal Life," Conference Report, Oct. 1947.

McKay, David O., "Counteracting Pernicious Ideas," Conference Report, Oct. 1951.

Oaks, Dallin H., "The Great Plan of Happiness," Conference Report, Oct. 1993.

Packer, Boyd K., "Why Stay Morally Clean," Conference Report, Apr. 1972.

Packer, Boyd K., "Little Children," Conference Report, Oct. 1986.

Packer, Boyd K., "For Time and All Eternity," Conference Report, Oct. 1993.

Packer, Boyd K., "The Touch of the Master's Hand," Conference Report, Apr. 2001.

Packer, Boyd K., "I Will Remember Your Sins No More," Conference Report, Apr. 2006.

Packer, Boyd K., "The Plan of Happiness," Conference Report, Apr. 2015.

Scott, Richard G., "The Power of Righteousness," Conference Report, Oct. 1998.

Wirthlin, Joseph B., "Deep Roots," Conference Report, Oct. 1994.

Resurrection and Restoration

Asay, Carlos E., "If a Man Die, Shall He Live Again?" Conference Report, Apr. 1994.

Goaslind, Jack H., "Happiness," Conference Report, Apr. 1986.

Johnson, Paul V., "And There Shall Be No More Death," Conference Report, Apr. 2016.

Nelson, Russell M., "Choices," Conference Report, Oct. 1990.

Oaks, Dallin H., "Resurrection," Conference Report, Apr. 2000.

Ridd, Randall L., "The Choice Generation," Conference Report, Apr. 2014.

Repentance: Wickedness Never Was Happiness

Benson, Ezra Taft, "Do Not Despair," Conference Report, Oct. 1974.

Hansen, W. Eugene, "The Search for Happiness," Conference Report, Oct. 1993.

Hinckley, Gordon B., "Converts and Young Men," Conference Report, Apr. 1997.

Nelson, Russell M., "Self-Mastery," Conference Report, Oct. 1985.

Scott, Richard G., "How to Live Well Amid Increasing Evil," Conference Report, Apr. 2004.

Wirthlin, Joseph B., "Running Your Marathon," Conference Report, Oct. 1989.

Judgment, Justice & Mercy

Bednar, David A., "We Believe in Being Chaste," Conference Report, April 2013.

Christofferson, D. Todd, "The Resurrection of Jesus Christ," April 2014.

Faust, James E., "Woman, Why Weepest Thou?" Conference Report, October 1996.

Oaks, Dallin H., "Cleansed by Repentance," Conference Report, April 2019.

Packer, Boyd K., "The Mediator," Conference Report, April 1977.

Scott, Richard G., "Finding Forgiveness," Conference Report, April 1995.

Scott, Richard G., "Jesus Christ, Our Redeemer," Conference Report, April 1997.

Scott, Richard G., "To Be Free of Heavy Burdens," Conference Report, October 2002.

Scott, Richard G., "Peace of Conscience and Peace of Mind," Conference Report, Oct. 2004.

Tingey, Earl C., "The Great Plan of Happiness," Conference Report, April 2006.

Uchtdorf, Dieter F., "Point of Safe Return," Conference Report, April 2007.

Wirthlin, Joseph B., "Christians in Belief and Action," Conference Report, October 1996.

Discourse 21: Helaman, "Remember; The Rock of Our Redeemer" (Helaman 5)

Arnold, Mervyn B., "What Have You Done with My Name?" Conference Report, Oct. 2010.

Asay, Carlos E., Family Pecan Trees: Planting a Legacy of Faith at Home. 1992.

Bednar, David A., "Therefore They Hushed Their Fears," Conference Report, Apr. 2015.

Davies, Dean M., "A Sure Foundation," Conference Report, Apr. 2013.

Davies, Dean M., "Come, Listen to a Prophet's Voice," Conference Report, Oct. 2018.

Eyring, Henry B., "O Remember, Remember," Conference Report, Oct. 2007.

Hales, Robert D., "Eternal Life – to Know Our Heavenly Father and His Son, Jesus Christ," Conference Report, Oct. 2014.

Hunter, Howard W., "Is a Church Necessary?" Conference Report, Oct. 1967.

Kimball, Spencer W., "Circles of Exaltation," CES meeting, June 28, 1968.

Kimball, Spencer W., "Hold Fast to the Iron Rod," Conference Report, Oct. 1978.

Nelson, Russell M., "How Firm Our Foundation," Conference Report, Apr. 2002.

Oaks, Dallin H., "Taking Upon Us the Name of Jesus Christ," Conference Report, Apr. 1985.

Oaks, Dallin H., "Have You Been Saved?" Conference Report, Apr. 1998.

Perry, L. Tom, "Born of Goodly Parents," Conference Report, Apr. 1985.

Scott, Richard G., "Finding Forgiveness," Conference Report, Apr. 1995.

Scott, Richard G., "Jesus Christ, Our Redeemer," Conference Report, Apr. 1997.

Warner, Susan L. "Remember How Thou Hast Received and Heard," Conf. Report, Apr. 1996.

Discourse 22: Samuel the Lamanite, "Signs of Christ" (Helaman 13-15)

Listen to the Prophets

Ballard, M. Russell, "His Word Ye Shall Receive," Conference Report, April 2001.

Causse, Gerald, "Is It Still Wonderful to You?" Conference Report, Apr. 2015.

Kimball, Spencer W., "Who Is My Neighbor?" Conference Report, April 1949.

Kimball, Spencer W., "Listen to the Prophets," Conference Report, Apr. 1978.

Oaks, Dallin H., CES fireside for young adults, May 1, 2005.

Uchtdorf, Dieter F., "O How Great the Plan of Our God!" Conf. Report, Oct. 2016.

Repent and Re-Turn to God

Andersen, Neil L., "Repent . . . That I May Heal You," Conference Report, Oct. 2009.

Burton, Theodore M., "The Meaning of Repentance," *Ensign*, Nov. 1988.

Nelson, Russell M., "Repentance and Conversion," Conference Report, Apr. 2007.

Packer, Boyd K., "The Plan of Happiness," Conference Report, Apr. 2015.

Renlund, Dale G., "Repentance: A Joyful Choice," Conference Report, Oct. 2016.

Uchtdorf, Dieter F., "Point of Safe Return," Conference Report, Apr. 2007.

Discourse 23: Mormon, "Faith, Hope & Charity" (Moroni 7)

Real Intent: Motives and Actions

Dyer, Alvin R., "The Laws of Man and God," Conference Report, Oct. 1965.

Oaks, Dallin H., "Why Do We Serve?" Conference Report, Oct. 1984.

Oaks, Dallin H., Pure in Heart. 1988.

Peale, Norman Vincent, Enthusiasm Makes the Difference. (1958).

Romney, Marion G., "Mother Eve, A Worthy Exemplar," *Relief Society MagaziNephi* Feb. 1968.

Romney, Marion G., "Living Welfare Principles," Conference Report, Oct. 1981.

Sill, Sterling W., "What About the Man?" Conference Report, Oct. 1962.

Good Comes from God

Andersen, Neil L., "Beware the Evil behind the Smiling Eyes," Conference Report, Apr. 2005.

Christiansen, ElRay L., "All Good Cometh of God," Conference Report, Apr. 1957.

Christiansen, ElRay L., "Blueprint for Life," Conference Report, Apr. 1958.

Faust, James E., "The Healing Power of Forgiveness," Conference Report, Apr. 2007.

Teixeria, Jose A., "Gifts to Help Us Navigate Our Life," Conference Report, Apr. 2009.

Light of Christ

Andersen, Neil L., "Beware the Evil behind the Smiling Eyes," Conference Report, Apr. 2005.

Bednar, David A., "Bear Up Their Burdens with Ease," Conference Report, Apr. 2014.

Eubank, Sharon, "Christ: The Light That Shines in Darkness," Conference Report, Apr. 2019.

Faust, James E., "The Restoration of All Things," Conference Report, Apr. 2006.

Faust, James E., "Communion with the Holy Spirit," Conference Report, Apr. 1980.

Hales, Robert D., "Out of Darkness into His Marvelous Light," Conference Report, Apr. 2002.

Hales, Robert D., "The Holy Ghost," Conference Report, Apr. 2016.

Oaks, Dallin H., "The Light and Life of the World," Conference Report, Oct. 1987.

Oaks, Dallin H., "Always Have His Spirit," Conference Report, Oct. 1996.

McKay, David O., "Christ, The Light of Humanity," Conference Report, Apr. 1968.

Packer, Boyd K., "The Candle of the Lord," *Ensign*, Jan. 1983.

Packer, Boyd K., "Personal Revelation," Conference Report, Oct. 1994.

Packer, Boyd K., "The Light of Christ," *Ensign*, Apr. 2005.

Packer, Boyd K., "These Things I Know," Conference Report, Apr. 2013.

Light of Christ (cont.)

Packer, Boyd K., "The Plan of Happiness," Conference Report, Apr. 2015.

Scott, Richard G., "Peace of Conscience and Peace of Mind," Conference Report, Oct. 2004.

Uchtdorf, Dieter F., "Bearers of Heavenly Light," Conference Report, Oct. 2017

Wirthlin, Joseph B., "Peace Within," Conference Report, Apr. 1991.

Faith

Andersen, Wilford W., "The Rock of Our Redeemer," Conference Report, Apr. 2010.

Edgley, Richard C., "Faith – The Choice is Yours," Conference Report, Oct. 2010.

Eyring, Henry B., "The Spark of Faith," Conference Report, Oct. 1986.

Eyring, Henry B., "Walk in the Light," Conference Report, Apr. 2008.

Hunter, Howard W., "Faith – The First Step," Conference Report, Apr. 1975.

Maxwell, Neal A., <u>Lord, Increase Our Faith</u>. 1994.

McConkie, Bruce R., "Faith," Conference Report, Oct. 1953.

Nash, Marcus B., "By Faith All Things Are Fulfilled," Conference Report, Oct. 2012.

Oaks, Dallin H., "Faith in the Lord Jesus Christ," Conference Report, Apr. 1994.

Scott, Richard G., "Obtaining Help from the Lord," Conference Report, Oct. 1991.

Hope

Ballard, M. Russell, "The Joy of Hope Fulfilled," Conference Report, Oct. 1992.

Faust, James E., "Of Seeds and Soils," Conference Report, Oct. 1999.

Maxwell, Neal A., "Brightness of Hope," Conference Report, Oct. 1994.

Maxwell, Neal A., "Hope Through the Atonement of Jesus Christ," Conf. Report, Oct. 1998.

Uchtdorf, Dieter F., "The Infinite Power of Hope," Conference Report, Oct. 2008.

Charity

Allred, Silvia H., "The Essence of Discipleship," Conference Report, Oct. 2011.

Ashton, Marvin J., "The Tongue Can Be a Sharp Sword," Conference Report, Apr. 1992.

Benson, Ezra Taft, "The Book of Mormon: Keystone of Our Religion," Conf. Report, Oct. 1986.

Caldwell, C. Max, "Love of Christ," Conference Report, Oct. 1992.

Cook, Gene R., "Charity: Perfect and Everlasting Love," Conference Report, Apr. 2002.

Holland, Jeffrey R., "He Loved Them unto the End," Conference Report, Oct. 1989.

Kimball, Spencer W., "Becoming the Pure in Heart," Conference Report, Apr. 1978.

McKay, David O., "Untitled," Conference Report, Apr. 1951.

Monson, Thomas S., "Charity Never Faileth," Conference Report, Oct. 2010.

Monson, Thomas S., "Love – The Essence of the Gospel," Conference Report, Apr. 2014.

Oaks, Dallin H., "The Challenge to Become," Conference Report, Oct. 2000.

Oaks, Robert C., "The Power of Patience," Conference Report, Oct. 2006.

Parkin, Bonnie D., "Choosing Charity: That Good Part," Conference Report Oct. 2003.

Peterson, Mark E., "We Believe in Being Honest," Conference Report, Oct. 1966.

Soares, Ulisses, "Abide in the Lord's Territory," Conference Report, Apr. 2012.

Taylor, Henry D., "Thou Shalt Love the Lord," Conference Report, Apr. 1969.

Uchtdorf, Dieter F., "Your Wonderful Journey Home," Conference Report, Apr. 2013.

Wirthlin, Joseph B., "Cultivating Divine Attributes," Conference Report, Oct. 1998.

Discourse 24: Mormon, "Baptism of Little Children" (Moroni 8)

Baptism of Little Children

Bowen, Shane M., "Because I Live, Ye Shall Live Also," Conference Report, Oct. 2012.

Lybbert, Merlin R., Conference Report, "The Special Status of Children," Apr. 1994.

McConkie, Bruce R., "The Salvation of Little Children," *Ensign*, Apr. 1977.

Oaks, Dallin H., "Sins and Mistakes," *Ensign*, Oct. 1996.

Packer, Boyd K., "Funerals-A Time for Reverence," Conference Report, Oct. 1988.

Baptism: A Gateway to Perfect Love

Goaslind, Jack H., "Our Responsibility to Take the Gospel," Conference Report, Oct. 1983.

Vinas, Francisco J., "Applying Simple and Plain Gospel Principles," Conf. Report, Apr. 2004.

Discourse 25: Mormon, "Persevere Despite Wickedness" (Moroni 9)

Persevere Despite Wickedness

Eyring, Henry B., "The Spark of Faith," Conference Report, Oct. 1986.

Hanks, Marion D., "What Manner of Men?" Conference Report, Apr. 1973.

Maxwell, Neal A., "Deny Yourselves of All Ungodliness," Conference Report, Apr. 1995.

Oaks, Dallin H., "World Peace," Conference Report, Apr. 1990.

Oaks, Dallin H., "He Heals the Heavy Laden," Conference Report, Oct. 2006.

Robbins, Lynn G., "Agency and Anger," Conference Report, Apr. 1998.

Stapley, Delbert L., "The Power of Example," Conference Report, Apr. 1969.

Wirthlin, Joseph B., "Never Give Up," Conference Report, Oct. 1987.

Discourse 26: Mormon, "Invitation to Believe" (Mormon 7)

Holland, Jeffrey R., "My Words . . . Never Cease," Conference Report, Apr. 2008.

Nelson, Russell M., "Scriptural Witnesses," Conference Report, Oct. 2007.

Sill, Sterling W., "God and Country," Conference Report, Oct. 1970.

Discourse 27: Moroni, "Voice of Warning; The Last Days" (Mormon 8-9)

Ballard, M. Russell, "The Joy of Hope Fulfilled," Conference Report, Oct. 1992.

Benson, Ezra Taft, "The Book of Mormon: Keystone of Our Religion," Conf. Report, Oct. 1986.

Christensen, Joe J., "Rearing Children in a Polluted Environment," Conf. Report, Oct. 1993.

Packer, Boyd K., "We Believe All That God Has Revealed," Conference Report, Apr. 1974.

Perry, L. Tom, "Behold, the Lord Hath Shown unto Me Great and Marvelous Things," Conference Report, Oct. 1992.

Peterson, Mark E., "The Last Words of Moroni," Conference Report, Oct. 1978.

Romney, Marion G., "And the Lamanites Shall Blossom as the Rose," Conf. Report, Apr. 1963.

Romney, Marion G., "America's Destiny," Conference Report, Oct. 1975.

Miracles

Callister, Tad, "The Book of Mormon," Conference Report, Oct. 2011.

Hales, Robert D., "Personal Revelation: The Teachings and Examples of the Prophets," Conference Report, Oct. 2007.

Hinckley, Gordon B., "The Miracle That Is Jesus," Conference Report, Apr. 1966.

Hunter, Howard W., "The God That Doest Wonders," Conference Report, Apr. 1989.

Kimball, Spencer W., "Continuous Revelation," Conference Report, Oct. 1966.

McConkie, Bruce R., "Faith," Conference Report, Oct. 1953.

Oaks, Dallin H. "Miracles," *Ensign*, June 2001.

Reynolds, Sydney S., "A God of Miracles," Conference Report, Apr. 2001.

Tanner, Susan W., "Stand as a Witness," Conference Report, Apr. 2008.

Discourse 28: Moroni, "Revelation & Gifts of the Spirit" (Moroni 10)

Revelation: Promise of the Book of Mormon; The Holy Ghost

Ashton, Marvin J., "There are Many Gifts," Conference Report, Oct. 1987.

Bednar, David A., "The Tender Mercies of the Lord," Conference Report, Apr. 2005.

Benson, Ezra Taft, "The Book of Mormon Is the Word of God," Conference Report, Apr. 1975.

Benson, Ezra Taft, "A New Witness for Christ," Conference Report, Oct. 1984.

Cook, Gene R., "Moroni's Promise," *Ensign*, Apr. 1994.

Eyring, Henry B., "Opportunities to Do Good," Conference Report, Apr. 2011.

Hinckley, Gordon B., "A Testimony Vibrant and True," *Ensign*, Aug. 2005.

Hinckley, Gordon B., "The Stone Cut Out of the Mountain," Conference Report, Oct. 2007.

Martino, James B., Conference Report, "Turn to Him and Answers Will Come," Oct. 2015.

Maxwell, Neal A., "Remember How Merciful the Lord Hath Been," Conf. Report, Apr. 2004.

McConkie, Bruce R., "What Think Ye of the Book of Mormon?" Conference Report, Oct. 1983.

Nelson, Russell M., "A Testimony of the Book of Mormon," Conference Report, Oct. 1999.

Nelson, Russell M., "Ask, Seek, Knock," Conference Report, Oct. 2009.

Nelson, Russell M., "The Book of Mormon," Conference Report, Oct. 2017.

Oaks, Dallin H., "Always Have His Spirit," Conference Report, Oct. 1996.

Oswald, William D., "Gospel Teaching – Our Most Important Calling," Conf. Report, Oct. 2008.

Packer, Boyd K., "Personal Revelation," Conference Report, Oct. 1994.

Packer, Boyd K., "The Book of Mormon: Another Testament of Jesus Christ," Conference Report, Apr. 2005.

Perry, L. Tom, "That Spirit Which Leadeth to Do Good," Conference Report, Apr. 1997.

Perry, L. Tom, "Blessings from Reading the Book of Mormon," Conf. Report, Oct. 2005.

Peterson, Mark E., "The Last Words of Moroni," Conference Report, Oct. 1978.

Romney, Marion G., "Magnifying One's Calling in the Priesthood," Conf. Report, Apr. 1973.

Scott, Richard G., "Realize Your Full Potential," Conference Report, Oct. 2003.

Smith, Eldred G., "Gain a Testimony," Conference Report, Apr. 1963.

Uchtdorf, Dieter F., "The Power of a Personal Testimony," Conference Report, Oct. 2006.

Uchtdorf, Dieter F., "Have We Not Reason to Rejoice?" Conference Report, Oct. 2007.

Wirthlin, Joseph B., "Pure Testimony," Conference Report, Oct. 2000.

Gifts of the Spirit

Ashton, Marvin J., "There are Many Gifts," Conference Report, Oct. 1987.

Beck, Julie B., "Mothers Who Know," Conference Report, Apr. 2007.

Packer, Boyd K., "Gifts of the Spirit," BYU Fireside, Jan. 4, 1987.

Richards, LeGrand, "The Promise Unto the Children," Conference Report, Oct. 1943.

Richards, Stephen L., "Gifts of the Gospel," Conference Report, Apr. 1950.

Romney, Marion G., "Gifts of the Spirit," Conference Report, Apr. 1956.

Be Perfect in Christ: Developing Divine Attributes

Bednar, David A., "Ye Must Be Born Again," Conference Report, Apr. 2007.

Bednar, David A., "Clean Hands and a Pure Heart," Conference Report, Oct. 2007.

Christofferson, D. Todd, "As Many as I Love, I Rebuke and Chasten," Conf. Report, Apr. 2011.

Hales, Robert D., "Becoming a Disciple of Our Lord Jesus Christ," Conf. Report, Apr. 2017.

Maxwell, Neal A., "Education of the Whole Man," Conference Report, Apr. 1970.

McKay, David O., "The Mission of Lay Members," Conference Report, Oct. 1958.

McKay, David O., "Christ, The Light of Humanity," Conference Report, Apr. 1968.

McMullin, Keith B., "Welcome Home," Conference Report, Apr. 1999.

Nelson, Russell M., "Perfection Pending," Conference Report, Oct. 1995.

Snow, Lorenzo, "Untitled," Conference Report, Apr. 1898.

Uchtdorf, Dieter F., "Christlike Attributes: Wind Beneath Our Wings," Conf. Report, Oct. 2005.

Wirthlin, Joseph B., "Christians in Belief and Action," Conference Report, Oct. 1996.

Wirthlin, Joseph B., "The Time to Prepare," Conference Report, Apr. 1998.

Wirthlin, Joseph B., "Cultivating Divine Attributes," Conference Report, Oct. 1998.

Wood, Lowell D., "Come unto Christ," Conference Report, Apr. 1993.

Word Index

A

accountability 80, 229, 230, 231
Adam... 30, 31, 32, 33, 36, 37, 50, 60, 73, 90, 124, 146, 152, 187, 191, 200, 207, 230, 249, 252, 253
addictions 38, 177
afflictions 54, 65, 77, 136, 185, 223, 267
agency 24, 30, 34, 36, 37, 38, 39, 69, 109, 156, 191, 218, 232, 234, 264
aircraft .... See plane
America 40, 54, 55, 56, 166, 243, 273, 278, 281, 284
angel ... 31, 46, 49, 50, 55, 58, 60, 72, 90, 97, 105, 112, 113, 115, 135, 145, 173, 195, 196, 197, 211, 236, 260, 267, 271, 273
anger ... 65, 79, 101, 115, 123, 143, 178, 183, 214, 234, 236, 242
atonement 19, 51, 73, 86, 87, 88, 89, 90, 91, 92, 93, 98, 110, 112, 114, 115, 146, 165, 166, 167, 189, 201, 208, 216, 223, 224, 225, 230, 232, 267, 268, 269
Atonement 16, 19, 30, 31, 33, 34, 35, 39, 42, 51, 66, 72, 86, 87, 89, 90, 91, 92, 93, 98, 110, 115, 133, 136, 137, 138, 146, 148, 157, 164, 165, 166, 167, 168, 170, 174, 176, 193, 200, 201, 202, 204, 208, 210, 214, 223, 227, 229, 230, 246, 255, 264, 265, 266, 267, 268, 278, 279, 288, 294, 300, 316, 317

B

B-17 "Flying Fortress" 251
baptism 50, 81, 83, 84, 90, 92, 132, 137, 221, 229, 230, 231, 232, 239, 260, 266
Benjamin Franklin 56
Bible 40, 41, 42, 45, 46, 49, 58, 59, 63, 71, 80, 89, 155, 177, 214, 221, 238, 239, 240, 260, 272, 278, 280
biotechnology 142
bishop 175, 192, 193, 216
body 33, 34, 38, 50, 90, 91, 98, 105, 124, 145, 146, 147, 148, 149, 157, 170, 189, 190, 191, 194, 195, 196, 197, 198, 199, 201, 236, 269, 270
boldness 183, 184
Book of Mormon... 1, 2, 3, 16, 19, 24, 28, 40, 41, 42, 44, 45, 46, 48, 49, 54, 57, 58, 59, 60, 61, 62, 63, 64, 65, 66, 68, 71, 72, 73, 74, 79, 80, 81, 87, 89, 102, 103, 105, 106, 110, 122, 125, 126, 130, 147, 151, 163, 165, 166, 168, 170, 172, 178, 179, 184, 189, 194, 199, 200, 208, 213, 214, 215, 216, 225, 231, 235, 238, 239, 240, 241, 242, 243, 244, 249, 250, 251, 252, 253, 254, 255, 256, 259, 262, 264, 265, 266, 270, 271, 272, 273, 274, 275, 276, 277, 278, 280, 281, 288, 307, 309, 310
bridle 33, 115, 140, 183, 184, 185
building . 16, 20, 21, 22, 23, 54, 55, 101, 103, 149, 178, 209, 210, 273, 274

C

Camelot 185
charity 73, 101, 109, 138, 140, 142, 143, 170, 183, 187, 202, 215, 222, 224, 225, 226, 227, 228, 229, 232, 233, 261, 269
chastity .... See immorality
checklists 251, 252
children 16, 19, 24, 25, 26, 28, 29, 30, 32, 33, 34, 35, 37, 55, 56, 58, 66, 69, 72, 74, 75, 76, 78, 79, 84, 87, 90, 103, 109, 110, 113, 116, 120, 121, 125, 126, 142, 148, 152, 153, 185, 186, 191, 195, 196, 200, 202, 206, 207, 209, 229, 230, 231, 247, 248, 251, 253, 259, 261, 263, 265, 266, 267, 268, 269, 272, 278
chocolate 142
Christ 2, 16, 17, 19, 21, 30, 33, 34, 35, 38, 39, 42, 45, 46, 47, 48, 49, 50, 51, 58, 61, 62, 64, 65, 66, 67, 69, 70, 71, 72, 73, 74, 75, 77, 78, 80, 81, 82, 83, 84, 85, 87, 88, 89, 90, 91, 92, 93, 94, 97, 98, 101, 105, 109, 112, 113, 114, 115, 116, 119, 120, 121, 122, 123, 124, 125, 126, 127, 129, 130, 132, 133, 134, 135, 136, 137, 138, 139, 142, 143, 144, 146, 148, 149, 150, 154, 155, 157, 158, 159, 160, 164, 165, 166, 167, 170, 172, 173, 174, 176, 178, 179, 184, 187, 193, 194, 195, 197, 199, 201, 202, 204, 205, 206, 207, 208, 209, 210, 211, 212, 214, 216, 217, 218, 219, 220, 221, 222, 223, 224, 225, 226, 227, 228, 229, 230, 232, 233, 236, 237, 238, 239, 240, 241, 242, 243, 246, 247, 248, 249, 250, 251, 253, 254, 255, 256, 259, 260, 261, 262, 264, 265, 266, 267, 268, 269, 270, 272, 273, 274, 275, 276, 277, 278, 279, 280, 281, 282, 283, 284, 288, 292, 294, 297, 305, 310, 316, 317
Christlike attributes 142, 144, 264
cocoa butter 142, 143
Columbus 49, 55
commandments ... 19, 20, 21, 24, 26, 27, 28, 29, 36, 39, 42, 56, 59, 62, 64, 68, 78, 82, 84, 87, 92, 94, 103, 104, 110, 111, 112, 115, 116, 118, 119, 121, 122, 126, 138, 145, 149, 150, 152, 153, 161, 162, 171, 172, 174, 177, 182, 183, 187, 190, 191, 194, 199, 204, 205, 206, 211, 217, 224, 229, 231, 232, 259, 263, 265, 266, 267, 273
condescension 47, 50, 51, 266
Confucius 220
conversion 120, 129, 130, 132, 135, 145, 172, 173, 174, 177, 226, 235
Could any man have written this book 254
creation 28, 32, 36, 113, 127, 148, 190, 191, 192, 246, 247, 252, 253, 271
Creation 30, 31, 278, 282
creditor 203, 204
crucifixion 49, 50, 88, 123, 124, 239, 267

Page | 313

D

debt 25, 34, 105, 106, 110, 167, 203, 204, 265
deliverance 35, 56, 57, 154, 172
desire 22, 33, 34, 39, 47, 48, 55, 59, 63, 100, 109, 115, 123, 133, 142, 160, 161, 168, 186, 199, 203, 214, 216, 217, 218, 222, 223, 228, 232, 249, 254, 262, 264, 272, 273, 277
devil .. 21, 31, 38, 54, 55, 69, 71, 72, 77, 78, 79, 80, 90, 165, 169, 188, 193, 208, 218, 219, 222
diligence..109, 131, 138, 141, 142, 162, 178, 179, 182, 183, 231, 232

E

earthquakes 88, 213, 242, 245
education 57, 95
evil 27, 31, 36, 38, 39, 49, 68, 69, 79, 80, 96, 101, 102, 107, 122, 126, 133, 140, 144, 152, 154, 175, 177, 178, 184, 189, 197, 198, 199, 202, 208, 214, 216, 217, 218, 219, 221, 222, 225, 231, 233, 235, 237, 269
experiment 38, 160, 161, 163, 198

F

faith. 2, 21, 22, 24, 25, 27, 33, 38, 43, 48, 55, 64, 69, 72, 73, 81, 83, 84, 87, 90, 95, 96, 106, 109, 115, 116, 118, 120, 125, 126, 129, 130, 131, 132, 133, 135, 138, 139, 140, 141, 142, 146, 152, 154, 155, 157, 158, 159, 160, 161, 162, 163, 164, 167, 168, 170, 171, 172, 174, 178, 179, 181, 183, 185, 187, 209, 211, 214, 215, 216, 222, 223, 224, 225, 226, 229, 230, 231, 232, 233, 235, 237, 239, 241, 242, 246, 248, 250, 251, 253, 254, 260, 261, 262, 263, 265, 266, 267, 268, 269, 270, 273, 274, 276, 277
faithfulness 28, 111, 112, 114, 182
Fall 30, 31, 32, 35, 200, 255, 267, 278
family .. 15, 16, 17, 18, 39, 40, 59, 61, 62, 65, 66, 67, 68, 90, 99, 106, 107, 109, 123, 127, 145, 148, 170, 175, 178, 186, 190, 191, 194, 208, 227, 231, 248, 268, 277, 278
forgiveness 19, 34, 39, 91, 115, 135, 162, 169, 174, 175, 176, 193, 199, 201, 204, 208, 225, 226, 232, 268
foundation 32, 36, 73, 85, 95, 103, 138, 156, 159, 164, 204, 205, 206, 208, 209, 210, 224, 229, 268, 269

G

genes 142, 143
Gentiles 46, 49, 54, 55, 56, 57, 58, 62, 66, 71, 72, 75, 97, 239, 240, 266, 278
gifts 76, 84, 110, 156, 232, 236, 246, 250, 253, 261, 262, 263, 264
good name 207
grace 34, 90, 95, 98, 125, 135, 144, 146, 167, 201, 207, 250, 264, 265, 266, 268, 270
grammar 255, 256
great and abominable church 55, 62
great and marvelous work 57

H

happiness 27, 29, 37, 39, 108, 111, 147, 153, 177, 181, 189, 190, 192, 193, 194, 195, 196, 197, 198, 199, 223, 227, 228, 249, 277
harrow 162, 173
Holy Ghost 18, 55, 64, 72, 75, 81, 82, 83, 84, 85, 92, 115, 118, 128, 130, 135, 139, 157, 174, 175, 184, 187, 188, 190, 204, 206, 221, 222, 225, 229, 231, 232, 239, 250, 251, 253, 254, 259, 260, 261, 262, 263, 266, 270, 271, 273, 274, 275, 276, 280
hope 22, 24, 25, 29, 39, 57, 61, 62, 65, 69, 83, 93, 105, 109, 118, 138, 142, 150, 159, 160, 176, 180, 193, 194, 202, 209, 215, 216, 222, 223, 224, 225, 227, 228, 231, 232, 233, 236, 237, 239, 267, 269, 270, 277
house of Israel 16, 40, 50, 58, 61, 62, 65, 66, 75, 87, 89, 97, 156, 238, 239, 255, 266
humility 22, 34, 95, 106, 115, 135, 140, 142, 143, 158, 159, 160, 174, 183, 184, 188, 225, 229, 232, 272, 277
Humility 7, 101, 106, 115, 141, 158, 159, 160, 184, 279, 296
hypocrites 170, 212, 217, 243

I

idleness 183, 185
immorality 73, 80, 100, 104, 190, 191, 193, 208, 245
intelligences 33, 156
Internet 118, 133, 199
Isaiah ...57, 60, 61, 62, 63, 64, 65, 66, 67, 69, 70, 71, 72, 86, 87, 88, 89, 94, 95, 97, 122, 123, 124, 127, 195, 200, 202, 217, 266, 267, 277, 278, 286, 316

J

Jehovah 34, 50, 73, 113, 127
Jerusalem 21, 40, 44, 66, 71, 88, 137, 155, 172, 239
John ...17, 19, 48, 49, 51, 60, 64, 89, 92, 106, 123, 124, 149, 150, 161, 167, 181, 187, 219, 227, 259, 271
John Adams 181
Joseph Smith 2, 25, 33, 40, 41, 42, 43, 44, 48, 55, 57, 58, 60, 64, 69, 80, 81, 95, 103, 110, 111, 122, 146, 147, 148, 149, 156, 170, 184, 200, 212, 218, 226, 230, 231, 233, 254, 256, 259, 260, 262, 271, 272, 273, 274, 276, 278, 283
justice 25, 30, 34, 58, 65, 91, 92, 93, 105, 125, 142, 167, 189, 200, 201, 203, 204, 205, 208, 211, 230, 266, 268, 269

K

knowledge 41, 45, 61, 66, 72, 76, 84, 87, 88, 95, 98, 105, 106, 115, 116, 126, 138, 139, 140, 142, 149, 150, 153, 160, 163, 178, 183, 195, 199, 200, 219, 223, 247, 253, 254, 259, 261, 262, 263, 271, 272, 274, 275, 276

L

Laban 59
Lamanites 46, 49, 54, 99, 211, 215, 235, 238, 239, 240, 241, 242, 250, 278, 280
land of promise 26, 55, 57, 97, 242, 266
Liahona 178, 179, 268
Light of Christ 219, 221
love 16, 19, 22, 24, 29, 34, 35, 47, 50, 51, 58, 65, 68, 74, 76, 80, 83, 96, 101, 102, 106, 107, 109, 112, 115, 116, 132, 133, 134, 135, 142, 147, 150, 158, 163, 166, 167, 170, 171, 179, 182, 183, 184, 185, 187, 188, 191, 192, 193, 197, 202, 212, 216, 217, 218, 224, 225, 226, 227, 228, 229, 231, 232, 233, 234, 253, 263, 264, 265, 266, 269, 270, 275, 277

M

marriage 65, 93, 103, 104, 190, 191
mediator 125, 203, 204
meditation 48
mercy .. 34, 65, 66, 74, 90, 92, 115, 125, 131, 133, 135, 136, 152, 158, 159, 165, 166, 167, 168, 169, 173, 174, 176, 177, 189, 193, 200, 201, 202, 203, 204, 208, 229, 230, 234, 236, 237, 265, 267, 268, 269, 270
Messiah. 34, 62, 68, 72, 73, 86, 88, 122, 123, 155, 213, 265, 266, 285
microalgae 142, 143
miracles 50, 114, 175, 178, 213, 222, 228, 242, 244, 246, 247, 248, 249, 261, 262, 270
missionary 107, 120, 141, 145, 158, 171, 182, 183, 188, 217, 231, 255
Mohammed 220

N

natural man .. 9, 33, 106, 114, 115, 142, 143, 144, 185, 234, 265
Nazi holocaust 237

O

obedience 22, 34, 35, 38, 42, 59, 82, 83, 90, 94, 95, 111, 112, 114, 120, 125, 129, 130, 135, 137, 138, 142, 154, 156, 178, 181, 196, 201, 208, 209, 217, 218, 224, 232, 262, 263, 265, 267, 275
opposition 30, 31, 36, 37, 104, 217, 235
outer darkness .... *See* spirit prison

P

Parable of the Sower 23
passions 33, 114, 115, 140, 183, 184, 185, 194, 261
patience 34, 37, 94, 138, 139, 140, 162, 163, 182, 183, 223, 225, 226, 227, 264
perfection 37, 142, 144, 147, 218, 264, 265
Plan of Salvation 30, 31, 50, 80, 278, 284
plane 180, 251, 252
pollution 245
ponder . 48, 61, 162, 186, 222, 224, 251, 253, 254, 263, 273
pondering 46, 48, 83, 203, 253
poor ... 27, 74, 75, 87, 96, 102, 116, 135, 158, 202, 223, 243
pray 24, 48, 85, 113, 118, 157, 162, 168, 169, 170, 184, 186, 206, 216, 217, 222, 226, 237, 248, 253, 254, 269, 275
prayer 28, 38, 48, 56, 85, 106, 110, 129, 130, 131, 135, 138, 141, 158, 162, 163, 165, 168, 169, 170, 175, 181, 187, 206, 222, 231, 232, 243, 253, 254, 263
preparation 64, 171, 179, 180, 181, 186, 204
pride 20, 54, 71, 77, 95, 96, 99, 100, 101, 103, 115, 130, 133, 134, 142, 143, 144, 159, 160, 162, 183, 184, 187, 190, 236, 243, 244, 255
priesthood 130, 151, 155, 156, 157, 188, 193, 247, 248, 259, 276
Procrastination 165, 268, 279, 317
promised land 21, 40, 42, 49, 54, 58, 61, 70, 86, 97, 278
prophet .3, 22, 26, 29, 41, 43, 49, 50, 57, 58, 61, 62, 63, 74, 87, 88, 104, 105, 110, 115, 119, 123, 145, 154, 155, 156, 167, 175, 182, 185, 193, 196, 197, 198, 199, 208, 211, 212, 215, 225, 230, 235, 236, 237, 238, 243, 259, 273, 274, 277
prophets 10, 18, 28, 29, 38, 40, 44, 58, 60, 62, 63, 64, 80, 91, 103, 111, 120, 122, 125, 126, 128, 154, 156, 161, 186, 190, 191, 206, 210, 211, 212, 214, 223, 232, 234, 235, 236, 239, 241, 243, 255, 259, 268, 274
punishment 34, 109, 168, 188, 195, 200, 201, 202

R

real intent. 81, 216, 217, 218, 251, 253, 254, 270, 273, 274, 276
records ... 40, 43, 49, 54, 57, 58, 59, 97, 120, 134, 149, 172, 178, 182, 199, 211, 241, 242, 250, 273, 274
redemption 19, 32, 34, 35, 62, 89, 120, 125, 126, 127, 151, 152, 153, 154, 168, 172, 189, 194, 200, 204, 231, 238, 246, 249, 269, 270
remember 3, 62, 73, 100, 102, 106, 108, 131, 133, 156, 159, 170, 174, 175, 176, 178, 189, 192, 202, 206, 207, 210, 222, 251, 252, 253, 259, 275
remission of sins ... 72, 81, 82, 105, 115, 116, 125, 174, 229, 230, 231, 232, 266, 269, 270, 271
repentance ... 27, 34, 35, 79, 80, 81, 83, 84, 87, 90, 92, 100, 112, 117, 125, 129, 130, 137, 144, 151, 152, 154, 155, 159, 165, 167, 168, 170, 171, 172, 173, 174, 175, 176, 177, 187, 188, 189, 193, 198, 199, 200, 201, 202, 203, 207, 208, 211, 212, 214, 221, 229, 230, 231, 232, 235, 236, 238, 239, 265, 266, 267, 268, 269
restoration 35, 43, 49, 57, 59, 62, 66, 71, 89, 103, 146, 148, 189, 197, 199, 231, 247, 259
resurrection.. 32, 34, 71, 74, 87, 89, 90, 91, 92, 94, 98, 120, 126, 137, 146, 147, 148, 149, 150, 151, 152, 153, 166, 189, 194, 195, 196, 197, 199, 200, 211, 223, 224, 246, 259, 267, 268, 269, 270

Resurrection 90, 126, 145, 146, 147, 148, 149, 150, 164, 188, 189, 194, 195, 223, 255, 268, 279, 280, 288, 295, 301, 316

revelation .. 18, 43, 48, 58, 63, 68, 85, 95, 96, 131, 135, 157, 196, 212, 223, 246, 253, 256, 259, 260, 262, 266, 271, 273, 275, 277

Revolutionary War 49, 56

riches 20, 21, 23, 87, 95, 96, 99, 100, 101, 102, 103, 104, 105, 133, 134, 145, 207, 267

righteous need not fear 62, 68

rod of iron 18, 20, 21, 22

S

sacrifice ... 50, 64, 90, 91, 105, 112, 113, 120, 122, 165, 166, 167, 193, 201, 208, 225, 255, 266, 268

salvation 25, 27, 30, 32, 34, 35, 40, 42, 55, 66, 71, 72, 74, 87, 88, 112, 113, 115, 120, 124, 126, 127, 139, 146, 148, 154, 164, 167, 170, 172, 176, 178, 181, 190, 200, 201, 203, 207, 208, 209, 225, 226, 235, 238, 246, 249, 259, 266, 267, 268, 269, 275

sanctification 65, 157

Satan . 31, 38, 62, 68, 69, 72, 78, 79, 80, 101, 118, 124, 134, 139, 154, 174, 175, 176, 184, 192, 205, 229, 230, 234, 236, 254

Savior .. 21, 23, 28, 30, 34, 35, 39, 48, 50, 51, 57, 62, 63, 66, 72, 73, 74, 80, 81, 82, 83, 87, 88, 90, 91, 92, 93, 102, 110, 114, 115, 120, 123, 124, 132, 133, 136, 137, 138, 140, 141, 146, 149, 150, 158, 162, 164, 167, 170, 174, 175, 179, 185, 187, 189, 193, 196, 197, 202, 206, 210, 211, 213, 219, 223, 227, 228, 255, 259, 264, 265, 266, 267, 272, 273, 292, 297, *See* Christ

scriptures .. 17, 18, 21, 22, 28, 42, 45, 48, 58, 61, 62, 64, 65, 79, 83, 84, 85, 94, 125, 127, 131, 132, 139, 141, 142, 151, 154, 161, 166, 167, 169, 173, 175, 178, 186, 187, 189, 197, 206, 214, 216, 217, 218, 221, 222, 223, 224, 246, 248, 253, 256, 260, 268, 277

seed .. 23, 40, 42, 54, 97, 103, 120, 127, 158, 161, 162, 163, 239, 268

sexual sin .... *See* immorality

Shakespeare 198, 203

shub 177

signs and wonders 212, 213

small and simple things 172, 173, 178, 181

sober 183, 186

spirit prison 195, 196

spirit world 48, 150, 156, 170, 196

Spiritual death 31

Sullenberger 180

T

teaching 40, 50, 96, 104, 105, 107, 132, 136, 138, 152, 153, 170, 172, 173, 178, 183, 186, 187, 188, 193, 235, 236

temperate 114, 138, 139, 183, 187

temple 25, 38, 67, 84, 99, 104, 105, 114, 123, 140, 159, 192, 222, 259, 278

temptations 18, 21, 23, 31, 37, 54, 80, 93, 118, 128, 132, 157, 190, 192, 193, 208

terrorists 237, 244

testimony . 2, 28, 58, 60, 64, 71, 81, 85, 116, 120, 129, 130, 131, 133, 135, 146, 161, 162, 163, 165, 172, 173, 186, 189, 204, 206, 225, 231, 235, 236, 242, 248, 251, 254, 256, 259, 263, 266, 267, 268, 271, 272, 273, 274, 275, 276, 277

three-legged stool 224

time 22, 24, 28, 33, 34, 39, 44, 48, 50, 56, 57, 60, 62, 68, 71, 78, 87, 91, 92, 99, 102, 103, 107, 109, 111, 118, 123, 124, 126, 128, 130, 131, 132, 133, 135, 139, 144, 145, 148, 151, 152, 154, 156, 160, 162, 163, 165, 170, 171, 173, 174, 175, 179, 180, 182, 185, 186, 187, 191, 195, 196, 197, 199, 201, 203, 207, 209, 217, 222, 223, 224, 225, 227, 228, 230, 232, 236, 237, 239, 240, 243, 245, 247, 248, 251, 252, 253, 254, 256, 259, 262, 266, 269, 275

tree of life 3, 16, 17, 18, 19, 20, 21, 23, 24, 27, 31, 35, 37, 50, 55, 167, 266

W

war 63, 235, 238, 239, 254, 277

wealth 100, 101, 102, 103, 135, 184, 242, 254

wickedness 62, 66, 71, 77, 99, 130, 145, 154, 171, 189, 195, 197, 198, 208, 233, 234, 235, 236, 237, 242, 270

Book of Mormon Discourses
Doctrines and Commentary: A Study Guide

"This morning I speak about the power of the Book of Mormon and the critical need we have as members of this Church to study, ponder, and apply its teachings in our lives. The importance of having a firm and sure testimony of the Book of Mormon cannot be overstated. . . . If you are not reading the Book of Mormon each day, please do so. If you will read it prayerfully and with a sincere desire to know the truth, the Holy Ghost will manifest its truth to you. If it is true – and I solemnly testify that it is – then Joseph Smith was a prophet who saw God the Father and His Son, Jesus Christ. Because the Book of Mormon is true, The Church of Jesus Christ of Latter-day Saints is the Lord's Church on earth." (President Thomas S. Monson, "The Power of the Book of Mormon," Conf. Report, April 2017).

The 28 Discourses

1. **Lehi**, to his family while traveling in the wilderness, "*The Tree of Life*" (1 Nephi 8)

2. **Lehi**, to his children, Laman and Lemuel, "*Awake and Repent*" (2 Nephi 1)

3. **Lehi**, to his son, Jacob, "*The Plan of Salvation; Agency*" (2 Nephi 2)

4. **Lehi**, to his son, Joseph, "*Joseph - A Choice Seer*" (2 Nephi 3)

5. **Nephi**, to future readers, "*Panoramic Vision of the Future*" (1 Nephi 11-14)

6. **Nephi**, to the House of Israel, "*Hope in the Lord (Isaiah)*" (1 Nephi 19-22)

7. **Nephi**, to his people and future readers, "*Press Forward in Christ*" (2 Nephi 25-33)

8. **Jacob**, to the people of Nephi in a gathering, "*The Infinite Atonement*" (2 Nephi 6-10)

9. **Jacob**, to the people of Nephi at the temple, "*A Warning about Sin*" (Jacob 1-3)

10. **King Benjamin**, to the people of Zarahemla, "*Service and Salvation*" (Mosiah 2-5)

11. **Abinadi**, to Noah's court in Shilom, "*Redemption through Christ*" (Mosiah 13-16)

12. **Alma**, son of Alma, to the church in Zarahemla, "*A Mighty Change of Heart*" (Alma 5)

13. **Alma**, son of Alma, to the church in Gideon, "*Divine Attributes*" (Alma 7)

14. **Amulek**, to the people in the city of Ammonihah, "*Resurrection*" (Alma 10-11)

15. **Alma**, son of Alma, to the people in the city of Ammonihah, "*Life Is a Probationary State; The High Priesthood*" (Alma 12-13)

16. Alma, son of Alma, to the Zoramites, "*Nourish Faith with the Word of God*" (Alma 32-33)

17. Amulek, to the Zoramites, "*Atonement, Prayer & Procrastination*" (Alma 34)

18. Alma, son of Alma, to his son, Helaman, "*Repentance; Simple Things*" (Alma 36-37)

19. Alma, son of Alma, to his son, Shiblon, "*Effective Teaching*" (Alma 38)

20. **Alma**, son of Alma, to his son, Corianton, "*Chastity, Justice & Mercy*" (Alma 39-42)

21. Helaman, son of Helaman, to his sons Nephi and Lehi, "*The Rock of Christ*" (Helaman 5)

22. Samuel the Lamanite, to the people in Zarahemla, "*Signs of Christ*" (Helaman 13-15)

23. Mormon, to the people of Nephi in a synagogue, "*The Light of Christ; Faith, Hope & Charity*" (Moroni 7)

24. Mormon, to his son, Moroni, in an epistle, "*Baptism of Little Children*" (Moroni 8)

25. Mormon, to his son, Moroni, in an epistle, "*Persevere Despite Wickedness*" (Moroni 9)

26. Mormon, to the Lamanites (present and future), "*Invitation to Believe*" (Mormon 7)

27. Moroni, to future people who receive the record, "*A Voice of Warning; Tthe Last Days*" (Mormon 8-9)

28. Moroni, to the Lamanites and future readers of the record, "*Promise of the Book of Mormon; Gifts of the Spirit*" (Moroni 10)

Made in the USA
San Bernardino, CA
23 April 2019